Columbia Journals

Bicentennial Edition

Columbia Journals

DAVID THOMPSON

Edited by Barbara Belyea

McGill-Queen's University Press
Montreal & Kingston · London · Ithaca

© McGill-Queen's University Press 2007
ISBN 978-0-7735-3325-7
Legal deposit fourth quarter 1994
Bibliothèque nationale du Québec

Printed in Canada on acid-free paper
First edition 1995
First paperback edition 1998
Reprinted 2002

Published simultaneously by the University of
Washington Press

This book was first published with the help of grants
from the Social Science Federation of Canada, using
funds provided by the Social Sciences and Humanities
Research Council of Canada, and the University
Endowment Fund of The University of Calgary.

McGill-Queen's University Press acknowledges the
support of the Canada Council for the Arts for our
publishing program. We also acknowledge the financial support of the Government of Canada through
the Book Publishing Industry Development Program
(BPIDP) for our publishing activities.

Canadian Cataloguing in Publication Data

Thompson, David, 1770–1857
    Columbia journals
    Includes bibliographical references and index.
    ISBN 978-0-7735-3325-7
    1. Northwest, Canadian – Description and travel –
    To 1821. 2. Northwest, Pacific – Description and
    travel. 3. North West Company. 4. Fur Trade –
    Northwest, Pacific. 5. Thompson, David, 1770–
    1857.
    I. Belyea, Barbara II. Title.
    FC312.1.T46A3 1993   971.2′01   C93-090505-9
    F1060.7.T46 1993

This book was typeset by Dynagram Inc.
in 10/12 Sabon.

Contents

Preface, Bicentennial Edition   vii

Acknowledgments   xiii

Introduction   xv

Signs and Abbreviations   xxxi

COLUMBIA JOURNALS

Journey to the Kootanaes   3

Journey to the Bow River   12

Journey to the Rocky Mountain   21

Across the Mountains   35

Building Kootanae House   54

Journey to the Lake Indian Country   75

From Boggy Hall to Kootanae House   96

Along the Saleesh River   104

Athabaska Pass   117

The Lower Columbia   142

Return Upstream   157

NOTES TO THE TEXT

Journey to the Kootanaes   181

Journey to the Bow River   195

Journey to the Rocky Mountain   202

Across the Mountains   209

Building Kootanae House   218

Journey to the Lake Indian Country   231

From Boggy Hall to Kootanae House   239

Along the Saleesh River   243

Athabaska Pass   249

The Lower Columbia   264

Return Upstream   280

Maps   291

List of Sources   321

Index   331

Preface, Bicentennial Edition

In 1845 poverty impelled David Thompson to write a popular book about his travels in the Northwest. R. M. Ballantyne's success with yarns about life at Hudson Bay spurred the old man's competitive nature: he would describe the regions he had explored during twenty-eight years in the fur trade. In his *Narrative* Thompson recast the terse but wide-ranging statements of his journals as a story of fulfilled ambition. He had surveyed the Northwest from Hudson Bay to Athabaska, from the Great Lakes to the Pacific Ocean. Looking back on his fur-trade years, Thompson presented the Northwest as if he were once more mapping it and his trading career as if it had been less important than his survey work.

Since the tone of the *Narrative* is quiet, even modest, it may seem chary to point out the book's artfulness. But Thompson, even as he continued to write with the low-key, self-effacing emphasis on places and events that was characteristic of his journals, highlighted three dramatic moments of his long years in the fur trade: his decision to join the North West Company, his crossing of Athabaska Pass, and his arrival at the mouth of the Columbia River. Presenting his past in this way suggested that recent governmental indifference to his maps and Sir George Simpson's refusal of support were comparable to an earlier failure to employ his considerable abilities. The North West Company partners, "gentlemen of enlarged views," had allowed him to survey when the Hudson's Bay Company's "mean selfish policy" had not. Thompson had proved himself worthy of the North West partners' "liberal and public spirit"[1]:

---

1. J. B. Tyrrell, ed., *David Thompson's Narrative of his Explorations in Western America* (Toronto: Champlain Society, 1916), 169-71, 502; Richard Glover, ed., *David Thompson's Narrative* (Toronto: Champlain Society, 1962), 131-2, 359.

he had crossed the continental divide and mapped the great river sought by generations of explorers.

Thompson's recasting of events is apparent when the *Narrative* is compared with his journals and when these journals are in turn compared with other fur-trade documents of the period. His decision to change companies, the pivotal event of the *Narrative,* is a good example. Thompson's journal entry for 21 May 1797, the day he set out to join the North West Company, is a statement of fact: "This day left the Service of the Hudsons Bay Co^y and entered that of the Company of Merchants from Canada May God Almighty prosper me."[2] Malcolm Ross, who had wintered with him, recorded what Thompson said at the time: "This morning Mr David Thompson acquainted Me with his time being out with your Honors and thought himself a freeborn subject and at liberty to choose any service he thought to be most to his advantage."[3] Whether Thompson was attracted to the North West Company by a promise of more opportunity to survey is an open question. Contemporary documents leave no doubt that the Hudson's Bay Company appreciated and rewarded Thompson's ability to make accurate maps. In 1791 the company gave him instruments worth more than his annual income as a "writer"; four years later he was appointed the HBC's leading surveyor at a generous salary of £60.[4] Whatever Thompson's real reason for changing sides, it could not have been HBC's indifference to his surveying skills.

The *Narrative*'s protagonist is portrayed throughout as exceptionally competent and determined: Thompson repeatedly distances himself from his peers and distinguishes his own perceptions from those of his companions. One of his schoolmates sent to Hudson Bay had been poorly trained; another "had lost all his education."[5] A lucky break allowed Thompson to spend the winter of 1790–91 with Philip Turnor, the HBC's first appointed surveyor, but when injuries prevented him from exploring the Athabaska region with Turnor, "a Mr Peter Fidler took my place."[6] Although Fidler's postings and surveys paralleled Thompson's for twenty years, this is Thompson's only mention of him in the *Narrative*. And although cooperation, camaraderie, and family ties were essential to the North West Company alliance, only a few of the

2. AO F4425, David Thompson, journal no. 5, 21 May 1797.

3. HBCA B.14/a/1, Bedford House post journal (Malcolm Ross), 21 May 1797.

4. HBCA A.5/3, HBC Committee to Joseph Colen, May 1791; HBCA A.30/6, "Servants at York/ Inland."

5. Tyrrell, 27–8, 53–4n, 173–4; Glover, 20, 43, 133.

6. Tyrrell, 53–4n; Glover, 55.

partners figure individually or favorably. Thompson also distinguishes himself from the engagés and freemen with whom he worked for years. They could not share his great moments at Athabaska Pass and the Pacific coast: "the height of land ... was to me a most exhilarating sight, but to my uneducated men a dreadful sight, they had no scientific object in view ... a full view of the Pacific Ocean ... to me was a great pleasure, but my Men seemed disappointed ..."[7] The *Narrative* leaves an impression of heroic solitude, as indelible as it is artful and untrue.

In contrast, Thompson's journals document a succession of days, seasons, and routine tasks in a spare style that deflects attention from the writer. The prescribed range of topics – weather, the daily tasks of individuals and groups, letters from fellow post masters, trade with Native people, the routes taken from place to place, animals hunted for food – is covered systematically, without emphasis, as uncommented statements of fact. Thompson learned to keep such records during his years with the Hudson's Bay Company. His trip journals follow the format of Turnor's running surveys and served as the reference base for his maps. His post journals were written in the format required of all the inland post masters; their annual records were sent down to the Bay factories, then forwarded to London, where the company's directors examined them with great care and attention. In both kinds of journals, Thompson responded to established categories of information and used conventional turns of phrase. These journal requirements forestalled the process of shaping by choice and omission that later characterized the *Narrative*.

North West partners and clerks also kept journals, but since they were required to make only financial reports, the kinds of journals they wrote varied widely. The Agreement by which the company was reorganized in 1802 stipulated that each wintering partner send "a true faithful and exact account and Inventory" to the summer rendezvous of partners and agents. "Account" in this context meant a list of goods and returns, the sales record of each post – a meaning made clear in subsequent annual minutes.[8] Since the North West Company was a coalition of partners rather than an overseas service directed from a distance, there was less need for written journals and uniform standards of reporting than in the Hudson's Bay Company. Nevertheless the number and wide provenance of extant North West Company journals indicate that such records were kept

---

7. Tyrrell, 446, 500–1; Glover, 321, 358.
8. W. Stewart Wallace, ed. *Documents Relating to the North West Company* (Toronto: Champlain Society, 1934), 115–16, 250, 255.

more often than not.[9] They registered private reflections, logged trip routes and landmarks, kept track of trade, visits, correspondence, employees' daily tasks, and small debts. Entries in these journals followed a looser, less comprehensive format than the HBC journals: the writer chose whatever topics he wished to cover and passed over others with little or no mention. Several North West partners and clerks followed published models. Alexander Mackenzie's editorially enhanced *Voyages from Montreal* echoed James Cook's famous journals, also polished for the press; in turn, Simon Fraser's journals imitated Mackenzie's. For his pious reflections, Daniel Harmon adopted the vocabulary and reasoning of contemporary devotional works. Alexander Henry the Younger had his famous uncle's book in mind as he wrote detailed explanations of fur-trade life and descriptions of Native tribes.[10] Harmon published his journals; Fraser and Henry planned to publish as well. Thompson's *Narrative* reflects the themes of these contemporary accounts.

However, as a North West Company clerk and partner, Thompson continued to keep journals in the Hudson's Bay Company formats and style. He wrote journal-based reports for the North West Company agents in 1798, 1801, and 1807, the years he hunted for the Mississippi's source and for a pass across the continental divide.[11] But he wrote his almost unbroken daily record for himself, just as his surveys were conducted for the most part on his own initiative and at his own expense. The journals make clear that Thompson's daily work was trade. His exploration of the Mississippi in 1798 and the lower Columbia River in 1811 are the only surveys for which there is evidence of direct company support.

The texts of *Columbia Journals* span twelve years of Thompson's career in the Northwest but they cover no more than seventeen months of activity. The daily record has been cut and shaped to

---

9. See, for example, Charles M. Gates, ed. *Five Fur Traders of the Northwest* (Minneapolis: Minnesota Historical Society, 1965); W. Raymond Wood and Thomas D. Thiessen, eds., *Early Fur Trade on the Northern Plains* (Norman: University of Oklahoma Press, 1985); Lloyd Keith, ed. *North of Athabaska* (Montreal: McGill-Queen's University Press, 2001).

10. Lamb, W. Kaye, ed., *Journals and Letters of Alexander Mackenzie* (Toronto: Macmillan, 1970); Lamb, W. Kaye, ed., *Letters and Journals of Simon Fraser* (Toronto: Macmillan, 1960); Lamb, W. Kaye, ed., *Sixteen Years in the Indian Country: the Journal of Daniel Williams Harmon* (Toronto: Macmillan, 1957); Barry Gough, ed. *Alexander Henry the Younger's Journal*, 2 vols. (Toronto: Champlain Society, 1988 and 1992).

11. Tyrrell, 242; Glover, 181.

present Thompson's search for mountain passes and exploration of the Columbia watershed. Post journals detailing trade in the Peace River region and the "Rat Country" west of Hudson Bay, trips to the rendezvous at Lake Superior, even winters in Thompson's new Columbia department – all are omitted. The reason for these omissions is simple: when I edited *Columbia Journals* I accepted without question Thompson's *Narrative* promotion of himself as an explorer and surveyor. The cost of the omissions appears higher with each year of hindsight, since the journal entries detailing seasonal routines of the fur trade are essential to understanding Thompson's historical role. As it stands, the selection of texts for *Columbia Journals* is logical and rigorous in its adherence to the theme of exploring the great river. But if I were to make a new selection, I would be tempted to give a better sense of the relationship between Thompson's surveys and his work as a fur-trade partner.

Acknowledgments

I would like to thank the following people for their generous friendship, help, and advice. Any remaining errors or omissions are mine alone.

Christon I. Archer, Judith Hudson Beattie, Catherine Belyea, Ronald B. Bond, Jennifer S.H. Brown, Linda Cameron, William H. Cooper, Edward H. Dahl, John G.N. Davidson, Olive Patricia Dickason, John Ferris, Lloyd Gallagher, Jeff Gottfred, Barb Harrison, Al Judson, Joyce Kee, Doug Leighton, Carlotta Lemieux, Alan H. Macdonald, Allan J. MacDonald, Elona Malterre, David B. Mason, Leslie Potter, Sabrina Reed, Anthony L. Rees, Aylene Reynolds, Bob Reynolds, Kevin Root, Valli Sheuring, Donald B. Smith, Jānis Svilpis, Walter Volovsek, Véronique Vouilloz, Anthony Wall, Helen Wallis, and Barry Whitehill.

I am grateful to the University of Calgary for two six-month sabbatical leaves, a research grant, and a publication grant. I am also grateful to the Izaak Walton Killam Foundation for a four-month resident fellowship.

Introduction

David Thompson's Columbia journals require of the reader a perseverance that is well rewarded. Laconic in style, filled with measurements and calculations, these journals nevertheless record events of the fur trade in the period of its greatest expansion. They document Thompson's establishment of transmontane trade and his exploration of the North Pacific watershed. They describe landscapes which have since been transformed by settlement and industry, and provide a glimpse, albeit one-sided, of Natives at the moment of contact with Europeans. Filled with geographical detail as well as the fur trade's daily business, they are the record on which Thompson's maps and the second part of his better known *Narrative* were based. The information they furnish would be enough, one would think, to have interested generations of historians. Yet all but fragmentary sequences of these journals and a few details of the maps have remained unpublished.

This indifference to Thompson's journals may be due not so much to their technical detail as to their lack of transparency. Apparently historians have sensed that Thompson's text does not yield easily to historical methods and aims. Despite the immediacy of the genre – the writer tells of his own experiences as they occur – Thompson's journals resist attempts to go "behind" the textual surface in order to reconstruct the author and his times. As with any narrative text, the reader responds not to the events recorded but to the record of events, to a textual filter that selects, judges and presents deeds as words. In the case of Thompson's journals, access to the writer's experience is doubly problematic. There is no concession to or acknowledgement of an outside reader, as in the published journals of Cook, Hearne, Mackenzie and others – or even in the company journals that were circulated among partners and clerks. Thompson's journals are an *aide-mémoire*, not a communication in the usual sense. There is no authorial persona to engage in dialogue with an outside reader. The journals therefore make it difficult to invent a distinct personality which can motivate and "explain" the written words. The hundreds of daily entries form a pattern at once intimate and impersonal, candid and purely professional. Thompson's journals are less and more than a clear window on the past. The reader must make an effort to define their textual status in order to assess their informational, "historical" value correctly.

REGARDLESS OF IMPORTANT TEXTUAL DIFFERENCES, a biography of David Thompson has been pieced together from his own *Narrative* and letters, together with a few contemporary documents.[1]

Thompson reached the Pacific Ocean in 1811, twenty-eight years after his arrival at Churchill, where he began an apprenticeship to the Hudson's Bay Company. Although scarcely into his teens, he immediately set himself to learn new skills of living along the bleak subarctic coast, at the same time insisting on practice for skills he had learned at school: writing, accounting and navigation. While apprentices sometimes became "reprobates" and a former schoolmate "lost all his education," Thompson prepared for his long life as a fur trade bourgeois and surveyor. In 1787 he wintered with Peigans in the Rocky Mountain foothills; in 1790 he and Peter Fidler learned "practical astronomy" from Philip Turnor.[2] Thompson affirmed his sense of independent purpose in 1797 when, unlike Fidler, he left the HBC for the still loose association of "Merchants from Canada," the North West Company. His first trip for this partnership was a visit to the Mandans on the Missouri River, during which he surveyed the area La Vérendrye had explored sixty years before. His next postings were to the Athabaska and Fort des Prairies departments, the farthest extensions of the fur trade at the close of the eighteenth century.[3]

Following Turnor's example, Thompson observed, mapped, kept a journal and looked forward to the senior partners' approval of expe-

1. See Nick's account of Thompson in the *Dictionary of Canadian Biography*.
2. Umfreville (63–4); PRO letters FO5/441: Thompson to Sir James Alexander, 9 May 1845; AO journals 1–6, which cover the years 1790–97; AO journals 28, year-by-year summary; HBCA A11/117: Thompson to HBC Committee, 30 August 1790; *Narrative* (Tyrrell, 3–54/Glover, 3–56).
3. AO journals 7–12, which cover the years 1797–99; AO journals 6, 13–17, which cover the years 1801–06; AO journals 28, year-by-year summary.

ditions to the west side of the continental divide. In 1793 Alexander
Mackenzie, an associate of the North West Company, had joined the
fur trade's knowledge of the interior to Vancouver's coastal survey.
But Mackenzie's route was not a practical one, and it left many questions unanswered: it appeared on Aaron Arrowsmith's 1795 map of
North America as a zigzag line across a blank space almost twenty
meridians wide. Thompson's interest in Mackenzie's explorations and
his transcription of the parts of Vancouver's journal relative to the
Columbia River show him determined, as early as 1800, to penetrate
this unknown space.[4]

Mackenzie's voyage to the Pacific encouraged others as well as
Thompson. Fidler, though interested, never went farther west than
the Rocky Mountain foothills.[5] But Duncan McGillivray, already a
partner in one of the North West Company's coalition of firms, led
two exploratory trips from Rocky Mountain House in 1800 and authorized two more. McGillivray's poor health and the difficulties of
organizing a unified North West Company delayed western expansion
of the trade until 1807. That summer Thompson crossed the divide to
the "Kootanae" (Columbia) River and wintered at its headwaters. He
was to spend the next four years solving the puzzle of the Pacific drain-
age. After comparing his own explorations with the discoveries of
Mackenzie, Fraser, Lewis and Clark, he produced the first accurate
picture of the river systems between Stuart Lake and Astoria.

At the same time, from 1807 to 1812, Thompson established the
routes and posts of a Columbia Department: from Rocky Mountain
House to Kootanae House via Howse Pass, by water and overland
from the Columbia headwaters to Kullyspel House and Saleesh House
on the Clark Fork River, and overland again from Pend Oreille Lake
to Spokane House. During his last two years in the West, Thompson
crossed the divide via Athabaska Pass and travelled the entire length of
the Columbia River. He discovered and mapped what Mackenzie had
failed to find: a navigable route from the Rocky Mountains to the
western ocean. Fur traders, immigrants and adventurers followed this

---

4. Mackenzie, "A Map of Mackenzie's Track from Fort Chipewyan to the
   Pacific Ocean in 1798" (facing 239); VPL journal: "Extract from *A
   Voyage of Discovery Round the World* by Captain George Vancouver,
   regarding the North West Coast of America".
5. Fidler copied passages from Mackenzie's *Voyages* and Dalrymple's *Plan* of
   1789 (HBCA E3/2).

route until the Canadian Pacific Railway was completed seventy-four years later.[6]

In 1812 Thompson settled at Terrebonne, near Montreal, where he spent the next two years correcting his area charts and drawing a comprehensive map of the Northwest. He then advertised for subscriptions to a printed map or atlas, but apparently there were no takers. Thompson's maps were never published in his name, or to his profit. Even after amalgamation with the North West Company in 1821, the Hudson's Bay Company showed unrelenting hostility to a man who had left its service; at the same time it recognized, covertly, Thompson's cartographic knowledge. George Simpson, the governor of the new Northern Department, continued the HBC practice of forwarding information to Aaron Arrowsmith, who used it to update his own map of North America.[7]

In 1817, Thompson was engaged by the International Boundary Commission set up by the Treaty of Ghent to survey the Anglo-American border from Lake of the Woods to the Eastern Townships of Quebec. From this time until 1846, Thompson witnessed, with partisan interest, the British and American scramble for the Oregon Territory. Hard times followed his work with the boundary commission. The two themes of patriotism and indigence appear together in Thompson's representations to Sir Charles Metcalfe, governor general of Canada, and to the Earl of Aberdeen, the British foreign secretary. Lord Aberdeen belatedly paid Thompson £150 for information forwarded to Arrowsmith, but he refused to acknowledge or return the maps which Thompson sent to the Foreign Office in 1843. Further pleas for remuneration fell on deaf ears. In one of his letters to an official on the ascending scale of patronage, Thompson sketched "a brief memoir of [his] life," the germ of his *Narrative*. He had certainly done, as he himself claimed, "all that one man could hope to per-

6. AO journals 13, 18–28, which cover the years 1800–01 and 1806–12; *Narrative* (Tyrrell, 375–536/Glover, 273–382); Simpson (Rich, 170).

7. AO journals 28, which covers the years 1812–14; RCSL "Remarks on the Countries westward of the Rocky Mountains, with references to the Rough Chart, by D.T. Terrebonne, 19th April 1813"; AO "Map made for the North West Company in 1813 and 1814 and delivered to the Honorable William McGillivray then Agent"; PRO FO925/4622; "Maps of North America"; NA MG19 A8: "Prospectus" (undated); Simpson (Merk, 112–13); Arrowsmith, "A Map of all the New Discoveries in North America ... 1795 with additions to 1814." See also Ogden, ed. Davies and Johnson (xxvii–ix), and Harris (1:67).

form," but without support in high places, so many years after he had left the Northwest, the aging explorer remained isolated and obscure.[8]

ALTHOUGH THOMPSON WAS FEARFUL THAT his "mass of scientific materials ... of surveys, of astronomical observations, drawings of the countries, sketches and measurements of the Mountains &c &c &c [would] all soon ... perish in oblivion," these "materials" have been well preserved. An early map of the Hayes, Nelson and Churchill rivers is in the Hudson's Bay Company Archives. His border survey maps and all but one of the journals are kept in the Archives of Ontario; an early notebook has found its way to the Vancouver Public Library, while a report of the 1801 expedition is in the National Archives of Canada. A second report, of Thompson's first year on the Columbia, is in the Royal Commonwealth Society Library, together with "Remarks" that accompanied a rough version of the North West Company map. This map, which hung in the hall of the North West Company's western headquarters at Fort William, is now displayed in the Archives of Ontario. The maps which Thompson sent to the Foreign Office, and which he regarded as his best work, are housed in the Public Record Office at Kew; another set is in the British Library. Most of the *Narrative* manuscript is kept at the University of Toronto Library, but a "missing chapter" has been found among the journals in the Archives of Ontario.

Thompson's *Narrative* has run through two Champlain Society editions, by Tyrrell (1916) and Glover (1962). In his popular compilation, Hopwood (1971) included passages of the *Narrative* as well as excerpts from the journals and reports. Coues (1897), Elliott (1914–32) and White (1950) published journal fragments; recently Wood and Thiessen (1977, 1985) edited the Mandan journals. Except for occasional illustrations, the maps have remained unpublished.

If Thompson was indeed a great explorer and cartographer, as most of his editors claim, his work has yet to be generally acknowledged in histories and geographical studies, particularly of the Oregon region. Despite Tyrrell's admiration, which was repeated in scholarly articles

---

8. NA MG19 A8 letters: Thompson to Lord Sydenham, 24 May 1840 and 30 May 1841, Thompson to Lord Stanley, 27 December 1842, Thompson to Sir Charles Metcalfe, 9 May 1843, 7 July 1843, 21 November 1843 and 1 December 1843; PRO FO5/402, 5/418, 5/421, 5/415 letters: Thompson to the Earl of Aberdeen, 26 August 1843, 29 November 1843, 10 September 1844, 28 October 1844 and 2 December 1844; PRO FO5/441: "Remarks on the Oregon Territory" and Thompson to Sir James Alexander, 9 May 1845.

and public addresses between 1888 and 1939, Thompson's work is seldom mentioned. This, despite Tyrrell's praise – or, one might argue, because of it. Not content to point out the explorer's technical excellence, Tyrrell lauded his moral austerity: Thompson's self-control and moral rectitude were exceptional in the rowdy, drunken milieu of the fur trade. "There were few men in the West," commented Tyrrell, "who bore so consistently as he did the white flower of a blameless life." This unfortunate emphasis shifted attention from Thompson's real achievements to vain speculation on the saintliness of his character. Apparently Thompson could do no wrong. The disciple was also quick to defend Thompson's actions in what proved a controversial problem of fur trade history, the "race to the sea" against John Jacob Astor's Pacific Fur Company in 1810–11. While Elliott and White, who edited fragments of the journals, echoed Tyrrell's praise of Thompson's character, historians made much of Thompson's inability to defend British interests in Oregon.[9]

The historian A.S. Morton first advanced the thesis of the North West Company's "Columbian enterprise" and blamed Thompson for failing to carry it through. Thompson had not played his part at the decisive moment: "No Alexander Mackenzie or Simon Fraser this, but a scholarly surveyor, not without an element of timidity in him. In this crucial hour of his life, David Thompson was weighed and found wanting ... The Canadian patriot may deplore Britain's failure through him to establish a first claim by settlement to the Pacific coast of the Oregon." Thompson's journal for the critical weeks of October 1810, which might have provided evidence of his intentions and certainly would have accounted for his actions, had since disappeared. Anxious to fit the (absence of) data to his theory of the "race," Morton hinted darkly: "It is not safe to rely on evidence of the man Thompson himself, all the more so since there is a strange, perhaps a determined silence in his journals at this point."[10]

Confusing, as Tyrrell had done, the roles of historian and editor, Glover took up the "race" debate in the second edition of the *Narrative* and decided in favour of Morton. Tyrrell's picture of Thompson, a "hagiographical myth," deserved attack; Glover would replace the hero with the truth. He began by drawing larger historical lines, as Morton had done with his theme of the "Columbian enterprise." Glover credited the fur companies with Thompson's carto-

9. *Narrative* (Tyrrell, lvii, liii); Tyrrell-RSC 243–5. See Ronda (62–4, 232–4, 248, and 443) for a conclusive review of the "race to the sea."
10. Morton, CHR 17:284; Morton, *History* (491).

graphic work: the Hudson's Bay Company had trained Thompson, and the North West Company had allowed him to explore. Then Glover questioned Tyrrell's characterization of the explorer. In place of "the white flower of a blameless life," Thompson's character was reduced to "the more commonplace Puritan virtues" and even "that common Puritan disease," an inability to admit mistakes. Glover contended that Thompson lied by omission: his *Narrative* account of joining the North West Company "leave[s] the reader with a very falsified impression of the whole picture of what actually happened." Thompson also lied by suppression: Glover pointed to the missing journal of 23 July – 28 October 1810, asserting that Thompson had deliberately destroyed it, that he had recoiled from leaving a record of shameful behaviour during these three months.

What Thompson could not bear to reveal, Glover undertook to re-constitute: "If one cannot tell what Thompson actually did from day to day all through this long episode, one can perhaps fathom his state of mind." From inference to conjecture, from action to intention, Glover built his loss-of-nerve theory: Thompson failed to arrive at the Pacific coast before Astor's men because he had failed to confront Peigans at Howse Pass – and this because at the critical moment he was "in a state of fear, which numbed his powers of decision." Glover multiplied his accusations: not only was Thompson a coward, he was "an inept businessman"; his desperate poverty late in life was unrelieved because of an "apparent failure to inspire the most commonplace family affection among his children." In Glover's view, Thompson was notable as a devious bungler – he could do no right. But far from arriving at the truth about Thompson, Glover engaged in the same myth-making process as Tyrrell and merely served up an anti-hero.[11]

Tyrrell and Glover shared a weakness for excessively interpreting and historicizing the text they edited. Tyrrell constructed a moral character for Thompson, and Glover believed he could recount "what actually happened." Both editors were eager to pose and answer historical questions before they had recognized to what extent formal, textual considerations should have limited their speculation. This oversight was especially problematic when the editors indiscriminately applied their characterizations of Thompson to both the *Narrative* and the journals. To focus on a supratextual identity – "the man Thompson himself" – is to overlook the real editorial issues: the tex-

---

11. Glover, CHR 31:1–25; *Narrative* (Glover, xii-xiii, xli, lvii–lviii, lxv); Dempsey (22–8).

tual determination of authorial persona, and the kind of information that each kind of text can be expected to provide.

The *Narrative* was Thompson's adaptation of his professional journals for "the general reader," that is, for a popular audience more interested in adventure than discovery. It is surprising that historians and geographers, as readers with professional concerns, have neglected the explorer's scientific journals in favour of the popular work. But as Coues remarked, "So much of Thompson's manuscript consists of astronomical calculations, traverse tables, and other mathematical detail, without which the matter would cease to be Thompsonian, yet with which it would be largely unreadable and unsalable." Glover concurred: "Much in any journal is apt to be waste material, so far as any reading interest goes." Hopwood looked for "anecdotal units" hidden in the "almost infinite factuality" of Thompson's daily record.[12] What these editors wanted from the journals, and found only in the *Narrative*, was a series of dramatic incidents and vivid descriptions of fur trade life. Tyrrell repeatedly refers to the journals as Thompson's "notes." So they were, in the sense that they were cartographic notes, a sort of verbal map which the explorer consulted when preparing his maps; they were also the mnemonic stimulus for his *Narrative*. But the journals are more than the preparatory stages of Thompson's maps and memoirs. They form a distinct and self-sufficient text; they are Thompson's detailed, contemporary record of measurements, events and impressions during the day-to-day business of trading and surveying. Readers less informed than Tyrrell about Thompson's scientific work, and as negligent of textual considerations, have assumed with Glover and Hopwood that the *Narrative* is equal in authority to the journals on which it is based. Hopwood commented on the "stylistic strength" of the *Narrative*, and praised Thompson as "a master story teller" who knew how "to bring the story line to the front."[13] These are admirable traits in the *Narrative*, but the journals have other virtues.

For the editor and reader in search of "the man Thompson himself," the most disturbing difference between the *Narrative* and the journals is their striking disparity of style. In the journals the "master story teller" seems disappointingly arid, and annoyingly hard to define. The generic nature of each text explains this stylistic incongruity, for the two genres present the writer in different relationships to the events and impressions he records. The autobiographical *Narrative* assumes

12. Coues (1:xxi–xxii); *Narrative* (Glover, lxv); Hopwood (25, 21).
13. Hopwood (20–35).

a continuing personal identity of the "I" who writes and the "me" who is written about. Autobiography views past activities and perceptions as they are measured and coloured by the writer's present; it also presents the writer as the main textual subject. By contrast, a journal is divided into daily entries that follow each other like snapshots in an album, without the transforming perspective of hindsight and the sense of personal identity that this perspective creates. Moreover, Thompson's journals adhere to a standard fur trade format – in style they are official rather than introspective accounts. Since it is based on the journals, even the *Narrative* retains some of the emphasis and restraint of the earlier text.

Consequently, "the man Thompson himself" is exceptionally elusive. The persona of the journals, which is retained in great measure in the *Narrative*, defeats the efforts of Tyrrell, Glover, Hopwood and others to characterize and identify the writer apart from his distinct functions in the two texts. These editors, and the historians who followed their lead, tried to invent a single, consistent character rather than contenting themselves with the separate authorial masks presented in each text. Almost nothing is known of Thompson apart from the documents he himself produced. That "the man Thompson himself" is so obviously an interpretive tautology, a figure derived from the documents in order to explain them, should serve as a caution to any editor bent on biographical explanation and/or historical reconstruction.

This is not to say that the standard format of fur trade journals prevented them from becoming a medium of individual expression. But the journals are filters rather than mirrors. Mackenzie's journal relates the incidents of the day to his "darling project" of reaching the Pacific; Fraser's journal obsessively recounts the dangers of his voyage; Simpson's ruminates on the reorganization of the Columbia Department. Thompson's journals are easily distinguished from these others, yet like them they are professional records. All of the fur trade journals exclude vicarious references to private life, general statements of intention, retrospective analysis and comment on anything but the task at hand. Even concerning work they are restrictive: they record the writer's activities and the "remarkable occurrences" of his immediate neighbourhood, but they are silent about company policy or long-term projects. Within a genre already limited and controlled, Thompson's discretion is exemplary, just as his emotional reticence is extreme. He comes closest to giving vent to his feelings when he makes a few ironic comments on his mutinous men in entries for January 1811. Admiration and discouragement alike are expressed in conventional phrases such as "It was a grand sight" and "I was at a loss what

to do." Any intensity of emotion is transferred to the event or phenomenon that forms the subject of the entry: the tone does not vary, but
the subject is described at length and in detail. Of Thompson's con-
temporaries, only Turnor and Vancouver kept journals as purely professional and as rigorously void of emotion. This may be mere
coincidence; it is nonetheless true that Turnor and Vancouver were
Thompson's cartographic models.[14]

Thompson's journals are useful as historical sources only insofar as
these generic traits and limitations are recognized. Given the controversy over his "missing journal," it is important to note that the kind
of information provided in fur trade journals concerning policy and
intentions is negligible. As well, the repetition of daily activities
implies rather than emphasizes progression towards some goal. In his
extant journals, Thompson rarely states his own plans or preferences,
and never discusses his role in carrying out those of the company. This
reticence explains much of the mystery surrounding the "race to the
sea." If the *Narrative* account of first crossing Athabaska Pass is compared with journal entries covering the same event, it will be seen that
the *Narrative* transforms weeks of repeated activities and recalci-
trance, recorded at the time in daily entries, into a turning point in the
explorer's efforts to reach the sea.[15] Yet even while it concentrates
repetitive day-by-day progress into a single decisive moment, the
Narrative preserves the journals' narrow preoccupation with an individual enterprise, without reference to company directives or contemporary events. Thompson's silence in both texts concerning the North
West Company's plans is a discretion of form, not necessarily of guilt.
Even if the missing journal of July–October 1810 were to be recovered, historians might well be disappointed in their search for proof of
Thompson's role in the "Columbian enterprise." All that the extant
journals record of the matter is one laconic entry for 10 July 1811:
"Heard news of the American Ship's arrival." The journals do not
deny that Thompson had a special role to play in a "Columbian enterprise," just as they do not confirm it. They are simply not occupied
with the question – nor by their generic nature can they be.[16]

14. HBCA A11/117: David Thompson to HBC Committee, 30 August 1790; VPL
   journal: "Extract of *A Voyage of Discovery* ..."; PRO (1): "The whole of the
   Sea Coast is taken from Vancouver's Survey."
15. *Narrative* (Tyrrell, 446–9/Glover, 321–3).
16. The reticence of Thompson's journals may be compared with his style in
   reports and letters – for example: concluding remarks in the VPL journal/NA
   report (1801); RCSL report (1807); pencilled draft letter in AO journals 19

This narrow focus notwithstanding, the historical value of Thompson's journals is considerable. Instead of circulating them among colleagues or revising them for publication as Hearne, Mackenzie and Fraser did, Thompson seems to have written these journals for himself, preferring to send reports to senior partners while still a trader, and later to write the *Narrative* as a separate text. Consequently, Thompson's journals, so precise and rich in detail, are exceptional as an unretouched, contemporary record of the fur trade during its period of greatest expansion. This period left so few physical marks that Dr James Hector of the Palliser expedition wrote as if he were distanced by centuries rather than decades from its activity. Indeed, by the mid-nineteenth century a number of abandoned posts could scarcely be located, portages had disappeared, and most of the North West Company's records had been lost or destroyed. Since Hector's time, settlement and hydroelectric dams have radically altered the territory in which the traders worked. Thompson's journals are the textual trace of the fur business in its most extended phase, just as his maps preserve the traders' image of the country.

IN EDITING THE JOURNALS WHICH THOMPSON WROTE between 1800 and 1812, I have perceived and responded to three problems: selecting the journal sequences to be edited, determining the relationship of variants, and presenting the text.

Journal sequences selected for this edition demonstrate Thompson's role in the European discovery of the Columbia River, the long-sought "river of the west." Until the end of the eighteenth century, the Plains tribes' geographical knowledge was bounded by the Rocky Mountains; of the Europeans, only Mackenzie had pushed through to the Pacific Ocean – but not by the river whose mouth had been charted by Gray and Broughton. From the Columbia's source in the Rocky Mountain Trench, Thompson doggedly charted every bend and sandbank in its course to the sea. His complete and methodical account of the river can nevertheless be lost in the repetitiveness of his trips from supply depots to the posts he built in his new department. Unlike the accounts of Hearne, Mackenzie, Lewis and Clark, which relate singular and exceptional journeys of discovery, Thompson's daily record reflects the fact that his explorations accommodated the main job of trading.

(1807); NA MG19 A17: Thompson to Alexander Fraser, 20 December 1810; Thompson to Duncan McDougall, David Stuart and Robert Stuart, 15 July 1811 (Bridgwater, 52).

I have selected those passages of Thompson's journals which describe each stage of his exploration of the Columbia, beginning with his first attempts to cross the divide and concluding with his ascent of the river from Astoria to Boat Encampment. The first three parts of the edited text describe early efforts to gain access to the upper reaches of the Columbia River. Thompson's successful crossing of the divide in 1807 and his establishment of Kootanae House are recounted in the fourth and fifth sections. Part seven, a trip in 1808 "from Boggy Hall to Kootanae House," retraces the Howse Pass route of the previous summer, and is included to show Thompson's minimal style when he travelled over old ground. As well, the seventh part contains details that shed some light on the controversial month of October 1810. The sixth and eighth sections relate Thompson's advance south of the Columbia's source to two of its tributaries. Parts nine and ten record Thompson's first crossing of Athabaska Pass and his voyage to Astoria. The eleventh section completes his survey of the Columbia River.[17]

The second editorial problem was to determine, if possible, the relationship between variants. Thompson's early editors, because they were preoccupied with historical rather than textual questions, did not consider this aspect of the journals. Wood and Thiessen gave it cursory attention: they confidently classified the two versions of the Mandan journals as "the original copy of [Thompson's] field notes" and "a later copy, a 'fair journal,'" but they did not explain how they made this distinction.[18] Among the Columbia journals, multiple versions exist for two sequences: 10 May 1807 to 8 February 1808, and 20 April to 8 June 1808. Thompson wrote his journals in foolscap memorandum books which were ordered, together with ink and quills, as items in his requisitions of goods. The following list indicates the relevant memorandum books and the journals they contain:

13 5–23 October 1800
    17 November – 3 December 1800
18 11 October 1806 – 26 July 1807
19 18 July 1807 – 4 August 1808
20 10 May 1807 – 8 February 1808
21 20 April – 8 June 1808
22 27 September 1809 – 22 July 1810
23 4 August 1808 – 16 September 1809

---

17. See Thompson's itinerary in the *Narrative* (Tyrrell, lxxix–xcvi).
18. Wood and Thiessen (93–4).

25 29 October 1810 – 2 July 1811
27 3 July 1811 – 28 April 1812[19]

No. 24, the "missing journal" that so intrigued Morton and Glover, presumably covered the period 23 July to 28 October 1810; no. 26 is a set of traverse tables for the Columbia River. No Journal is extant for the abortive expedition of 6–30 June 1801, but the two reports of this trip appear to be based on a journal, since they reproduce certain passages in daily entry format.

Of more interest to an editor than missing evidence are the variants for 1807–08, which form an overlapping pattern. No. 20 begins on 10 May 1807 and overlaps no. 18, dating from the previous fall. No. 18 ends on 26 July 1807, but not before no. 19 has been started, so for the week of 18–26 July there are no fewer than three journals. For the period 20 April to 8 June 1808, no. 19 is doubled by no. 21. No. 20 ends on 8 February 1808, but no. 19 ensures continuity through the summer of 1808 until 4 August, when a successive pattern takes over; for the later journals there is only one account for each time period. The overlap seems to have been caused by Thompson's simultaneous adherence to two journal subgenres: the post journal, which kept a continuous record of trade and occurrences at a given place, and the travel journal, which described a "voyage." Nos. 18 and 19 begin as post journals but include, respectively, the voyages of 10 May – 18 July 1807 and 20 April – 8 June 1808. No. 20, on the other hand, begins as a travel journal but is maintained as a record of the winter at Kootanae House. Although no. 21 repeats part of no. 19, in form it is a travel journal, the account of Thompson's first trip down "McGillivray's" (Kootenay) River.

One might assume, as Wood and Thiessen did for the Mandan journals, that these overlapping accounts are an original and copies, but it is impossible to define their relationship with any certitude. The physical state of the manuscripts is not a reliable indication: all of the Columbia journals are written right to the margins in a fairly cramped hand, as if paper were at a premium; all are worn at the edges and some pages are stained. In other words, they all look like original "campfire" journals. The variants are distinguished by slight alterations of word and phrase; although these changes point to a concern for style, overall they do not allow classification into "rough" and

---

19. The book numbers are Thompson's own. The books have been grouped, bound and assigned volume numbers which have no historical relevance and are quite confusing. Hence my practice of citing only the book numbers.

"fair" copies, as Fraser's variants clearly do. Why Thompson would make, and then keep for himself, more than one version of these journals remains a baffling question.

Whatever their exact relationship, all the manuscripts of the 1807–08 journals seem to have been written before 1817, the year in which Thompson began his surveys for the International Boundary Commission. By 1820 his handwriting had changed significantly, becoming at first larger, with the letters more widely spaced, then showing the first signs of deterioration to the tremulous, detached characters of the *Narrative* manuscript. This change in handwriting also dates the maps that Thompson submitted to the Foreign Office. They appear to have been drawn very soon after the North West Company map completed in 1814, and to have been merely touched up in 1842–43. Within the ten-year period of 1807–17, the evidence of dates and revisions of the variants is inconclusive. Rather than establishing what would be at best a tenuous, at worst an erroneous series of textual relationships, I have preferred to treat the multiple versions simply as parallel texts. Where possible, I have shown variation by angled brackets in the printed text, and where this is not possible, I have indicated divergences in the notes. The dates of the other, successive journals are not in doubt.

A final editorial problem, that of adapting the manuscript text to print, has necessitated minimal changes in punctuation as well as a reduction of the course notations and astronomical calculations. Verbatim reproduction of the manuscripts can be tiresome and confusing in a long text, as a glance at the editions of White, and Wood and Thiessen will show. Elliott's editorial solution was to make sentences of Thompson's phrases. Hopwood edited even more boldly in an attempt to provide "an accurate, easy to read" text; he omitted repetitions, altered the syntax and "regularized" (modernized) spelling and punctuation, so as "to avoid intruding questions of correctness on the reader."[20] Given the fact that Thompson's journals are now almost two hundred years old, no editor in the world can produce a text of these manuscripts that is at once "accurate" and "easy to read." By seeing period spelling and syntax as problematic, Elliot and Hopwood revealed their uneasiness when faced with the eighteenth-century conventions of Thompson's style. Even Wood and Thiessen, who prided themselves on exactly reproducing the manuscript, interjected names, comments and question marks into the printed text, and let their own notes effectively intrude into the text by placing both on the same

20. Hopwood (35–8).

page. Like Elliott and Hopwood, the editors of the Mandan journals wanted to bring Thompson's text within easy reach of modern readers.

However, a document may be clearly presented without being unduly modernized, and the period differences remind readers of the distance that separates the text from their own habits of mind and expression. Thompson's capitals and contractions, like his science and religion, are of his own time, not ours. Although I have grouped phrases to make the text clearer and more fluent, I have done so only by altering punctuation and spacing at certain points; here, as in the manuscripts, the phrase remains the syntactical unit. The astronomical calculations and most of the lengthy course notations have had to be omitted. Their scientific value is better expressed in Thompson's maps and they occupy one-fourth to one-third of each journal. I have kept a vestige of them by including lists of ten or fewer courses, and have retained the positions determined by astronomical observations. Explanations of Thompson's survey techniques are given in the notes. These explanations, which have not been given in previous edited accounts of fur trade and northern exploration, provide more information about Thompson's method than would be furnished by inclusion of all the courses and calculations.

In providing notes to the text, again I have avoided excessive modernization and have worked to keep editorial interference to a minimum. The notes are unkeyed and placed after the text so that it retains, as much as possible, the impact of the manuscript journals. At all times the notes are suggestive and tentative rather than explanatory. With few exceptions the textual cross-references work forward rather than back so that the reader is progressively liberated from this editorial support system. To further this liberation and to avoid needless repetition, contextual quotations are referenced to the list of sources rather than introduced here and there in the notes themselves. Together the period sources furnish a contemporary commentary in response to questions that modern readers are likely to ask: What was the fur trade milieu of which Thompson was a representative? What navigational instruments and skills did he use to carry out his surveys? What scientific ideas influenced his observation of natural phenomena? And what were the impressions of other early travellers in the territory he explored? The sources are not embedded in a historical commentary that weighs and adjusts their "accuracy"; instead, they form the documentary context on which subsequent historical appraisal of Thompson's work must be based. They give a one-sided, European evaluation of events, conditions and customs, just as Thompson's own journals do: Thompson never forgot that he was a stranger among the "strange Indians" of the trade frontier. Although specialists may not need to consult all of the notes, other readers will find that they supply useful information.

The list of sources is confined to a bibliography of Thompson's own texts and maps, the contemporary works referred to in the notes, and a very few specialized studies. I have not listed scholarly commentary on Thompson's work because such a list would soon be out of date and, even more importantly, because Thompson's journals themselves constitute a source document. To look at them from a previously developed historical perspective would be like looking through the wrong end of a telescope. While it is true that no text can be read except by interpretation, the process can be usurped by the editor or left as much as possible to each reader. This is the first major edition of Thompson's journals, and as such it is a source book: it provides the materials for history; it does not rely on ready conclusions. The journals are dry and difficult, editorial guidance is deliberately minimal, and the reader must work hard to create his or her own pattern of understanding. Such effort will be repaid, for there is much in this text to discover and enjoy.

Signs and Abbreviations

[ ]	illegible in manuscript	In	inch
[added]	dubious reading:	Inst	of the present month
	added word or phrase	Isl^d	island
〈 〉	variant in parallel texts	lbs	pounds (weight)
&	and	LL UL	sun's lower limb, upper
&c	et cetera		limb
£	pounds (currency)	Lat^de	latitude
X	cross, across	Long^de	longitude
°	degrees	[MS]	manuscript
′ ″	minutes, seconds	M	mile
ab^t	about	MM	memorandum
Am	morning,	Merid	meridian
Pm	evening	N S E W	north, south, east, west
Amm	ammunition	NW Co	North West Company
com	common	obs^d	observed
Co	course	p^r	per
DT	David Thompson	perpend	perpendicular
Dec^n	declination	pt	point
dist	distant	R	rapid
d°	ditto	Ro^ds	rounds of ammunition
Doub	double	SC	strong current
Exp^d	expended	SRC	strong rapid current
Ex^d	extended	SS	stroud
fm	fathom	Ther	temperature
ft	foot		(Fahrenheit)
FDP	Fort des Prairies	Tob	tobacco
G	good	Var^n	variation
H	hour	VG	very good
Ho	house	VS	very strong
[HBC]	Hudson's Bay Company	Y^ds	yards

Columbia Journals

Journey to the Kootanaes

5–23 October 1800

October 5th [1800] Sunday A fine cloudy Day. At 8 Am the Men
crossed the River, La Gassé, Beauchamp, Morrin, Pierre Daniel,
Boulard & myself, with the He Dog, a Cree, and the Old Bear, a
Pekenow Indian, our Guide. We had an assortment of Goods,
amounting to about 300 Skins, & each of us a light Horse, belonging
to himself, and 3 Horses of the Company's to carry the Baggage.
We met several Blood Indians going in to trade. Our Co, the crossing
Place of the Clear Water River, may be about SEbE 2½M. After
crossing that Stream we went on about SE ½M to the parting of the
Roads, where finding we had forgot to take a Kettle with us, I sent
La Gassé back again to the House for one. Mean Time we went on to
the Bridge, which is a few Sticks laid across a Brook – our Co^s
during this Time thro' mostly thick Woods of Pine and Aspin may have
been SEbs 1½M to a small Brook with very little water and which
we crossed – it goes into the Clear Water River. Then sbw 10½M to the
Brook Bridge: here we put up to wait La Gassé, who came in the
Evening with 2 Kettles. Fine weather.

October 6th [1800] Monday In the Morn Cloudy, with a small shower
of Rain – afterwards fine. At 6 Am set off – lost ½ Hour in crossing
the Bridge, which we found very bad. We went on thro' a willow Plain
about SE 4M, then we entered the Woods, then Co SE 4M South 3M
very bad swampy Ground thick Woods of Pines. Co sbE 2M small
Plains, saw a Herd of Cows – end of Co stopped an Hour at 10 to
a bold Brook – Co along it mostly SEbE 1M when we crossed it, then
Co SE 6M to a Plain in which we went ab^t So 3M, at end of Co a

Rill of Water – crossed it. Co sbE 4M when we came to 5 Tents of
Pekenow Indians, with whom we staid to smoke about ¼H. We then
went on sbE 1¼M and crossed a Rivulet, which a small Distance below
us falls into the Red Deers River.

Co ssw 2M to the Red Deers River, which we also crossed – we then
went on up along the River, mostly on the Gravel Banks, which
formerly in high Water were part of the Bed of the River.
swbs 2M sw 2M in these Co⁵ several crossed & recrossed the small
Channels of the River, as they came in our Way, and at end of Co
recrossed the River altogether, and went on thro' a tolerable fine
Plain sw 2M to a bold Brook, which falls into the last mentioned River.
Here we had a grand view of the Rocky Mountains, forming a
concave segment of a Circle, and lying from one Point to another about
sbE & Nbw. All it's snowy cliffs to the Southward were bright with
the Beams of the Sun, while the most northern were darkened by a
Tempest; those Cliffs in the Concave were alternately brightened
by the Sun & obscured by the Storm, which spent it's Force only on the
Summits. All the above Co⁵ by the Sun. We then crossed a Plain
abounding with small Willows. The Co s65w 6M by the Compass, to
the Foot of a high woody Hill extending along those Mountains,
where we found 5 Tents of Pekenow Indians – into one of them belonging to our Guide we went & put up at 5 Pm.

It is surprising what a quantity of Ground ... In some Places, it was
not less than 500 Y^ds broad, by different Channels, with gravel
Banks between them – while at present it is contracted into a Stream
of from 40 to 50 Y^ds and it's Depth upon a Medium about 2 ft at
ab^t 3½M p^r Hour, with here and there a few small insignificant
Channels occupying rarely more than 200 Y^ds and in general much
less. Let us ask the Cause of this: is it that the heavy Rains and melting
of the Snows have carried away such Quantities of the Particles of
the Mountain as greatly to have diminished it's height and therefore
does not attract the Clouds & Vapours so strongly as formerly; or
that the Earth and Ocean in these Climes do not yield the Vapours so
freely as of Old; or if they do, are they driven by some unknown
Cause, to break and dissolve before they reach the Mountains?
Whatever Opinion we may form, the Fact is certain, that at present
and for several Years past the Mountains do not send forth above two
thirds of the Water they did formerly, for we see upon the Banks
of all the Rivers large Trees that have been carried down by the Stream,

and left either a great way from their present Boundaries, or a great Height upon the Banks far above the greatest known Level of the present Times. These Trees are not only to be found singly, but in vast Numbers, piled so intricately together that it is next to impossible to disentangle them.

October 7th [1800] **Tuesday** In the Night an exceeding heavy Fall of Rain, which in the Morning changed to Snow, and continued all Day; in the Even the weather moderated – the Snow is now about 1 foot deep.

October 8th [1800] **Wednesday** A Cloudy Day, with at times small light Snow. Went a hunting with a Pekenow Indian – killed a Jumping Deer, very fat, & my Companion killed another, which we brought with us to the Tents, where we arrived in the Evening. In this Excursion we crossed the Red Deers River, which here is mostly confined to one Channel of about 40 Y^{ds} & very strong currents, with Banks of Rock. Found the Country very bad, full of large Swamps and high Knowls covered with thick Woods, that were in many Places burnt. Animals of all Kinds were numerous, but the Weather was too Calm for Hunting.

October 9th [1800] **Thursday** A very fine Day. We wait a Pekenow Indian who is to come with us by his Promise to [be] our Guide. In the Afternoon he came, but I soon found by his conversation that his Company like the rest of his Nation now present was intended only for that Spot, for the sake of Smoking and what else they can get. They are so jealous of the Kootanaes coming in to Trade that they do all they can to persuade me to return, assuring me that it is impossible for me to find them, and that in endeavouring to search them out, our Horses will fall by Fatigue and Hunger, and perhaps also ourselves. At Noon Obs^d Merid Alt^{de} of [sun's] LL Lat^{de} 51°:47′:21″ N Decⁿ 6°:23′:59″ s.

October 10th [1800] **Friday** A cloudy stormy Day, with high Drift & Snow 'till 10 Am, when it cleared & became tolerable fine. Went a Hunting with our Guide & a young Man – killed a Bull of which we brought 2 Horse Loads to the Tents. Every where thick Woods of Pines with Spots of Aspin and much, very much deep swampy Ground.

The Indians dissuade us all they can from going any further, but our Guide tells me, they purposely misrepresent the Country for their own private Views.

October 11th [1800] **Saturday** A very fine Day, but the Snow thawed very little. At 10 Am we set off & went about sbw 3M ssw 1M sbw 2M end of Co passed a small Brook, which falls close by us into the Red Deers River, which last may be about sse 1M from us. Put up at end of Co – but I went a hunting with La Gassé and our Guide on the Heights of the River, where I killed a Bull with Horns of a remarkable Length, measuring 35 inches along the Curve – we brought most of the Meat to the Tents where we arrived in the Evening. Cloudy.

October 12th [1800] **Sunday** Lat^{de} 51°:42′ N Long^{de} 114°:45′ w. At 9½ Am set off – Course along the Red Deers River, over a high Point of Land, with thick Pines sw 3M then West 2M wnw 2M nwbw 1½M along the Red Deers River – at end of Co came to 2 Tents of Pekenow Indians, who were Eagle Hunting, and put up with them. I went up a high Knowl & took a rough Sketch of the Appearance of the Mountains. Killed a Fisher to Day – there are many of this Animal about these woody Hills, as also of Wolverenes – Buffalo, Red Deer, Moose & small Deer are also plenty, and Grisled Bears but too many. In the evening the Indians, having finished their Eagle Hunt and having killed 8 this Day, they made a Feast. A clear Place being made within the Tent, at the back Part, the Eagles were all laid there upon clean Grasses with their Heads towards the Fire – very little Ceremony of any kind was used, except in smoking, when the Eagles had, each separately, the pipe presented to it. As the Pipe went round, the People who were seated on each Side of the Tent and of the Eagles, sung & took the Rattle alternately – this lasted about 3 Hours when the Company broke up. From the top of a very high knowl, I had a very extensive View of the Country: from the southward extending by the westward to the North, it was every where Ranges of woody Hills lying nearly parallel to the Mountain, and rising one behind another higher and higher to the snowy Summits of the Mountain.

October 13th [1800] **Monday** A snowy Morn. At 10 Am it cleared away & became tolerable fine. Obs^d Merid Alt^{de} of [sun's]

LL Lat^{de} 51°:41′:41″ N Dec^n 7°:54′:36″ s. Our Guide and three Men
went a Hunting, but soon returned without Success. The Day has
been very stormy with Showers [of] Hail & Snow. In the Evening 2
Pekenow young Men (who have stolen two fine Mares from the
Kootanaes) arrived – they brought word that the Kootanaes would be
on the Heights of the Mountain the Morrow.

October 14 [1800] **Tuesday** A very fine Day. At $7\frac{1}{2}$ Am I set off for the
Mountains with three Men, our Guide and several Pekenow
Indians, who came with us from Hopes of Plunder. I left two Men in
care of our Baggage, which was unnecessary to take with us, as the
Kootanaes are to pass by the Camp. We went on about West 22 Miles
to the Foot of the high Cliffs, where at $2\frac{1}{2}$ Pm we met the Kootanae
Chief attended by about 26 Men and 7 Women. They had 11 Horses
with a few Furrs in Beaver & Bears. The Chief made me a Present
of his Bow & Quiver of Arrows and of a Red Fox Skin which he had
for a Cap, also of a yellow Horse with about 50 Beaver Skins – but
I told him to keep Possession of the Horse & Furrs 'till he came to the
House, when I should be able to reward him for the Present. The
others I took upon. He spoke; we then all sat down & smoked together.
I cut a fathom of Tobacco which I had brought with me among
them – after having sat about $\frac{1}{2}$ Hour, I proposed going to some Place
where we could Camp, which we instantly did, returning back
about 1 Mile. These poor Fellows are but poorly clothed notwithstanding the rigour of the Cold in these Mountains; they give me to
understand that the Pekenow Indians have stolen most of their Horses.
I said all I could to encourage them to come on to the House, and
they assured me they would persevere. Our Road to day has been
mostly along small Brooks – the Scources of the Red Deers River
– which every where intersect the Hills. These Streams in general form
narrow Bottoms among the Hills, where they wind about in all
directions from North by the East to South – after crossing & recrossing
[one] of them several Times 'till we found a convenient Place to go
up the Hill which formed it's western barrier, we left the Brook
& crossed the Hill where we, on the other side, were sure to find
another small Brook, which we again crossed & recrossed, as we did
the one before, until we gained the heights of the Mountain –
where we found the road dry, very Hilly & stony. The Hills of all this
Day, 'till we began to get above the Scources of the River, were
extremely swampy for about half way up them, the Water oozing out

every where, and in many Places formed Bogs impassable to large
Animals. They were in general well clothed with Woods of Fir very tall
& straight, tho' not large, as I did not see one that exceeded 7 or
8 Feet in Girth. The Swamps had small dwarf Pines, in many Places
burnt. When we arrived on the Heights of the Mountains, at the
Foot of those high Craigs that brave the storm in all it[s] Force, I wished
to climb them to gain a View of the back Country, but they were
inaccessible to human Feet, and the Care of the Kootanaes called for
all my Time & Attention. A very clear, cold Night obliged to tye
our Horses as there was little or no Grass for them.

October 15 [1800] Wednesday A very fine Day, but sharp Morning.
We set off very early, the Kootanaes taking the Lead; we arrived
at the Camp, about an Hour after Sun Set, very much fatigued with
the Badness of the Roads. The poor Kootanaes were hardly arrived
when one of the Pekenow Scoundrels took a Fancy to a Black Horse
belonging to them, & wanted to take him by Force – but the
Kootanaes bravely springing upon their Arms, he was obliged to
relinquish his Prize but it raised a small Tumult in which our
Guide, a Chief & distinguished warrior of the Pekenows, went out
& made a Speech suitable to the Occasion, bidding the young Men
remember his Example: that when he wanted Horses, he went & took
them from his Enemies bravely, and that it was an Act neither
brave nor manly to rob a few Strangers, their Allies, of their poor
starved Horses. They dispersed, but the Kootanaes from such a
Prelude were many of them determined to set off back for their Country
in the Night. I went with Boulard to them, & by Entreaties
& encouraging Conversation brought them from their Fears
& prevailed on them all to come in to the House – at Midnight I left
them & went to sleep.

October 16 [1800] Thursday A very fine Day. In the Morn, on assembling the Horses the Kootanaes found that the Pekenows had
stolen 5 of their Horses in the Night, and among them my yellow
Horse. They also stole a Horse which one of my Men traded from
them last Night; the rest of them they were obliged to exchange for
the worst Horses the Pekenows had, getting with those bad Horses
a Knife, a few rounds of Ammunition, a bit of Tobacco &c &c. I was
much distressed to get them in the Temper to come on, which with
much ado I brought about, lending them a Horse to carry part of their

Baggage on. By 10 Am we set off with the Kootanaes and 2 Tents in Company – our Guide and another.

As I kept among the Kootanaes to encourage them, and to learn their Sentiments of what had happened, I soon found they did not bear the repeated Injuries of the Pekenow's with entire resignation, but only wait a convenient time to retaliate. They complained much & bitterly to me of what had been stolen & plundered from them, & declared they would revenge such Treatment – several of the principal of them went so far as to kneel down and swear by the Sun, the Skies and Earth that they would revenge themselves on the Pekenows and never forgive them. After we had gone about 7 or 8 Miles, the Pekenows wanted to put up, for the sake of drawing from them every thing they had of worth. This I perceived & was aware; I had therefore previously given orders to the Men, in case the Pekenows should wish to put up very early, to pass on with the Kootanaes. They did so, but no sooner did the Pekenows see them pass, than 3 young Men took hold of the foremost of the Kootanae Horses, to make them turn round – I rode up & with the assistance of Boulard made them relinquish the Horses & get out of the Road. This done I instantly went to where our Guide was about pitching his Tent & told him to come on if he had any Friendship for us, and wished to avoid the spilling of Blood; to this he consented, & begging me to tell his Women to follow on he went off.

We went on & put up early at the little Brook Wt^d of the Water Campment. I tried all I could but without effect to get one or two of them to go after my Horse – they could by no means be persuaded and seemed to consider whatever had been stolen as lawful Plunder. I cannot help admiring the Spirit of these brave, undaunted, but poor Kootanaes; they have all along shown a courage and Fortitude admirable – not the least sign of Weakness or Cowardice, altho' they are in the Power of a large Party of Indians, who are at least 20 to one. They are conducted by 4 old Men who seem worthy of being at the Head of such People. This day when the young Pekenow Men seized the Heads of their Horses, they all as if acted by one Soul bent their Bows, got ready their other Weapons, and prepared to make their Oppressors quit their Horses or sell their Lives dearly – hardly a single Word was spoken among them.

October 17 [1800] Friday A very fine Day. At 8$\frac{3}{4}$ Am set off & went on to about the mid of the Plain of the grand View, where the

Pekenows pitched their Tents. We however with the Kootanaes passed on without Molestation & leaving our former Road on the right, took the Woods. At $4\frac{1}{2}$ Pm we camped about 1M N^d of the last Camp of the Pekenows. The Chief of this Camp kindly invited us into his Tent, where he gave us something to eat; he then called all the Kootanaes & made them a Feast. In the Evening some of the Pekenow young Men challenged the Kootanaes to a Gambling Match, which was readily accepted by the latter: they assembled round our Fires, but the Pekenows were by no means a Match for these Strangers – they lost every Game. At Midnight they separated.

October 18th [1800] **Saturday** A fine Day. In the Night a Pekenow Scoundrel stole one of the Kootanae Horses – they have now but Two. At 7 Am I set off with one Man on light Horses for the House, in order to arrange Matters there, & to get two or three light Horses to assist the Kootanaes, who are all very much fatigued. I arrived at 3 Pm & found all well, thank God.

October 19th [1800] **Sunday** A very bad Night of Sleet & Rain, & in the Morn of Snow, 'till $9\frac{1}{2}$ Am when it ceased & became fine. At 8 Am I set off with 3 Men & two light Horses to meet the Kootanaes – when I arrived at the Bridge, I left the Men and Horses & went on alone. About 1 Pm I met them coming on – they had killed two Cows, & several of them were carrying Meat on their Backs; however, late in the Evening they all arrived at the Bridge & put up.

October 20th [1800] **Monday** A fine Day. At 8 Am having lent the Kootanaes Two more Horses & arranged them, we set off & with much Trouble and Dispute with the Pekenows, even to drawing of Arms, we arrived at the Fort at 3 Pm, thank God. An Old Man with 3 Bear Skin's went to the English. Made them a present of near half a Keg of Rum, as also of about 3 Gallons to the Pekenows and my Guide who have assisted me.

October 21st [1800] **Tuesday** A fine Day. Paid the Old Bear our Pekenow Guide & the three other Pekenows as p^r Expence List. In the Afternoon traded with the Kootanaes – their Trade amounted to $110\frac{1}{2}$ Beaver, 10 Bears 2 Wolverenes and 5 Fishers. Conversed much with them about the Mountain and the Rivers and Lakes on the other Side – I also laid strict Injunctions on them to come again in

the Spring to guide us to their Country – also fitted La Gassé & Le Blanc
to winter with them.

October 22nd [1800] Wednesday About Noon part of the Kootanaes
went away. Lent a Horse to the Chief, which he is to pay in the
Spring, for he has none to carry his Things on, as the two Men who
are to go with the Kootanaes cannot find their Horses. The Chief
with part of his young Men wait them. In the Evening 10 Pekenows
on Horseback were seen on the other Side of the River, which made
me suspect they had come to know what Road the Kootanaes would
take to pass the Mountains & lay wait & rob them. I immediately
ordered off all the Kootanaes, & told them not to stop 'till they came
up with the others – however, it proved to be only a false Alarm,
as they came to Trade and made no Enquiries after the Strangers.

October 23rd [1800] Thursday A fine Day. Early at $7\frac{1}{2}$ Am I set off with
La Gassé & Le Blanc after the Kootanaes – following their Road
'till $\frac{1}{4}$ past Noon I came up with them when, bidding Adieu to the Men,
I returned home. On my arrival found Mr McGillivray on the other
Side the River, and soon after he came with Mr Bird, 2 Men
& 3 Indians. The Route the Kootanaes took to cross the Mountain
& avoid the Indians is on this side this River, where they also take the
Mountains. The Country is exceeding Woody, without any Plains
– at a small Distance from here the Woods are mostly of Pines, many
of them fallen down & rendering the Road very bad.

Journey to the Bow River

17 November – 3 December 1800

November 17th [1800] Monday A cold cloudy Day with light Snow at Times. We could not cross the River for driving ice 'till $11\frac{1}{2}$ Am, when we set off – Mr Duncan McGillivray, Boulard, Charron, Dumond, Bapt[iste] Regnie & myself. At $3\frac{1}{2}$ Pm we came to the Bridge, where we warmed ourselves a few Minutes and then came off with a Pekenow young Man, whom we have engaged to guide us, and whom we found waiting us here. We then went SE 10M to where we found 2 Tents of Indians with whom we put up at 5 Pm – after having gone about 3 Miles we found ourselves close to a Brook, whose current went towards the Red Deers River, the whole of this Co on the left hand side of a large Swamp intersected every where by a Brook – saw two or three Beaver Houses. The Road was at Times in the Swamp which is froze & at times on Knolly Meadow Ground with Points of Wood of Aspin.

Novr 18th [1800] Tuesday A cold cloudy Day. One of the Men could not find his Horse 'till $9\frac{1}{4}$ Am. At $9\frac{1}{2}$ Am set off – Co along the great Swamp & Brook which is increasing its Waters fast, it's Current running into the Red Deers River. ESE 14M we made a few Turns in this Co from the winding of the Swamp & Brook – near end of Co the Swamp became lost in the Brook, which has moderate Banks & is increased to a Rivulet. Our Road very uneven Meadow Ground, strong Woods close on both Hands. End of Co crossed the Brook and went thro' burnt Pines SE 1M when we came to the Red Deers River, which we crossed in Three Branches – the 1st small, the mid

Branch was the main Channel & large, the 3rd small – but before we crossed the mid Branch we went about ssw $1\frac{1}{2}$M upon it's gravel Banks, formerly all covered by the River – end of Co we left the River & went on thro' woods and Swamps with much Larch. South 2M then Swamps with burnt Woods SE $1\frac{1}{2}$M – we then came to tolerable Meadow Ground, but from it's uneven Surface not good footing for the Horses. We kept along a Brook ESE $4\frac{1}{2}$M, we then crossed to the right & went SEbE 5M to a small River on our Right where we put up at $2\frac{3}{4}$ Pm – a fine place. Small Snow with a cold easterly Gale all Day.

November 19 [1800] **Wednesday** A cold cloudy Day, with light driving Snow all Day. At 9 Am set off, Co ESE $1\frac{1}{2}$M when we crossed the Rivulet – it falls into the Red Deers River – then Co SE 3M where we turned off. sbw 10M where we fell in with the Rivulet this Morn, when we stopped to refresh our Horses & take Breakfast at Noon. The Indian informing us that we should find no Woods in our Road fit for Tent Poles, we cut Poles sufficient for that Purpose, & took them with us. At 1 Pm we resumed our journey Co S10W 12M – 3 Miles gone we came to a tolerable Brook which I suppose falls into the last. The Weather being very bad, & plenty of small Deer being about us, we put up at 3 Pm – went a hunting, but had no Success; saw no Buffalo. Most of this open Meadow Ground, upon our Right a bow of straggling Woods but the left seems to be boundless Meadow – bad footing for the Horses from the uneven Surface, called by the French Tate des Femmes.

Novr 20th [1800] **Thursday** A fine Day – Gale at sw^t. At $8\frac{1}{2}$ Am set off, Co South $1\frac{1}{2}$M S22E 11M to a bold Brook which we crossed at 11 Am – we stopped to Breakfast & I obs^d Doub Merid Alt^{de} of [sun's] LL Lat^{de} 51°:33′:23″ N Decⁿ 19°:4[8]′. At $\frac{1}{2}$ past Noon set off – Bow Hills in Sight S12E 12M where we put up at a Spring at 2 Pm. The latter part of this Day, the Ground became Knolly & the Surface tolerable good – all fine open Meadow with chance patches of Willows. We go in a Line parallel to the Mountain which every where is covered with Snow & seems to present an impenetrable Bank. The View is grand in a high Degree: on our right we have the Bow Hills, lofty in themselves and Brown with Woods, above them stately rises the Rocky Mountain vast and abrupt whose Tops pierce the clouds –

on our left, before & behind us, a verdant Ocean. Ran a Bull Buffalo, the first we have seen this journey – took part of the Meat; our Guide killed another.

November 21st [1800] Friday A very fine Day. At 8¾ Am set off, Co thro' wide Plains, keeping the Mountain about 40 Miles to the Right or wsw from us. sse 13m when seeing a fine Herd of Cows before us we stopt abᵗ 50′ for one of the Men to approach them, but not killing any – I ran a fine young Bull. Our Co s20e 2m then Co sse 12m to a Brook where we stopped a Moment for our Horses to drink, then Co s20e 11m to the Bow River where we put up at 3½ Pm – we found the Marks of Indians having gone from here to Day, as their Fire was still alight. The Bow River is here abᵗ 150 to 180 yᵈˢ wide, a fine equal Stream say 3½ feet deep at 2¼ Miles an Hour. We have had tolerable good Surface to day except in the Morn, when the footing was very bad for the Horses. All the Meadows about the Branch may be said to be barely white with Snow, and except close along its Shores the Bow River is entirely clear of Ice.

Novʳ 22nd [1800] Saturday A very fine Day. At 8¾ Am set off, Co across a Point of Land – the River running about 2½ Miles on our Right. s20e 17 Miles when, seeing Indians, we made Signs to them & a Horseman turned about & came towards us. We then descended the Banks of the Bow River and crossed it – it may be here abᵗ 200 yᵈˢ wide and 2½ feet at 2m an Hour, with a Bottom of Gravel & Pebbles. On the South Side we met a Blood Indian, a stupid looking Fellow, from whom we could get no Information. Having smoked with him about 20′ we set off & went down along the River se 4m where we came to where the Women were preparing to Camp – but on our coming up they reloaded their Horses & came off. We staid there smoking about ¼h when we resumed our Journey. Our Course to the Spitchee River s25e 5m which we crossed & came to a Camp of 7 Lodges of Pekenows, with whom we put up at 2 Pm. The Ground has been very fine & equal to Day, without any Snow whatever. The Spitchee falls into the Bow River about 2½ Miles below us going off in a South Direction to it's Junction – the Bow River hereabouts takes a course about ese as far as we can see it. It is to be observed all the Courses of this Journey are by the Compass.

In the Evening the Sac o tow wow, the principal Chief of the Pekenows, paid us a visit with a few Men. He spoke to us upon

several Subjects – about the Kootanaes &c &c; he complained of our
having armed them by which means the Flat Heads would also
acquire Arms to their great Hurt. To this I replied that they themselves,
the Pekenows, had first & principally armed the Kootanaes in
exchange for Horses &c, & replied to all the other Parts of his
Argument. We then spoke to him about introducing a Number of
Iroquois & Seauteaux into this Country about the Mountain. We
informed them that their Country was so very poor, as to be utterly
incapable of maintaining them – for which reason they had applied
to us to bring them up to the Mountains, which request we had not
complied with, as we did not know how they would be pleased with
it. We also added that those Indians would behave quietly, would
reside in the woody Hills at the foot of the Mountain & serve as a
Barrier between them & their Enemies – upon these Terms they
gave us Permission to bring them up as soon as we pleased. Cut a Pipe
of Tobacco to each Man & gave them a few pints of mixed Rum
to Drink.

November 23rd [1800] Sunday A fine mild cloudy Day. At 10 Am
Mr McGillivray & 3 Men went off to the Sac o tow wow's Tent,
where they smoked & distributed a Trifle of Tobacco to the Indians –
in the Evening they returned. Obs^d Merid Alt^{de} of [sun's] LL
Lat^{de} 50°:46':38" N Dec^n 20°:27':6". The [sun] was very cloudy
& faint but the Obs^n is better than Nothing – it is near the Truth.

Novr 24th [1800] Monday A very fine Day. At 9$\frac{1}{4}$ Am we set off for
a Camp of Tents above us – we amused ourselves with running
Buffalo, of which there were vast Numbers – we killed 2 cows 1 calf
& 1 Bull. Our Road was over fine level Plains & our Co S1OE 12M.
At 1$\frac{1}{2}$ Pm we crossed the Spitchee & arrived at the camp – about
40 Lodges. Mr McGillivray & two Men went into the Old Bear's
Tent, & I with 2 Men went into the Foxe's Head's Tent. We were all
very well received; here we discoursed about the Country, & again
introduced the Subject of the Iroquois & Seauteaux, which met with
a better & more ready Reception here – indeed they were all well
pleased with it. They told us, from where they are now Tenting to the
Missisouri was 10 days Walk & no more, and a Horseman would
only sleep 5 Nights to that Place. We mentioned our Intention of going
close to the Mountain, & if possible into it, when they warned us
in a friendly manner to beware of the Flat Heads, who were constantly

hovering about there to steal Horses, or to dispatch any small weak Party they might chance to fall in with. After much Discourse on various Subjects not worth inserting here, and getting information of all the Brooks & Rivulets which fall into the Bow River from the Mountain southward of its Scource, we parted & went to Bed.

Novr 25th [1800] **Tuesday** A very fine Day. We had the Pleasure of running a few Cows – I assisted at the Death of Two.
Mr McGillivray assembled the Chiefs & gave them each a small piece of Tobacco. At Night I Obs^d Doub Merid Alt^{de} of Rigel
Lat^{de} 50°:35′:30″ N.

Novr 26 [1800] **Wednesday** A fine Morn but ab^t 10 Am the Wind sprang up a Gale from the North & NW and at 11 Am came on heavy Snow. At 9$\frac{1}{4}$ Am took leave of the Pekenows, a few of whom accompanied us a little Distance on our way – we went N30W 4M then crossed a small Brook, then Co N75W 13M to a Rivulet, which we crossed at 1 $\frac{1}{4}$ Pm. Went on nearly on a Line with the Rivulet, Co N80W 8M, where we put up at 2$\frac{3}{4}$ Pm at a Hommock of Woods. Run a Cow at 4 Pm. The Weather became fine & clear – Obs^d Doub Merid Alt^{de} of Rigel mean Longitude 114°:11′:7″ W.

Novr 27th [1800] **Thursday** A fine Day. At 8$\frac{3}{4}$ Am set off, our Co N50W 5M, where we came to large Herds of Cows: twice we attempted to approach them, but the wind was too calm & unsteady – I run a tolerable good Cow, and another old Cow – also assisted Dumond in Killing a Calf. We then made a fire & having satisfied our Appetites we set off at 1:50 Pm, our Co N75W 5M approaching the Mountain NW 2M – end of Co crossed a Rivulet and followed it NNE 1$\frac{1}{2}$M North 1M. Then leaving the Rivulet going off NE for the Bow River – we went NW 2M where we put up at 3$\frac{3}{4}$ Pm in a large Hommock of Aspins & Poplars. Saw many small Deer to Day – where we put up our Guide fired at a Buck Moose, but missed him – saw plenty of Cattle all Day. The Bow River may be ab^t 20M NNW of us. Cloudy Night – watched our Horses all Night. The Road of [to] day extensive Meadows with every where Patches of Wood and Willows; the Ground was broken into high Knowls and Vallies and the Surface very uneven – Tate des Femme. The Ground the Latter part of the Day is barely white with Snow.

Novr 28th [1800] **Friday** A very fine clear warm Day. Saw many Herds of Cows in the Morning. At 8:50 Am set off, Co N65W 10M where we stopped 20′ to wait the Indian, who was running after the small Deer, which are very Plenty about here. We then in ½M crossed a Rivulet in several small Channels, with excessive strong Current – it may have as much Water as the Spitchee. We then came towards the Mountain N60W 4M, when I stopped to observe Merid Alt^{de} of [sun's] LL Lat^{de} 51°:3′:32″ N. The nearest part of the Mountain bears now from me S38W 25M. At ¾ Pm set off, Co NW 2½M to the Banks of a Brook; here not finding Mr McGillivray, after having searched about 1 Hour for him, we saw him at a Distance before us. We then crossed the Brook & went off N75W 3½M, when seeing only high Ridges or Hills before us, we struck off N35W 9M to a Gully with a Spring of water near the Bow River – where we put up at 4½ Pm within 1¼M of the Bow River, NW^d of us. The Ground of this Day fine Meadow with very little Wood – the latter part of the Day [h]illy. Saw many large Herds of Bulls, but few [or] no Cows.

Novr 29th [1800] **Saturday** A fine Morn. At 8:50 Am set off for the Rocky Mountain, leaving Boulard in charge of the Baggage & Baggage Horses. Our Road lies along the Bow River, which all along to the very Mountains has beautiful Meadows along its Banks: those on the South Side the River tho' the most extensive are so frequently cut by Brooks, whose Banks here are always high & often very steep, and Ravelines, the remains of old Streams whose waters have failed; on the North Side the Meadows are not extensive, but they are the best Road, as they are not so often intersected by the small Streams which come pouring from the Hills. After having gone S50W 3M we crossed the Bow River, deep & Strong Current as usual – we then on the North Side went S50W 9M when I stopped to Observe Doub Merid Alt^{de} of [sun's] LL. Here Mr McGillivray, a Man & the Indian set off ahead to hunt the Mountain Goat, several Herds of them feeding a little Distance before us in our Road. Went on S50W 2M S15W 1M where we put up at 4 Pm, having amused ourselves the whole After noon with running after the Goats – 3 of them were killed by the Indian & a large old Buck by Mr McGillivray, which we skinned round – we found their Meat to be exceeding sweet & tender and moderately fat. The she Goats might weigh ab^t from 120 to 140 lbs, as alive; the Buck that was killed

might also weigh ab^t 190 or 200 lbs – 30 of which may be the
weight of his enormous Horns which, measured along the Curve, were
$3\frac{1}{2}$ feet long and 15 Inches in Circumference. About 1M sw^d of
where I Obs^d, a Brook with exceeding high steep Banks and $\frac{1}{4}$M farther
another small Brook; also close to where we put up on each Hand,
a small Brook. The Bow River for the last 3 Miles has many strong
Rapids with several Falls but none of these above 8 or 10 feet
perpen[d] height & in general not above two or three feet: the most
considerable of these Falls are Three which all lie in the same bend
of the River, and may be all avoided by one Portage across the Point
of ab^t 300 Y^{ds} – the River every where navigable for large Canoes,
loaded with 20 Pieces and so even at this time of Year, when the Water
is lowest. Its Banks hereabouts are very high, and in some Places
almost perpendicular to the height of 200 feet; they are composed of
a black slaty Rock, not extremely hard – but steep as these Banks
are, the Mountain Goats are seen to take to them (*if not prevented*)
on the least Alarm and seemingly run along the steeps as securely
as on the Plains. Indeed this Animal is remarkably agile, and jumps
both well and sure; his make is strong, at the same time light, his
Hoofs pointed, & somewhat soft in the hind Part [which] enables him
to climb with Ease. The She Goats have a simple mild Look, and
are curious to approach and examine with their Eyes whatever they
see moving, if it does not appear in too formidable a Shape; the
Bucks divested of their Horns would have nearly the same Appearance,
but their large weighty Horns superior size & Strength and more
ardent curiosity, which makes them advance before the Herd, give
them an Air [of] daring with a Dash of the Formidable. They are
not remarkable for their Swiftness and are easily overtaken by a good
Horse in a Plain. We lay under Arms and mounted Guard all Night
by Turns, to secure ourselves from any Attack of the Flat Heads.

Nov 30 [1800] Sunday A very fine Day. At 7:50 Am we set off for the
Rocky Mountains, and went on s30w 4$\frac{1}{2}$M – at end of Co we left
our Horses and went up along the River on Foot s15w 2$\frac{1}{2}$M to a Point
of the Mountain which we thought practicable, for the Mountain
all this last Course presents an inaccessible Steep: from where we set
out this Morn to the end of the first Course the River gradual[ly]
widens, and the Banks lower, until there is hardly any Bank at all. In
this Distance very few Rapids and for the last Mile of the first
course the River may be ab^t 250 Y^{ds} to 300 Y^{ds} over with several small

Islands – all the last Course it has the same Appearance – beyond
that it winds in the Mountain about wsw for 3 or 4 Miles as seen from
the Heights. At end of the last Course Mr McGillivray, Dumond
and myself began to ascend the Mountain – we found it very steep with
much loose small stones very sharp, but as we got higher & higher
the loose Stones became less frequent; when the Rock was solid, it was
extremely rough and full of small sharp Points like an enormous
Rasp – this enabled us to mount Places very steep, as the footing was
good & sure, but it cut our Shoes, Socks &c all to pieces in a Trice.
The Rock of the Mountain all the way to the Top is one and the same,
of a dark Grey, with few or no Veins, very hard & Glassy, and upon
rubbing Two Pieces of it together for a Moment produces when held
near the Nose a strong disagreeable Smell, somewhat Sulphurous.

Our View from the Heights to the Eastward was vast & unbounded
– the Eye had not Strength to discriminate its Termination: to the
Westward Hills & Rocks rose to our View covered with Snow, here
rising, there subsiding, but their Tops nearly of an equal Height
every where. Never before did I behold so just, so perfect a
Resemblance to the Waves of the Ocean in the wintry Storm. When
looking upon them and attentively considering their wild Order and
Appearance, the Imagination is apt to say, these must once have
been Liquid, and in that State when swelled to its greatest Agitation,
suddenly congealed and made Solid by Power Omnipotent. There
are low Shrubs of Fir & Canadian Pine almost to the very Top in Places;
we also found the Dung of Cows for about two thirds up the
Mountain, tho' we saw no Grass. After having spent 4 Hours there,
we returned to our Horses from whence we set out with
Expedition, and having come below the Falls &c we re-crossed the
River and went down on the south Side to our Gully where we
arrived at $5\frac{1}{4}$ Pm – all well, thank God.

Decr 1st [1800] Monday A fine Day. At 7:50 Am set off, Co N15W $1\frac{1}{2}$M
where we crossed the Branch or Bow River and a few yards below,
the Bow Rivulet. We then came on over the Bow Hills N10W $2\frac{1}{2}$M –
end of Co a Brook, then N5E 5M to a Brook which we crossed. Co
along the Bow Hills in the Plains – tolerable level Ground like the most
of the last. N5E 10M to a Brook which we crossed at Noon –
stopped to refresh our Horses. On our left the Bow Hills close with
thick Woods of Pines &c; the right is extensive Meadow. At 1:5'
Pm set off, Co mostly North 18M good – at $4\frac{1}{4}$ Pm put up close to a

small Brook. Cloudy Night with Rime. We begin to get among
Tate des Femme.

Decr 2nd [1800] **Tuesday** A Cold Cloudy Day with an easterly Breeze.
At 7:20 Am set off, Co N15E 2M North 8M where we crossed a
small Brook – on this Co Points of Wood, our old Campment of the
3rd Day's Journey 1M short of course. Co 10W 2M then Co among
Hommocks of Wood N40W 8M where we came to a Bold Brook or
Rivulet – where we stopped at 11 Am and took Breakfast. At 20′
Pm set off, Co N20W 10M thro' Woody & Marshy Ground to the Red
Deers River, at the same Place where we crossed it going to the
Kootanaes. We now follow the same Track; it is therefore needless to
set down the courses, as they have been better taken on that
Journey. We went on thro' the Woods past the Pekenow Campment
and to the edge of the Plain, where we put up at the small Brook
on the So end at 4$\frac{1}{4}$ Pm. Small Snow in the After noon – we have had
Snow on the Ground all this Day, which [it] is to be remarked has
not been the Case since the Fall of Snow beyond the Bow River, and
which extended but a small Distance.

Decr 3rd [1800] **Wednesday** A cloudy cold raw Day, with light Snow
at Times. At 6 Am set off, & walked in to the middle of the Plain
– we then mounted our Horses and pursued our Route. When we came
to the parting of the Pekenow Roads, we found the Indians had
taken the right Hand Track, which being the longest we took the Left
and at 11:20 Am arrived at the Bridge. At 35′ Pm we again set off
& by 4 Pm arrived at the House – all well, thank God. All our Horses
have held out exceeding well this Journey, which has been upon
the whole very hard marching.

Journey to the Rocky Mountain

6–30 June 1801

Account of an attempt to cross the Rocky Mountain by Mr James Hughes, nine men & myself on the part of the NW^t Company in order to penetrate to the Pacific Ocean, 1801.

On the 6th of June ⟨1800⟩, every Thing being ready for our Journey to the Rocky Mountains, being in number Eleven Persons –
Mr Hughes, nine Men & myself: we had thirteen Horses belonging to the NW^t Company, of which ten were loaded either with trading Goods, Provisions or other Necessaries; each Horse had a Burthen of from 120 to 130 lbs.

 For a Guide to cross the Mountains, we had a Nahathaway Indian named the Rook, a Man so Timourous by Nature, of so wavering a Disposition, & withal so addicted to flattering & lying, as to make every Thing he said or did equivocal & doubtful – such was the Character of our Guide, & bad as he was, ⟨situated as we were then,⟩ there was no possibility of getting a better. Of his character Mr Duncan McGillivray was aware when he engaged him, & as he could not change it, he did every Thing that lay in his Power to counteract its Effects, by making him large Promises if he performed his Part well, & by severely threatening him if he did not – and added to these, the awful act of making him smoke & imprecate the Wrath of the Great Spirit on himself, his Wife & Children, if he did not fully perform his Promise of guiding us across the Mountains. We had also with us an old Kootanae Woman who many years ago had been taken Prisoner, & had since mostly resided with the Canadians in the Company's Settlements.

Thus arranged, & carrying with us Birch Rind sufficient to make a Canoe, in the Morning we loaded our Horses and set out. Our Course sw 4 Miles thro' Points of Woods & small Plains up along the Saskatchewan River, when we stopped to refresh the Horses 'till 11 Am. We then went sw $8\frac{1}{4}$ Miles in a tolerable Road, thro' mostly burnt Woods, to a small Meadow with 3 Rills of Water; here we again stopped to refresh our Horses, & at $3\frac{1}{4}$ Pm we continued our Route N82W $4\frac{1}{2}$ Miles when we left the Banks of the River, & turned up along a small Brook N70W $2\frac{1}{4}$ Miles; we then left it & went on thro' a bad Swamp, with small burnt Woods, N82W 3 Miles to a wet Meadow of about 3 Miles in circumference where, at $7\frac{1}{4}$ Pm, we put up on the Banks of a Brook which traverses the Meadow. About 1 Mile sbw of us flows the Saskatchewan River. The whole of our Road to day, considering the Country, would have been tolerable had it not been for the late heavy Rains, which have so soaked & over flowed the Ground as to occasion the Horses often to sink to the mid Leg.

June 7th [1801] Sunday A very fine Day, except a few light Showers of Rain. Early in the Morning we collected the Horses, & at $4\frac{1}{2}$ Am we set off, our Guide & one of the Men having gone ahead to hunt. We went thro' the Meadow N70W $1\frac{1}{4}$ Mile, when we went up a Bank thro' burnt Woods N62W $1\frac{1}{2}$M – in this Distance we crossed several Rills of Water with miry Banks. Then N60W $1\frac{3}{4}$ Miles to a Plain, where we found the Man that was a hunting had killed 2 Bull Buffalo; having taken as much Meat as we wanted, we went on N70W $1\frac{1}{2}$M thro' Woods & Meadow, when we stopped to Breakfast & I obsd for Latde by two Altitudes double. At $11\frac{1}{4}$ Am we again set off & went N60W 3 Miles without a Road, over very bad wet uneven broken Ground, thro' burnt Woods tumbled down by the Storms in every Direction.

We now came to the Banks of the River, which were very high and steep, & cut in a perpendicular Direction by the craggy Sides of a Brook – which obliged us to descend & gain the River Beach; in doing this, one of our loaded Horses fell, & rolled down close to the edge of a Precipice at least three Hundred Feet high, but by good Fortune he brought up against a Pine Tree & recovered his Feet. When near the River, another of our Horses fell actually into the Stream, but

luckily made a shift to gain the other Side – but how to recover the
Horse & his Load was the Difficulty: we had no Canoe, & the Current
was too deep & rapid to be crossed on a Raft. La Ramme, one of
our Men, attempted to cross on Horseback – this he effected 'till about
the middle of the Stream when, the Waves washing over the Head
of the Horse, he reared up & threw his Rider. Fortunately La Ramme
could swim; he strongly exerted himself & gained the Shore, where
he secured the loaded Horse & lead him up along the River – we went
on a little distance higher up, & made a Skin Canoe, with which we
recrossed the Man & Goods, & put up.

June 8th [1801] **Monday** A Day of variable Weather, with frequent
Showers of Rain – after 3 Pm the Rain became constant. Early in
the Morning we began to cross our Horses & Baggage, but from the
Rapidity of the Current, we did not get all across 'till 10 Am. We
had then a very high Bank covered with small Pines to ascend: the
strongest of our Horses made a tolerable shift to get up it, but the
others with much Difficulty: two of them, when about half way up,
lost their footing & rolled down 'till brought up by the Trees; we
then unloaded them & part of us carried up the Baggage, while others
of us attempted to get the Horses up the Bank; but they rolled
down so often, and received such violent Shocks from the Trees against
which they brought up, as to deprive them for a Time of Motion
– after several Attempts, we at length succeeded in getting them up the
Bank.

   Without entering into a too minute Detail, we now held on for the
Mountains West 1 Mile wsw 4M sbw ½ Mile wbs 3 Miles
sw 2 Miles – the first Mile we had firm Ground with much fallen
Wood; for the next four Miles the quantity of fallen Wood was so
great as to render the Country almost impassable, with now & then a
Bank & very many small Bogs, in which the Horses sometimes sunk
up to their Bellies. We then had about three Miles of tolerable Ground,
but the last two and a half Miles was along a Brook, in the first
Mile of which we saw 10 or 12 Beaver Houses, & killed three Beaver
& a Doe Moose with her Fawn. The rest of the Brook being stony,
& having nothing but burnt Woods on its Sides, prevents the Beaver
from building higher up; but below where we fell in with the Brook
the Beaver seemed to have several Houses, from the level Country the
Stream coursed thro' & from the sound of the Water falling over
the Beaver Dams – but none of us went to examine, our whole

Attention being taken up in conducting our Horses over the bad
boggy Ground that lay along the Brook. At $7\frac{1}{4}$ Pm we camped at the
Foot of the first Chain of Mountains. ⟨This Evening we found
Snow in several Places.⟩ In the Course of the Day, we saw a Red Deer,
and a small herd of Bulls – one of the latter we killed. ⟨The scene
around us has nothing of the agreable in it: all Nature seems to frown,
the Mountains are dreary, rude & wild beyond the power of the
Pencil.⟩

June 9th [1801] [Tuesday] A tolerable fine Day. At $\frac{1}{2}$ past 5 Am we set
off & went up along the Brook to cross the first Chain of Mountains
East $\frac{1}{2}$ Mile ENE 1 Mile, thro' thick Pines with wet Ground. Following
the Paths of Animals we now came to a Brook, the Current running
to the eastward, which we followed SEbE 2 Miles, when another fell
into it from the Southward – this we went along South $\frac{1}{4}$ Mile,
when we left it & came to several fine little Meadows, our Course SE
two Miles, the latter part of which took a Point of Woods,
& brought us to a rapid Brook, whose Banks we followed WSW 6 Miles,
when we stopped to refresh our Horses & I obs^d for Latitude. Here
we dried many Things that had got wet by the Rain & in the Swamps.
We then continued up along the Brook, crossing several Rills
which fell into it. Our Course was SW 2 Miles West 2 Miles, when we
crossed one of the Forks of the Brook, & went on the right Side of
the eastern one West 3 Miles; we then crossed the Brook altogether,
& cut a Point of high rising Ground covered with Pines. Our Course
West $\frac{1}{2}$ Mile, when we saw a small Rill whose Current we followed
West 1 Mile, & then put up on its Banks at $3\frac{1}{2}$ Pm, our Guide
informing us that if we went farther, we should not be able to find
Grass for our Horses ⟨before it would be dark⟩.

   Considering the Country, the Road of to Day has been tolerable,
altho' we have had much wet Ground, & many small Bogs, with
now & then fallen Wood. We are now behind the first Chain of
Mountains, which from the Valley where we are now camped,
appears to be as firm, as compact, & as high, tho' not so abrupt, on this
Western Side, as on the Eastern. The Tops of them are every where
covered with Snow, tho' farther down on the northern than on the
southern Aspects; they are wooded for about two thirds up, with
small Pines and Firs, & on some chance Cliff, there are dwarf Shrubs
almost to the very Top; they are composed of a very hard, dark
grey Rock, and may be estimated at 1600 Feet above the Level of their

Base. ⟨The Hills to the Westward somewhat soften the rude scenery with their verdant Appearance.⟩ Saw the Tracks of several Grizled Bears, & a small Herd of Bulls – one of the latter we killed; we also saw several mountain Goats, but they were ⟨feeding near the Tops of the Mountains,⟩ far enough above our reach.

June 10th [1801] Wednesday A rainy Morn 'till 7 Am, when it ceased a little. We made ready our Horses, & by 8 Am set off & went along the Rill for about 200 Yards, when another fell into it from the westward – we continued along this Water SSE $\frac{1}{2}$M tolerable Ground, when it ran into a bold & very rapid Brook, which we followed going SSE 1 $\frac{1}{2}$M over part small Meadow, part wet muddy Ground with strong Woods; we then left the Brook and going West 1 Mile thro' a Hollow of Firs & Pines, we came to the South Branch of the Saskatchewan, a bold & very rapid Stream of about Thirty Yards wide; we went on it's Banks West 2 Miles WNW 1 Mile good Road, when we came to one of the Channels of the River, which tho' not above twelve Yards wide, took us a full Hour to cross our Horses & Baggage – we attempted to make a Bridge, but the Current swept it away. Having at last got all safe on the Island, we went WNW $\frac{1}{2}$M & recrossed the Channel. Heavy Rain, which had broke out while we were attempting to make a Bridge, now became so violent as to oblige us to put up at 11 $\frac{1}{2}$ Am. The Country thro' which we have come to Day, & which lies about us, is not mountainous, but very hilly, & in Appearance all the Hills are covered with a green Sod, or Moss, & well wooded for the Country; the Valleys have Grass, which is every where becoming green; the Leaves as yet have not made their Appearance, neither on the Willows, nor on the chance Aspins we have now & then met with. By the Evening the Rain had become uncommonly heavy – the Water descended in Sheets from the Hills & flooded the Country; the River, at all times Rapid, was now an over flowing Torrent that bore down every Thing that opposed it's Course; the Thunder rolled along the Hills ⟨& added Horrour to the Darkness of the Night; we wished for the morning Light⟩.

June 11th [1801] Thursday Early in the Morn the Rain ceased. We dried our Things & collected the Horses that were scattered by the night Storm, and by 11 Am were ready to set off. Our Guide, whose Spirits had visibly begun to droop ever since we entered the Defiles of the Mountain, was last Night presented by Mr Hughes with some

Rum to keep him hearty in the Cause. Upon this he had made a
shift to get Drunk with his Wife, and this Morning complaining that
his Head & Stomach was out of Order, he asked for a little
Medicine, which was given him; but finding it did him neither good
nor Harm, he called his Wife to him where he was sitting amidst
us, at a large Fire we had made to warm ourselves. She readily came:
he asked her i[f] she had a sharp Flint, & upon her replying she had
not, he broke one & made a Lancet of it, with which he opened a Vein
in her Arm, she assisting him with great good Will; having drawn
about $\frac{3}{4}$ pint of Blood from her into a wooden Bowl, to our
Astonishment he applied it to his Lips quite warm, & drank it of[f]
— what of the Blood adhered to the Vessel he mixed with Water, so as
to clean it, and also drank off.

While I was considering from whence so savage an Action could
arise, one of our Men with Indignation exclaimed to our Guide,
I have eaten & smoked with thee, but henceforward thou & me shall
never eat & smoke together — what, drink warm from the Vein the
Blood of your Wife? Oh oh, my Friend, said the Indian, have I done
wrong? — when I find my Stomach out of order, the warm Blood
of my Wife in good Health refreshes the whole of my Body & puts me
to rights; in return, when she is not well I draw Blood from my
Arm, she drinks it, it invigorates & gives her Life. All our Nation do
this, and all of us know it to be a good Medicine; is this the first
Time you have seen it — from whence comes your Surprize, my Friends?
But looking round on us all, & perceiving in our Countenances
marks of an utter Abhorrence of what he had done, he said no more,
for however it might be the Custom of his Nation, he saw plainly
he had done wrong to transact it before us.

He smoked his Pipe with great Tranquillity, then getting up, he
proceeded with us along the River s70w 2 Miles over mostly
meadow Ground s80w 2 Miles West 2 Miles — near end of this Course
the River obliged us to go edging along side of a steep Hill where
there was much Ice. The Feet of one of our loaded Horses slipping, he
rolled down the Hill, fairly into the River, & was nearly drowned;
but fortunately the River was not wide, & he made a shift to gain the
other Side; one of the Men about 1 Mile above forded the River
on Horseback & brought back the Horse & his Load, but every Thing
was quite wet. A little way beyond this, as we were going along
another steep Place, another of our Horses missing his footing rolled
down with his Load; from the Height, we concluded he was killed,

but on coming to him, found the Horse only somewhat stunned. We now dried the Goods &c that had got wet ⟨but unfortunately all our Sugar and Salt, making part of the Load of the Horse, was totally lost. We⟩ went onwards, & crossed a bold Brook, our Road at Times lying over small low Points, but mostly along steep sloping Hills, very dangerous for the Horses – our Course sw 4 Miles following the River, which is now not above 20 Yards wide, but very rapid. We killed this Day 2 Bull Buffalo & a Buck Moose, & at $6\frac{1}{2}$ Pm put up at the foot of the great chain of Mountains ⟨they are clothed with Snow & present a most formidable View, the Clouds breaking about their rugged Heads⟩. The Country we have come thro' to day is much the same as that of Yesterday.

June 12th [1801] Friday A fine Day, but heavy Gale at sw. Not readily finding two of our Horses, we did not set off 'till 7 Am, when we entered a Defile of the great Chain of Mountains, going s1 5E 2 Miles – in the beginning of this Course we crossed a Fork from the westward nearly equal to half the River; we then went South $2\frac{1}{2}$ Miles following the eastern Rivulet, which has now but little Water & is about 10 Yards wide. The whole of this Distance has been over tolerable hard Ground, in a Valley between two high Mountains of Rock – the width of the Valley may be from $\frac{1}{4}$ to $\frac{1}{2}$ Mile. Then sw 4 Miles – when we had gone about $\frac{1}{2}$ Mile of this Distance, we found a small Brook with 6 Beaver Houses, all of them having their Complement of Beaver; in this Course we often crossed & recrossed the Rivulet, & had much fallen Wood with sharp rocky Ground, & the defile of the Mountain became quite narrow. We continued on sw 2 Miles over much the same kind of Ground, except the last $\frac{1}{2}$ Mile, which was in a wet Willow Plain of about $\frac{1}{2}$ Mile in width – here at Noon we stopped to refresh our Horses. Every Thing about us wore the Face of Winter: the Willows [as] yet had not budded, nor the Ground brought forth the least Verdure. We staid $2\frac{1}{2}$ Hours to give time to our Horses to pick up the miserable remains of the Herbage of last Summer. We then went off s1oE $1\frac{1}{2}$M, when the Rivulet separated & became a mere shallow Brook; we still held on s1oE $4\frac{1}{2}$ Miles in a very narrow bottom between two stupendous Ridges of rugged Rock. For the last two Miles we walked on small, sharp, broken Pieces of Rock, which cut our Shoes to pieces & crippled our Horses. We still followed the Brook, which is but trifling, & is supplied by the Rills from the Snows; the little Space

that is between the Mountains is filled with fallen Wood, & piled
so high as obliged us often to walk in the Channel of the Brook, & to
cross & recross it every Moment. At 6 Pm we put up where formerly there had been a little Grass, some trifling Vestiges of which still
remained, and this was all our Horses had to pass a bleak cold
Night on, nor could we find a better Place. ⟨In the Course of the Day
we killed three mountain Goats, but they were very poor & shed-
ding their Hair. We saw a Bull Buffalo but he escaped us.⟩

Late in the Evening our Guide came to us ⟨with a woful
Countenance⟩, desiring Permission to return, that he might still live
& see his Children. Mr Hughes asked him what he had to apprehend,
that for his Part he saw nothing more formidable than the
Mountain Goat, from which he promised to defend him if ever they
became daring enough to attack him; this however had no Effect
on our Guide, who replied in a whining Tone, This is the way of all
you white Men – you joke at every Thing 'till you are fairly killed;
for my Part, I am certain there are strange Indians ⟨near us⟩ who will
kill us – I dream continually of them. We told him plainly that we
were far too advanced to think of returning, that we had not come thus
far for that Purpose, & in short that right or wrong he must accompany us. Why, said he, at all Events we cannot go much farther; some
of your Horses are already quite feeble & others nearly cripple[d],
& we have still the worst of the Mountain to pass. That is nothing to
you, my Friend, we replied; we will go on while we have a Horse
left. Oh, but I will not follow you to be killed, said he; it is true I have
drank your Rum, you have given me a good Horse &c, but I love
my Life better than all this. I will pay you for what I have had: I have
three Horses at the Fort & I have two here – take the whole, I will
begrudge nothing, only turn back. We told him, that while there was
a possibility of going forward, nothing could alter our Resolution;
he retired saying, Well, you will see if we go much farther. Mr Hughes
was for keeping an extraordinary strict Eye over him for the Night,
but I thought it unnecessary; for I knew the Dastard was more afraid
to return all alone, than even to remain where he was, while in our
Company.

June 13th [1801] **Saturday** A very cold frosty Morn, but fine Day. By
$5\frac{1}{2}$ Am we got ready & set off – our Course in a narrow Bottom ⟨of
a Defile⟩, between two lofty Mountains S15E $4\frac{1}{2}$ Miles. We had not proceeded more than $\frac{1}{4}$ of a Mile, when we came to Snow regularly

from 2 to three feet deep, & in places more than this; the night Frost
had made a hard Crust on it, but not strong enough to bear the
Horses; with the greatest Difficulty we made our way thro' it, tho'
sometimes we avoided the Snow altogether for a little Distance by
getting into the Channel of the Brook, which was now almost dry. But
we were seldom able to go above 50 or 60 yards in it at a Time for
the great Banks of Snow, which had come shelving down from the
Mountains, & blocked up the Brook to the Height of from 15 to
20 feet perpendicular; & when we had gone about three Miles, even
this failed us, for the Brook was totally lost in the minute Rills
which dripped from the Rocks. For the last $\frac{1}{4}$ of a Mile we were on a
bare Spot tolerably exposed to the Action of the Sun – here we were
obliged to stop, for at the end of this was a deep Lake lying South one
Mile by a quarter of a Mile wide, whose eastern Side rose abrupt
& hid it's Head in the Clouds, accessible to the Eagle only, & it's western
Side, equally lofty but broken, denied us a farther Road with
Horses.

At this Sight I could not help scrutinizing our Men, in whose
Countenances I read, with Ease & Concern, the Pleasure with
which they viewed this impassable Place. We asked our Guide if this
was the Road by which he had passed; he replied in the
Affirmative. Pray, said we, in what Manner did you get your Horses
to the other end of the Lake? Oh, replied he, we had no Horses
with us – we left them with our Families, at the Entrance into the
Mountains. Why you Scoundrel, we said, did you not tell us at the
Fort that you had Horses with you the whole of the Road across the
Mountains, & was it not upon the Supposition that you knew a
good Road for Horses across them, that we engaged you for our
Guide? Otherwise we would have followed, the best Way we
could, the Banks of the Saskatchewan River. All this is true, said our
worthless Guide, but I thought where we had gone on Foot, Horses
might possibly go – but I forgot this Part of the Mountain: you see
plainly as well as me that if we go farther, we must leave our
Baggage & Horses.

At a Loss what to do, we unloaded our Horses; & then Mr Hughes
proposed that [at] all Events we should go & examine the western
Side of the Lake, as that perhaps a Road for light Horses might be
found; & if so we could make a Skin Canoe & ferry the Goods to
the other end of the Lake. This the Men objected to as Fatigue utterly
unnecessary, but Mr Hughes insisting upon it, he named Meillet

& Gladu to accompany us. We now set off & after going about $\frac{1}{4}$ Mile, up to our middles in Snow, we went along the lower Bank of the Lake, but it was so steep that, however necessary it was to be well armed in such a Country, we were all of us soon obliged to leave our Arms, & get along the best we could on all Fours – our Situation was often dangerous, as the least Slip would have precipitated us into the Lake, from a height of above 100 feet. Having at last got round the Lake, we found ourselves on a narrow piece of level Ground, still between the same two lofty Mountains; having advanced about three hundred Yards farther, we began to descend a very narrow Defile, over very sharp ugly broken Rocks which cut our Shoes to Pieces in a Moment. Here Meillet sat down, & Mr Hughes asking him if he intended to go no farther, he said that he had already seen too much, & that he would stay there. Mr Hughes & me still continued on, & having descended about 200 Yards more, we found a Brook issuing out from under the sharp broken Rocks, and among large Fragments of which it held it's Course down the Mountain – we fol-lowing the Stream & walking in the Water among the Rocks, which were so slippery that it was with Difficulty we could keep our Feet.

Having descended a considerable Distance, we sat down to rest our-selves, & consider what was to be done. We saw plainly that it was impossible to bring the Horses any farther, for tho' we should even make them swim the Length of the Lake, they would not be able to descend this Defile among the broken Rocks; the only way that appeared to us, would be to leave as much of the Goods as possible, & make a Skin Canoe to ferry the rest over the Lake – from thence to carry them on our Backs to the Saskatchewan River, which we thought could not be above a Day's Journey from us, & there make a Canoe & proceed as far as possible. I was for immediately return-ing, & hurrying the Men into this Scheme before we had seen too much, or the Men had had Time for Reflection; but Mr Hughes judged it necessary to examine the Defile to the Bottom, lest after having taken a great deal of Trouble we should find Precipices lower down.

We accordingly rose to continue our Route when Meillet joined us, who it seems had become ashamed of staying behind; we found as Mr. Hughes had judged, tho' not Precipices, yet very bad broken Rocks, among which we still walked in the Water, for the Breadth of the little Stream was the whole Space that lay between these enor-mous Mountains. At last we reached the Bottom, when we came to a bold rapid Brook which came from the ENE to the wsw^d, towards the Saskatchewan, somewhere about the Kootanae Plain, which

we supposed to be about 10 or 15 Miles wsw^d of us. Having stopped
a few Minutes to examine this Stream, we found that it also ran
between two very high Mountains, & the Country by no means seemed
passable for Horses, even allowing that we had got them down this
far – our Course, from the Lake to this Place, about ssw $2\frac{1}{4}$ Miles. We
now returned & I found by my Watch that altho' we made as much
Speed as possible, yet we took two Hours to get back to the Lake, not
counting the Time we rested ourselves, & all this way up a steep
Ascent – & yet when at this Height, we were evidently not half way up
the Mountain. We then began our crawling Road along the Lake,
& came to our Men.

Mr Hughes now proposed to them to send back the Horses with our
Indian Guide & as much of the Baggage as we could possibly do
without, & what we took with us to be equally divided among the
whole of us, we offering to carry our Share; but the Men by no
means liked this Proposal. They said that even allowing them to get
all well down to the Bottom, who could tell at what Distance the
Saskatchewan River lay from us; it might be a great way (for our
Guide, while we were gone, had insinuated to them that he no
longer knew the Road with certainty, & that the Saskatchewan was a
long way off), beyond their Power to carry thereto, & that they
were not engaged to carry at that Rate &c &c. But Meillet & Gladu who
came with us finished the Dispute, by declaring it to be a Thing
impossible for Men even lightly loaded to get down the Mountain without breaking their Limbs, & that they could not think of such an
Undertaking. Mr Hughes now saw plainly as well as me that we had
too many Men: they had began the Journey with the greatest
Reluctance as Mr Duncan McGillivray well knows, & they had all
along hoped for, & now found, a fine Occasion of getting off –
however we must do them the Justice to say, that it was improbable
that they could have got down the Mountain with the Baggage,
without at least one half of them being crippled. The only hope that
now remained was to return to the Saskatchewan near the
Entrance into the Mountains, & there build a Canoe & try what could
be done by that Means; it was however but too plain that our
Journey was finished for this Season at least. We therefore reloaded
our Horses & resumed the Road we had come, & put up about
2 Miles N10W of where we started from this Morning.

On the Morrow we continued our Return, & without any Thing
worth remarking arrived in the Evening of the 16th at a Place of
the Saskatchewan River where 5 or 6 years ago the Nahathaway

Indians had made a War Tent – we crossed over & camped. We found the River had rose to a great height. We now set to work to build a Canoe, but having little else about us than burnt Woods & a few green Firs, we had much Trouble to get, & lost much Time in procuring, the Wood necessary for a Canoe.

By June 23rd the Canoe was pretty forward, when Mr Hughes, knowing that his Presence was absolutely necessary for regulating the Affairs of the different Settlements [o]n the River, returned to the Fort, taking with him one Man & our worthless Guide, with the Horses &c – leaving me with 8 Men to prosecute our Voyage up the River as far as possible.

By the next Day our Canoe was ready to be gummed, but the continual Rains which now unfortunately fell delayed us 'till the 26th. During all this Time the Water had kept rising, & the River was now flush from Bank to Bank, bringing down great Quantities of Wood. We however set off, hoping that by the Line or the Pole we should be able to stem the Current – this we effected, tho' several Times at the most imminent hazard of our Lives, crossing & recrossing the River at every Point, 'till in the Afternoon of the 29th, when we were obliged to desist altogether. For the last 3 Miles the Banks were steep & covered with fallen Wood, great Quantities of which were lying in the Water – of this we came up a small Distance with the Line, altho' it was as much as five of us could [do to] make the light Canoe move against the Current; for the rest of these 3 Miles, as we could make no further use of the Line from the extreme badness of the Banks, we poled now & then a few Yards, but in general hauled ourselves up by laying hold of the Trees; at length, from the badness of the Banks, the Depth & extreme Rapidity of the Current, we could not gain an Inch in spite of all our Efforts.

I now ordered the Canoe to where they could get ashore, & hoping that this bad Road did not continue any great Distance, took two Men with me to examine the River above us. We proceeded to nearly passing the first great Chain of Mountains, being about 5 or 6 Miles above where we left the Canoe; but instead of finding this Part better, to my great Disappointment we found it much worse: the River was every where bounded by Craigs, whose height w[as] never less than 300 feet & often rose to 500 feet perpendicular above the level of the River.

Here then for the Present was my last Hopes destroyed. I felt this more keenly than ever from seeing before me, for a great Distance to the Westward, a Country not very Mountainous but covered with green Hills which seemed to promise a much better Road; & had the Waters been two Feet perpendicular lower, we might perhaps have succeeded; for notwithstanding the Craigs, still it was easy to be seen that in low Water there are all along narrow Beaches, by which means People may get up, by the Line or by the Pole; and I am pretty confident that the first Chain of Mountains passed, the River will be found better.

It may perhaps be necessary to explain the Nature of the River near the Mountains. It may be remarked that in general all Rivers from Bank to Bank have a greater Space than what is occupied by the Stream: after this Manner is the Saskatchewan River below us, and a River thus formed has Place for the great Flushes which rise in the Summer, without increasing its Current beyond what the natural weight of water gives it. But a River, or part of a River such as the Saskatchewan in it's Passage thro' the first Chain of Mountains, where it's Banks are high Craigs that rise nearly from the margin of the Stream, has not the advantage of a vacant Space for the Waters as they swell; in such Places the Stream rises perpendicularly, & must compensate in Depth & Velocity what it wants in Breadth. I measured the Rate of Current & found it to be, where easiest, 9 Miles p^r Hour & where quickest from 12 to 15 Miles an Hour. For a proof of the great Velocity with which the Current moves in Summer: from where we turned about, we took only 5 Hours & 50 Minutes to the Rocky Mountain House, altho' the distance is about 74 Statute Miles, & we paddled no more than what was barely necessary to keep the Current from carrying us on the Rocks or against the Craigs of the River. We arrived at the Fort on the 30th of June.

How unfortunate has this Journey been from the beginning, when we had got all ready, & waited a long Time! At length a Kootanae came to guide us, & he when within a few Miles of the Fort was murdered; Mr Duncan McGillivray, who was to have headed the Party, from his weak state of Health was obliged to abandon it; & we, attempting to cross the Mountains with loaded Horses, for want of a better Guide were obliged to trust ourselves to the Guidance of a worthless, cowardly Indian who led us into defiles impassable to Horses; and by the Time we had returned & got a Canoe built, the River had rose so uncommonly high, & ran with such impetuousity, as to preclude all human Means from being able to stem the Current in it's Descent from the Mountain. So greatly indeed had the waters swelled that the oldest People do not remember ever to have seen the River so high, even in the Vicinity of the Cedar Lake, except once about 23 years ago – & in this State the River continued 'till the latter end of August.

However unsuccessful this Journey has been, it has not been wholly without it's use: it has taught us to make a better choice of our Men, & take fewer of them; & never to employ an Indian of this Side the Mountains for our Guide; it has also shewn us plainly, that to employ & depend on Horses for carrying the Goods &c in such Expeditions is the most uncertain, & most expensive, of all the Modes of Conveyance. Whoever wishes to attempt to cross the Mountains for the Purposes of Commerce ought to employ a Canoe, & start early in the Spring, say the beginning of May, from the Rocky Mountain House, the Water for that Month being low & the Current not half so violent as in the Summer; there are then also Beaches all the way, either on one Side or the other of the River even in the Mountains, by which People may track on the Shore where the Pole cannot well be used. In this Season, they would cross a great Part of the Mountains without any extraordinary Difficulty, and meet the Flushes of high Water where they would have need of it, that is, near the Head of the River – from whence there is said to be a short Road to the waters which flow on the other Side the Mountain.

It is a Maxim pretty well received, that Success in Enterprizes justifies all the Measures that have been taken in such Enterprizes; on the Contrary, whatever is unsuccessful must be accounted for: it is on this Account that I have been so tedious in detailing so minutely the trifling Occurrences of the above Journey.

DAVID THOMPSON

Messrs William & Duncan McGillivray
Agent[s] of the NW^t Company

Across the Mountains

10 May – 18 July 1807

May 10th [1807] **Sunday** A very fine day. At $9\frac{1}{2}$ Am sent off Mr Finan McDonald & 5 Men in a Canoe with Goods & Necessaries to the expedition across the Mountains on which I pray the blessing of Heaven. Yesterday I sent off 2 Men with 6 lean Horses, for want of better, with Provisions &c for the above purpose. At 10 Am I set off with Bercier on Horseback – we arrived at the Horse Tent, but could not get the Horses 'till $2\frac{1}{2}$ Pm, when with very hard riding thro' thick woods very much fallen down we arrived at the Round Plain. Camped, with the Horses & Men sent ahead, at the Brook [passed] in my former Journey.

May 11th [1807] **Monday** A very fine day, wind variable. Sent Men a hunting, but they killed nothing, altho' they saw both Buffalo & Red Deer, the Dogs having followed them & started all the Animals, without being able to stop a single one. Obs^d [sun's] LL Doub Merid Alt^{de} Lat^{de} 52°:24':13″ N.

May 12th [1807] **Tuesday** A fine day. At 8 Am Clement with my self went ahead with 2 loaded Horses to the Long Plain, where leaving them we went afoot. About the mid of the Plain at the Brook, we saw a Bull, which we killed after a hard chace up high Knowls & thro' thick fallen down Woods – sent five Horses for the Meat which they brought. Obs^d for Lat^{de} by 2 Alt^{des} Ther +70° Lat^{de} 52°:31':32″ N Decⁿ 18°:4':28″ N. We seem now to have marched obliquely to a chain of Mountains whose southernmost Point bears S32E by the Compass.

May 13th [1807] Wednesday A fine day, but cloudy. At 8 Am went off with Clement, but saw nothing. The Canoe & Men with Mr F. McDonald arrived safe at 9 Am where they staid all day. At 2 Pm the Wolverene, a Nahathaway Indian, arrived – he informs me an Indian, The Iron, is shot, was killed; our Guest may do to hunt. Rain all the Evening – see May 17th.

May 14th [1807] Thursday A morn of very cold thick Snow, & all day 'till Noon when it ceased & the evening became tolerably mild. Did not decamp on acc^t of the bad weather.

May 15 [1807] Friday A very fine day. At $7\frac{1}{2}$ Am went off with the Wolverene a hunting – about Noon killed a Doe Red Deer, poor. Went into the Little Plain of the War Tent where we arrived at $1\frac{1}{2}$ Pm – the People followed at $8\frac{1}{4}$ Am, but did not arrive 'till 4 Pm. Very bad Road, much fallen burnt Woods as usual. A Horse was missing with the leather Tent – sent a Man to look after both, but he did not find either. Cloudy. Killed 1 Cow & Calf, poor.

May 16th [1807] Saturday A very fine day, cloudy. At 8 Am having brought all the Horses sent off a Man to look after the Horse & Tent missing yesterday, which he found, & brought. At 11 Am came to Jaco's Brook, where the Canoe & Men were waiting; brought 2 Horse Loads of Meat – they had also killed a good Bull & a Red Deer. Got a quantity of the Meat split & dried for the use of the Canoe Men. The River is now very shoal & full of Rapids, but still the Navigation is not worse than about the Fort below & for about 7 Miles above it. We now turn to the right to go up along the Brook – our Co will be ab^t s70w, that of the Canoe between the 2 Mountains ab^t s25w, & the Mountains may be about 6 or 8M distant.

May 17th [1807] Sunday A fine day, cloudy – showers of Rain in the Afternoon & Evening. Being now to go over Ground I have not yet passed, I will take the Courses, the best the nature of the thick woody Country will permit me. At $8\frac{1}{4}$ Am set off, Co s72w 6 or 7M – we followed the north Brook, very often crossing the Stream, the first 3M burnt Woods with high Banks, then flat low wet Points of green Pines, small & full of branches. Put up at $\frac{3}{4}$ Pm as our Horses are very weak & poor – the first Grass is just showing itself in a few advantageous Spots. Went up the Bank & set our Co for the Morrow which

will be ab^t West 1M then turns to the [left], but the Co between the
2 Mount^{ns} is straight s66w. The Mountain between this Brook & the
River is a detached Mass of ab^t 10M long or so; the Mount^n on the
right of our Road is Rocks, tolerable even surface, as they all are for
ab^t 1M then falls into a chain of Hills, wooded with small Pines.
The detached Mountain is mostly bare of Wood, but may almost every
where be climbed by an active Man. They may be elevated ab^t
1600 ft above their Bases – there is no convenient Place to measure
their height. The Snow lies in the hollows & furrows of the Rocks
& no where appears to be deep. Animals are Buffaloe & Red Deer with
Moose tolerable plenty. MM: There are 4 Brooks that fall into the
Long Plain; west^d of the Brook of the green Hummock of Firs, all these
sink into the Ground as well as the latter, & disappear soon after
they leave the inner Bank.

May 18th [1807] **Monday** All last Night a high Gale of NW Wind with
showers of Hail & Rain – in the morning Sleet & Rain, which
continued all day.

May 19 [1807] **Tuesday** A day of fly^g Clouds 'till the afternoon, when
Showers of Hail & Sleet. We were a long time in finding all the
Horses; we then set off & camped at the upper War Tent, where the
Nahathaways formerly entrenched themselves with Pickets &c.
Our Co may have been s80w 6M – 5M gone Brook from the west^d, as
we have not gone to between the Mountains, but towards the right
hand one. Set the Course I think we shall go the Morrow: it appears
to be s28w to between the Mountains before set. The Mountain
between us & the Saskatchewan s70E & N70w – they have 14 Ranges
of Trees say 840 feet above their base here. Our Road has been
mostly over bare low Points, no Banks, but in general wet – the Woods
are all green, but small; the foot of the Mountains may be ab^t 1M
or so from us – those on the [right] ab^t 3M, & the Land between is very
swampy. The Wolverene killed a fleshy Bull: Buffaloe have been
plenty – they are now few here & the Country too wet for Red Deer.
Many Porcupine – killed one, very poor. Saw a few Geese & Ducks.

May 20th [1807] **Wednesday** A very fine clear Day. At setting off
[crossed] the Brook, our Co ab^t 82w 6M – bad woody swampy
country. Here we found the Wolverene had killed a tolerable good Bull
– staid 1 Hour & then went on for about 1 Hour more sw 2M when

we put up at 2 Pm. The Mountains above are 1 or $1\frac{1}{4}$M behind us to the NE^d, and are more abrupt on this side than as seen elsewhere. Our Road has been all along near & [crossing] the Brook of this Morning which may be from 6 to 10 Y^{ds} wide & now diminished to 4 Y^{ds} at times, for the last 3M forming a narrow shoal Pond of ab^t 100 Y^{ds} x. Woods always of Fir or Pine: no Aspin or Poplar since our Brook's sortie. Killed also 1 Bull, 1 Cow & Calf, & 1 Porcupine. The Horses fell down frequently with weakness & bad Roads, altho' carrying no more than ab^t 130 lbs each. Lat^{de} 52°:35′:56″ N.

May 21 [1807] **Thursday** A very fine day of fly^g Clouds. As one of the Horses was missing, we did not set off 'till $9\frac{1}{2}$ Am, leaving Boulard to look for the stray Horse. At $\frac{1}{4}$ Pm put up at the NE end of the Lake, our Co S42W 3M – we have taken as many Hours for as many Miles: the Road is very bad, many small swamps, Banks & much fallen Wood – $\frac{3}{4}$M gone we crossed the main Branch of the Brook & kept along the south one; the other comes from the west^d. The little Brook that we followed, seeing it at times but did not x it, came direct from the Lake. The Lake may be $1\frac{1}{4}$M long in a S18W Co & $\frac{1}{2}$M wide – the longest Bay is due South, Water very clear. Woods of small Pine & Fir, no other. Saw ab^t 40 or 50 black Ducks, & altho' the Lake is $\frac{5}{6}$ covered with weak Ice yet there are Loons in it, probably also Fish. The Wolverene killed a Bull Buffaloe, but from the badness of the Roads we could take none of the Meat.

May 22nd [1807] **Friday** A fine day, as usual flying Clouds. At 9:5′ Am set off Co along the Lake – say South $1\frac{1}{4}$M then S20W 2M a very small Brook S16W 2M, the latter 4M tolerable good Road, latter $2\frac{1}{2}$M of this along a bold Brook, at which we camped at $\frac{1}{4}$ Pm. The Saskatchewan bears S60E 1M, to which I went: westward of the first range of Mountains, the River runs between ridges of high rocky Hills, in some places bare Rocks but mostly wooded with small Pines, or a swath of Weeds & short Grass.

May 23rd [1807] **Saturday** A Stormy Day with flying Clouds, mostly Cloudy. Obs^d for Lat^{de}, very hazy but will serve to correct the Courses: Ther +66° Lat^{de} 52°:24′:17″ N Dec^n 20°:31′:2″ N. The Brook is still covered with Ice so as to form strong Bridges of 100 Y^{ds} long, but it is decaying fast. Went with Bercier to the next Camp^t across the River, saw about 20 Buffalo, 10 Sheep, & 2 Red

Deer – wounded a Cow, but the Gun is too short to throw a Ball any distance. In the Even^g heavy Rain which lasted all Night.

May 24 [1807] Sunday At 6 Am the Rain ceased – very heavy Showers from 10 Am to 5 Pm, when fine Weather. All the Mountains that before were bare of snow, as well as the high Hills, are now covered with it, but in the afternoon thawed on the lower part. Much of the Mountains about us are abrupt, almost perpend & bare black & dark grey Rock.

May 25th [1807] Monday A very fine day. As I was doubtful whether the Canoe & People had passed us or not, I sent down Clement & Bercier to go below along the Banks of the River to where the Goods of the Winter were put in Hoard. They went & found the canoe had passed; in the evening they returned. At the Sortie of the Brook from the Camp^t set the Courses – Co from the Camp^t S71E $\frac{3}{4}$M, Co to the Plains of our next Camp^t S7W 5M. The perpend of the River here is S52E 1M: the west End of the River as it seems to come from the Mountains is N68E 18M & then winds to the north^d & this is nearly the Course of the River. From this plain the River runs N66E then turns a little to the east^d – this all the bend it makes to the Mountain below, except the windings of the Channels backwards & forwards among the Gravel Banks. Ther +60°.

May 26th [1807] Tuesday A very fine day. At 8 Am the Wolverene with a Woman set off to find her countrymen to the NE^d. At 9 Am we set off & kept on 'till we came to the [crossing] Place of the small Plains – but finding the Water too high, we did not cross, but camped. Our Course has been S71E$\frac{3}{4}$M along the Brook then Co up along the Saskatchewan S10W 4M – 3M of this gone a bold Brook from the NNE^d. Clement went a hunt^g & killed a Bull. Bercier with myself went to find a Road to pass by that may avoid the high Banks of the usual Route – we found one, but finding a still better, we followed it 'till late without knowing where it ends.

May 27 [1807] Wednesday A fine but stormy Day 'till Evening, then Rain, Sleet & finally Snow. Early sent off Boulard with a Note to Mr F. McDonald at the Kootanae Plains, to return directly & bring up the rest of the Goods as the Water is rising fast. Went & followed up the Road of yesterday – found it to be tolerable good & entirely

keeps clear of the high Banks so dangerous to the Horses
& Property. Killed a Ram but lost him at the foot of a high Hill – saw
ab^t 70 or 80 Buffalo, all across the River.

May 28th [1807] **Thursday** A very snowy Night & Day – Snow lies
thick on the Ground & on all the Trees. Cloudy evening.

May 29th [1807] **Friday** A fine day; most of the Snow of yesterday
thawed. Went a hunt^g – killed a Cow, & Clement a Bull, neither of
them fat. The Canoe & People with Boulard arrived here at $\frac{1}{2}$ past Noon
– they repeat that there is neither Grass for our Horses nor Animals
for hunting at the Kootanae Plains, from the long Residence of Jaco
& Family there with the 2 Indians. We shall stay here 'till the return
of the Canoe & People from the Hoard.

May 30 [1807] **Saturday** A very fine day. At 7$\frac{1}{2}$ Am the Canoe & People
set off to go to the Hoard for the rest of the Goods &c – gave them
a few pairs of Shoes, as the whole way up is with the towing Line. They
describe the River as having a constant rapid Current, with a few
dangerous places – & their Lines tho' of the best Cod Line, often broke
& endangered the Canoe & Property. Obs^d for Lat^{de} [sun's] LL
Lat^{de} 52°:20':39" N Dec^n 21°:42':32" N.

May 31st [1807] **Sunday** A very fine warm Day. Water rising fast; the
Woods of Aspin, Poplars &c turning Green & the Leaves unfolding
fast; the Grass springing up to 2 In long, but the hard Soil does not
provide much. At Noon the Canoe & Men arrived safe with the rest
of the Property – they have come fast on.

June 1st [1807] **Monday** At 7 Am the Canoe & People set off to go to
the Kootanae Plains. At 8 Am we also set off – 10 Am to the
Brooks, the latter one 2 Y^{ds} x. 11 Am a Brook of 3 Y^{ds} x, but much
wider when the Snow thaws in the Mountains – then none of consequence 'till 1$\frac{1}{2}$ Pm when we crossed 4 Brooks, say 4 to 6 ft wide at
nearly equal distances from each other. Put up at the Muleton
Plains at 3 Pm ab^t $\frac{1}{4}$M past the last Brook. The Tops of the Mountains,
which before appeared so elevated, sink down in appearance as we
approach them. We are near some of the elevated, tho' they appear
more so to the west^d – these do not appear high tho' quite close to
us; their Bases may be 1M wide dist from each other – they are remark-

ably rugged & lightly covered with Snow. Our Campment is the best & most pleasant we have yet had. No Sheep to be seen – killed a Calf, wounded a Cow; there was a herd of Cows but the Dogs drove them away. Our Course has been s20w 12M – 6 Hours of marching. The Place where I think the Kootanae Plains are bears s30w from a Hill near the Tent.

June 2nd [1807] **Tuesday** A very fine day. Went a hunting & killed a Ram, but not fat. Rested the Horses as they are very poor.

June 3rd [1807] **Wednesday** A morning of small Rains, but fine day. At 8$\frac{3}{4}$ Am set off Co s30w 7M – 1 M gone [crossed] the Muleton Rivulet, bold 20 Y^{ds} x, very strong Current & to the Sides of the Horses – *when very high cannot be forded* – besides 7 or 8 small Channels: these change with almost every flush of water. Co s22E 4M thro' the Kootanae Plains, where we put up near the Canoe & People at 1 Pm – we came fast on, often at a sound Trot. The Valleys, notwithstanding the rugged snowy appearance of the Chain of Mountains about us, are pleasant, & one might pass an agreeable summer in such places as we have come thro' the last 4 Miles – the Hills on the [right] have also a smooth verdant appearance. 3M below us a bold Rivulet from the sw^{d} – I suppose it to be the one Mr Hughes & me saw formerly; $\frac{1}{2}$M below where we are now another bold Brook from the sw^{d}.

June 4th [1807] **Thursday** A day of variable weather. My Watch has lost Time – I missed a Merid Obs^{n} of the [sun]. Ther +60° Lat^{de} 52°:2':6" N Dec^{n} 22°:24':40" N Kootanae Plain.

June 5th [1807] **Friday** A Day of variable Weather. Having arranged several little Affairs, at 7:35 Am we set off, Co s18w 1$\frac{1}{2}$M Co s55w 7M put up at 1$\frac{1}{2}$ Pm – perhaps we have gone 8M instead of 7M as above. At 5 Pm the Canoe & People came to us. We have passed thro' a barren hard woody country: the Banks are only thick Woods of Pine & Fir very full of Branches & the Ground covered mostly with their Leaves & a few scattered Blades of Grass in places – the low Points are marshes with very rank short coarse Grass.

June 6th [1807] **Saturday** A day of variable Weather, wind NE – much Rain in the Afternoon. The Horses finding no good Grass crossed the River in the Night, upon which we also crossed over our Baggage

to the So Side, & at 8½ Am set off, Co s30w 5M – 4M gone a bold
very rapid Brook, end of Co the Forks; we take the So Branch, which
is by much the least, leaving the main Stream to the nw^d. Our Co
s80w 1M s20E 2M – I lost my Compass for the present – at end of Co
camped at a remarkable little Knowl. At 2 Pm the Canoe & People
also arrived; they took a Meal & at 3 Pm set off on their return to the
Kootanae Plain for the rest of the Property. Bercier with me in care
of the Goods &c here – spent the rest of the Day in arranging ourselves.
We lost the Black Horse: as he is a stallion, we suppose he is
returned to the Herds of Mares at the Kootanae Plains.

June 7th [1807] **Sunday** Variable Weather – much Rain in the morn^g
& even^g. The Country is very mountainous & all nearly perpendicular; the Hills at the base of the Mountains are very wide & high,
clothed with mostly small Firs & in places fine Grass for the
Animals – there seems to be plenty of Buffaloe, Moose & Red Deer in
the Summer, which however has not yet begun here. The
Mountains are loaded with Snow, the continual rushing down of which
makes a Noise like Thunder.

June 8th [1807] **Monday** A fine day. Went a hunting but saw nothing;
dried most of the Cargoe landed here. A few Moose here but the
Woods are too close for me to hunt them.

June 9th [1807] **Tuesday** A fine day, flying Clouds. Went a hunting up
the mid Rivulet but saw nothing – Co to it from the Campment
sw 2M Co up it West 1M to a Lake of sw 3M by 1M wide. It appears
deep; it is bordered on the [right] with Woods, but much torn
down by the rushing Masses of Snow from the Mountains – in one
place in particular the Snow, in rushing from the Side of the
Mountain, had swept & broken all the Trees to a considerable distance
& carried them all before it clean, except a Fir Pine of ab^t 3 fm
round, beautifully made. It alone had withstood the ravage & the other
broken Trees were piled about it to the height of about 12 or
15 feet – it stood most majestically erect amidst such vast Ruins; its
bark was about 4 or 5 In Thick, of a very firm close Grain. On the
west Side the Lake, the rushing of the Snows from the height & Sides
of the Mountains has destroyed almost all the Trees & their fragments strew the sides of the Lake. At the end of the Lake the Rivulet
comes from the sw^d from the very large Glaciers, & runs from there

thro' a low marshy stony Soil; it then turns from the WNW^d at the foot of the Glaciers. Saw no Animals of any Kind, altho' there are many Moose Tracks – at end of Lake &c the cuttings of ab^t 5 or 6 Beavers.

June 10th [1807] **Wednesday** A day of much Rain, with squalls of Wind. At 8 $\frac{3}{4}$ Am, Canoe & People arrived with the rest of the Merchandize. At 10 Am sent off 4 Men in the Canoe, light for the Kootanae Plain, there to live for the time the Portage is blocked up with Snow. Kept Boisverd with me as I think the Merchandize will require to be put in Boxes of thin Boards, in order to be safely transported across the Mountains; I looked out for Wood proper to split into such Boards but could find none – the Woods are of such a twisted knotty growth.

June 11th [1807] **Thursday** A fine day. Sent Bercier & Buché with Horses to bring us Meat from the People at the Kootanae Plain, as there are no Animals about us here – went a hunting towards the Height of Land, but saw nothing.

June 12 [1807] **Friday** A stormy, cloudy Day. Went a Moose hunting but saw nothing; the Woods are too close, altho' their Tracks are plenty in the Moss.

June 13th [1807] **Saturday** A cloudy cold Day, many small Showers of Rain. Bercier & Buché returned with the Meat of a Cow & a calf.

June 14th [1807] **Sunday** Almost continual Cold Rain – Snowing for about more than half way down the Mountains.

June 15th [1807] **Monday** A fine Morning, stormy Afternoon, fly^g Clouds. Went across the Rivulet & split out ab^t 130 small fir Boards for Boxes to put the Goods in. The Snows that have plentifully fallen on the Mountains these three days are now rushing down with such a Noise that we can hardly persuade ourselves it is not Thunder – we hear it at least every Hour, & sometimes oftener.

June 16th 1807 **Tuesday** A fine day, but as usual stormy. Spent the day in squaring &c the Boards of yesterday – got it done. Sent Bercier to tell one of the Hunters to come & hunt here, also a Note to Mr F. McDonald. Lat^{de} 51°:50′:31″ N Dec^n 32°:21′:27″ N.

Measured the Height of 3 peaks of the Mountains about as from the
Gravel Banks of the Rivulet – they give 4707 ft, 5200 ft & 5057 ft
perpend above their Bases.

June 17th [1807] **Wednesday** A fine Morning but rainy Afternoon.
Went up the North Branch – an aft Wind prevented hunting with
effect. At 4 ½ Pm Bercier & the Hunter arrived.

June 18th [1807] **Thursday** Showers of Rain at Times. Working at the
Boxes &c. The Hunter killed a Buck Red Deer, but very poor; I killed
a black Bear, also very poor – it was astonishingly tenacious of Life.

June 19th [1807] **Friday** A rainy Night & Day. Sent Men for the Red
Deer, which they brought. At dawn of Day the Hunter killed a
black Bear at our Tent Door – we had fired at him last Night at our
Door, but it was too dark to aim with precision. The Hunter went
off to the Kootanae Plain. The Boxes are 23 In by 23 In & 8 ½ deep.

June 20th [1807] **Saturday** A fine day but surly Morn^g. Working at the
Boxes – packed up 5 d°.

June 21st [1807] **Sunday** A very fine day, the best we have had yet. Put
the major part of the Goods in 5 more Boxes – I reserve the rest 'till
I am come from visiting the Portage. The Heights of the Mountains
still present that cold clear shining white Snow which is never seen
but in the depths of a rigorous Winter in [all but] a very severe Clime.
They have all Rocky Peaks which for several hundred feet are destitute of all verdure, & uniformly present a dark grey or blackish rugged
Rock, seemingly very hard; they all appear of the same kind of
Rock: no variation of Matter, except with regard to its state of preservation – some being in a state of decay, much split by Lightning
& Frost, & more in the primeval quality. Some have about 2000 ft
perpend of greenish Ice, which seemingly never thaws, & the slip-
peryness of which no doubt causes many of those rushes of Snow that
overwhelm everything in their way, besides the Cavities that at
length become overcharged – & for want of a sufficient Basis, the Snow
is hurled down, or poured down like a Torrent of Water, with a
Noise that is not easily distinguished from Thunder.

June 22nd [1807] **Monday** A very fine day. At 5:40 Am set off with
Bercier and two light Horses to visit the Portage of the Mountains,

if yet passable, as not having had of late fine weather. Co s1ow 2M –
near opposite end of Co the main Stream of this Rivulet falls in
from a Lake – see June 9th. Then Co s27E 1M Red Berry Campment
SE 4M Kootanae Pound s27E 1$\frac{1}{4}$M we leave the Rivulet. We leave
the Rivulet we have followed coming from the west^{d} and take a Brook
on the [left] N55E $\frac{1}{2}$ M s60E 1$\frac{3}{4}$M – near the Place where we leave
the Brook there are on the [right] 2 Bodies of Rocks close to each other,
detached by a Rent, whose strata incline very much to the SE^{d}. We
then enter a low Point where there are Tent Poles & a marked Path:
from this place on the ground Flats, we perceive the Brook come
from the [right] & in the bight of the Concave are Banks of blackish
Gravel – on seeing which is the mark for us to enter & find the
above marked Path, which leads to the Height of Land. Co thro' this
Point SE $\frac{3}{4}$M – last $\frac{1}{4}$M along a Rill, which here rises & whose Current
descends to the Pacific Ocean. May God in his Mercy give us to see
where it's waters flow into the Ocean, & return in safety. Several
small Rills fall in from all Sides – it is now 2 Y^{ds} wide, but very shallow.
At 9 Am stopped to bait our Horses – several Patches of Snow still
on this bit of Meadow & the Grass just beg^{g} to spring. At 9$\frac{1}{2}$ Am set
off down the Rill Co SE 4M soon becomes a Brook – at 2$\frac{1}{2}$M a bold
brook from the [left]: the Brook is now 6 Y^{ds} wide, 2 ft deep with a
rapid Current, which indeed belongs to it every where. Many Falls
– the descent is every where very great. As we had now passed the
narrowest part of the Defile & had descended very considerably,
we found no Snow whatever but the Grass somewhat long, the Leaves
in the Willows somewhat large & all the appearance of Spring. We
thought proper to return as in all probability there is no snow to stop
us in the rest of our Road. From 11 to 11$\frac{1}{2}$ Am repacked our Horses
– at 1 Pm arrived at the Height of Land w[h]ere we again stopped to
bait the Horses 'till 2 Pm, when we again mounted & pushed
forward 'till 5 Pm, when we arrived at our Tents. Water rising much
from the melting of the Snows.

June 23rd [1807] **Tuesday** A fine day but cloudy. Early sent off Bercier
with a Note to Finan to come with the People, Horses & rest of the
Baggage, Provisions &c as soon as possible. I spent the day in arranging
Pieces &c in order for the Horses to transport over the Mountains.

June 24th [1807] **Wednesday** A very fine day. Arranging our little
affairs &c &c. Mean Lat^{de} 51°:57′:38″ N. At 7 Pm Mr Finan
McDonald with the Men, Horses & Baggage arrived, but brought not

a mouthful of Provisions. Assigned to each two Men 3 Horses with their Furniture, consisting of each Horse 1 Saddle, Saddle stuff, Cords for the Lead, & their Load, weighing ab^t 130 lbs.

June 25th [1807] Thursday At 3$\frac{1}{2}$ Am started the Men, who gathered the Horses, arranged the Loads &c, & by 6 Am were all ready & set off – for our Course, Dist^{ce} &c see June 22nd. At 9 Am stopped near the Rocks of the Kootanae Plain to bait the Horses. Seeing 5 white Goats on the Mountain I went off after them, but they eluded my pursuit by taking to the perpendicular Craigs – when near them a large Rock gave way & bounced down touching the Mountain only in a few places, & immediately after a great rush of small Stones, Water &c – I supposed it to be bursting of some Cavern. The whole passed within ab^t 100 Y^{ds} of me, & made me set off as fast as I dared to go. I found the Mountain, altho' apparently not above an [angle] of 45°, almost too steep to climb: when I breathed a few Seconds I was obliged to keep hold with my Nails & feet to prevent myself slid-ing down – at the same time keeping fast hold of my Gun, which otherwise would soon have found the foot of the Mountain in pieces. Returned to my people & directly at 11$\frac{1}{4}$ Am again set off – [crossed] the Rivulet twice, deep & rapid, very muddy from the rising of the Water by the melting of the Snows in this fine Weather, but the Ice does not seem much affected by it. At 1 Pm arrived at the Height of Land & put up on acc^t of the weakness of our Horses. This is a low Bottom of Moss & a little marshy Meadow full of springs at the foot of the surrounding Mountains, forming a hollow – not to be noticed at any dist^{ce}. The Mountains around are of the highest & yet from this place, their Base, they may not measure more than those of my Campment. They & these are [a] vast Mass of Matter, fixed in an inclined Plane, whose vertex is here & thus these Mountains may be geometrically measured & no one of them be found considerably higher than the others yet the Mountains placed on the vertex are actually perhaps a full 1000 feet, or more higher than near the foot of the inclined Plane. Ther +76° Lat^{de} 51°:48':25" N Dec^n 23°:25':12" N Height of Land.

June 26th [1807] Friday A very fine day. Arose early, & by 6$\frac{1}{2}$ Am got ready & set off, Co SE 4M + 2M – 2M gone a Brook from the [left] – at 2$\frac{1}{2}$ d^o from the [right] – small Rills very many. The Brook is very much increased by the melting of the Snows in this fine Weather

— so much so with the rapid Current as to endanger not only the wetting of the Goods, but also the Lives of the Men, who are all afoot: they can cross only by clinging fast to the Horses. Co s35e 2m – 1½m gone a Brook from the [left]. Co s7e 1¾m – ½m gone a bold Brook from the [left], 1m gone dº from the [right]. Put up at end of Co at 2 Pm – at 11 Am stopped 1¼H to refresh the Horses, but no Grass for them. Opened several Boxes & dried the Goods that has got wet. Gave the Men a large Dog of which they made a hearty Meal. The Road of to day was between 2 Hills of Rock nearly perpend, always very steep; between these Hills the Brook runs which we have followed, it's Banks covered with large hard Pines, much of two unknown Species. The Trees every where fallen down & the Moss overgrown with a kind of wild willow vine & very sharp prickly Shrubs – we had to cut much wood away & widen the Path. Add to this, the Horses were obliged to jump with their Loads over much wind-fallen Wood; & as the Brook now struck to the foot of this or that steep Hill, so we were obliged to x to the opposite low shore, then the whole valley was often not above 100 y^{ds} x. The Men had much ado to save themselves. Ther +78° Lat^{de} 51°:20':21" N Dec^n 23°:23':30" N Dog's Campment.

June 27th [1807] Saturday A fine day except a few light Showers. At 6¾ Am set off, after having cut a Road thro' about ¼m of strong Wood Co s5e 4m – Co s30e 2½m to 10½ Am when we refreshed our Horses. We have [crossed] the River at times, part good, part bad – especially that thro' the first Cedars along a steep Hill on the [right]. Cut away much wood, yet the Horses were continually bucking the Cords that held on the loads, the Road is so very narrow & bad. At ¼ Pm set off, & was continually cutting away much Wood 'till we got in the Flats of Gravel: here the Hills separate much, leaving sometimes a Mile nearly, frequently less – here we [crossed] [and recrossed] every hundred Yards, the Stream winding continually from the foot of one Hill to the foot of the other, besides sending off many Channels. Co So 2m s30w 5½m when we put up on the [right] at 5¾ Pm. We have come hard on since we came on the Gravel Flats – the Current is so very rapid & deep, that I often expected to see the Men & Horses with their Loads swept away before it, but thank God all got safe hereto, tho' much wilted. I rode before the Men on a capital Horse, sounding all the Fords, & when too deep, looking out others. The Mountains to the sw^d before us appear lower than those

we have left – it is thus also on the east Side: while going up the
inclined Plane, the Mountains towards the vertex appeared very high,
& yet as we passed them, & from the vertex Land looked back on
them, they then appeared to have lost much of their height – no doubt
much of this arose from the elevated Ground on which we viewed
them. Saw much fine Cedar, white-fir Pine & Fire Pines &c, [&] much
of that very sharp prickly Shrub. The prickles are all in the Shrub
Bole; it has long Leaves & the under Side of the Leaves are full of sharp
Prickles also – we hurt our hands much as we caught at it, in saving
ourselves from a fall.

June 28th **[1807] Sunday** A fine day. Early got our Horses collected
& by $6\frac{1}{4}$ Am set off – [crossed] the River almost directly & went
over a flat Point on the left tolerable open, then thro' quite pathless
Woods & so thick set, that one may say the [sun] never saw their
Stems, with hilly rocky Ground. Left our Horses, & Axe in hand four
of us cut a Road thro' it, which took us a long Time – at length by
Noon we got to a low small flat Point, fine open Ground. Our Horses
hav^g been loaded these 6 Hours, we stopped to refresh them & ourselves, from very heavy fatigue & Labour. After taking a mouthful of
Pemmican 5 Men went off to cut a Road & it was $4\frac{1}{2}$ Pm before they
returned – when a Thunder Storm with Rain coming on & every one
tired, we camped for the Night, as there is no Grass for the Horses
for a considerable distance. Our Course s30w $1\frac{1}{2}$M or $1\frac{3}{4}$M at most.

June 29th **[1807] Monday** A fine day. At $5\frac{1}{4}$ Am set off & went thro'
the Woods s30w $2\frac{1}{2}$M to a bold & exceeding rapid Brook. Here the
water being far too violent to ford the Horses, we examined the Brook
upwards & found a place where a Bridge might be thrown across
(which with some Trouble we got done) of 2 large Fir Pines. We then
crossed all the Goods & horse Furniture on our Backs; we then
[crossed] the Horses one at a time, by tying a strong Halter to them
& 3 or 4 Men hauling them x in the Water – for altho' not more
than 3 ft deep, such was its extreme descent & velocity, that our best
Horses were immediately thrown off their Legs & swept under. We
held on thro' very thick Woods to the foot of a high Bank – here at
11 Am we stopped to refresh our Horses, that they might have
strength to go up it, & the Men cleared the Road. We then went to the
little Rill of saltish Water where we stopped 2 Hours in the Hills
to fetch the Meat of a young Buck Red Deer killed by the young

Seauteaux. We then held on over much very woody bad Road, & passed the high steep Bank which borders close on the River, with a Precipice close along which we walked – the least slip would have tumbled our Horses to the bottom. Close below this, on the Bank of the Stream, we camped at 6 Pm. Our Course I suppose to have been s30w ab^t 8M in all, mostly near the River, tho' not seeing it from the rugged Hills which line it. It is always a Torrent which seemingly nothing can resist, always boiling with its velocity against the inequalities of the Bottom.

June 30th [1807] Tuesday As we were getting our Horses saddled a heavy Rain broke out, which obliged us to let our Horses loose again, but clearing up at 8$\frac{1}{2}$ Am set off. Co may be South 2M a Brook – [crossed] then along the River, clearing the Road at times + 6M, the last 2M over a high Point of fine Woods that lies between this Portage River & the Kootanae River. At 1$\frac{1}{4}$ Pm, having descended the Hills, we stopped in a grassy Marsh to refresh our Horses – at 2$\frac{1}{2}$ Pm we again set off & went upwards round the grassy Marsh to the Kootanae River. Our Co may have been s30e 1$\frac{1}{4}$M when we arrived at 3$\frac{1}{2}$ Pm, thank God all safe. As soon as we unloaded the Horses, we untied the Goods to dry them, which fine weather enabled us to do tolerable well, & the Morrow if fine will complete the business. Visited the Canoes left by Jaco – found them unfit for carriage but handy for light voyaging.

July 1st [1807] Wednesday A very fine day. Finished drying all the Goods; looked out a place for building canoes, as the old place is full of Rubbish – removed with all the Goods &c about 200 Y^{ds} lower down & then put all in good order. Long^{de} 116°:47':8" w.

July 2nd [1807] Thursday A very fine day. At 3 Am sent off Bercier & Clement to look for the Kootanaes; sent 4 Men off with ab^t 12 Horses to bring the rest of the Goods, that are left in charge of Mr Finan McDonald at my Campment. Staid with Beaulieu & Boisverd to make a large Canoe if we can procure Materials.

July 3–4 [1807] Employed in getting Materials for the large Canoe.

July 5th [1807] Sunday Very much in want of Food – sent word to the 2 Seauteaux that are here, that if they did not pay me part of the

Meat they owed me, I would kill one of his Horses for Food – on this
he brought me ab^t 30 lbs of a small Deer & a small Beaver.
Lat^{de} 50°:59':2" N Dec^n 22°:50':7" N.

July 6–7–8 [1807] Working at a large Canoe with Boisverd. Clement
& Bercier arrived & with 3 Kootanaes – they brought part of a Chevreuil which was highly acceptable, as we were at our last mouthful.
Beaulieu has been these ten days so very ill that he could not help
us, & at length so much so that we dispaired of his Life – his Complaint
a violent dry Colic & Pain under his Ribs on the [left]. This Morn^g
perceiving a small Swelling close under his left Ribs mid of the Side to be
enlarging, he was feeling it with attention, & by his fingers feeling
something rough he sent for me. It appeared to be a small splinter – I
extracted it, & to our great surprise found it was a porcupine Quill,
that had made its appearance from the inwards – it was of the short
thick ones on the Rump & Tail of the Porcupine. It can be accounted
for only by supposing that, when he eat part of the Dog the day we passed
the Height of Land, he had in eating the Meat swallowed the
Porcupine Quill in the Meat, as he is a voracious eater. All our Dogs have
been more or less wounded by the Porcupines, & no doubt some of
their Quills have worked themselves into the internal of the Skins of the
Dogs. The Porcupine Quill thus extracted was ab^t 1 In long, yellow,
dry & hard & not the least matter ab^t it – but seemed to have a kind of
dry Sheath, altho' the flesh all around from the inflammation at-
tending its passage was hard like an egg of a Pigeon.

July 9th [1807] [Thursday] Sent the three Kootanae young men a
hunting.

July 10th [1807] Friday About Noon Mr F. McDonald with the Men
& Goods arrived safe – they say the River & Brooks of the
Mountain have lowered much, & scarce any of the Goods are wet.
Shared the last morsel with them.

July 11th [1807] Saturday A fine day. Early sent off Mr F. McDonald
& 2 Men to look after our Kootanae Hunters, but they saw nothing
of them – nothing to eat.

July 12th [1807] Sunday A rainy Night but fine day. The two Seauteaux
& Family went off for FDP – gave them a Letter for Mr Hughes. We

had tied up all our Things, the large Canoe was finished, the cargoe given out &c, ready to embark – when we heard 2 Shots fired below us. Judging this to be our Kootanae Hunters, went to the place & found them with ab^t 20 lbs of good dried Meat of a Buck Red Deer, killed beyond the range of Hills close opposite us – the fat was nearly as soft as that of a Cow, & remarkably well smoked & preserved – shared it among the Men. Agreed with Boulard & the three Kootanae Lads to take the Horses up to the Kootanae Lake, while the whole of us took up the Goods & Baggage in 2 small & one large Canoe. I set off in one of them with a Man & the other small Canoe, also 2 Men, the large canoe 4 Men & Mr F. McDonald – at $3\frac{1}{2}$ Pm set off. As I am obliged to paddle I cannot take the courses of the River, but refer it to some other more convenient opportunity. At $7\frac{1}{4}$ Pm camped. Very strong rapid Current.

July 13th [1807] Monday A very fine day. At $5\frac{3}{4}$ Am set off. Our Co may be, at half-guess by the Compass, noticing only the lead of the Banks & not of the many windings & turnings it makes, S55E $1\frac{1}{2}$M to opposite the Rapid River – 'till now in many Channels, & including Islands ab^t 1M wide, but the major part is Isl^{ds} all low & wooded with Red Cedar, but small dwarf & full of Branches. Poplars very fine – Birch, White & Red [Fir] d^o – fine Willow, especially of Arrow Wood & Choak Cherry – Poplar & Pines d^o. We are now up the Rapids nearly, which from the flush of Water are very strong – went ab^t $\frac{3}{4}$M farther & stopped to gum our Canoes. Up the last Rapid, we hauled the Canoe & ourselves by clinging to the Branches, & even then with great difficulty. At 9:20 Am set off, Co S55E 2M – the other Canoe went straight into the Eddy. I went up a Lake & fortunately killed 9 Swans – thank Heaven for this Relief. The Current above the Rapid River, which falls in from the NE^d, is mild to the Eddy, but the Rapid River itself is a very Torrent from between steep Mountains. At the Eddy we camped to await the large Canoe – & in the Evening finding they did not arrive fired 2 Guns, which they answered from the Rapid River. Saw a few Beaver Houses & many Paths & tracks of Red & Small Deer; caught only 5 Mullets by fishing. Several Partridge Nests have been taken in the Mountains, & only 4 to 6 Eggs, while those to the east^d of the Mountains have from 11 to 15 Eggs.

July 14th [1807] Tuesday A fine Morn^g, then Rain & heavy Storm from the South. The Canoe not arriving, I became anxious & at $10\frac{1}{2}$ Am

embarked in a small Canoe with 2 Men, went down the River to the
end of the Swan Lake where we met them & brought them in to the
Campment – separated the Swans among them & at 1 Pm set off, leaving the other 2 Canoes to follow. At 5½ Pm put up, quite tired with
paddling against a strong deep Current. The country is all over flowed,
not getting ashore any where. Our Co has been ab^t s60E 4M
s68E 5M. The Mountains are now much lower & descend often in one
slope to the River, which is winding at times but keeps mostly the
[left] Side – the other Side is a Lake to the foot of the Hills. Saw only
1 Swan, a few Ducks & one Chevreuil, but none within reach of our
Guns.

July 15th [1807] Wednesday A very fine day. At 4:10 Am set off from
a bad Campment. Our Co may be s68E 15M when we stopped at
11¾ Am to pitch the Canoe & wait the others – at 3½ Pm they arrived.
I took Mr F. McDonald on board with me, & told the Men to keep
on the best they could 'till I could procure provisions, when I would
wait them. At 4 Pm set off, Co about s68E 8M to near & past the
Gooseberry Hill on the [right] – at 7½ Pm put up supperless. Strong
Current since 5 Pm. The country improves, but still very dark
rocky woody Hills bound the River on each Side & all from Hill to Hill
is overflowed. Saw nothing.

July 16th [1807] Thursday A very fine day. At 4¾ Am set off s62E 8M
– for ab^t 6M of this we were in the River that comes from the NW^d
– we then made a Portage of 8 Y^{ds} into the Kootanae River. At 9 Am
a Kootanae young Man & his Wife in a Pine Bark Canoe came up
to us – we stopped 1½H while he was calling to others of his Tribe. At
10½ Am set off with him & at ¾ Pm turned into a small Channel that
led us to their Campment – 6 Men & their Families. I traded from them
ab^t 6 lbs of dried Provisions & a Goose; gave them a little
Ammunition with which they went a hunt^g – they killed 3 Swans,
which they soon eat up without giving us a mouthful, tho' we had
repeatedly informed them we were all starving.

July 17th [1807] Friday A very fine day. At 4¼ Am set off & went to the
head of the small Channel, where I waited the Canoes – at 6¼ Am
they came. Shared with them the mouthful we had got. We then set off,
Co ab^t s55E 4M, where seeing fine clear Woods & kind of Meadows
we stopped to Hunt 1½ Hours, but got nothing – several Chevreuil

Tracks. At 10 Am set off, Co s55e 14m – the River is pretty straight
& easy Current – stopped to hunt, but not long. At $5\frac{1}{4}$ Pm put up
& Bercier went to look for the Kootanaes, while we hunted & fished
but all of us without success – a Partridge among us all for Supper.

July 18th [1807] **Saturday** A very fine day. At $4\frac{3}{4}$ Am set off, Co
s48e 10m – 8m gone left the main River, which has thick muddy
strong Current & comes from the sse^d, took the left hand Channel in
a small shoal Pond, then into the River of the Lakes, about 40 y^{ds}
x & very clear, but strong Current – saw many small Fish in it. At Noon
arrived at the Kootanae Lake – along the Road saw 6 Chevreuil.
Boulard with the three Kootanae Lads arrived on three nw Horses,
hav^g left all the others behind from the badness of the Roads & his
being a complete Rogue. They gave us ab^t $1\frac{1}{2}$ Chevreuil which with a
few Berries made a kind of a Meal for us all, hungry & starved this
long time. Set three Nets in the Lake – it has a fine appearance: the
Banks are high say 200 ft, all Meadow, with straggling Trees & d°
in Clumps; the Water is very clear & the Country on the whole has a
very romantic appearance.

Building Kootanae House

19 July – 6 October 1807

July 19th [1807] Sunday A very fine day. Early set off to look for a Spot
to build a House in & put all our Baggage & Goods in security, as
this bad turn of hav^g all our Horses left behind distresses us much. We
are also much worn down by Hunger & Fatigue so that we have
hardly any strength left – but we hope so soon as we can procure
Provisions & some Knowledge of the Country we shall be able to
penetrate farther. Found no fit Place for several Miles, returned
& crossed over to the sw^d but also no fit Place – & I was obliged to
pitch upon a Spot ab^t 200 y^{ds} above the Level of the Lake, where a few
straggling Fir Pines may be got to build with. The Country affords
wood only in Ravines & Gullies from whence it cannot be got – the
Timber is large, dwarf & very straggling. Took up the Nets – not
a single Fish. Brought part of a dead wild Horse that was killed yesterday, & has lain without being unembowelled 'till 9 Am this
Morn^g – we boiled it & eat of it but it made us very sick, being half
rotten. Most of the Men went angling of a kind of Mullet, of which
they caught wherewith to make a single Meal; traded ab^t $\frac{3}{4}$ of a
Chevreuil from the Kootanaes weighing ab^t 36 lbs at most. Put all
the Goods to the top of the Bank near to where we intend to build,
& pitched our Tents. Talked a long time with the Kootanaes, but
find by their information that little can be done in the present circumstances. The Country is extremely poor in Provisions beyond us,
& even about us, & nothing larger than a Chevreuil, whose weight when
poor may be about 50 lbs & when fat ab^t 70 lbs – & we are in all
17 mouths to feed.

July 20th [1807] **Monday** A very fine day. Early traded with a few
Kootanaes – they have sold me about half a Pack of very ordinary
Beaver Skins, badly stretched – they went off to the south^d & by them
I sent a small Present of Tobacco to the Lake & Saleesh Indians –
traded 9 dressed Skins which I gave to the Men. Sent ab^t 6 Miles for
Birch Wood to helve our Tools with – looked for Pine Bark to
cover a House with, but found none. Arranged 2 New Nets, backing
Lines &c – put them well in order & set them one on each side the
Lake. Traded ab^t 12 lbs of Beat Meat at a very dear rate. Sent Boulard
to stay with the Kootanaes, induce them to Hunt & bring us Meat.
Helved 2 fish Darts & got wood for Flambeaux to spear Fish with, but
the water is too deep & the Current too strong: Mr F. McDonald,
who is the most clever, speared only 1 Mullet & 1 small kind of Herring.

July 21st [1807] **Tuesday** A very fine day. The Men cut wood of Fir
Pine for the warehouse, & made a Horse Slay to haul it on, but we
can turn very little of the time to building, as we are in want of
Provisions. No fish in the Nets. As there are very many small Fish
in the strong Current of the River, we staked across at the dist^{ce} of
ab^t 20 ft from one stake to another, to set our Nets by & keep them
steady to the Current. Had only 6 lbs of Beat Meat among us all. Obs^d
for Lat^{de} Ther +85° Lat^{de} 50°:31′:32″ N Decⁿ 20°:33′:53″ N.

July 22nd [1807] **Wednesday** A very fine day. Nothing in the Nets but
one Mullet. Began to build the walls of the Warehouse, 16 ft by
16 ft, but the wood is very heavy & large, the Men too weak to work
hard – got it half up. Had only the remaining 6 lbs of Beat Meat
'till evening when Boulard arrived with most of the Meat of two
Chevreuil from the Kootanaes. He says the Kootanaes are pitching
off to a great dist^{ce} – this cuts off all hopes of any further supply 'till
a few more Indians visit us. But we afterwards learnt that Boulard
only lied to us thro' laziness; he is a complete Scoundrel & want of Men
only obliges me to employ him. Mr McDonald hunted the whole
day, for only a single Partridge. Shared all the Meat equally among us,
each to do the best he can with his share.

July 23rd [1807] **Thursday** A very fine day. Nothing in the Nets. Found
a few Pines, & off them with much Trouble rose ab^t 43 pieces of
poor Bark to cover the Roof of the Warehouse. Got the walls of the

Warehouse up & the gable Ends finished also, & brought most of
the roofing Poles on the Spot. Merid Alt^de of [sun's] LL
Ther +78° Lat^de 50°:31':24" N Dec^n 20°:10':52" N.

July 24th [1807] Friday A very fine day. Working at the warehouse:
finished half the Roofing with Bark & put Earth upon it, but could
do no more for want of Bark – sawed wood for a Door with very much
Trouble – put the Goods in the Warehouse. Early sent off Bercier,
Clement & Le Camble to bring up the Horses from the Portage, as we
are in great want of them. In the Evening 3 Kootanae Men & their
Families arrived – they traded with us a little good Meat, thank
Heaven, for we are much in Want.

July 25th [1807] Saturday A very fine day. The Fire that is burning the
Country below us approaches fast & is now within a few Miles of
us. Sent off the Men each to raise 25 pieces of Pine Bark, which they
procured with much Trouble as the Pines are very few & those full
of Branches. The Indians went a hunting & to look after a Hoard of
Skins & Provisions.

July 26th [1807] Sunday A very fine day. Obs^d for Long^de
& Time Long^de 115°:57 $\frac{1}{4}$' W.

July 27th [1807] Monday A very fine day, latter part Cloudy. Sent the
Men to collect Wood to make a Weir. By 3 Pm they supposed they
had enough & began to place the Triangles of heavy green Aspin loaded
with Stones – but there are none of the latter near at hand of any
size, which finished the day's work. Ther +64° Long^de 115°:58 $\frac{3}{4}$' W.

July 28th [1807] Tuesday A very fine day. Men working at the Weir,
but when nearly completed, the strength of the Current & the depth
of the Water was found too great, & the Weir was broken up & carried
away. Being now better acquainted with the Country ab^t, which
is full of Ravines & Gullies capable of concealing Armies from our View
& rendering us liable to an Attack every minute – which, should
it happen, we must perish with Thirst only – I resolved to see if any
place more eligible could be found ere we advanced too far in the
Building intended, as the prime Objects for which we built here have
deceived us – viz the Fisheries – for we get nothing, besides really
having no Wood worth while to build with. I took 2 Men with me

& luckily found a Place where a good House &c may be built & not
easily attacked, close on the Banks of a rapid Stream. On my return
I found every Body under the alarm of a Band of strange Indians
hav^g pursued the Women who were out gathering Berries &c. I directly
ordered the Men to fill the Kettles with Water & get all ready for
defence – but it fortunately turned out to be only 3 Kootanae young
Men, who in a frolic gave a fright to the Women; they came from
a small Band of Kootanaes who are about a long day's March off.

July 29th [1807] **Wednesday** A very fine day. Early began to tye & arrange all our Goods up for leaving this place, pitched the canoe,
got everything down the Hill & at 7 Am set off – landed our Canoe
Load of Goods, Lumber &c &c – sent the Canoe off for the rest,
with which they returned by $\frac{3}{4}$ Pm. We pitched our Tents, & at $4\frac{1}{4}$ Pm
began cutting Wood for the Warehouse – cut 27 Pieces & hauled
12 d° of 18 ft long. Sent two Men for Helves [of] Birch Wood for Tools,
with which they returned at 8 Pm. A morsel of Beat Meat is all we
have.

July 30th[1807] **Thursday** A very fine day. Sent three Men to finish the
weir, but when they had nearly compleated it, about one third of
it gave way from the depth & rapidity of the Current & we were obliged
to abandon it as hopeless – at least 'till the water lowers considerably. Cut the rest of the Timber for the Warehouse & with hard
Labour hauled it all, & put the walls up to the intended height of
$6\frac{1}{2}$ ft – cut the Door Way & Windows &c, also cut part of the Wood
for the Roofing. Received from the Kootanaes half a Chevreuil
& half a small Bear in Meat – sent them off again to hunt for us.

July 31st [1807] **Friday** A fine Morn^g, but soon cloudy – at 11 Am Rain,
which soon became heavy & continued all the afternoon. Began the
Beams, Roofing &c, but was obliged to leave off on account of the
Rain.

August 1st [1807] **Saturday** A day of constant Rain, tho' sometimes
very light. Finished roofing the House & covered it with Pine Bark
– mudded the Warehouse on the outside, & finished most of the inside
work, hung the Door, put in the Windows & placed the Shelves for
the Goods &c. In the Evening put the Goods in. Only 4 lbs of poor
Scraps for this day.

August 2ⁿᵈ [1807] Sunday A very fine day. Not a mouthful to give the
Men – they get a Supper by angling Fish. Got all the Kootanaes off
a hunting.

August 3ʳᵈ [1807] Monday A very fine Day. As we have no Provisions
& are too weak to build without Food, the [Men] went an angling
of Fish & got 8 small Mullets to make a Supper. The Nets yield nothing
at all in our distress, tho' I attend to them myself & remove them
from place to place – went with Lussier & set them far off in the Lake,
tho' without Hope.

August 4ᵗʰ [1807] Tuesday A very fine day. Went with Lussier & visited
the Nets – not a single Fish in three well set Nets of 150 fms long
in all. Went round the Kootanae Lake & a little way up the mid Rivulet
– saw a Swan, a few Geese &c, but they were too shy to be shot at.
Returned by 7 Pm quite tired and famished – but thank Heaven the
three young Men whom I had sent a huntᵍ returned with 2 poor
small Chevreuil each weighing about 30 lbs, of which we made a
Supper. Boulard declared off Duty.

August 5ᵗʰ [1807] Wednesday A very fine day. Early Boulard who had
gone a huntᵍ yesterday returned – he had killed a she black Bear
& her Cub; I lent him a Horse to bring the Meat on. Set the Men to
cut wood to haul it. In going round the Lake yesterday, I remarked
the Lake to be abᵗ 8M long but nowhere above 1M wide & some places
not more than ½ Mile: the North End fine deep clear Water 3 to
5 fms, the So end shoals considerably to 6 & 7 ft. Saw no place where
a House could be built on it's Banks. On the East Side there are
seemingly many small springs in the bottom of the Lake, the Mud being
hollowed in very many places like conical Kettles of 2 & 4 ft across
& seemingly deep. By 2 Pm Beaulieu returned with the Meat. Cut all
the Wood for the House & hauled the major part. At 4 Pm the three
Men sent for the Horses to the w End of the Portage returned, bringing
with them all the Horses of private Property, but they have
marched in such bad Countries that they have hardly any Skin on their
Legs, & their feet, Ancles &c [are] much swelled. The Company's
Horses remain there, as to have brought them would only to have had
the Trouble to have taken them down again in a short time.

August 6th [1807] Thursday A very fine Day, but too hot. Three Men raising Pine Bark for the House, the others building – put the walls of the House up to the intended height of $6\frac{1}{2}$ ft, took Pine Bark for to make two small Canoes with. The Hunters brought us 2 Chevreuil. Late in the Evening a few Kootanaes arrived.

August 7th [1807] Friday A very fine day. Put the Beams in the House, the Needles & Roof Beam, cut the roofing Poles, filled up the gable Ends & brought 97 Pieces of Pine Bark. At Noon a Storm from the westward arose which blew down the Tents & endangered every thing, so that we could not work 'till the evening. Traded a few Furrs & a little dried Provisions, for which I paid them very dear, to encourage them.

August 8th [1807] Saturday A fine day. Men roofed the House, covered it with Bark, put the Chimney up ab^t $3\frac{1}{2}$ ft. A Man with myself split out 4 large Boards, trying to make a Pine Bark Canoe.

August 9th [1807] Sunday A very fine day. Finished the Pine Bark Canoe but it is of little service, partly from the injuries the Bark received when raising of it. 4 Tents of Kootanaes have arrived, who have passed the greater part of the Summer in the Mountains among the Buffalo. They traded only wherewith to give us a scanty day's Provisions – indeed they put a very high Value on all their Provisions, especially when dried.

August 10th [1807] Monday A very fine day. Heightened the Chimney about 18 In & mudded the House inside & outside. Buché began a Wood Canoe of 18 ft long of Fir Pine, ab^t 3 ft diam. Another Tent of Kootanaes arrived with Provisions, but will not trade it.
Mr F. McDonald & 2 Kootanaes went to the Head of the Lake River to look for Salmon – they saw one, but could not spear it.
Ther +68° Merid Alt^{de} of [sun's] LL Lat^{de} 50°:32':15″ N
Decⁿ 15°:42':5″ N Variation by the [sun's] Transit $20\frac{3}{4}$° East
Long^{de} 115°:41′ W.

August 11th [1807] Tuesday A fine day 'till 4 Pm when a Storm of Thunder, Lightning, Rain & Wind came on & lasted 'till the evening. Nearly finished the Chimney, laid the Sleepers in the Ground

for the flooring, finished the covering of the House, split out
32 pieces of flooring & also wood for a Door. Got the Nets ready to
set. Traded a little dried Provisions & 4 dressed Red Deer Skins.

August 12th [1807] Wednesday A very fine day. Working a little at the
House, then set to work to cut wood for a Hall – hauled part of
it. Finished splitting out the flooring & sent it down the River piece by
piece which we caught as it passed, but lost a few pieces.

August 13th [1807] Thursday A fine day. The Kootanaes representing
to us that we should catch much fish by making a Weir, & the
Water hav^g fallen, I again sent 4 Men to aid 2 old Kootanaes to make
a Weir on the Lake River; the rest of us laying the flooring &c.
About Noon 2 Kootanae Men arrived from afar – as soon as they
entered the Kootanae Camp, the news they brought caused such
Cries & Shrieks among the Kootanaes that we thought an attack at
hand from the Meadow Indians, & ran to Arms. After remaining
about half an Hour in this state of suspense, they came & informed us
that it was on account of the Death of the Old Chief's son, who had
lately been killed by the Peagans – they also added that a Battle had
been fought a few days ago, between the Peagans & the Saleesh
Indians, in which the latter were victors & had killed 14 of the former
with the loss of 4 of their own Party.

August 14th [1807] Friday A very fine day. Working at the fishing Weir,
making a Wood Canoe, laying the Floor of the House, making
Doors &c. Traded 1 Chevreuil which served us for Supper.

August 15th [1807] Saturday A very fine day. Early the Kootanae
young Men went off – I sent Tobacco by them to the Old Chief,
& told them to tell him to hasten his coming here with what Indians
he could collect. Working at the Weir & finished damming the
River in, but the Kootanaes have added nothing to catch the Fish in.
Took up our Nets – not a single Fish of any Kind in the Nets for
these three Nights they have been standing. Flooring the House – put
in the Windows. Finished the Wood Canoe. Traded ab^t 20 lbs of
dried Provisions, 1¾ Chevreuil & a few Berries. Took up my Residence
in my Room.

August 16th [1807] **Sunday** A very fine day. Several of the Kootanaes pitched away. Gave the Men a Breakfast & they angled Fish for Supper.

August 17th [1807] **Monday** A very fine day. Sent a Kootanae a hunting – he brought us a poor Chevreuil, also traded $1\frac{1}{4}$ d°. Began to build the Hall, the walls of which with the gable Ends were put up and the major part of the roofing.

August 18th [1807] **Tuesday** A very fine day. Covered in the Hall with Pine Bark & Earth – mudded it both inside & outside. Set a Net at the Weir. Our Hunter killed a Beaver. Traded about $\frac{2}{5}$ of a large fat Buck Red Deer & paid as much for it as if I had had the whole.

August 19th [1807] **Wednesday** A very fine day. Nothing in the Net as usual. Made half the Chimney; cut all the Wood for the Men's House. Killed a large fat buck Chevreuil, but it had been too much run by the Wolves.

August 20th [1807] **Thursday** A very fine day. Hauled most of the Wood for the Men's House & put the Walls up to $3\frac{1}{2}$ ft high – it is 16 ft by 18 ft in the Clear. Split out 70 Pieces for the flooring. Saw a fine herd of wild Horses.

August 21st [1807] **Friday** A very fine day – a little Rain in the morning. Floated down all the flooring. Working at the Men's House & also at the Chimney in the Hall.

August 22nd [1807] **Saturday** A very fine day. Hauled all the flooring up the Bank; finished the hall Chimney & covering of the roofing of the Hall, which for want of Bark was done with Grass. Made the Hearth in my Room, squared Wood for a Door &c &c. From 4 Pm heavy Rain, Thunder & Lightning.

Aug 23rd [1807] **Sunday** Moderate Rain all day.

August 24th [1807] **Monday** Moderate Rain 'till Noon, when the weather became fine. Finished the Walls of the House – floored the

Hall. Went a hunt^g & saw a Herd of wild Horses & 3 Chevreuil, but killed nothing.

August 25th [1807] Tuesday A very fine Day – foggy morning. Finished the gable Ends & half roofed the Men's House; made the Hall Floor level with the Adze. Went a fishing – got only 5 small Mullets. 2 Men lame.

August 26th [1807] Wednesday A very fine day – foggy Morning. Finished the roofing of the Men's House & all the stone Work of the Chimney. Traded 2$\frac{1}{2}$ Chevreuil, thank Heaven – I had just given out the very last mouthful we had for breakfast.

August 27th [1807] Thursday A very fine day. Men finished half the roofing with Hay & Earth, & the Chimney entirely. About 2 Pm, 12 Peagan young Men & 2 Women arrived – they are come to see how we are situated. I had expected them long ago, & it must be their Policy to be highly displeased with us for being here, as we thus render all these Indians independent of them over whom from time almost immemorial they have held in dependence or as enemies, & destroyed them. They have it in their Power to be very troublesome to us, & even to cut us off; we however hope in the Care of good Providence. They say that the Peagans are pleased that we are here – but they are professed dissimulators. Several Salmon seen.

August 28th [1807] Friday A fine but blowy Day. Men working at their House – mudded it both inside & outside. Rain at Night.

August 29th [1807] Saturday A very fine day. Men working at their House – covered the other half with Hay & Earth & split out their flooring. Finished the Provisions brought us by the Peagans, 1$\frac{1}{2}$ day. In the Evening Mr F. McDonald & 2 Men went off to spear salmon in the Night. They returned with 5 Salmon – one of them weighed 26$\frac{1}{2}$ lbs.

August 30th [1807] Sunday A very fine day. Two Kootanaes arrived with most of the Meat of 4 poor small Chevreuil.

August 31st [1807] Monday A very fine day. Tried to get the Peagans off, but they insist on waiting the band of Kootanaes daily expected. Finan speared 1 Salmon; arranged the Wood Canoe for the purpose of spearing Salmon in. Hauled all the Wood of the Hangard & put the Walls 6 ft high up – floated down the flooring of the Men's House.

September 1st [1807] **Tuesday** A very fine Day, cool & cloudy – all those past have been with a burning Sun from 9 Am to 3 Pm, but a fine dry Heat. At length the troublesome Band of Peagans went off. They confess they came to steal Horses &c, which I also appre-hended, & on seeing them, had all the best of our Horses hid far in the Hills to the north^d. On their going away they stole 3 of the Horses of a poor old Kootanae Man – 2 Kootanaes went after them, came up with them, & had much altercation with them, but the Peagans listened to no Arguments, chased the Kootanaes away & kept the Horses. The Kootanaes in return fired on the Peagans, without effect, then flew back to the Ho & put all their Goods &c under our Protection, camped close to the Ho & kept themselves under Arms, with a continual good lookout for their Enemies. Roofed the Hangard &c – split out Gunwales & Timbers for the bastard birch rind Canoe, which is all going to Pieces it is so badly made. In the evening Le Muet, a Kootanae, arrived – he informed us that 30 Peagan Men were on their way hereto, & would arrive in 2 days hence. They have nothing to trade, & only come to see what they can get & how we are situated; it is fortunate that I am not off on Discovery. Late arrived 2 Kootanaes with Meat. Heard a Shot across the River, but did not answer it.

Septr 2nd [1807] **Wednesday** A very fine day. Very early three Peagan Men arrived – they say they come ahead to see if we were built here or not. Almost finished flooring the Men's House. Cut Wood, hauled it, & put up 2 strong Fences – one of 27 ft long the other of 51 ft d^o, with a Gate – to prevent the Indians approaching the Houses in too great numbers. Traded the Meat of 2 good Chevreuil. Early sent Bercier & a Kootanae to the great Camp to hasten their arrival. In the Evening Showers of Rain, with Thunder & Lightning. In the Night a Kootanae arrived very ill from the Camp – they sang around him all Night. He related that the Camp is very sick, & several Children dead.

Septr 3rd [1807] **Thursday** A cold stormy Day with showers of small Rain. Two of the Peagans went off to meet the others, & to hasten them here, with word of the Sickness broke out in the Kootanae Camp – they asked for Tobacco, but I sent only 6 In among them all, with word that I had nothing to trade with them. The Men entered their Ho as their residence. Began a Salmon Nett of 17 fms wrought of twisted holland Twine.

September 4th [1807] Friday A day of variable Weather – snowed in the Mountains, the upper parts all white, which is the first time this season. Made 9 fms more of Net but havg sprained my wrist I was obliged to give over. Lussier at do. [The Men] mudded the outside of the Hangard – working at their own House. 3 Peagans & 1 Kootanae arrived, the latter ill of the distemper. Traded 1 Chevreuil.

Septr 5th [1807] Saturday A fine day. Traded a Doe Chevreuil. Mr F. McDonald & 4 Men from spearing of Salmon – they brought 7 do but they are very poor, quite exhausted with spawning & the vast distce against a very Rapid Current from the Sea hereto. One of them, poor as it is, weighed 34½ lbs – many escaped from the bending of the iron Darts. Backed & set the Salmon Net. Gave Turlington to those afflicted with this endemic Distemper, which seems to relieve them a little. About Noon 23 Peagan Men with a few Women arrived: as usual they asked for Rum & could not be persuaded that we had none; they smoked, but I kept them without the Fence – they have nothing. Traded a small Chevreuil.

September 6th [1807] Sunday A fine day. The Peagans traded a few Scraps of Meat, which made us a Meal – 1 Salmon in the Net. All the Indians are now Gambling, so that we cannot get them to hunt. Bercier & a Kootanae arrived: they saw only one Tent of the great Band, who say the Indians are all ill, but will be at the House with what Furrs they have as soon as possible.

September 7th [1807] Monday A very fine day. 1 Mullet & 1 Salmon from 2 Nets. Traded ¾ of a poor small Chevreuil, but very acceptable as we are at short allowance. Raised Birch Rind to mend the Canoe & made new Gunwales for do – the Canoe is so badly made as to be already to pieces. Made a Door for the Hangard.

Septr 8th [1807] Tuesday A very fine day. Working at mending the Birch Rind Canoe. Traded part of a poor Chevreuil – & 1 Mullet

& 2 Salmon from the Nets. 4 Kootanae Men arrived: the[y] tell us that the others will not be here for some time, that they are all very much reduced by sickness, that about 10 Saleesh Indians were with the Kootanaes to accompany them, but turned ab^t on hearing so many Peagans (their Enemies) were on the Road. Speared 4 Salmon.

September 9th **[1807] Wednesday** A very fine day. Finished the Canoe & got it ready to be pitched. 4 Kootanaes arrived & brought a little Provisions; almost all the others pitched away, to avoid the troublesome Peagans who are always taking their little Property, Horses &c from them. 1 Salmon & 1 kind of red Carp from the Nets – 1 Duck. Spoke to the Peagans to decamp, as we wish them off from here very much; they are of a nature so full of dissimulation that we can trust them no longer than we are armed & ready to repel any insult – they say they will wait the Kootanaes here.

September 10th **[1807] Thursday** A very fine warm day. Gummed the Canoe &c. 1 fine Salmon from the Net. Kootanaes arrived with a little Provisions; those of yesterday traded for 8 Skins & these to day for 12 Skins value – say about 12 or 15 lbs per skin. Little Hunter killed a Buck Red Deer, & gave us about $\frac{1}{8}$ of the Meat – we should have got much more, but the Peagans are so very importunate with the Kootanaes for Meat &c.

September 11th **[1807] Friday** A very fine warm day – as usual the weather, when fine, is dry warm hazy & smoky. Only 1 Carp from the Nets. Sent Clement for Meat, who returned with the half of a Red Deer, very good Meat. Engaged Boulard at 400 Livres, no Equipment – he is useful as an Interpreter in these troublesome Times, but good for nothing else, as no reliance can be placed in him. Sent Beaulieu & Buché for Timbers of Cedar for the large Canoe & other Purposes. Speared 1 Salmon & 1 Trout. Set the Net close below the Weir.

September 12th **[1807] Saturday** A very fine day. 6 Salmon from the Net; traded the meat of a Sheep. The Peagans, thank Heaven, are preparing to go away the morrow – spoke to them not to steal any Horses from any party, which they promised to listen to. Hunger makes them decamp. The Men are employed about various jobs – as Saddles for the Journey, Halters &c – as I shall send them across the Mountains to fetch Goods in a few days. Almost every one is more or less afflicted with a violent Cold.

September 13th [1807] Sunday A very fine day, too warm – in the Evening Showers of Rain with Thunder & Lightning. At length the Peagans decamped. Gave each Chief 1 ft of Tobacco & 5 Rods of Amm & each of the young Men 2 In of Tob & a paper of Vermillion – this was given to prevent horse stealing and other disagreeable Circumstances, which in the end might have brought on a much greater Expence. After the major part were gone I learnt that some of them had threatened that we should not be long time here, & had told the young Men not to steal Horses now, as they should have them all in a short time. I spoke to those few who loitered behind: they denied any Intention of the Chiefs of bringing on a Quarrel but owned the young Men would be glad of it, that they might have a Pretence to plunder all Parties – I assured them that whenever they might think proper to begin they would meet with a warm reception, however numerous they might be. That the Peagans are highly jealous of the Kootanaes' having a trading Post in their Country is certain, & equally so that they wish to find some means to drive us hence, but how they will act is yet to be learned. 6 Salmon in the Net & one speared, but they are very poor.

September 14th [1807] Monday A rainy Day but fine evening. Sent a Kootanae Man with Clement to spear Salmon – they soon brought in 9, which I had split; I doubt they [will] dry, as they are so very meagre & flabby.

September 15th [1807] Tuesday A fine day. Sent off a Man & Horse with a Kootanae for some Provisions laid up in a Hoard a few Miles to the southd.

September 16th [1807] Wednesday A very fine day. At $8\frac{1}{2}$ Am a Lake Indian came for Tobacco for a few of his Tribe that are close here. At 9 Am 12 Lake Indian Men with one Woman arrived: they have passed along the Kootanae River thro' the Mountains – they have never before seen white People & have very little or nothing. Gave each of them 3 In of Tobacco. We conversed much about their Country, which they say has plenty of Beaver, Chevreuil, Red Deer &c, but how far they speak Truth or not is hard to say. They appear to be a hardy race of active People, are very muscular, equally so with any white man of the middle stature – mild Countenance, yet manly.

September 17th [1807] Thursday A fine but cloudy day. Put a small Canoe on the Bed & got it all done to the putting in of the Timbers. Bercier & a Kootanae from the band of Kootanaes – he says they are so ill & weak, that they cannot probably be here for some time yet. I conversed much with the Lake Indians: they speak well of their Country, which I wish much to see, but the old Chief wishes to revenge the death of his Son & thus bring on open war.

Septr 18th [1807] Friday A very fine day. Working at the large & small Canoes. Traded with the Lake Indians – they brought 29 Skins value in different Furrs, mostly Beaver, which they traded for Amm, Axes & Tob with a Kettle. They also brought ab^t 1 Bushel of very fine dried Arrow Wood Berries, & a little Sturgeon Oil, part of which was mixed with Berries for food. I wished them to conduct me directly as far as the junction of McGillivray's River with the Kootanaes d°, but they said they had left their Families far on this Side that Place, that the Season was too far advanced, & that not one of them were Men of consequence – that Ugly Head, their Chief, was the most fit Person to apply to, as he was best known to the neighbouring Indians & most respected. In the evening they made a gambling Party with the Kootanaes here, but staked scarcely any thing of what they had come so far for. Gave each old Man a small Present as p^r Expence Book. Speared 4 Salmon.

Three of our best Dogs died: the Kootanaes had often warned us of the fatal Effects to Dogs if permitted to eat raw Salmon which, they said, constantly 9 times out of 10 were sure to bring on the Death of the Dog – we had paid no attention to this Point, as thinking it the Effect of Superstition. But for about 6 days past our Dogs have been dying, & this day made their exit. The next Day after they had eaten raw Salmon, they became dull & lethargic, always lying down in some lonesome place & sleeping, refusing all food, & scarcely after the 3rd day lifting their Head even at the voice of their Master, never of their own Will getting up – except when, urged by extreme Thirst, they ran down to the Brook & drank heartily, then immediately returned & resumed their former lethargic state. When near dying, they almost always retired to some dark [place] & there quickly expired.

Septr 19th [1807] **Saturday** A very fine day, but like the three Mornings past a strong hoar frost. The Lake Indians, after passing the Night in gambling, lost their Stakes & early set off on their return – they pass by the foot of Nelson's Mountain. Sent off Mr F. McDonald & 2 Men to the Kootanae Camp to trade Horses to bring Goods across the Mountains with.

September 20th [1807] **Sunday** A very fine day. Traded $\frac{1}{2}$ a Red Deer & 2 Chevreuil for Amm & Tob.

September 21st [1807] **Monday** A windy Morning & rainy Day. Finished mending the Canoe & put several things in order.

Septr 22nd [1807] **Tuesday** A fine day. Finished making the small Canoe for hunt^g – gummed the large Canoe. Collected the Horses & got all ready to send off the People. In the evening Mr F. McDonald & party returned, hav^g been able to trade only one Horse; they thinking that we stood highly in need of Horses asked very high Prices – add to this Mr McDonald lost all the Ball, the most valuable Article to them. I spoke to the Kootanaes here: they promised to sell me two Horses, altho' they are by no means rich. Traded 2 Chevreuil & 3 Skins in Bear's & dried Meat.

Septr 23rd [1807] **Wednesday** A fine day. Sent off Mr F. McDonald & 2 Men in a large Canoe for the Portage. The Men who are to go across the Mountains passed the day looking for the Horses, & could not find 3 of them, altho' they were close here last evening. The Kootanaes here brought me three Horses for sale – but the Prices were so high that I could afford to buy only one of them, for which I was obliged to give a new Gun & a foot of Tobacco. The Gun, altho' not the best in the World, is still worth more than any common Horse on this Side the Mountains, where a Gun ought to be double the value of one on the east Side the Mountains.

September 24th [1807] **Thursday** A cloudy Day, at Noon very stormy which was followed by moderate Rain. The Little Hunter found the Horses lost, one of which belongs to the Co^y, & the Men set off for the Portage with 6 NW Horses in good condition – one of them belonged to Buché but he readily gave him up to the Co^y in this emergency, & I am to trade another for him. Speared 3 Salmon, but they are too meagre to be eaten but by People who are starving which, thank Heaven, is not our case at present. Three Kootanae Men arrived – they smoked & then returned to their camp; they say they will all be in the Morrow.

September 25th [1807] Friday A fine cloudy Day. The two Chiefs of the Kootanaes & Lake Indians arrived. They smoked; in the course of conversation they informed me that in the month of July a large Party of Peagans, Blood & Blackfoot Indians had come on this Side the Mountains, to where they were tenting with a camp of Saleesh & Shawpatin Indians. The Peagans said they & their Allies were come by order & request to make Peace with the Saleesh & Shawpatin Indians – that they all remained about 6 or 7 Days peaceably smoking, each Party having agreed upon a mutual Oblivion of all past Injuries, & even for the future to act as Friends & Allies, without any reserve whatever. When the Peagans & their Allies were raising camp the Blackfoots began to put on a hostile plundering appearance, & as the women had got at some distance, they began by seizing upon a very swift Mare, tossing the Owner off her Back – a young Saleesh Indian. But the latter losing no Time, sent an Arrow thro' the Heart of the Aggressor, which directly brought on a Battle – wherein the Peagans & their Allies lost 14 dead on the Field with many wounded & they were obliged to fly, throwing away every thing they had to aid their flight. The Saleesh Indians lost 4 killed & a few wounded, but not badly. The Spoils of the Peagans & their Allies being gathered up and worn by the Saleesh &c &c brought on the distemper before noticed, which had been previously among the Peagans & their Allies, & lodging in the hair of the Robes &c, had spread the infection. They also informed me that when camping with the Peagans & their Allies, while making Peace they learnt from private information, that the Blackfeet had plundered Fort Augustus to equip themselves more ably for War. $\frac{1}{2}$ Chevreuil.

September 26th [1807] Saturday A cloudy cold Day. Kootanaes traded 128 Skins in Beaver, 6 Bears, 7 Fishers, 3 small Otters & ab^t 1 Bushel of Arrow Wood Berries. $\frac{3}{4}$ of a Red Deer from my Hunter. Backed a Net of 50 fms & a small Net of 12 fms for Herrings – the salmon still very plenty but worse than ever. A part of the Kootanaes

are not yet arrived: they are gone to kill Beaver &c – I found here
that 120 large Beaver weigh 179 lbs – their Trade was for Arms, Amm,
Tob, Kettles & Axes.

September 27th [1807] Sunday A moderate fine day.

September 28th [1807] Monday A day of variable windy Weather.
Conversed much with the Kootanaes of the Country & Indians
around us but no information that can be wholly relied on, as they
rarely speak without prejudice in favour of their Friends & against
their Enemies or those who care little about them. The Old Chief
& others related that in the Woods of the Mountains there is a very
large Animal, of ab^t the height of 3 fms & great bulk that never lies
down, but in sleeping always leans against a large Tree to support
his weight; they believe, they say, that he has no joints in the mid of
his Legs, but they are not sure as they never killed any of them, & by
this acc^t they are rarely or never seen – this is no doubt some Animal
of their Nurses Fables, as they cannot say they ever saw the least
remains of a dead one. These People the Kootanaes were once numerous, but being continually at war with Nations more powerful
& far better armed than themselves, they diminished continually, 'till
at length the Small Pox almost entirely rooted them out, leaving
them only about 40 Families, & now they may count about 50 Families
of 6 & 7 to a Family.

Septr 29th [1807] Tuesday A moderate fine day. A Tent of the
Kootanaes pitched away. After much conversation about the Lake
Indian Country, I asked the Chief of those Indians if he would accompany [me] in about a month's time hence to see & examine that
Country – to this he objected, on account of the Cold & the Snow
becoming deep in the Passes of the Mountains thro' which our
Road will lie. I again hesitated to go now, as while the weather is
moderate the Meadow Indians may attack & destroy the
Settlement here – but the Old Chief assuring me with the other old Men
that they did not think an Attack at this Season was to be appre-
hended, I agreed to go off with the Lake Indian Chief in a few days,
as by personally examining that Country I may be enabled to form
a judgement whether we can with any hopes of Profit form a trading
Post. But principally I wish to see if the large River to the south^d
of us, which I name McGillivray's River, is navigable – part of it is

represented so, & others again say that it is navigable with safety
only in places – and I wish to see a few Indians who are that way, to
encourage them to work Beaver.

Septr 30th [1807] **Wednesday** A tolerable fine day. The major part of
the Kootanaes pitched away to hunt Beaver – as they say.
Yesterday I set a Net of $3\frac{1}{2}$ In Mesh in the little Lake before the Ho,
which gave us 5 small Fish something like a Herring – they seem
to be a species of the white Fish.

October 1st [1807] **Thursday** A very stormy Night & Day – the most
elevated Mountains appear like a Mass of Snow. Several of the
Kootanaes pitched away. $\frac{2}{3}$ of a Chevreuil from the Hunter. Took up
the large Net – one Carp & Salmon, the last good for nothing. A
few Geese & Ducks about, but too shy to be shot at.

October 2nd [1807] **Friday** A very fine day – high wind at SE. At
9:50 Am set off with 2 Horses, a few scraps of Provisions & the
Lake Indian Chief Ugly Head for my Guide. Co to the Head of the Lake
River, our Old Hut, S67E $1\frac{1}{4}$M then along the Lake, leaving it at
unequal distances of ab^t 1 to $1\frac{1}{2}$M on the right according to the even-
ness of the Ground. Our Course ab^t S50E 8M much uneven
Ground, but the Country finely variegated with Hill & Valley: fine open
spreading forest Trees & Lawns & Plains while on the [left] the
close, near abrupt dark Hills & Rocks rose like an impassable
Boundary. On the [right] the distant Hills kept parallel with us,
leaving a bold Valley on whose extreme east Margin we have our Road
– 4M gone a small Brook, $5\frac{1}{2}$M a small Brook, 7M a small Brook
– lost $\frac{1}{2}$ Hour by my Horse getting loose & endeavouring to return to
the Ho. At $1\frac{5}{6}$ Pm stopped $\frac{3}{4}$ Hour to refresh our Horses, opposite
& close to the Head of the Rivulet from the southern Lake; Co has been
S25E 4M – this Brook or Rivulet between the Lakes has many large
Ponds & Plashes of Water on each side of it & runs thro' a low, marshy
woody vale. Held on: Co of the southern Lake is ab^t S25E 7M – opposite the north end of the Lake at the head of the Brook, the Road
takes along a steep shelving Rock, somewhat dangerous, especially
to loaded Horses. On the whole the Road along the second Lake is
tolerable good 'till the end of it, when it crosses rocky Hills & follows the shelves of a steep Rock Hill, at the end of which the Path,
always narrow, becomes still more so among black broken frag-

ments of Rocks. This Lake is always pretty close to the foot of the
Mountains, which leaves but a small space for the choice of Road
& often none at all – the Country is but thinly wooded & the soil very
stony & hard, affording there low but sweet Grass for Animals.

At 5 Pm passed the Lake, Co over McGillivray's Portage s30E $1\frac{1}{2}$M
– very good Road among Red Fir Trees, the first I have seen – none
are to the north^d of the Portage along the Lakes, but up the Rivers only.
To McGillivray's River, a bold clear rapid Stream of ab^t 150 y^{ds}
wide, besides much extent of gravel Flats – we quickly forded it on
Horseback over a bottom of fine large Gravel. On crossing we
followed the Path over a low Point & up a moderate Bank, along which
we kept verging within to the east^d; Co s30E $2\frac{1}{2}$M downwards to
a Rill of Water, at which we camped at 6:35 Pm. We have passed
among clear Woods of the Mountain Larch, a beautiful tall
straight timber Tree admirably adapted to Ship uses, now beginning
to shed their foliage. The other Trees were mostly of the Red Fir
& a Kind of Cypress, with a Chance small Aspin & a few Shrubs – the
Ground a Meadow of short thin sweet Grass. Saw no Animals, but
had not so many Indians been lately passing & tenting this way, we
should probably have seen plenty of Chevreuil or the Virginian
Deer, wild Sheep & a few Red Deer. In to the Brook between the two
Lakes, 4 small Brooks from the Mountains on the east^d empty
themselves near the north end of the Lake, also 2 small Brooks, & near
the south end also 2 small Brooks.

October 3rd [1807] Saturday A very fine day. At 6:50 Am set off, Co
s35E 7M s23E 5M – at end of Co at 10:25 Am came to the River
& stopped to refresh our Horses: here a Brook gushed out of the Bank
& mingled with a bold Brook below. At 11$\frac{1}{2}$ Am set off & went
s23E $\frac{1}{2}$M – passed 4 Rills of Water & came to a bold rapid Brook, which
we crossed near the River, then went over a low Point close along
down the River – near the end of which, opposite an Island, we forded
the River on horseback to the west side, very good bottom & only
deep to the belly of the Horse. Our Road hitherto has been between
a Hill which forms the east Banks of the River & the Mountains –
the Land such as that described yester evening. On [crossing] we came
to fine Plains with very much gravel mixed with the earth: this produced a fine sweet Grass, but the Soil was so uneven that our Horses
trotted with uneasiness over it 'till 1$\frac{1}{4}$ Pm, when we passed these
Plains. Our Co has been s23E 7M Then sw 1M to a Brook s10E 2M over

a Point of high woody Land, the Woods very open affording fine
Road & Shelter with plenty of Grass. At 2:20 Pm stopped to bait our
Horses, & at 3 Pm set off, Co SIOE 5M a Brook SIOE 6M to a Rivulet
which we crossed & put up at 5:50 Pm. The first Co is like the Country
latest described; the last Co has been over fine Plains, something
like those Meadows about Fort George, but the Rock
appears in many Places, & it would be dangerous running a Horse
at full Speed, if not previously acquainted with the Ground. About $1\frac{1}{2}$M
short of the Rivulet there is a small Lake.

   As me & my Guide converse together partly by signs & partly by
words, I supposed that when we left McGillivray's River it was
only to cut across some long winding Point of the River, & presently
fall upon it again, & such I understood was his intention when we
left the Banks of the River at $1\frac{1}{2}$ Pm. But my Guide now gives me to
understand that the Road he is on leads direct thro' the Mountains
before us, & always at a great dist^{ce} from the River – that after 4 day's
hard march, or 6 Days if we go moderately on, we shall again come
on the River Banks, & that the whole Journey will take us at least
17 or 18 days marching. As seeing the River & how far it is
navigable is one of my present Objects, & not crossing barren
Mountains, this Route renders useless the best half of my Journey;
besides, the length of Time, which in these perilous times I cannot spare
from my new settlement, is a very material Point – I shall therefore
proceed no farther on this Route, which presents nothing equal to the
loss of my Time. This, the Torrent Rivulet, is now low but in
Summer swells from the melting of the Snows to a bold dangerous
River, scarcely any where to be [crossed] even in a Canoe – it seemingly comes from a considerable dist^{ce} from the west^{d}. The Marks of
very few Animals this way.

October 4th [1807] Sunday A very fine day. At 7 Am we began our
return, but the Horses of my Guide & his Wife were such poor ones
that continual whipping would hardly make them move. We put up
at [sun] set on the east Side the McGillivray's River, at the fountain
that gushes out of the Bank, having followed exactly the same Road
we went.

October 5th [1807] Monday A very fine day. At 7 Am set off & kept
on 'till 11 Am when we reforded the River to McGillivray's Portage
– came on over the Portage, & on along the southern Lake & on to

about half way between the Lakes & put up at [sun] set at a little Brook.

October 6th [1807] Tuesday Moderate Rain & Wind from 4 Am to 4 Pm. At $7\frac{1}{4}$ Am set off & rode 'till $10\frac{1}{2}$ Am, when we arrived & thank Heaven found all well. In my absence they have cut 200 Stockades, & hauled 40 d° – they have also traded 1 Red Deer & 1 Buck Chevreuil. They are under apprehensions of an attack, as well as the Indians, & my Presence was most welcome to all Parties.

Journey to the Lake Indian Country

20 April – 8 June 1808

1808 April 20 Wednesday A very stormy Morn^g with Rain. At 6 Am began to carry the Goods to the Junction of the Rivulets, & the rest went with Horses close to the Lake, or head of the River there, as the River is too shoal. Co down the Kootanae River from the House N35W $\frac{5}{6}$M, winding Co to the Junction of the Rivers N52E 5M. At 7$\frac{1}{2}$ Am arrived, loaded & set off thro' the little Lake. Co [16 courses] the Barrier or Weir (from hence to the Fort the straight Co is N76W & to this Co the others must come). Co in the River S30E $\frac{1}{6}$ embarked the Pieces & went to the Kootanae Lake, but as it blows a very hard head Wind, I went with the Horses by Land, to put a sixth hand in the Canoe. Co at 9$\frac{1}{2}$ Am to $\frac{1}{2}$ past Noon in the Lake S30E 3M S65E 4M. Hav^g put the Cargo ashore, which is a Load for 5 Horses, at 1 Pm we set off to go up the Rivulet – Co in the Reeds & Rushes S68E $\frac{1}{4}$M right hand Channel N63E $\frac{1}{6}$ – left off draw^g. Co [114 courses] an Embarras ⟨that nearly shuts up the River⟩ – much water passes under it; ⟨we round it on the left⟩ N65E $\frac{1}{20}$ S52E $\frac{1}{20}$SW $\frac{1}{8}$ NW $\frac{1}{6}$ end of Co come to the same Embarras. Co S65W $\frac{1}{6}$ S52E $\frac{1}{6}$ R S8W $\frac{1}{6}$ very shoal – carried; at 7 Pm put up. A fair Evening. The first part of this Rivulet had water enough for us, & plenty of Beaver; the mid part, full of embarras which took us much time to make a passage thro' them; the latter part, shoal rapids. Pines along this Brook but ⟨in patches & generally small, & each side extensive Swamps, Ponds & Marshes⟩. Beaver less plenty as we advance, but their marks are every where.

April 21st [1808] Thursday A fine frosty Morn^g. Gummed the Canoe

& at 6 Am set off, Co N75E $\frac{1}{10}$S5E $\frac{1}{10}$S25E $\frac{1}{7}$N35E $\frac{1}{10}$S80E $\frac{1}{10}$S40E $\frac{1}{2}$ the
beg^g of Co the Rivulet or Brook from the right 8 to 10 Y^{ds} wide –
in this Co passed 3 old Weirs – the Rivulet or Brook from the Lake is
now good ⟨[easy] Current & deep enough⟩. S22E $\frac{3}{4}$M close along the
left Bank, both Cos winding a little – finish at the Rocks. Co in the
Lake among Reeds, Rushes &c S10W $\frac{1}{4}$M. Came to the People with
the Horses & Goods, embarked the Pieces & set off, Co S20E 1M to the
Pines – they are low and swampy – S20E $\frac{1}{4}$M low pt of Willows
S25E 3M bold Point S43E 1$\frac{3}{4}$M or 2M to the left corner of the Lake. This
is a fine Sheet of Water: deep, clear, without Reeds, Rushes &c,
& seemingly much better for Fish than the other Lake.

At 10 Am put the Goods ashore & began to carry, the Horses taking
the Goods & most of the Canoe Men for the Canoe. The first part
of the Portage being bad & wet, lost much Time & the first Trip took
us 2$\frac{1}{2}$H, the next 2 Hours, when we got all over by 3$\frac{1}{2}$ Pm & the
2 Men, Clement & Bercier, with the Horses set off on their Return to
the Kootanae House. Gummed the Canoe & dried several Things
wetted by the Horses sinking in the Swamp close to the Lake. ⟨This
Portage I name McGillivray's Portage; its course⟩ S28E 2M full.
Once fairly clear of the Lake, very fine Road – here is the first Red Fir.
⟨The River I also name McGillivray's River.⟩ Co of it upwards is
N20E $\frac{1}{4}$M N80E $\frac{1}{2}$M – when turning round from the Mountains, it
appears to come from & thro' them from a N30W Co, inclining to
the north^d. Our Course downwards at 4$\frac{1}{2}$ Pm S15E $\frac{1}{5}$M (the general
Course of the River by the direction of the Hills N28E) Co [13
courses] on the left side Rocks begin S18E $\frac{1}{4}$ + $\frac{1}{3}$M – at mid of Co put
up at 6 Pm. Each point has a Rapid, but none any wise uncom-
monly strong or dangerous in the least – x 60 Y^{ds} ⟨in general, sometimes
less & sometimes a little more⟩. At the 3rd Co, which is the summer
crossing Place, obliged to take out a few Pieces, & every where the water
barely deep enough, ⟨altho' we are not half loaded⟩. A very fine
day. At the south end of McGillivray's Portage, obs^d for Lat^{de} by
2 Alt^{des} of [sun's] UL Lat^{de} 50°:9′:2″ N Dec^n 12°:1′:45″ N,
Lat^{de} 50°:16′:14″ N Dec^n 12°:5′:14″ N.

April 22nd [1808] Friday The morning a little Cloudy but clear in the
Afternoon, wind North^{ly} then variable. Gummed the Canoe, then
set off at 6:50 Am. The Mountains on the right are low & secondary,
& ab^t 2M dist. Co [33 courses] Mountains on the right 1M dist,
quite low & form a Point almost to the River Bank [13 courses] a low

Point of Poplars & Aspins – the Rocks on the left finish with this
Course. For the last $1\frac{1}{2}$H they have been separated at times by
pieces of meadow Banks. 11 Am small leaves on the Willows, Goose
Berry Bushes &c &c, & Aspins. [17 courses] – we are now opposite
a remarkable high Mountain whose Head is a Cone, on the left, & I
should judge it's perpend height to be ab^t 6500 or 7000 feet; the
Mountains on the left are ab^t 10M dist. Co s60w $\frac{1}{7}$ s40E $\frac{1}{5}$M end of
Co ⟨put ashore & obs^d for Lat^{de} by 2 Alt^{des} of [sun's] UL
Lat^{de} 49°:54′:15″ N Dec^n 12°:21′:35″ N.⟩ Co at 1:18 Pm Co [13
courses] Meadow on the right s16w $\frac{3}{4}$M Pine Island & Meadow
Co $+$ $\frac{1}{4}$M s8w $\frac{1}{2}$ $+$ $\frac{1}{2}$M Mountains on the left dist 8M [35 courses] at end
of Co seeing a few Red Deer on the Banks, went ashore & killed
a Buck – we put up at 6 Pm, thank God for this supply. Killed 1 Goose
& took 8 Goose Eggs – saw but few Geese but many Ducks, but
mostly of the whistling kind. A few Wolves & 6 or 7 Chevreuil with
2 small Herds of Red Deer.

In the early part of the Day every Point a rapid but not strong, with
pieces of easy Current. Where the low Points begin the River is
much more gentle, but many very shoal Places; since I observed, the
River in general has a very smooth easy Current with a sufficient
depth of Water, & where we are camped the Points are of fine Meadow,
& the first Ground I have seen that I think has sufficient moisture
to form a Garden for Herbs. The Woods of the Country are fine Red
Fir, Fir Pine, very fine Mountain Larch, & along the River Pines,
but of the swampy kind; the low Points have small Aspins & Willows.
Very few Beaver hitherto in this River, altho' the Banks begin to
wear a favorable appearance for them. At 7 Pm moderate Rain, with
a southerly Wind which cont^d all Night.

April 23 [1808] Saturday All day lay by with moderate Rain. Large
Poplars opposite us with Ponds in the Meadows, & very many
Ducks in them. Plenty of small wild Onions.

April 24th [1808] Sunday A rainy Morning, at 10 Am ceased. We at
length got our Canoe gummed, and set off. If we approach the right
hand Mountains our straight Co is s53E, if the left hand Mountains
our Co is s64E. At $11\frac{1}{2}$ Am set off Co [15 courses] this last Co the
Woods on each Side of us Birch a few, a fine low Point on the left
for camping. s52E $\frac{1}{5}$M R N75E $\frac{1}{6}$ R s60E $\frac{1}{8}$ s7w $\frac{1}{6}$ fine Pine s20E $\frac{1}{6}$
beg^g of Co the Torrent Rivulet from which I returned last October:

it is ab^t 20 Y^{ds} wide, rapid Current, it's course from the Mountains
which we see clearly is N67W to it's falling into this River. Co
[31 courses] these long Courses all along fine low meadow Points
S80E $\frac{3}{4}$ S35E $\frac{1}{2}$M at end of Co at 5$\frac{1}{2}$ Pm, seeing a fine Beaver House
I set 2 steel Traps & we went a little farther & camped at 6$\frac{1}{4}$ Pm.
A fine day tho' cloudy. Our Course has been to the right hand
Mountains; our Course straight has therefore been S53E, & we are
close on the low pt of the Hills to which I set the compass. The Current
very fine 'till close on the Torrent Rivulet, then full of Rapids for
a small distance – but soon came to fine low Points, the water fine. Saw
2 Beaver & a few Beaver Lodges, but nothing else but a few Ducks
& 4 Swans. ⟨At times where the Current was strong & deep, the water
made a hissing Noise as if it had been full of small pieces of Ice or
Icicles striking on each other. Where so I always remarked the surface
very full of small whirlpools whose diameter seldom exceeded
2 Inches, & in general not half this Size. From the quick whirling of such
a vast number of small Vortices, each agitating & disturbing each
other, the drops of water appeared quite white, as if separate & distinct
from each other, and their clashing against each other occasioned
the hissing noise.⟩

April 25 [1808] Monday A very frosty Morn^g but fine, then cloudy –
at 10 Am cleared & fine Day. Nothing in the Traps. At 6$\frac{1}{4}$ Am set off,
Co N80E $\frac{1}{2}$M S80E $\frac{1}{2}$M – we are opposite to the end of that Chain of
high abrupt Mountains that have always been on our left – ⟨an opening
of $\frac{1}{2}$M wide bearing N50E, then secondary detached Mountains⟩. The
Point of the high Mountains may be ab^t 6M dist at their Base; Co
N75E $\frac{1}{3}$ S70E $\frac{1}{2}$ + $\frac{1}{2}$M passed the Bad Rivulet x it 8 Y^{ds} strong Rapid,
another Branch of the Bad River 15 Y^{ds} across, Co + 1M S35E $\frac{1}{4}$
R S42E $\frac{1}{4}$ R S30E $\frac{3}{4}$ S40E $\frac{1}{2}$M S15E 1M rugged woody Country SE$\frac{1}{2}$M x
120 to 150 Y^{ds} fine bold River [26 courses], mid of Co put ashore
at 11$\frac{1}{4}$ Am to gum the Canoe. Obs^d for Lat^{de} [sun's] LL Merid Alt^{de}
of LL 107°:41 $\frac{3}{4}$′ Var^n by the [sun's] Transit 20° East Latitude
49°:12′:42″ N Dec^n 13:19′:4″ N.

S12E $\frac{1}{2}$M S8W $\frac{3}{4}$ S23W $\frac{1}{4}$ S60E $\frac{1}{10}$S7E $\frac{3}{4}$ R beg^g of Co Stag River, x it
full 30 Y^{ds}, very rapid, comes seemingly from S60E, Co from the left
hand Mountains – perhaps from N40E a bold opening in the
Mountains, which last I think the most probable. To the north of this
N40E Co stands an isolated Mountain of ab^t 2M long, then the
opening & the secondary Mountain before mentioned from the north

of which comes the bad Rivulet. Co + $\frac{1}{2}$M R SW $\frac{1}{5}$ R S30E $\frac{1}{5}$ SR S53E 1M
SR S86E $\frac{1}{3}$ S40E 1M R S80E $\frac{1}{6}$ R S28E $\frac{5}{6}$ R S28E $\frac{3}{4}$M water makes a
Noise against the Canoe as if full of icicles S8E $\frac{1}{2}$M R S50E $\frac{1}{4}$
R N70E $\frac{1}{4}$ S53E $\frac{1}{4}$ S43E $\frac{1}{2}$ S58E $\frac{1}{2}$ + $\frac{1}{3}$ S40E $\frac{1}{2}$ S8W $\frac{3}{4}$ S40E $\frac{1}{2}$ [these] 3 last
Cos fine Meadows & red Fir ⟨high Ground rising always towards
the Mountains⟩. We now see a Ridge of low Mountains or woody Hills
coming from the east^d & stretching to the west^d, & a woody low
Mountain from the right stretching to the east^d, between which I think
the River will take it's Course. Co So $\frac{2}{3}$M, which is also the Course to
the opening in the Hills. The Mountains on the left now present
themselves abt 20M dist on the left, or east^d. Co S30W $\frac{1}{4}$ S8E $\frac{1}{4}$M fine
Meadow on the right S33E $\frac{1}{3}$ N80E $\frac{1}{6}$ S12E 1M went & viewed beau-
tiful Plains on the left S60E $\frac{2}{3}$ R S20E $\frac{1}{2}$M S8E $\frac{2}{3}$ S2W $\frac{2}{3}$ S40E $\frac{1}{3}$ saw a
Mark made by Indians S18W $\frac{1}{3}$M R end of Co camped at 5:25 Pm,
as the Canoe made much water. From this side the Stag River ab^t 2M
– the River may be computed at 150 to 180 Y^{ds} wide, the whole of
the distance since that time very strong Current & often Rapid – every
Inch must be gained by the Pole or the Line. Beautiful Meadows
on both Hands, even to the very Mountains on the left – nor have the
Mountains any great degree of elevation ⟨& appear thro' my
Telescope to be covered with Grass to a great extent⟩: a very fine
Country. Beaver very scarce indeed today, & saw no Animals. ⟨This
is the Place where the Indians speak so much of growing their Tobacco,
& we named them on that account the Tobacco Meadows.⟩

April 26 [1808] Tuesday A fine cloudy Day. Early sent Lussier to examine the Land to the West^d for Marks of Indians &c – at 7 Am
he returned, hav^g seen the Track of a Man close below us, perhaps ab^t
10 days ago. We directly crossed over & I sent Mousseau
& Beaulieu to the east^d on the same Purpose. Walking ab^t, I found the
Marks of 6 Lodges who have camped here a few days past & whose
Road leads straight down along the River. After crossing a bold
Rivulet, which I named Fine Meadow Rivulet – it is deep & ab^t
24 Y^{ds} wide – at 11 Am sent Lussier to examine this Road, but all to
return by [sun] set. Obs^d Merid Alt^{de} of [sun's] LL
Lat^{de} 48°:55′:54″ N Err[our] +1′:34″ – as the [sun] was very hazy
there may be an Errour of 1′ + or – but not more. Lussier
returned hav^g found that the Indians had crossed the Fine Meadow
Rivulet of ab^t 30 Y^{ds} wide ⟨& strong Current, which he could not
cross but by swimming⟩ – Beaulieu & Mousseau arrived at 8 $\frac{1}{2}$ Pm

havin^g seen nothing but a very fine open Country but no traces of Indians – they brought a Skunk which they killed close to us. Set the 2 Steel Traps.

April 27th [1808] Wednesday A fine mild cloudy Morn^g. Took up the Traps – 1 small & 1 mid sized Beaver: thank Heaven for this supply. At 6:50 Am set off, Co s1oE $\frac{1}{3}$M s22w $\frac{1}{4}$ s8w $\frac{1}{2}$M s8E $\frac{1}{2}$M to the junction of the Fine Meadow River with this River. x the Fine Meadow River 30 y^{ds} cold and deep, at its junction very still water like a small Lake – hav^g paddled up it s70E $\frac{1}{2}$M we set Beaulieu & Lussier ashore to follow the indian Road, & we went to the Junction of the River[s] to dry & arrange our Canoe. At all Events we must stay here-abouts for a few Days, as it is our Opinion we are before the Kootanaes except a small Camp & this is near the Place appointed for the Rendezvous, as the River close below enters the woody Mountains & seems to afford no farther any considerable Narrows. Obs^d Merid Alt^{de} of [sun's] LL Lat^{de} 48°:54′:15″ N. Here are fine Poplars, some near 2 fms round, also very fine Red Fir of the same size. A very fine place for a House in the last Course but on the west Side of the River. In the evening the 2 Men returned hav^g followed the Indian Road for 2 Campments, the Road always following close along the River. Set the Traps.

April 28th [1808] Thursday A cloudy Morning with a southerly Gale. Sent Beaulieu & Lussier a hunt^g, Mousseau & Le Camble to set up a Mark that we are proceeding down the River. Nothing in the Traps. ⟨We found 2 small Tortoise Shells where they had formerly sowed the Tobacco.⟩ Our Hunters were unsuccessful, & myself very lame with a sprained Knee.

April 29th [1808] Friday A fine Day, southerly Gale. Caught a mid sized Beaver, thank Heaven ⟨as we are much in want⟩. Water rose 6 In perpendicular since yesterday. At 6$\frac{1}{4}$ Am set off, Co s63w $\frac{1}{4}$ s20w $\frac{1}{8}$ s48E $\frac{1}{4}$ s5E $\frac{1}{6}$ fine Meadow s80w $\frac{1}{5}$ s35w $\frac{1}{4}$ s18E $\frac{1}{5}$ s42E $\frac{1}{2}$ s20E $\frac{1}{3}$ s25w $\frac{1}{2}$ beg^g of Co spent 2H after Red Deer, but without success. s8w $\frac{3}{4}$ s12w 1M banks of Rock on both Sides + $\frac{1}{3}$M x 150 to 100 y^{ds} s17w $\frac{1}{2}$M s8w $\frac{3}{4}$ s18E $\frac{1}{4}$ s22E $\frac{1}{2}$M s40E $\frac{1}{2}$M passed a white Cedar s65E $\frac{1}{4}$M s30E $\frac{1}{6}$M. At 11$\frac{1}{4}$ Am went ashore & arranged Beaulieu & Le Camble to follow after the Indians that are before us. We shall re-main hereabouts & do the best we can for a livelihood; we suppose part

of the Kootanaes still behind, but what Route they will take to the
Flat Head Country is unknown to us. Our Hunting procured us nothing ⟨tho' there are a few Chevreuil here⟩ – angled in every seemingly good place, but nothing bit.

April 30th [1808] **Saturday** A fine day, southerly Gale. Visited our
Traps, & caught nothing. At 8¼ Am we set off to go higher up the
River, where we hope to find a few Beaver. At 4 Pm put ashore:
2 of us went to make & set Traps [and] I went a hunt^g, but am so lame
of the Knee as to be obliged to walk with a Stick; the other Man
took care of the Canoe &c – but all without Success, & our subsistence
this day was a Dram of Rum & half a Partridge p^r Man.

May 1st [1808] **Sunday** A fine Day, heavy South Gale. Visited our
Traps – caught a mid sized Beaver, thank Heaven. At 8 Am heard
an Indian call on the other Side the River; we crossed him over to us.
He is the Monde, a Kootanae whom we had left at the Kootanae
Lake. He had with him 2 of our Horses which he says he found strayed
far away; one of them is lame in the fore foot. By 11 Am his Family
came here, & we sent him a hunt^g – 6 Balls & Powder; in the evening
he returned with the Meat of a small Chevreuil, thank Heaven.
Obs^d for Lat^{de} & Long^{de} by Doub Merid Alt^{des} of Capella, Arcturus
and Regulus Lat^{de} 48°:51':44" N Mean Long^{de} 114°:59' w Varⁿ
19½° East.

May 2nd [1808] **Monday** A fine Morn^g, cloudy afternoon, clear Night
but did not observe for want of Candles, hav^g only sufficient to
serve for 4 or 5 Nights more. Hunting on every Quarter but all without
Success.

May 3rd [1808] **Tuesday** A sharp frost, Ice ¼ In thick. Nothing in
the Traps – 10 Balls & Powder to the Kootanae for hunt^g, 6 In of Tob.
We set off & drove down the River; the Indian went a hunt^g
& wounded a Chevreuil, but lost him on the east Side. He killed a Kind
of Tiger: he was 3 feet high, long in proportion his Tail 2 ft 10 In
– of a Fawn colour, Belly white, very strong-legged & sharp Claws,
⟨upper part of the Tail of the Colour of the Back – that is, Fawn
– the under Side & Tip of the Tail white⟩. We put up at our Campment,
where I sent the Men on Discovery. Found the Tiger very good
Food, ⟨white,⟩ & yields as much Meat as a Chevreuil. ⟨Two of us upon

eating the Liver had a violent head Ache for a few Hours.〉 About us is very fine Larch – measured a common one 13 ft in girth 〈at 5½ feet from the ground; they are very tall, ab^t 150 feet〉. Many small Plane Trees, none above 2 to 4 In diameter; a few white Cedars but full of Branches, 〈very fine Red Fir & plenty of the Fir Pine, a few Poplars & Aspins〉. Late in the evening our Indian killed a Buck Chevreuil, thank Heaven. Obs^d for Long^{de} by Capella, Arcturus, Pollux and Spica Lat^{de} 48°:45¾' N Mean Long^{de} 114°:50':22" W.

May 4th [1808] Wednesday A very fine day. Early our Indian went out a hunt^g – fired several Shots at the Chevreuil without success. He returned, & finding he was not inclined to accompany us any farther 〈on acc^t of his Family & rugged Country〉, I gave him 1 ft of Tob & 10 Ro^{ds} of Amm, & recommended to him to take care of & look after the 2 Horses of the Company, which he promised. At Noon observed for Lat^{de} Doub Merid Alt^{des} of [sun's] LL Lat^{de} 48°:45':50" N. At ¾ Pm set off slowly down the River to look after my 2 Men who are on the scout after Indians. Co [19 courses], beg^g of [last] Co put up at 5½ Pm. Cedars all along the River, but not of size or goodness. The Hills are now quite low, of black & grey Rock & not more than 600 feet high, & yet many of them are covered with Snow half way down. Fine Current to day, except 2 Rapids. Woods mostly Larch & Red Fir with Fir Pine 〈& in the Hollows, Cypress〉 – one of the Fir Pine measured 3 fm round. The Larch & Fir also very fine.

May 5th [1808] Thursday A fine Morn^g, but like others very cold & frosty. At 6 Am set off, Co s40w ¼M s30w ⅓M s6e ¾M s5e 1½M s5w ¾M s22e ½M s35e ⅕ s5e ¾ s50e ¼ s18w ¾M beg^g of Co strong Rapid with huge Rocks in the mid – run it on the left, I think – it may be run close on the right with less danger. 〈At this place the River is not above 40 Y^{ds} wide but immediately opens out.〉 Co + ¼M s8w ¾M s48e ⅔M s5e ¼ s50w ⅙ s65w ¼. Finding that the indian Road no longer followed the River, returned back to close above the Rock River & camped at 11 Am. Find^g a fire but newly extinguished, we supposed our 2 Men have to have slept here – we fired several Shots but without answer. I sent a man on each Quarter, & ab^t 2 Hours after one of them returned in company with the 2 Men sent on the Scout, quite fatigued & half starved, hav^g found no Indians, & only a chance Partridge for food. We staid an Hour to refresh them. Obs^d Doub Merid Alt^{des} of [sun's] LL Lat^{de} 48°:22':24" N Var^n by the [sun's]

Transit $17\frac{1}{2}°$ East – this Obs^n is at end of Co s50w$\frac{1}{6}$M, close
above Rock River. At $2\frac{3}{4}$ Pm set off, Co West$\frac{1}{2}$M strong Rapid run on
the right – good s60w $\frac{1}{4}$ SR – mid good sw$\frac{3}{4}$M + $\frac{1}{4}$ R s75w$\frac{1}{2}$M the
River only 150 Y^{ds} wide, but bold & deep. West $\frac{1}{3}$M N86w $\frac{3}{4}$M R + $\frac{1}{4}$M
N65w $\frac{1}{3}$M N30w 1M NW$\frac{1}{2}$M s70w $\frac{1}{5}$M s40w $\frac{1}{3}$M sight tolerable high
snowy Mountains on the left, say 3000 ft perpend s48w $\frac{1}{2}$M s34w
$\frac{1}{3}$M s8w $\frac{3}{4}$M s70w $\frac{1}{2}$M R N72w $\frac{1}{4}$M s87w $\frac{1}{4}$M R N80w 1M s60w$\frac{1}{4}$M
NW 1M N82w $\frac{1}{2}$M mid of Co put up at $5\frac{1}{2}$ Pm to shave & wash ourselves
&c. Most part of the Day the Hills not above 500 ft high & mostly
verdant, often finely so. Red Deer & Chevreuil by their Tracks appear
plenty – no Beaver, nor Fowl nor Fish. Woods mostly of Larch,
with Red & Pine Fir, Cypress, a few Poplars, Aspins, Cedars, Alders
& Birch, with Willows & small Plane – but the Country in every
other respect forbids a Settlement hereabouts ⟨as the Hills are so very
close⟩. At the last Rivulet of 150 Y^{ds} x on the left, both Sides of the
River have extensive low Lands between the Mountains, seemingly
swampy & more extensive on the left than on the right hand – latter
part of the day the River banks quite rocky & the Hills dreary.

May 6th **[1808] Friday** A cloudy Morn^g, wind NW^{tly}. At $5\frac{3}{4}$ Am
set off, Co N85w $\frac{1}{4}$M Isle of Rock N70w$\frac{1}{2}$M R N75w $\frac{1}{2}$M s65w $\frac{1}{2}$M N80w
$\frac{3}{4}$M R end of Co strong Rapid – went down on the left with the Line ⟨an
Isle of Rock & Embarras⟩ s65w $\frac{1}{2}$M s60w $\frac{1}{2}$M SR shot it, to the right
mostly s75w $\frac{3}{4}$M to the upper end of the Fall. We put ashore at $8\frac{1}{4}$ Am,
rain & high Wind breaking out – we put [up] 'till better Weather.
The Morn^g & part of yesterday, the Rocks close to the River Side – Hills
ab^t 4 to 500 ft high ⟨& the Country very rugged⟩. Since the Rock
River ⟨where we embarked our 2 Men⟩ the Indian Road always on the
right Side the River. Large Cedars are now frequent but ⟨those
close to the River are⟩ full of Branches. Fished at the foot of the Fall,
but as usual caught nothing. After taking a mouthful, two Men
went off to examine the Portage on the left Side – they
returned at Noon, saying that the Portage was impracticable on
this Side, from the ⟨quantity of Wood to be cleared away &⟩ from the
Rocks coming steep down to the River. With 3 Men I immediately
crossed the River & we spent 3H in examining the north Side – we found
it very bad indeed but practicable with much care & precaution.
I went farther on & sent the Men back to bring all over to this Side, but
not to carry 'till I arrived beyond the last of the Fall; I saw nothing
extraordinary in the River ⟨except the difficulty of getting down the

Banks to the water Edge) & therefore went back, & found the Men
who had just put the Canoe & Cargo ashore. We began carrying at
$3\frac{1}{4}$ Pm with light Loads & went ab^t 1 Mile over a terrible Road, along
Side of a steep Hill nearly perpend, walking wholly among small
fragments of black broken Rock that had rolled from the Summit. Our
Height at times was ab^t 300 feet above the River, ascending and
descending as the steep Rocks obliged us; ⟨the least slip would have
been inevitable destruction, as the steepness of the Rock allowed
no return, or if once falling, to stop 'till precipitated into the River.⟩
We came to a Brook where we had a Bank of ab^t 200 ft to descend
without a halt, still among fragments of Rocks, not an Inch of Earth
⟨or Sand⟩ to ease the Foot. Each Trip took $1\frac{1}{2}$H, & by $6\frac{3}{4}$ Pm we
had got most of the Cargo to the Brook, where we put up. We had a
slight Supper, the very last of our Provisions. A very cold Night.

May 7th [1808] Saturday A very fine Day. Early began carrying to the
River Side which is ab^t 1M farther, but the Road passable good, the
Rocks bad to descend. At $6\frac{3}{4}$ Am set off to fetch the Canoe. I have
taken half the Timbers out to lighten it, & by 9 Am got it to the Brook
⟨altho' 4 able Men were continually bearing it, yet it was with
difficulty preserved from breaking against the Rocks from the badness
of the Road & short turnings⟩. We then took it to the Water Side
– I arranged the Canoe & the Men went for the rest of the Cargo, & by
$\frac{1}{2}$H past Noon we were ready, & set off. I had gone down by Land to
examine the River still farther & assure ourselves that the Falls
⟨& high steep Rocks⟩ were finished, as the Banks are [per]pend Rock
– & altho' I did not proceed more than a Mile in a straight Line, yet
the Hills were so bad & steep & I had such heights to Climb & descend,
that I was fairly fatigued before I could get to any Place where I
could approach the Canoe. Co of the Fall to the Brook s80w $\frac{1}{2}$M,
Co to the end of the Portage s44w $\frac{3}{4}$M, Co below the Portage s62w
$\frac{3}{4}$M – only 30 Y^{ds} wide in places, with violent Eddies which threatened to swallow up the Canoe & People. s60E $\frac{3}{4}$M Banks of Rock
but not so high & at times steep Earth &c. [19 courses] beg^g of [last]
Co found part of a Chevreuil, which the Eagles had more than half
devoured – it was almost putrified, but as we were without Food, we
were necessitated to take what remained, altho' we could hardly
bear the smell. Co [23 courses] – at $6\frac{1}{2}$ Pm put up as the Men had
tasted nothing all day & were much fatigued. Boiled our rotten Meat
– we eat of it but all of us became quite sick, ⟨& fatigued as we were,

they could not sleep). The first Co of this day among dangerous Eddies, then tolerable but strong Current – the Rocks again confine the River in a small space, & the water is driven from Side to Side as to form dangerous Eddies, especially above & at the rapid River from the right hand or north^d. From thence the Hills lower continually but almost always present a rocky Bank, frequently perpend to where we put up, & the Current always very strong. To stem this Current 6 good Men would be required, & with the best there are many places that could not be passed among the perpend Rocks ⟨without very hard work⟩ – they can neither pole nor line it, & to carry is ⟨often⟩ impossible.

May 8th [1808] **Sunday** A very fine day. At 5$\frac{1}{2}$ Am set off, Co S40E $\frac{1}{4}$M S38W $\frac{2}{3}$M N5W $\frac{1}{4}$ N60W $\frac{1}{4}$M SW $\frac{1}{6}$ S88W $\frac{1}{4}$ S33W $\frac{1}{2}$M S55W 1M N80W $\frac{1}{2}$M S30W $\frac{3}{4}$M 250 to 300 Y^{ds} wide, poplar Islands & low Points West $\frac{1}{2}$M to Rocks on one Side S38W$\frac{1}{2}$M N85W $\frac{1}{2}$M S82W $\frac{2}{3}$M beg^g of Co, thank Heaven, saw a Lake Indian who embarked with us. At end of Co came to the camp of the Kootanaes & Lake Indians, 10 Lodges – they have [neither] Beaver nor Provisions. At our starting this Morn^g, the River steep rocky Banks, but soon fine moderate deep Current; the Land on each Side of us low Points & tolerable wide at times – to the south a long view of low Land, seemingly fit for Beaver & Animals, but have seen no Marks of Beaver since the Fine Meadow River worth while; even here there are none. The Indians say there are Chevreuil, but the whole of their livelihood [is] small Carp ⟨& a kind of Bread made of Moss from the Trees, of a [s]lightly bitter insipid Taste⟩. They inform me that 47 Peagan Men crossed & stole 35 of their Horses, ⟨that one of the Peagans was killed by the old Chief⟩ – I wait Boulard for a more circumstantial account. As soon as I landed, smoked with the Indians for a few Minutes, when I got one of them to set off with Tobacco to the Flat Heads & the Old Chief, to be here as soon as possible – a Horseman also set off below to a Camp of Lake Indians who are to be here the Morrow or so. Put the Goods in order & camped close on the River Banks; the River here is ab^t 300 Y^{ds} wide & very deep, edged with Poplar, Aspin, Thorn, ⟨Choak Cherry, small Plane &c⟩ &c, & within Fir Pine & Red Fir ⟨with much Larch⟩, small Elder – the Woods in half Leaf & the Blossoms already falling off the Arrow Wood. Obs^d for Longitude by Capella, Arcturus and Regulus Lat^{de} 48°:42′:52″ N Var^n 19° East Mean Long^{de} 116°:00′:8″ W.

May 9th [1808] **Monday** A fine Day. Obs^d for Lat^{de} Doub Merid Alt^{de}
of [sun's] LL 116°:58':30" + 1'$\frac{3}{4}$" Lat^{de} 48°:42':44" N Var^n by the
[sun's] Transit 19° or 20° East. Capot Barré & Ugly Head arrived
− sent Indians a hunt^g − 1 small Chevreuil − Expence 14 Balls & Powder
& 9 In of Tob. Total Eclipse of the Moon. Ex^d Errour: + 1':$\frac{3}{4}$".

May 10th [1808] **Tuesday** A fine Day somewhat Cloudy. Obs^d for
Lat^{de} Doub Merid of [sun's] LL Lat^{de} 48°:43' N. Expences of
Hunt^g, 18 Balls & Powder − 1 Chevreuil & half of a good Bear. Traded
15 Beaver & 14 dressed Skins, of which 8 were directly sold to the
Men; we had not a single pair of Shoes. Water has rose ab^t 4$\frac{1}{2}$
feet since our arrival, bringing down much wood. Cloudy Even^g.

May 11th [1808] **Wednesday** A fine Day, Wind a Gale from the SW^d.
Sent Indians a hunt^g − in the Even^g traded $\frac{3}{4}$ small Chevreuil. A heavy
Storm all day.

May 12 [1808] **Thursday** A very fine day but very warm, a little
Thunder. Backed a Sturgeon Net − traded a few dressed Skins.
Agreed with the Ugly Head, Chief of the Lake Indians, to go the
Morrow & bring here quickly the Flat Heads &c &c, as the Season
advances fast. In the mean Time I propose to examine this River down
to the Lake & see if any eligible Place can be found for a Settlement.

May 13 [1808] **Friday** A fine Day. Early Ugly Head crossed to go in
quest of the Flat Heads. At 5$\frac{1}{2}$ Am we set off, Co down the River [105
courses]; at end of [last] Co 6$\frac{1}{2}$ Pm put up on the left, the Bank only
10 Y^{ds} wide & the rest to the foot of the Mountains & southward
one extensive Lake. Traded 1 Beaver & 2 Sheep Skins from the 4 Lake
Indian Families we saw − they were very civil & offered us Moose
& Sheep Meat, but it was too much tainted to be eaten. Met 2 Canoes
more − 1 very old Man & his Family.

May 14 [1808] **Saturday** A fine Morning − a few Musketoes for the
first Time this Season. At 5 Am set off, Co [15 courses] sight the
Lake: it bears N36W turning to the north^d, say the right hand Point 4M
dist and the left 7M dist. High steep rugged Mountains covered
with Snow bound the Lake on all sides − the Lake may be 3 to 4M wide
& seemingly very deep, but has not the least appearance of being
an eligible spot for a Building. Co N12E 1M − we wandered ab^t in this

Co for 4 Hours among back Lakes, looking for the Lake Indians whom at 11 Am we found & camped with – they have a few Beaver in Hoards. There are 18 Men with their Families, & ab^t the mid of the Lake there is another Camp of them. They received us very civilly & of such as they had they gave us to eat – Moss Bread & dried Carp. Obs^d for Lat^{de} Doub Merid of [sun's] LL Lat^{de} 49°:17':44″ N. Traded 1 Moose Skin, 35 Skins in Furrs, 3 good Horses for 27 Skins, & 4 Bows for Mr Duncan McGillivray, 1½ fm of Tob & 24 Ro^{ds} of Amm. Exp^d 18 [In] of Tob in Smoking. Traded a few Berries & dried Carp – they were stale but acceptable.

May 15 [1808] Sunday A fine Morn^g & Day. We loaded our Canoe early, but had much difficulty to find 2 Indians to take the Horses to the ⟨Camp we had left the morning of the 13th, as the low Lands are already overflowed to several feet, & the Hills are little else than bare Rock⟩. At 8 Am set off, Co up the main Channel S30E 1M River S52E 2M Lake SE 1M S65E^d ¾ SE ¼ River S36E 3M S25E½M + ½M beg^g of first half Mile Co indian fishing Grounds &c – latter half good Ground for building, but nothing else. S25E ⅓M So 1M fine Ground on the left – at end of Co carried 10 Y^{ds}. Cooked some dried carp, but found them bad food from their having been kept so long as they are last years drying. At 3:50 Pm embarked & set off, Co down a River So ⅙M to a Lake, but when the water is low, a Meadow. Co S30E 2M mid of Co saw 2 Chevreuil – the Indians went ashore but could not approach them. They put up at 5 Pm & we were obliged to do the same, as we are among back Lakes caused by the overflowing of the River – 8 Canoes of Lake Indians in company. The Moss Bread we have traded is very dirty, & scarcely eatable at all, hungry as we are, & gives the Belly Ache.

May 16 [1808] Monday A fine Day. Could not get the Indians to start till 6:20 Am when we set off & finished the Course: came to the River, carried over a portage of 40 Y^{ds} long – good, but burnt. Co up the River SW ⅙ S48W ½M S20 or 25E ½M S80E ¾ SE ¼ S30E ¾ high Land – it ends at end of Co. Here I finish taking courses, as those taken on descending the Current are more correct, & being obliged to paddle prevents me also. We paddled on to past where we met the Indians, where we made a Portage on the left into a back Lake & kept on a while; we then carried into the River, but soon again made a Portage at a [ ] into Lakes & continued on 'till 6½ Pm, when we put up. Met 2 Canoes of Lake Indians from whom we traded 12 singed Musk Rats & 2 Shoulders of a Chevreuil. ⟨All these Lakes are Meadows when the River becomes low.⟩

May 17 [1808] Tuesday A very fine Day. At 5 Am set off & paddled on thro' Lakes to the River, made a Portage & paddled a good Pipe in the River, at the Point of Rock into a back Lake, by a Portage of 300 Y^{ds}. These Lakes brought us to our old Campment, which is now under Water – we camped at 11 Am at ⟨a detached high Knowl⟩ & here received the disagreeable News of the Flat Heads & Kootanaes being unable to come here, on account of the flooding of the Country – thus all my fine Hopes are ruined. The Lake Indian Chief had arrived & brought 3 grand River Indians with him, who seemed very happy to see us & traded with me 2 Bears & 5 Beav^{r}, with ab^{t} 10 lbs of dried Meat & some Moss Bread, far superior to that made by Kootanaes and Lake Indians ⟨and very cleanly – the Men & all about them appear very cleanly⟩.

May 18 [1808] Wednesday A very fine Day. Conversing much ab^{t} the Country, & tried to make an arrangement to go to the Flat Head Country, but all to no purpose. Traded a Chevreuil, thank Heaven.

May 19th [1808] Thursday A fine Day. Tied up the Furrs traded, which amounts to 3 Packs, into Loads for the Horses. Traded also a strong Horse for the Co^{y}, & got ready to set off with our Kootanae Guide. As we were ready to start, he begged for another to come with him. The old Men made Speeches to encourage the young Men, but all to no purpose – ⟨none were found hardy enough,⟩ & we set off with our Kootanae at 2$\frac{1}{4}$ Pm. But the Hills were so steep & so high that the Loads slipped continually off the Horses, & it was 4$\frac{1}{4}$ Pm before we got to the top of the first Banks. Hav^{g} gone ab^{t} 2M our Guide found himself very uneasy, seated as he was on a loaded Horse, & requested to go back to procure a light Horse of his own. I sent Mousseau with him in case he should wish to ⟨give us the slip, &⟩ leave us. ⟨The rest of us – Lussier, Le Camble & myself –⟩ held on to a small Brook which runs to the west^{d} ⟨& that has high bad Banks from much fallen Wood⟩ – we crossed it & put up at 6:20 Pm. Our Co may have been N20E 4M by the [sun]. Woods of Red & White Fir, Fir Pine, Cedar & a few Pines ⟨with small Cypress – much of the Moss

of which they make their Bread is hanging on these Trees). Had a very
light Supper. At 9 Pm our Guide & Mousseau came to us.

May 20th **[1808] Friday** A very fine Day. At $6\frac{1}{2}$ Am set off & went
to the NE^d ab^t$2\frac{1}{2}$ Miles; we then turned along the Mountains,
down along the River towards the Lake & went on over very bad Road
& much fallen Wood to near a large Brook, when our Guide went
off a hunt^g, ⟨leaving us to go on the best we could⟩. We got to the Brook
over very bad Road. We found the Brook so deep & rapid that we
could not cross it, as it carried the light Horses under Water in an
instant. We threw down a large Cedar for a Bridge, on which we
crossed our Baggage & then with much Trouble crossed the Horses,
by hauling them with a strong Cord – this took us up near 2 Hours.
Went up the Bank & camped at 4 Pm to wait our Guide – at $\frac{1}{2}$ past [sun]
set he came to us. Went fasting to bed.

May 21st **[1808] Saturday** A very fine Day, Thunder in the Evening.
At 6 Am set off – our Guide set off ahead for a small Chevreuil he
had killed, & we went ⟨on the best we could⟩ thro' bad Grounds 'till
$7\frac{1}{4}$ Am when we came to where he had put the Chevreuil, but not seeing
him I fired 2 Shots, which brought him to us. We put the Meat on
our Horses & held on ab^t $\frac{1}{2}$M farther, where we stopped to breakfast, being very hungry. Our Guide again wished to leave us & go a
hunt^g: we could not consent to this from the badness of the
Country & hav^g no path to follow – he threw himself on the Ground
quite sulky & threatened to leave us, & at length we found ourselves
obliged to comply & he set off as if to hunt. We also went off, but
finding a Morass before us, we were obliged to return back to
where we breakfasted to try & round it to the east^d. Here we found our
Guide, who also returned & was eating the singed Skin of the
Chevreuil. It immediately struck me that he was about to desert: he
rose up ⟨& with a fawning look⟩ begged us to stay here, while he
would go & visit the Country for the best way to pass – he set off, but
did not return. Passed the evening reflecting on our forlorn situation ⟨without a Guide, Path or Provisions in these rugged Mountains⟩.

May 22nd **[1808] Sunday** A very fine day. Waited 'till $10\frac{1}{2}$ Am for the
return of the Scoundrel our Guide when, despairing of seeing him
& not being able to walk myself from a bad Knee, I sent off Mousseau

& Lussier to the Camp ⟨we had left⟩ to try & procure another Guide
– Le Camble stays with me in care of the Things.

May 23ʳᵈ [1808] Monday A very fine Day. Took a walk to the northᵈ
– found the Road that we are to follow & a large Brook that we
have to cross; saw 5 or 6 Chevreuil. Time hangs heavy with waiting
my Men & hopes of a Guide, which I pray God in his Mercy to send
us.

May 24ᵗʰ [1808] Tuesday A cloudy but fine Day. Passed the Time in
sad reflections; while I was wandering about ⟨examining the
Country⟩, Ugly Head & my 2 Men returned ⟨with Ugly Head for a
Guide⟩, thank God – they came at 6 Pm. He has received payment
for this Service: 1 Capot of 4 Ells, 1½ Yᵈˢ of com Red Strouds, 1 large
Knife, 1 small Axe, 10 Balls & Powder. Here we made a meal of a
few Berries.

May 25ᵗʰ [1808] Wednesday A fine Day. Early our Guide went off a
huntᵍ but without Success. At 9 Am we set off; we went 1M then
crossed a large Brook, very rapid, the same we had already crossed –
Beaulieu's Brook. Here we threw down a Bridge of a large Cedar;
in 1:20′H got all over. We then held on for abᵗ 3M tolerable good, when
thank good Providence we killed a small Chevreuil, of which we
stand in the greatest need, & on which we immediately made a hearty
Meal. At 2 Pm set off & went on thro' bad Woods, along high
sloping Banks, crossing Brooks frequently, in one of which a Horse
wet his Load of Furrs. We then came to a large Brook – our Guide
spent an Hour in examining it, & we spent 1½ Hours more in carrying
every thing across & crossing the Horses; this is the most northern
Scource of McDonald's River. We then held on thro' pathless Woods
'till 8 Pm, when we were obliged to put [up] ⟨for want of light⟩. Our
Co may have been NNE 7M – we lost ⟨very⟩ much Time by the derange-
ment of the Loads of the Horses from the ⟨extreme⟩ badness of the
Woods & Country.

May 26 [1808] Thursday A fine Day. At break of Day our Guide set
off to find the Road, which havᵍ done, he returned & we loaded our
Horses & set off. Went on crossing Brooks & Rills N[10]E 2M to
McDonald's River of 25 to 30 Yᵈˢ wide fully, bold & deep, very
strong Current ⟨as it is now swelled very much by the melting of the

Snows⟩ – held on along the River 'till Noon, when we stopped to
dry the Furrs. At $2\frac{1}{2}$ Pm we set off & held on up the River – often bad
Road from Rocks &c as the real Road crosses the River twice when
the Water is low – 'till $4\frac{1}{2}$ Pm, when our Guide informed us we must
make a Canoe to cross the River, as the Mountains on this Side are
too bad to be passed by Horses. Hav^g no Provisions we set to work
with a heavy Heart, & our Guide, like an honest Fellow, set off to
see if it was possible for us to pass. We got the Materials for a Canoe,
& late in the evening our Guide returned, but quite undetermined
what to do. Our Co this day has been ab^t NE 10M, sometimes over
broken Rocks, which has cut the Legs of our Horses very much,
so that we may trace them by the Blood only, poor Animals; sometimes
the Road has been tolerable for the Country.

May 27th [1808] Friday A fine Day. Could not find our Horses 'till
9 Am. Our Guide took the resolution of trying the Mountains: we
went on in most terrible Road – our poor Horses suffered most cruelly
from the Rocks & Woods. By 2 Pm we crossed a large Brook, over
which we were ab^t to carry our Things, but finding the Horses could
cross we reloaded them. At 3 Pm we came to the Road ⟨which here
re-crosses McDonald's River⟩ & followed it over tolerable Ground
⟨with small Cypress⟩ for $1\frac{1}{2}$ Hours, when we came to a Family of
Lake Indians of whom we got a good Bowl full of small Trout, ab^t 2 lbs
of dried Meat, & 4 Cakes of Root Bread, much better than any we
have hitherto had. We were very hungry, & fell on the dried fish with
a most keen appetite – our Guide told us to broil them, but we
found them excellent as they were, & eat them all fairly up. Here our
Guide told us to camp for the Night ⟨to refresh our Horses⟩, while
he got information of the Road before us &c – our Horses are much
harrassed & terribly cut. Exp^d 2 ft of Tob, 5 Ro^{ds} of Amm. Our Co
has been ab^t NE 10M, always along McDonald's River.

May 28 [1808] Saturday A very fine Day. At $5\frac{1}{2}$ Am set off, but soon
coming to overflowed Ground, we were again obliged to take to
the Mountains – but as usual made very little progress from climbing
& descending, at other times to the middle in water among very
thick pathless Woods. At $11\frac{1}{2}$ Am we stopped to refresh our Horses,
our Guide telling us that for the present the overflowed Ground
was passed. Hav^g lost a small Bag of Provisions our Guide has got from
his Countryman of yesterday, we spent 2 Hours looking for it, but

to no purpose. We set off & went on over tolerable Road for the Country, crossing high points of Hills &c, but always with a Path more or less perceptible, to a Lake from which McDonald's River issues – here we camped at $6\frac{1}{2}$ Pm. McDonald's River is here ab^t 30 Y^{ds} wide, & deep with even strong Current, & in Autumn is said to have plenty of Red Deer & Fish. Our Co N30E 5 or 6M NI0E 8M.

May 29th [1808] Sunday A very fine Day. At $5\frac{1}{4}$ Am set off & went on along the west Side of the Lake ⟨over very much fallen Wood⟩ North 3M – $1\frac{1}{2}$M gone a bold Brook from the east^d into the Lake. We then crossed Woods NI0E $1\frac{1}{2}$M to another Lake, seemingly larger than the last which appears to have 600 or 800 Y^{ds} width ⟨I think they are the same Lake; if not, they are connected by McDonald's River⟩. We went along the 2nd Lake North or NI0E 6M crossing several Brooks, at one of which we lost $2\frac{1}{2}$H in making a Bridge – here our Guide killed a Chevreuil, thank Heaven, of which we made a good Meal ⟨as we are very hungry⟩. At $\frac{1}{2}$ past Noon set off, & went on along the Lake NI5E 4M to the end of the Lake, & thro' Woods on the same Course 5M, the last Mile close along McDonald's River: here it comes ⟨from the perpend Rocky Hills⟩ from the west^d & ⟨directly⟩ makes a sudden bend to the sbE or so ⟨striking violently against the rugged eastern Rocks⟩, & here by one Means or other we must cross it. We examined it, but with [poor] Hopes of succeeding. At $6\frac{1}{2}$ Pm camped & began to throw ⟨down a large Fir Pine for⟩ a Bridge across it, but the Axe Helve breaking, & our Guide killing a Red Deer, we did nothing further this even^g than get the Meat to the campment. On the road this afternoon he had killed another Chevreuil – Animal Tracks are plenty on the Spot ⟨tho' the Country is exceedingly Rude⟩.

May 30 [1808] Monday A very fine Day. Early began to throw down large Trees for a Bridge, but the Current always broke them or swept them away. ⟨One of them was a very fine Larch of ab^t 2 fms round & its Butt lay ab^t 8 Y^{ds}in the Ground, but the Current turned it round & swept it off without the delay of even a minute.⟩ At $11\frac{1}{4}$ Am, seeing all hopes were vain, we desisted, loaded our Horses & at the very foot of a craggy Hill forded on Horseback, 4 Channels. The 5th d^o was deep & rapid – we unloaded our Horses on an Embarras, standing Knee deep in ⟨exceeding cold⟩ water & the whole Embarras shaking with the violence of the Current. Our Guide & Lussier crossed on Horseback swimming [their Horses]. They worked hard

'till 6 Pm throwing down ⟨large Aspins⟩ so as to fall on the
Embarras ⟨to make a Bridge to cross the Furrs on⟩, but all to no purpose
– the Current always broke them or swept them away. At length
we were obliged to tye each Parcel hard up in our Blankets &c, & a
strong line being tied to it, we threw it into the River, when it was
hauled across by those on the other Side as fast as possible. We then
crossed everything we had, except a Parcel cont^g ab^t $\frac{1}{2}$ Pack of
Beav^r, 2 very fine Bear Skins & all the little Property of Lussier & Le
Camble, which was totally lost by the breaking of the Line. We
then crossed on Horseback by 8 Pm, all safe thank God. We camped
on the waters Edge ⟨hav^g had a Day of extreme Danger & hard
work⟩ – I hope we have now done with this terrible River.

May 31 [1808] Tuesday A very fine Day. Early spread out every Thing
to dry & 10$\frac{3}{4}$ Am again arranged every thing & set off on our
Voyage, thro' close burnt Woods & over high Points of Rock. Hav^g
gone N20E 2M we crossed a Brook running into McDonald's River,
it's most northern water – in the upper part of this Brook ⟨in a Lake⟩
is where the Mountain ⟨Lake⟩ Indian caught the small Trout we
had from him. The Country now became more level & much better
⟨everything about us is green⟩. Our Road was ab^t ENE 4M – a small
Lake & fine Meadow Knowls on the left, which is probably our Road.
Held on, the Country having now a fine appearance like that at the
best part of the Kootanae Lake ⟨but the Grass thicker & longer⟩. NE 3M
to a Brook, which we crossed close to a large Campment of last
Summer – stopped half an Hour & then proceeded on our Journey
NE 2M to near the Torrent River, which I saw last Autumn, & from
where I turned ab^t, was ab^t North [or] NbW 3M from me. Here our
Guide questioning which I preferred – making a Canoe & crossing
the Torrent River & then McGillivray's River, or to turn out of our
Road, ⟨make a Canoe & ⟩ directly cross McGillivray's River, & thus
save the trouble of making a Canoe twice – I chose the latter as the most
expeditious, tho' it brought us direct on the War Road. We turned
off ab^t N8oE or East 7M to McGillivray's River & put up close on it's
Banks at 6$\frac{1}{2}$ Pm, now flush from Bank to Bank, ⟨very deep,⟩ with
a fine easy Current. Nelson's Mountains are still loaded with Snow,
the Rocky Mountains nearly bare.

June 1st [1808] Wednesday A very fine Day. Early our Guide & the
3 Men set off on Horseback to raise Pine Bark & Wood for a Canoe

— by 2 Pm they returned, & our Guide at 3 Pm with the Meat of a Chevreuil he had killed. Spent the rest of the Day in arranging Wood for the Canoe.

June 2nd [1808] Thursday A very fine Day, but stormy at times in the Morn^g, with small Showers. Early began our Pine Bark Canoe & by Noon we were all crossed – at $\frac{1}{2}$ Pm we set off & went on up the River 'till we came to Skirmish Brook at $3\frac{1}{4}$ Pm: this we attempted to throw a Bridge across but to no purpose till [sun] set, when we felled a large Red Fir ⟨of 10 ft girth⟩ – this broke but still answered our Purpose, tho' very hazardous as the Current rushed like a Fall over it – by $8\frac{1}{4}$ Pm we were thank God all crossed, & directly put up. I think we are opposite the Mouth of the Torrent River.

June 3rd [1808] Friday A fine Day. At 6 Am set off & went on over a tolerable fine Country, but no Animals. At $9\frac{3}{4}$ Am refreshed our Horses; at $11\frac{1}{4}$ Am set off & went on 'till 3 Pm when we came to Lussier's Rivulet of ab^t 30 Y^{ds} wide, ⟨rapid, but not so much as the others⟩ – we threw a Red Fir over the large Channel & with some danger crossed it, carrying all our Things. By 5 Pm again set off, & went on & put up at the small Lake & Plain at $7\frac{1}{2}$ Pm. ⟨At $7\frac{3}{4}$ Pm the noise of a falling Rock, or⟩ a Shot – ⟨we heard [it] distinctly ab^t 1 M from us⟩. Passed the Night in Arms – add to this it rained all Night.

June 4th [1808] Saturday A rainy Morn^g 'till $10\frac{1}{2}$ Am & small Showers after this, but fine Afternoon. Our Guide ⟨going his Rounds to see if there were no Tracks of Men near us⟩ killed a Chevreuil. At $11\frac{1}{4}$ Am set off, & went on to near the small Brook, where we stopped to take wood for the Canoe. At $5\frac{1}{4}$ Pm we arrived at the Crossing Place, thank God – spent the rest of the afternoon in arranging Wood for the Canoe ⟨as we cannot cross the River otherwise⟩. The Torrent River seems to come from SW to NE, & Nelson's Mountains go off nearly sbw.

June 5th [1808] Sunday A very fine Day. Early our Guide began his Canoe but taking extraordinary pains did not finish it 'till $2\frac{1}{2}$ Pm, when we began crossing the River. By 5 Pm were all landed on McGillivray's Portage ⟨thank Heaven⟩. Here we bid adieu to our humane Guide, without whose ⟨manly exertions,⟩ Perseverance & Attention we had certainly never been able to have reached this

Place. He descended McGillivray's River in his Canoe & we went on over the Portage, then along the Kootanae Lake to the Brook, where we camped at 8 Pm close to the upper Weir. Rain in the evening.

June 6th [1808] Monday A fine Day. At 5$\frac{1}{4}$ Am set off – by 11 Am came to the Brook below the long Plain, below our old House now desolate. Looked for the Wood Canoe, but the wind & Current had carried it off. Again set off at 2 Pm, held on & at 6$\frac{1}{2}$ Pm put up at the Lodge du Paille – a good day's Journey for Horses that are come so far ⟨& are so fatigued⟩.

June 7th [1808] Tuesday A day of variable Weather – at times Showers of Rain & mostly all the Afternoon. At 5$\frac{1}{2}$ Am set off & came on 'till 9$\frac{1}{2}$ Am when we breakfasted, but bad weather detained us 'till 11$\frac{1}{2}$ Am. We then set off & came on to where the Road falls on the Lakes of Grass & Water, now deeply overflowed. We held on thro' pathless Woods 'till 2 Pm, when seeing Pines of which I could make a Canoe, we brought the Furrs to the edge of a small Pond & began felling a large Pine, of which we took 3 fms of its Bark to make a Canoe. At 5 Pm sent off Le Camble & Lussier with the Horses for the Portage – Mousseau & me have to make a Canoe & transport the Furrs &c to the same place, unless we sooner meet the People I left. Put up the Tent, split out the Gunwales, & knifed 2 of them.

June 8th [1808] Wednesday A cloudy Day, fine Evening. Very early began working at the Canoe, but hav^g only a small Axe the work went on slowly. By 2$\frac{1}{2}$ Pm got the Canoe done, then looked for Gum, made Paddles – so that it was near 6 Pm when we embarked in a Pond of Water to get to the River. Here we were much embarrassed from the closeness of the Willows & badness of the Ground – fortunately the Men sent with the Horses had fallen in with Mr McDonald & Men, who came with a Canoe & relieved us. On proceeding down the River, killed a Beaver, which sank as we grasped him. At 8$\frac{1}{2}$ Pm arrived, thank God, at the Camp – ⟨found all safe⟩. They have had but poorly at times in Food & have eat most of the Dogs &c.

From Boggy Hall to Kootanae House

4 October – 10 November 1808

Octr 4th [1808] **Tuesday** A very fine day. Early sent the Men to collect the Horses to be taken to the Mountains belonging to the Co^y & the Men. At 3 Pm sent the Canoes off & myself with Le Camble. The Seauteaux & Ig[nace] Parizeau (& Lad) went on by Land with 7 Horses – 4 of which are the NW Co^y property & 3 belong to the Men. Put up below the Forks.

Octr 5 [1808] **Wednesday** A very fine day. Early set off & went on a day. Saw no Animals – camped at [sun] set.

Octr 6 [1808] **Thursday** A very fine day. Ab^t an Hour after [sun] rise set off. The Seauteaux killed 2 Red Deer, of which we took the meat of only the best Buck, the other being very poor. Men dried the Goods &c. At [sun] set put up.

Octr 7 [1808] **Friday** A fine day. Set off as usual – held on all day & put up below Baptiste's Brook at [sun] set.

Oct^r [8 1808] **Saturday** A very fine day. Set off – found Brière ab^t 2 points above Baptiste's Brook – had from him 4 split Beaver & 5 d^o Tails – told him to hasten to Boggy Hall for his Necessaries. Held on & put up at [sun] set, 2 points below the old Fort.

Octr 9th [1808] **Sunday** Rain in the Morn^g, then tolerable loud Thunder from NW^d. At 9 Am a very heavy Storm of Wind all day from the NW – threw numbers of Trees down. As usual set off & held

on all day late – camped close above Mr Pangman's marked Tree.
The Seauteaux killed a good Bull, a d° Cow & a poor buck Red Deer.

Octr 10 [1808] **Monday** A cold cloudy windy Day, moderate in the
Evening. As usual about an Hour after [sun] rise set off & held on
all day – at the War Tent brought to the Canoes the Meat of the Cow.
At [sun] set camped.

Octr 11 [1808] **Tuesday** A day of drizzling Rain 'till ab^t Noon when
it changed to Sleet & soon after to Snow. The Canoes held on 'till
at Noon when the Stones became so slippery they could not proceed
with the Line, the only means now to ascend the Current, & they
camped. At day set the Snow was 2 Inches deep & very much lodged
in the Trees & every branch, willow &c – Snow all night.

Octr 12th [1808] **Wednesday** A snowy Morn & afternoon – the
Weather too bad to proceed. People making Socks, Mittens,
Capots &c for Winter clothing as the cold is severe & the Snow about
mid Leg deep. Seauteaux killed a Chevreuil. Snow most of the
Night.

Octr 13 [1808] **Thursday** A cold cloudy day. Ab^t 10 Am, the Men hav^g
cleared the Canoes of Snow &c &c, set off & tracked on – gave them
the Meat of the Chevreuil – they held on 'till past [sun] set & put up
above the Round Plain.

Octr 14 [1808] **Friday** A cold day, with heavy Showers of Snow. The
Canoes held on from 9 Am 'till [sun] set & past, & then put up.

Oct^r [15 1808] **Saturday** A Morn^g of very heavy Snow. The Seauteaux
having killed 6 Red Deer brought the Meat of 2 good Does to the
Canoes, & at Noon the Weather becoming moderate they went off
& held on 'till past [sun] set, when they put up 3 points below Jaco's
Brook. Very cold Night & heavy Showers of Snow all the afternoon
– Snow near Knee deep.

Octr 16 [1808] **Sunday** A fine clear day, but very hard frost in the
Morn^g. At $9\frac{1}{2}$ Am the Canoes went off – pray Heaven send them
safe to the place of meeting beyond the first Mountains. Here at Jaco's
Brook saw the Canoes & we must now part as the River Bank no

longer allows from its rugged steepness any farther Road for Horses.
Accordingly we turned off to the north & rounded the Mountain
on the north side of the River, & put up at [sun] set at the Medicine
Knowl, having passed the Beau Parler's Tent & the War Tent.
Killed 4 Bulls.

Octr 17 [1808] **Monday** A very snowy Day. Set off & went on to the
little Lake where we killed 2 Cows & a young Bull – took as much
of the Meat as the badness of the Country would permit, say 1$\frac{1}{2}$ Cow
– they are small – & went on 'till [sun] set when we put up across
the Brook close on the Banks of the Saskatchewan. At camping, [the
Seauteaux] killed a poor buck Red Deer.

Octr 18 [1808] **Tuesday** A cold windy snowy Day. Early went
& brought the meat of the buck Red Deer to the campment. I then
sent the Seauteaux & the Lad off on Horseback to the Kootanae Plains
with a Letter to Messrs McMillan & McDonald to come down with
all the Horses & their Furniture – as from the state of the Weather & the
very low water in the River it is no ways probable the Canoes can
come even this far, 4 days March short of the usual place of laying up
the Canoes. Went myself below & looked for the Canoes but could
see nothing of them.

Octr 19th [1808] **Wednesday** A very cold but clear Day, much Ice
driving in the River & all the Brooks frozen over. Set off all alone
& passed the Day in looking for the Canoes, but to no purpose
– returned late to the Campment. Ab^t 2 Hours after [sun] set
Messrs McMillan, McDonald [as well as] Bercier, Buché, the Seauteaux
& the Lad arrived each on a light Horse; they have left the others
in a small plain ab^t 4 Miles off – thank Heaven they are well. 4 of the
Co^{ys} Horses which [were] knocked up last June west of the
Mountains & were left there they could not find – this is a hurt to us
as we are scarce of Horses for so long a Journey.

Octr 20th [1808] **Thursday** Mild cloudy weather. Sent off Bercier
& Buché to look after the Horses. All the rest of us took the Meat
& went off down the River over the Flats looking for the Canoes. Went
down to the Cache where we left the Meat, & set off light below
when, thank God, ab^t 1 Mile gone we saw the Canoes – they were all
well, but had suffered much from the extreme bad weather & their

Canoes were become unwieldy Masses of Snow & Ice, which they had thawed away by Fire the best they could. About 3 Pm the Canoes arrived at the Cache – had all the Goods brought above the Bank.

Octr 21st [1808] **Friday** A fine day but very cold. Early sent off 2 Men with Orders to bring down all the Horses. Had the Canoes well laid up for the Winter & a strong long Lodge of Brush Wood & Pine Trees made over them to defend them from the weight of Snow. Early cleared a piece of Ground from the Snow & Branches & made a kind of Lodge of the Canoe Sails where we undid all the Goods & remade them up into proper parcels for the Horses to pass the Mountains – nearly got all finished by Night. In the evening all the Horses arrived.

Octr 22nd [1808] **Saturday** A fine mild day – Wind from the South^d. Early the Men began to arrange the Horses & Goods – assigned to each 2 Men their proportion of the Horses & Goods, & by 10 Am got all ready & set off to cross the Mountains – pray Heaven send us a good Journey. Sent off Le Camble, Clement & Dupré for Fort Augustus, as these Men are not agreed to go any farther. Put up at the farther end of the east Plains above the Lake Campment, about 1H before [sun] set. The Seauteaux killed a Sheep. We have now a Journey of 16 days to go with Horses of which 10 days will be to the Kootanae River, where part of the Goods please Heaven will be embarked in the Canoe there, & the rest must be taken by Horses to the old Kootanae House. We have therefore to pay great attention to our Horses as we [have] none to spare to supply the place of any that may get lame – we must make short campments in order that they may hold out to the end of the Journey. Very little Snow where we are camped.

Octr 23rd [1808] **Sunday** Mild, blowy cloudy weather. Early began to collect the Horses – set off & went on to the Plains east below the Kootanae Plains, where we put up at $\frac{1}{2}$H before [sun] set. This day has been much too long for the Horses – several of them have their Sides swelled from the Kegs & Rolls of Tobacco pressing hard on them.

Octr 24 [1808] **Monday** A cold stormy Day. It was 10 Am before we could collect all the Horses – when ready to start, a Horse escaped us & I left a Man to look after & bring him. We set off & went to the

Kootanae Plains & past them, & put up west of the last point of Rocks on the right. 1 Porcupine. One of the Co^{ys} Horses quite lame – the Horse escaped the Morn^g could not be found.

Octr 25 [1808] **Tuesday** A very stormy Night & cold stormy Day. Early sent Mr [Mc]Millan & a Man for the lost Horse – the others collecting the Horses &c, & we set off. Mr McMillan hav^g found & brought the Horse, went on mostly over the Flats & put up opposite the Forks. The Seauteaux killed a fat he Goat from the inwards of which I got ab^t 12 lbs of grease.

Octr 26 [1808] **Wednesday** A moderate cold cloudy windy day. Early sent the Men for the Meat of the Goat, & the Seauteaux killed a she Goat & her young one which they brought. We set off & went on to the Point above the Red Berry Point on the west Side, & put up at [sun] set. The Seauteaux killed a Bull in the Campment of which we took the whole of the Meat, as we have very little Hopes of getting any more.

Octr 27 [1808] **Thursday** A fine tho' blowy day. 4 Buffalo came close to us but got off. Collected the Horses & set off & went on to the Height of Land. At the entrance of the last Brook, met the Snow again which we have not had since the even^g of the 22nd inst – where we camped it is ab^t 10 Inches deep & every thing looks like Winter. The Horses from such a sudden transition gaze at the ground & at each other as if quite lost & stupefied. The Seauteaux killed 2 Cows with the assistance of Mr McMillan, of which the Men brought ab^t the value of a Cow from the Kootanae Pound. Very cold. A Herd of Cows before us.

Octr 28th [1808] **Friday** A very fine day, but the Night has been so cold that every thing is quite froze – the water in the Kettle solid. The Horses went a long way off in quest of Food – as soon as they could be collected we set off & went down the Brook of the Columbia waters – as usual much bad Road. Came to the Flats where we put up $\frac{1}{2}$H before [sun] set. Very little Snow here for the first spot this day. Cows still going before us – saw 2 of them.

Octr 29th [1808] **Saturday** A fine day. It was late before we could get all the Horses found. At 9$\frac{1}{2}$ Am set off & held on first thro' the large point of Cedars, very bad Road, to the Flats – passed 6 Points, the 7th is the Campment du Prèle – passed it & went on & put up at [sun] set at the point below on the east Side. As usual froze hard.

Octr 30th [1808] **Sunday** A fine day tho' very hard frosty Morn^g. It was 9 Am before we found all the Horses – we then set off & held on over the Flats thro' the Woods, steep Banks &c, very bad Road to the last steep Bank, down which we led the Horses one by one, & got them all safe down. Went on to the Burnt Woods where we put up ½H before [sun] set, the Horses much fatigued with the badness of the Roads &c. Here the Country is much milder, but invariably every where the low Grounds are froze – where we were in the first Hills the weather was always more mild & the ground not froze, & the Herbs are green, some with Berries.

Octr 31st [1808] **Monday** A rainy Morn^g, about 7 Am ceased to a little small Rain. Gathered the Horses & set off & went on over the Flats to the foot of the last Hill – crossed it & along the great savannah to the Kootanae River at 2 Pm. We unloaded the Horses, put a part of the Goods for the Canoe & sent the rest off on Horses under the care of Mr McMillan & 7 Men for the place where the Cache is made, ab^t 3 days hence. Set the Men to gum the Canoe which is in very bad order. The water in the River very, very low.

Novr 1st [1808] **Tuesday** A rainy Night & very rainy day. Early the Men put bars in the Canoe & got Poles &c ready, but could not finish gumming the Canoe – employed myself in writing most of the day. The Rain continued.

Novr 2 [1808] **Wednesday** Rain ceased in the Night, Morn^g cloudy. Men gumming the Canoe but every thing was so wet that they could make little progress. At length ab^t 2½ Pm we got off &went on ab^t half way to the Rapid River & put up at ½ past [sun] set – Canoe so leaky that we were obliged to be constantly bailing the water out with a Dish. At 4 Pm we put ashore & split out 4 Paddles, as the Iroquois have stolen almost all those left in the Summer.

Nov 3 [1808] **Thursday** A cold cloudy Day – Even^g mild & southerly wind. Sent the Men to gather gum as the made Gum is too brittle for the present cold Water – when they had collected enough they began to gum the Canoe anew, covering all the Seams with Linnen, a troublesome & tedious but necessary Work. By 3 Pm got done & set off – got above the Rapid River where we put up at $\frac{3}{4}$H past [sun] set. We are now able to keep the water in the Canoe under with a Sponge.

Novr 4th [1808] Friday A fine day but cold. Early set off & held on all day. At $\frac{1}{2}$ past [sun] set put up above the long Point on the right Side. Killed 6 teal Ducks, very fat – many Geese, but very wild.

Novr 5 [1808] Saturday A snowy Morn^g. At $7\frac{1}{2}$ Am set off – at 8 Am the Snow ceased. Held on all day & at $\frac{3}{4}$ past Sun set put up in a shoal Channel opposite the Gooseberry Rocks, often hauling the Canoe over the Sands, &c. Killed 1 Goose & 1 Duck.

Novr 6 [1808] Sunday A snowy Morn^g, but soon ceased for a little while, then lightly for an Hour. Early set off & held on to the Hoard at 2 Pm – gave the Men to eat who, as well as us, are very hungry. Iroquois met us ab^t 8 Am this Morn^g & came on with us. Began to arrange the Goods, & got as much in order as possible.

Novr 7 [1808] Monday A tolerable fine day. Gumming the Canoes & arranging the Goods for the Lake Indian Country & for the Horses to take to the Kootanae House. At $2\frac{1}{2}$ Pm sent off 2 Iroquois with $2\frac{1}{3}$ Bags of Ball, 2 Rolls of Tob & 1 Keg of Powder – at 3 Pm sent off the large Canoe with Mr Finan McDonald, La Gassé, Methode, Mousseau & Crépeau, & an assortment of Goods as p^r Acc^t Book for the Lake Indian Country – pray Heaven send them well.

Novr 8th [1808] Tuesday A tolerable fine day. Early sent the Men for the Horses, but after much searching could not find 3 of them which we were obliged to leave. At 1 Pm set off with 14 loaded Horses & 13 light d^o – we are but 6 Men to manage all these in a pathless woody hilly Country; it is with the utmost difficulty that we can bring the Horses on. In the evening when time to camp found ourselves on burnt Ground, & in hopes of getting to some unburnt Meadow held on 'till dark, when we with much difficulty collected & unloaded the Horses, whom we were obliged to tie to the Trees all Night to prevent them straggling away. Buché: 1 ss Jacket, 1 Milled Cap.

Novr 9th [1808] **Wednesday** A rainy sleety Morn^g & Day. Early searched for 2 Horses that had broken loose in the night – hav^g found them we set off & were obliged to pass over almost continual fallen Woods without the least path 'till past Noon, when we fell into the Road, where we held on at a good rate & by 1H before [sun] set got to the Red Deer's Horns Meadow, where we put up. Our Horses are very hungry & fatigued, hav^g tasted nothing these 36 Hours. Our best Horse, Gros Ventre, has nearly killed himself by a stick running into the Brisket close to the left fore Leg – he is very much swelled.

Novr 10 [1808] **Thursday** A very snowy Morn^g 'till 10 Am when it ceased & became tolerable fine weather. Early gathered the Horses & set off to the Kootanae House of last year where, thank Heaven, we arrived ab^t 1 Pm.

Along the Saleesh River

20 August – 6 October 1809

Augst 20th [1809] Sunday A cloudy Morn^g & as usual very smoky. At
$4\frac{3}{4}$ Am set off & held on to the Lake, in which we had a fine aft
Wind. Jaco killed a good Doe Red Deer, & the Seauteaux a Sheep & her
young ones, one of a month, the other a year old – the last was ugly
for a lambkin. At 10 Am came to the Portage & by $4\frac{3}{4}$ Pm had crossed
the Portage & embarked – water in McGillivray's River is fine – fell
down to the campment of last spring & put up at $6\frac{1}{2}$ Pm. Thank God
for safety hereto & we hope for his goodness throughout.

Augst [21 1809] Monday A cold blustering Morn^g & Day with frequent
Showers & very cold. At $5\frac{1}{4}$ Am set off & ran down to the Aspin
Point where we put ashore at $7\frac{1}{2}$ Am to gum the Canoe & breakfast.
At 9:50 Am set off & held on 'till $\frac{1}{2}$ Pm when the weather becoming
too bad, we put up close below the fine plains, at the upper end of the
easy Current. Wrote my Journal in part &c &c. Note: $\frac{1}{2}$M or so
below where we started from this Morn^g, the same place where we
camped last year, is a bold Brook of 20 Y^{ds} wide from the Portage
Hand &c &c – say the Portage is full $2\frac{1}{2}$M long, but much less following
close below the Range of Hills.

Augst 22nd [1809] Tuesday A cold cloudy Morng, NE Gale. At $5\frac{1}{4}$ Am
set off & fell down to close above the Torrent Rivulet where we put
ashore at $8\frac{1}{2}$ Am & breakfasted. As we have no Birch Rind to mend the
Canoe with in case of accident, I sent 2 Men to raise a little for that
purpose – which they found & brought but in small Pieces, there being
no good Birch. At noon small Rain came on with calm weather.
At $\frac{1}{2}$ Pm set off & ran down to below the Torrent Rivulet Rapids & put

upon an Isle close below the junction of the Channels – at 2 Pm moderate Rain came on & staid us all day – we also wait for the Horses are with Jaco's things, who are not yet arrived. The ground Raisins ripe & good, but very tart. In the evening at 8 Pm all the Men & Horses arrived with Jaco's Baggage that he left in a Hoard – we crossed over the Men & they camped with us. A rainy Night.

Augst 23rd [1809] **Wednesday** A cloudy Morn^g, moderate day. We were 'till 6$\frac{1}{2}$ Am crossing the Men's Horses & things. We then set off & went down to a Point where we breakfasted – hereto the Peagans have crossed & re-crossed often, & one of their Roads is but a few days ago. Held on & came late to the Stag River which we passed & went on 'till 6 Pm when we put up.

Augst 24th [1809] **Thursday** A tolerable fine day. At 7$\frac{1}{2}$ Am set off having been thus detained with a thick Fog. Held on to the Tobacco River, where we staid near three Hours while two of us went to look how the garden Seeds that were sowed in the Spring had thriven. They returned hav^g found nothing of the Peas, the Turnips only in Leaves, & their very small Roots worm eaten – 5 or 6 grains of Barley that were sowed have thriven well, but not yet ripe. We then went off & drove down, took a little Time to hunt & ab^t 6 Pm put up. Caught 3 small Trout. Where we camp, 2 Canoes of Lake Indians have also camped a few days ago – they are going downwards.

Augst 25th [1809] **Friday** A very fine day. At 6 Am set off & went down to the Poil de Castor where we put up at 10 Am – here we expected to have met the Indians & Boulard, as this is the appointed place. I sent the Seauteaux to examine the Road & to Hunt – in about 2 Hours he returned saying that since the Spring neither Animals nor Men had passed. Jaco then went a hunting but got nothing, & we passed the day arranging our Canoe &c &c.

Augst 26th [1809] **Saturday** A very fine day. At 7 Am set off & went down to the Hangard of last Winter – here we put ashore & I arranged Mr McDonald & 2 Men to go down to the Lake Indians &c to trade Horses. In about an Hour's Time they returned having found 2 Kootanaes: one came with them, [and] there are 5 Men close to us who soon paid a visit. Thank God we now have Hunters &c, but they could kill us nothing here – we traded from them a quantity of dried Berries & ab^t 10 lbs of Meat.

Augst 27th [1809] Sunday A fine day. At 6 Am set off & went down to
the Indians. I left Mr McDonald to hasten them on to pitch downwards, as we stand much in need of their Help. We went on & came
to the Shoal Rapid, went down with the Line, then directly to the
Embarras Rapid – went down with the Line to the lower end, where
we made a Portage of ab^t 200 Y^{ds} – lowered the Canoe down with
the Line & breakfasted. We then went down to the next Rapid, where
we put out the Line, then ran down to the Fall, where we landed
the Goods &c & then made a Trip & hav^g found the Water low
& Current easy, returned & went to the other Side with ab^t 8 Pieces,
where they made a short Portage to the Brook – where we all put up
at 7 Pm. The Kootanaes arrived at 8 Pm, & took 8 Pieces this far
for us. Here are the small red Raisins of the Ground as at Montreal
&c – they are sweet & harmless.

Augst 28th [1809] Monday A very surly Morn^g, with Showers of Rain
& high Wind. At 6 Am began carrying the Canoe then the Goods
with the Kootanae Horses who lent us 6 for this purpose – got all over
& gummed. By 11:50 Am we embarked & ran down to the place
a little above the large Brook on the right below McDonald's Rivulet
& camped at 6$\frac{1}{4}$ Pm – hav^g in this Time waited near 2$\frac{1}{2}$ Hours for
Jaco & Family. The Rapids were all strong but not dangerous with Care
& the Rivulet quite low. Traded ab^t 86 lbs of Berries.

Augst 29th [1809] Tuesday A fine Morn^g & day. At 6 Am set off & went
down the Current – met a Kootanae who gave us much informa-
tion ab^t the others who, it seems, are all scattered ab^t Nelson's
Mountains. At 11$\frac{1}{2}$ Am we arrived at the Great Road of the Flat
Heads & camped as it is here we must procure Horses to take us to the
Flat Head River where we hope, please Heaven, to pass a good
quiet Winter. We pitched our Lodge & Tents – sent a hunt^g, but nothing. Angled Mullets – killed 1 Cormorant & 4 small Ducks – Teals
– & got for Supper ab^t 12 Mullets from the Kootanaes with us – 3 small
Lodges.

Augst 30th [1809] Wednesday A very fine Morn^g & day. Early began
to arrange our Goods for the Horses &c, & examine & dry every
thing so as to have the whole in good order for Trade & Preservation.
Sent Buché to angle Fish – Beaulieu & the Thunder to go to the
Grand River Flat Heads to procure Horses &c &c – got 5 Bales packed

up. Mr McDonald 2 Ducks, & Buché 2 Mullets. 2 Kootanae Men
arrived.

Augst 31st [1809] Thursday A very fine Day. Arranging Goods &c. Set
a Line with 16 Hooks &c below – all the small Fish have left the
small Channels of the Lakes so that we have no dependance – nor will
the Mullets & Trout in the River bite.

Septr 1st [1809] Friday A very fine day. Finished all the arranging of
Goods &c early 'till we can determine what further is to be done
by the arrival of the Indians whom we daily expect. In the evening a
distant Indian & his 2 Wives arrived late at Night with a few Skins
– traded a small Tiger & Crane.

Septr 2nd [1809] Saturday A very fine day. Indians all a hunt^g. 2 dist
Indians arrived & a Lake Indian – they brought nothing.
Obs^d Lat^{de} 48°:42$\frac{3}{4}$′ N Long^{de} 116°:00′ 8″ w.

Septr 3rd [1809] Sunday A very fine day. Traded with the distant
Indians – they preferred Cloth & Iron Works with Tobacco to all
other Things. In the evening 2 Grand River Flat Heads arrived – they
brought a few Berries & ab^t 2 lbs of dried Salmon which they gave us,
& say Beaulieu is ill but will be here with many Flat Heads on Tuesday.

Septr 4 [1809] Monday A very fine day, southerly Gale as yesterday.
The Hunters all arrived, but brought nothing but the Mack of a
Beaver.

Septr 5th [1809] Tuesday A fine day. Ab^t Noon the Flat Heads, 16 Men,
arrived with ab^t 25 Horses – they lent us Lines, with which we tied
our Goods & Lumber & got as much as possible ready for the Morrow
– traded Berries & Fish for 2 ft of Tob & 4 Ro^{ds} of Amm.

Septr 6th [1809] Wednesday A very fine day. Early began arranging,
but the Lake Indians trading a few Skins with us prevented us from
getting ready. The Flat Heads lent us 13 Horses & Bostonan one d^o,
which we loaded & at 9$\frac{1}{4}$ Am – thank Heaven got all [ready] & set
off, & went to the foot of the high Banks S1 5E 3M. At 11$\frac{1}{2}$ Am we had
much Trouble to get up it, the Horses often rolling down with their
Loads. At length by 3 Pm we had got all up, taken a mouthful to eat

& reloaded & set off – we had now tolerable good Road 'till 6 Pm
when we put up, near a small Brook. Our Co may have been s20w 2M
s8w 2M s60E 1M – the Road was good yet narrow, & having many
small Trees to cut away to widen the Road, we did not hold on at a
good pace. Note: from where we started this Morning is 25′ good
walk to our old campment of last year.

Septr 7 [1809] **Thursday** A very fine day. Early brought part of the
Horses, but did not find the others 'till 7 Am. At 7$\frac{1}{2}$ Am set off, Co
s8E 1M, to a Brook + $\frac{1}{2}$M to another Brook. Held on 'till 10$\frac{1}{2}$ Am
s15E 4$\frac{1}{2}$M to a Brook of ab^t 9 y^{ds} wide, but much wider in high
water. Co s18E 6M to recrossing the Brook Co s18E 1M crossed a small
Brook Co s18E 2$\frac{1}{2}$M to recrossing the same Brook then Co s18E
1$\frac{1}{4}$M – put up at 4$\frac{1}{4}$ Pm. Much fine Woods to day of several Kinds of
Fir & Pine & plenty of Cedar.

Septr 8 [1809] **Friday** A fine day, but very cold Night – Ice was formed
– but the Leaves are yet every where very green, except a few on
the Ground, which in places are a little faded. At 7$\frac{1}{4}$ Am set off, Co s20E
$\frac{1}{2}$M to a Brook which we followed s40E$\frac{1}{2}$M then crossed it – it is
15 y^{ds} wide, deep & very easy Current. Co s20E 6M to a Rill of water
which we followed down s40E 1$\frac{1}{2}$M to the Lake. I do not pretend
to take any Courses further, as I hope for a better opportunity. We
went ab^t 1M then met Canoes who embarked ab^t 20 Pieces of
Lumber & Goods. We held on SE^d 4 or 5M & put up at 2$\frac{1}{2}$ Pm, the Wind
blowing too hard for the Canoes to hold on. Killed 2 Geese,
Mr McDonald 1 d^o, & Buché 1 d^o; Beaulieu 1 Crane, & the Flat Heads
3 Ducks.

Septr 9th [1809] **Saturday** A fine day. The Wind moderating, the
Canoes got off & we following, but the Wind rising, the Canoes
were obliged to lighten & reload part of the Horses. We all at length
arrived in safety, thank God, at the mouth of the River (at 2 Pm)
where we camped for the Night. They all smoked – say 54 Flat Heads,
23 Pointed Hearts & 4 Kootanaes – in all ab^t 80 Men. They then
made us a handsome present of dried Salmon & other Fish with Berries
& a Chevreuil &c.

Septr 10 [1809] **Sunday** A very fine day. Early set off with 2 Flat Heads
to look for a place to build a House on – at length found a place

somewhat eligible but labours under the want of good Earth. I returned
& we got all the Goods embarked by the Flat Heads & landed the
whole by 3 Pm, when we set up our Lodge & Tents &c.

Septr 11 [1809] **Monday** A cloudy day with a little Rain. We made a
scaffold for our Provisions & got Birch for Helves which is very
scarce, & helved our Tools &c &c.

Septr 12 [1809] **Tuesday** A rainy Night but very fine day. Began our
Warehouse. The Ground is so very full of small Stones that the
Holes for the Posts &c &c is a long time making – got the Posts
& Needles ready, & threw down a Red Fir of 2 fms round to make
a Canoe for fishing &c. 16 Canoes of Pointed Hearts passed us
& camped with the other Flat Heads.

Septr 13th [1809] **Wednesday** A fine Morning, but at 10 Am a heavy
Gale from sw which soon brought on moderate Rain, which lasted
nearly all Night. Buché & the Chien Foux brought 2 Chevreuil. Cut
& hauled Wood, the Needles, & arranged a Horse Collier which
broke towards evening – we then got Wood for another. Spent much
of the Day in trading with the Indians who brought ab^t 120 or
130 Skins – put out a fire the Indians kindled.

Septr 14th [1809] **Thursday** A blowy Day, but fine – wind SE^{tly}. Set up
the Posts & the Needles & raised the Warehouse ab^t 2$\frac{1}{2}$ ft high.
Made a Horse Collar, which is however too narrow. The Wood is so
very heavy that it requires the force of 4 or 5 Men to lift a single
piece of 10 or 11 feet. Traded ab^t 20 Skins & looked for Wood for a
Horse Collar &c.

Septr 15 [1809] **Friday** A fine day but blowy South. 3 Canoes arrived
last Night & put up at the Island – they made us a present of Berries,
which we paid for. Put the House up the intended height [of] 7 feet.
Indians traded a few things &c & promised to bring all they have
presently – traded a Canoe for fishing &c.

Septr 16 [1809] **Saturday** A tolerable fine day. Put the Beams, Plate
& Roof Trees on the Warehouse, & cut Wood of Birch for Helves
& f[o]r Nails, also Cedar for Net Floats. We arranged & set 2 Nets to
the north^d.

Septr 17 [1809] **Sunday** A fine Morn^g, but very rainy Day. All the Indians arrived with what they have remaining to Trade, ab^t 1$\frac{3}{4}$ Packs & much Berries – we spent the whole day in this Business &c. 6 Mullets & 2 small Trout, thank God.

Septr 18 [1809] **Monday** A rainy Night & Morn^g, & 'till 2 Pm when it ceased. We arranged 3 other Nets & set them, & began cutting the Roofing of Cedar which must be hauled ab^t 400 Y^{ds}, as the Wood ab^t us is too large & too heavy. Traded a Horse for 15 Skins value.

Septr 19th [1809] **Tuesday** A blustering Morn^g, but fine day. Caught 20 Mullets from the Net at the Door, & 4 from the others – the Nets of 4$\frac{1}{2}$ In Mesh are much too large & catch nothing. In the evening set 3 Nets at the Mouths of the Channels of the River, as the Indians say there are plenty there. Traded 3 Horses which now makes 7 for the company. Pointed Hearts to their own Country.

Septr 20 [1809] **Wednesday** A very fine day. Visited our Nets – the small one here caught three small Trout & 8 Mullets, those at the River channels 1 good Trout, 1 small & 2 Mullets – took all the latter up, & set them near hand about us. The Flat Heads broke up their Camp & part pitched away to the south^d.

Septr 21 [1809] **Thursday** A very fine day. Caught 24 small Fish from the 2 small Nets. Working at the small Net – roofed the Magazine and brought Grass for to work in the Mud that the roofing is to be made tight with. Took a walk around the Peninsula on which we are, which took me 4 Hours. In the evening Jaco & Family arrived. Set the large Nets at the Isles.

Septr 22 [1809] **Friday** A very fine day. Caught 15 small Fish in the small Nets, nothing in the others – we find them useless in this Lake. Men making mud Torches for the Roof of the Magazine – & Mousseau & me working at the Nets. Mr McDonald hung the Door & put the Windows of the Magazine in, &c. Much Thunder & Lightning.

Septr 23 [1809] **Saturday** A stormy Night, fine day. Mudding the Covering &c – working at Nets. 15 strange Indians arrived from the west^d; they are quite poor in every thing seemingly – they each made us a small present of dried Trout or Salmon. 13 small Fish from the Nets. Obs^d [sun's] LL 82°:48$\frac{1}{2}$′ Errour 1′:30″ Lat^{de} 48°:12′:14″ N Dec^n 7′:44″ by 116°.

Septr 24 [1809] **Sunday** A rainy Morn^g 'till 10 Am. 2 Green Wood Indians arrived; they made me a present of a Bear Skin, 1 Beaver d° & 5 Rats, with 2 parcels of dried Fish & 2 Mares – for which I shall pay them. A Lad brought 1 Beaver in Meat. Beaulieu, 1 Duck. 7 Mullets.

Septr 25 [1809] **Monday** A fine day. Finished mudding the Roof & got all the Goods &c in the Warehouse, thank Heaven. The lower Indians went away – gave each a bit of Tob & an Awl – showed them how to stretch the different Skins & they promised to be here by the time the Snow whitens the Ground. Rainy Afternoon & Even^g.

Septr 26 [1809] **Tuesday** A blowy Day with cloudy cool weather, in the evening Rain which lasted all Night. Men cutting, hauling & squaring Wood for the upper Floor of the Warehouse. Got ready to set off the Morrow to examine the Country below us.

Septr 27 1809 **Wednesday** A rainy cold Morn^g & blowy cloudy Day. Crossed the Horses & sent those not wanted to the north^d Bay. 2 Fish in the small Net – the other 2 have stood 2 Nights: one of them set parallel to the Beach caught 11 Fish, the other tho' twice its length was set perpendicular to the Beach & caught nothing. At Noon in company with Beaulieu & an Indian Lad, with 4 Horses, I set off to examine the Country below us – that we may if possible change our Route to the Mountain Portage, for the one we now practise is entirely open to the incursions of the Meadow Indians. We set off, but I did not take the Courses as I wish to get first a good Idea of the Lake &c. We took $\frac{3}{4}$ of an H to cross the Isthmus – here we took the 4 Horses. At 1:12 Pm round the Bay, then onward to the green bay & brook where we camped in the beg^g on this month, where we put up at 5:25 Pm. Killed a dwarf Goose – there are many Cranes, dwarf Geese & Ducks, but the Marsh is open so they cannot be approached.

Septr 28th [1809] **Thursday** A cold cloudy Morning, wind northerly. At 6:50 Am set off. Upon taking out my Compass, found by accident the Glass had fallen out & the Needle lost, which I much regret, especially as the weather is cloudy. We held on along the Lake 'till 10½ Am having gone abᵗ 12[M] to the Head of the River, on a jog Trot all the way. The Ground near the Lake is low & often muddy & wet, with high Hills a small distance within – plenty of water Fowl, but no shelter for the Sportsman. For these 5 days past the Leaves have been withering much on the Hills; half of them are already fallen off & those of Willows &c are in the same state – the Poplar, Aspin, Birch, Alder &c are getting part yellow, & a few falling off. At 10½ Am we stopped to breakfast & refresh our Horses ¼M down the River. The River is here abᵗ 350 to 400 Yᵈˢ wide, very easy Current & shoal near the Shore – & it's sides are fine covered with Grass & Woods. At ½ Pm we again set off, soon after the [sun] appearing. I take the Courses to be, from where we started, abᵗ sw 2M s30w 1M s25w 6M s60w 4M s75w 1M n35w 2M mid of Co put up at 5:35 Pm, having trotted along with very little delay. Abᵗ 4½ Pm our Baggage got partly wet by the Horses going into the River & swimming a few Minutes, which wetted all our dried Salmon – we dried it in the evening. At Night cleared & I observᵈ the Merid Altᵈᵉ of Aquilae 100°:26′ Good. Killed 1 dwarf Goose & 3 Partridges – many Swans, Geese, Ducks & Cranes abᵗ the head of the River & all along hereto except the Swans, the River always 350 to 400 Yᵈˢ wide with very easy Current. The woods of Poplar, Aspin, Cedar, different Firs & Fir Pine, with a few White & Red Pines – Plane & Alder & a variety of Shrubs &c – many fine grassy Points & Bays all along the River & the Grass every where quite green, havᵍ sprung up since the water has lowered. Latᵈᵉ 48°:9′:4″ N Decⁿ 8°:22′:8″.

Septʳ 29ᵗʰ [1809] Friday A cold Night & cloudy foggy Mornᵍ. Killed 2 Duck & boiled the inwards. At 8½ Am set off & finished the Course of yesterday, then went West 5M n80w 2M to the Falls which are in 2 Channels separated by an Isle of Rock, on which is the Portage of abᵗ 20 Yᵈˢ, seemingly good – safe. Fished abᵗ 20′ but got nothing. Held on n70w 1M, where at 11¾ Am I stopped to observe Merid Altᵈᵉ [of the sun's] LL 79°:9′ – tolerable good, tho' much flyᵍ misty Clouds. Refreshed our Horses & took a Meal. Rain then coming on, we camped & the Rain soon became tolerable heavy – shaved, wrote off my Journal &c &c. Ther +64° Rained all the evening. Beaulieu, 3 Morgansers. Latᵈᵉ 47°:51′:22″ N Decⁿ 2°:48′:17″ s.

Septr 30 [1809] **Saturday** A rainy Night & cloudy drizzling weather all day. At 7 Am set off & went on down the River, keeping mostly in the Woods which are of fine Red Fir, many Trees ab^t 3 fms round & a chance one a little larger, but the common Size is ab^t 1 to 2 fms round – much gummy white Fir, but very few of the real white Fir – plenty of Fir Pine &c, but no Cedar or Birch – Poplar & Aspin in places along the River. The Ground is very dry & finely hilly, but very much of it level & the high Hills seemingly distant, but we cannot see to any dist^ce on acc^t of the bad weather. This prevents me also knowing the Course, tho' I estimate it at N70W 20M or 18M, having from 7 Am to Noon kept always on a jog Trot except in a few places & the Road has been in general good. At Noon we came to where the River seemingly falls into wide marshy Ground – here we saw the Tents of a few Indians. We went to the woods & made a Fire to refresh our selves & bait our Horses. Our Indian Guide called to them & they crossed [to] him – ab^t an Hour after, 6 Men 2 Women & 3 Boys came to us; the oldest Man according to custom made a Speech & a Present of 2 Cakes of Root Bread, ab^t 12 lbs of Roots & $2\frac{1}{2}$ dried Salmon, with boiled Beaver Meat. I gave them all 6 Inches of Tob [to] smoke, & each Man 2 In. of d^o – to the old Man 4 In, a Steel & 2 Flints, for which they were very thankful. They tell me there is plenty of Beaver all about them, but they cannot work them except with Sticks & Snares, having neither Axe nor Chissel among them; the Spokanes & another Tribe are ill, they say, & cannot do anything. I inquired of the Road before me; they say there is only another Fall to go to the Columbia of which they drew the Chart. This was good news to me, who expected to have heard of ab^t $1\frac{1}{2}$ days' March of Falls & no navigation among them as the Lake Indians had informed me – but they inform me that the Road thereto is very bad for Horses. I requested the loan of a Canoe & one to guide us, to which they readily consented & we are to go the Morrow, please Heaven who I hope will prosper our Voyage. Our Horses will stay here under the Care of the Lad & will be ready for our Return.

Octr 1st [1809] **Sunday** A Night of smart Rain & Morn^g of d^o. We got ready & went down to the water Edge with our Baggage. The Canoe brought us was old & nearly useless – we asked for another, which was lent us, but before we had gummed &c &c it was 9 Am when we set off, with an Indian to conduct us in a small Canoe, hav^g left part of our Baggage. We went down the River 'till $11\frac{1}{2}$ Am, when we put ashore to gum our Canoe which was very leaky & had wet much of our Things – this took us nearly an Hour. At 20′ Pm again embarked & went on, always drizzling Rain; at $1\frac{3}{4}$ Pm it became heavy & we were obliged to put up. The River hitherto is fine & the Current very easy, but as we descend, the width is contracted & the velocity augmented. Very many Fowl, but cannot get a single Shot at them.

Octr 2nd [1809] **Monday** A cloudy Day. At $6\frac{3}{4}$ Am set off & ran down a steady, sometimes a swift Current 'till 9 Am. I asked our Guide if we were near the Falls, but he informed us he had never passed in a Canoe. We found we had no Time to go any great distance & there-fore began our Return, as we shall have barely time to get to McGillivray's River before the Canoes arrive. The [sun] now at times showed itself, by which I take the Courses to be, up the River, S15E 3M + $2\frac{1}{2}$M this last Co easy Current S25E $2\frac{1}{2}$M S25OE $\frac{1}{2}$ N8OE $1\frac{1}{2}$M – 3 Pm passed most of the strong Current S60E $\frac{1}{2}$M S30E $\frac{1}{2}$M South $\frac{1}{2}$M end of Co where we camped last Night – Co S60E 1M SE $\frac{3}{4}$M S25E $\frac{3}{4}$ So 1M – 5 Pm S20W $\frac{1}{4}$ SW $\frac{1}{2}$M S60W 1M – $\frac{1}{2}$ of Co gone put up at $5\frac{1}{2}$ Pm. The [sun] set somewhat clear, by which I think the Courses are as well as can be expected in such cloudy weather. From where we turned ab^t this Morn^g the Co of the River below may be estimated at N2OW 8M to the foot of a Range of broad high woody snowy Mountains, which turns the River to the So^d of them, running ab^t WNW. Since the 26th of Septr much Snow has been always on the top of the Mountains & Hills, even of Hills not above 600 feet high, & the Mountains are tolerably loaded with Snow, as was it the depth of Winter. The woods of the River is mostly Red Fir & well wooded, interspersed with Larch & Fir Pine &c with Poplars & Aspins near the River, but no marks of Beaver, or indeed of any Animals whatever. Killed 3 dwarf Geese & a Teal Duck. The Snow no doubt renders the Country in the Winter very bad for Animals; otherwise there is plenty of Provender.

Octr 3rd [1809] **Tuesday** A rainy Night, cloudy misty Morn^g but no Rain – tolerable fine Weather & saw the [sun] at times. At 6:50 Am set off having gummed the Canoe &c – finished the Co of last Night & went S30W $\frac{1}{2}$M S20W $\frac{1}{2}$M – $7\frac{1}{2}$ Am then the Long Reach. Co by the [sun] S1OW 3M + $1\frac{1}{2}$M end of Co Obs^d Merid Alt^{de} of [sun's] LL 74°:40$\frac{1}{2}$′ – G, but flying Clouds. Co S15W $1\frac{3}{4}$M to the Indian

Camp at 1 Pm. We had set Beaulieu ashore to kill Geese &c, which
made us lose much time. When arrived, we found our Lad had
gone off with one of my Horses to the Green Wood Indians – we were
therefore obliged to wait – at 4 Pm he arrived. We killed 7 Geese
& 2 Teals. The Indians gave us a good Chevreuil & some Salmon, which
thank Heaven makes us Rich. A rainy Night.

Octr 4th [1809] **Wednesday** A night of heavy Rain but very fine day.
Hearing some of the Indians wishing to see me & that would arrive
by Noon, awaited them. At 11 Am, 4 Men arrived; they made me a
present of a Horse & a few Rats – they smoked a few Inches of
Tobacco, all I had left; they seem to be of the Spokane Tribe with one
that is yet more distant. At 1 Pm, having procured a Saddle from
the good old Man, we set off. Our Co is ab^t S15E 2$\frac{1}{2}$M + 2$\frac{1}{2}$M + 2$\frac{1}{2}$M
keeping the Woods as p^r Map – then Co SE 2M passed the Fish
Wier of the Summer, now dry. Co S70E 1M to the River NE $\frac{1}{2}$M
slippery along the water Edge to avoid a Bog in the Woods, then Co
S80E 8M S70E 1M – at 6$\frac{1}{4}$ Pm put up near where we camped for Rain.
I Obs^d Merid Alt^{de}. Fine cloudy evening. Killed 6 dwarf Geese & 1
large Goose, thank Heaven – our Provisions are now 15 Geese,
1 Chevreuil, 1 small Beaver, ab^t 50 lbs of Salmon & as many Roots
&c. By the star Aquilae, the Course we have come for a dist^{ce} passed
is not more than SSE – this must be noticed, & the Obs^{ns} will perhaps correct this, but it must fall entirely on the last 5 Miles – perhaps
on only 2 Miles.

Octr 5th [1809] **Thursday** A fine Morn^g for the Season but had several
small Showers all Night. At 6:50 Am set off & held on to the place
I obs^d, say 1$\frac{1}{4}$M or 1M the Co ab^t S30E, this rounding a Point of the
River – then to the Falls, say 2 Miles. Co is I think ab^t S50E. From
thence at 8 Am we went S70E 4M to the River, then SE 4M – $\frac{3}{4}$M gone
came to the Rivulet of 25 Y^{ds} wide – 3M gone to our Camp^t where
I obs^d Aquilae, then Co S35E 1M – 10 Am. This brought us to the Rock
where we wet our Things, but we avoided it this time by going up
the high Bank. Co to 11 Am is I think ab^t N70E as we frequently see
the [sun] – 4M. Stopped at 11:8 [Am] to refresh our Horses, this
directly opposite to the Skeetshoo Road & River, but perhaps the Co
of this part & from the Lake is best taken on the outgoing. At
50′ Pm set off & held on – at 3:20 Pm came to where we baited on the
outgoing. I [think] the dist^{ce} we have come is ab^t 10 Miles & the

Co ab^t East, especially the latter part of it. We then went thro' a point of Woods & to the wide part of the River, our Co N50E 2$\frac{1}{2}$M – ab^t $\frac{1}{2}$M short of Co we were obliged to put up with heavy Rain at 4$\frac{3}{4}$ Pm, hav^g lost full 20′ after a Chevreuil in the River which escaped us. The Ground is quite soaked with the late & continual Rains. Great Numbers of Cranes mostly all grey, a tolerable number of Swans, plenty of dwarf Geese & a few flocks of Ducks – Teal & Stock – but cannot be approached. Saw the [sun] the greater part of the Afternoon. Killed 1 large Goose. In the 10M Course there are 3 great Points, especially one of Cedar & Maple, which lie ab^t N10E & S10W.

Octr 6th [1809] **Friday** A cloudy misty Morn^g. At 7 Am set off, Co $\frac{1}{2}$M then open out in the Lake. Co to a large Point, the one this side of the Rivulet, is ab^t East 5M, but we have to go round a deep Bay to a Point ab^t N50E 2M then to the other Point S70E 3M then to the House Point about S40E 6M. Having rounded the Bay to the gravel Point we baited at 10:35 Am – from hence the Co to the Point we left is ab^t West 1$\frac{1}{2}$M. Obs^d Merid Alt^{de} of [sun's] LL 72°:32$\frac{1}{2}$′ Good Lat^{de} 48°:16′:55″ N Dec^n 5°:11′:5″ N. At $\frac{1}{2}$ Pm set off & at 3 Pm arrived safe – thank God, we found all well. Mr McDonald had traded ab^t 2 Packs of good Furrs in my Absence, mostly from the Pointed Hearts, of whom there are ab^t 44 Men, several Women & Children here. They have ab^t 110 Horses, & have traded 3 of them with us. Rainy Evening.

Athabaska Pass

29 October 1810 – 26 January 1811

Journey from Boggy Hall on the Saskatchewan to the Athabaska River, 1810

October 29th 1810 Monday A cloudy Morn^g & day, but mild. Early began collecting the Horses: 24 in Number belonging to the NW Company, each loaded with the weight of 180 to 240 lbs of Goods for Trade, Provisions & Necessaries. We in all 24 Men including myself – 2 Men are absent at old White Mud Brook to bring up Dogs & dressed Leather as soon as the River is fast with Ice; 4 Men more are [gone to] old Rocky Mountain House, for Lodges & Provisions &c &c; 2 Men are to hunt, 2 Men to clear the Road & the other 12 Men manage & take care of 24 Horses, each loaded with Goods & other Necessaries for our journey & the Trade – besides Boussé & Du Nord to aid in hunt^g. We have 2 professed Hunters in Bap[tiste] Bruneau & the Yellow Bird; & Thomas an Iroquois for our Guide across the Mountains when we have ascended the Athabaska River, for which place we now bend our Course. At 10 Am we were all ready & set off – pray Heaven to send us a good Journey. We went up along a small Brook which falls into the River close below Boggy Hall. Our Course by the [sun] & guess about West 4M winding, especially at our out set – here we left the Brook, which is ab^t 2 ft wide & hardly any Water. This Course had several Banks to go up & down, but the Road on the whole tolerable for the Country. Woods green Pine & Aspin – latter part burnt Woods. We then turned to the left to

avoid the marshes & went to a Hill of green Woods sw 1M then
over the Hill sw 1M to a Brook, up along which we went, all burnt
Woods N20W 1M or 2M in a wet willow Plain, with several pieces
of boggy Ground. We put up at $2\frac{1}{2}$ Pm – Horses fatigued, as the
Road is bad tho' full as good as could be expected in this part of the
Country. No supper.

October 30th [1810] **Tuesday** A cloudy day with Showers of Snow & an
easterly Gale of Wind, but mild. Bap[tiste] Bruneau & the Yellow
Bird hav^g killed a Cow & a large grisled Bear, & Boussé 1 Cow,
Mousseau, the Hunters & myself went off to bring the Meat to the
Road, which we got done by $11\frac{1}{2}$ Am & waited the Men, who
arrived by 1 Pm. Our Course has been North 3M up along the Brook,
very bad wet boggy Ground with burnt Woods – the Brook ab^t
2 y^{ds} wide diminished to a mere Rill, & we held on up rising Ground
3M to where we camped – the Horses much fatigued with the
badness of the Road. Du Nord & myself spent the afternoon in examining the Country before us, which we found passable.

October 31st [1810] **Wednesday** A cloudy day – at times the [sun] made
a momentary appearance – & warm. Set off with 4 Men to clear
the Road; we came to the Pembina River at 4' past Noon, having
walked from 8 Am. Our Co down a descending, sloping Hill – ab^t
N20W 3M to a small Lake, mostly green Woods N30W 3M N60W 3M
N80W 2M; close to the end of Co fell upon a bold Brook of 55 y^{ds}
wide, up along which we went ab^t $\frac{1}{4}$M then crossed & camped in a
small Plain – good Grass for the Horses. Bap[tiste] killed a Doe
Chevreuil, fat & good, but the Tail is not so large nor so long haired
as those of the Columbias – the other Hunters killed nothing. In the
evening Pichette & Coté arrived from the RM House with Letters
& Provisions from Mr Henry – the Provisions they have left in the care
of Pareil & St Pierre – Mr Henry asks the Horse Le Caille & has
given a large Roan Horse of the NW Co^{ys} to Pichette – which leaves
us 4 Pieces without any Horse to carry them. The Cut tailed Red
Horse for Meat & myself will replace Le Caille – to replace the Roan
Horse I am obliged to buy a stout Red Horse of Brière for 34 Skins
in Goods, part of which he takes the Morrow.

Novr 1st [1810] **Thursday** A fine cloudy day. Wrote a letter to
Mr A. Henry – sent off Pichette, Coté & Bap[tiste] Delcour: the

former takes Mr Henry's Horses to him, & the latter with Pareil & Coté
return with the Provisions &c – sent 5 Horses with them. The
Hunters & Thomas went ahead to search out a Road; in the Even^g
the[y] returned hav^g found a Road, but killed nothing. Arranged
my small Compass.

Novr 2nd [1810] Friday A fine cloudy warm day – clear afternoon. We
set off to clear the Road at 8:20 Am & at Noon arrived at a Brook,
where we camped – some of the People did not arrive 'till 2½ Pm.
Our Co by the Compass ab^t s75w 1¼M – ½M gone crossed the Pembina
River, say 40 Y^ds wide but shoal, full of gravel Rapids with scarcely
1 ft of Water on them. The River seemingly goes to n65e or 70e by the
range of Hills – the rest of the Co up along the River & oblique,
leaving it on our left ab^t ½M; it then comes from s25w 1M, where
a bold Brook falls in from the South^d. Perhaps this large Brook & the
one at our Camp^t comes from the Chain of Lakes to the sw^d of us
at the Cow Knowls. Our Co west 5M to the high Knowl: here is an old
Camp^t & an extensive view of the Country to the So^d which is the
nearest point of the rocky Mountains – from hence the River is ab^t 1½M
on our left, very bad swampy burnt Ground. Held on n70w 2½M
to a Brook of 4 Y^ds wide, across which we camped. Our Hunter killed
nothing. The Road of to day, except a Morass of ab^t 40 Y^ds, tolerable good & open burnt Woods. Obs^d for Long^de 114°:57¼' w
Aquilae for Time & Lat^de 53°:8':3″ n Dec^n 8°:22':17″ n Ther
+16°.

Novr 3rd [1810] Saturday A hard frost last night Ther +1° very fine
day. Sent off D'Eau & Methode for the Pieces that were left, with
which they came in the Even^g. The Hunters nothing. Thomas & La
Fontaine searched out & marked the Road for ab^t 6 or 7M. Obs^d
for Lat^de, Long^de & Time Ther +26° Mean Lat^de 53°:7':57″ n.

Novr 4th [1810] Sunday A cloudy Night & Day Ther +20° did not
thaw any & the Brooks closing with Ice. Sent Bercier & Canada
with a Horse before the Men who are coming behind, to bring
Provisions as the Men have fasted since the Even^g of the 2nd Nov^r.
The Pembina River seems to come from s75w & our Co for the next
Campment seems to be ab^t n65w or 70w at most to a Hill of mixed
Woods. At 11 Pm the Men sent for Meat arrived – they brought 2 Bags
of Provisions, greater part of which we directly distributed among

the Men who, late as it was, made directly a hearty Meal, hav^g tasted nothing but a Dram of Rum these 3 days.

Novr 5 [1810] Monday A snowy cloudy Morn^g, which soon ceased & became fine Weather. The Hunters cannot hunt, as the Ground is too hard for the Animals to mark it with their feet – we wish much for Snow, but the little that falls always directly thaws. Ther + 22° at 7 Am. In the Evening the Men with the Provisions &c arrived – the Horses are very much fatigued.

Novr 6th [1810] Tuesday Ther + 5° Very fine warm day. The Swamps mostly bore up the Horses, but in the afternoon the thaw rendered them impassable to loaded Horses. At 10$\frac{1}{2}$ Am set off & held on N65W 2M to a very small Brook; here at Old Fort Peles we turned off N40W 1$\frac{1}{2}$M N5W 2$\frac{1}{2}$M – here we camped at 3 Pm. North $\frac{1}{3}$M to a small Rill going to the East^d & very swampy beyond – here we turned ab^t. Bap[tiste] informs me that at N5W there is a Brook of 4 Y^{ds} wide going northerly & beyond that a River of 30 to 40 Y^{ds} wide also going northerly – the Brook may be N5W 5M dist & the River N5W 6M dist from us. The Buffalo Dung Lake bears from us N5W [ ]M dist. The Hunters had no success – each 2 Men & Women a double handful of Beat Meat with the side Fats of Buffalo.

Novr 7th [1810] Wednesday Ther + 34°, at noon + 52° Very fine warm cloudy day with light Showers at times. Sent Thomas & La Fontaine to examine the Road before us, as we now turn off the Stone Indian Road we have been so long following. The River of yesterday mentioned falls into the Pembina River somewhere ab^t opposite Boggy Hall. The Buff Dung Lake is supposed to be ab^t North 50 Miles from us.

Novr 8th [1810] Thursday Ther + 28°. At 9$\frac{1}{3}$ Am set off to clear the Road – we returned ab^t 1$\frac{1}{4}$M back, & then turned off about s80w 6M to a Brook, the one I observed on. We crossed it & went s80w $\frac{3}{4}$M to one of its small Branches, on which we camped at 2 Pm. We have had on the whole tolerable good Road, with small pieces of Marsh but not bad. We made a Road ab^t 1M farther to the w^{td} but finding ourselves on the verge of a large Morass, we turned about to the Rill of Water. Our Hunters, still unsuccessful for want of Snow, say that we cannot pass to the West^d & it is by this account uncertain if we can get from where we are, as the Marshes are not froze to any depth sufficient to bear up the Horses.

Novr 9 [1810] **Friday** Ther last Night at -14°, this Morn^g +18° with Shower of light round Snow which hardly whitened the Ground. At 8 ½ Am set off to clear the Road – we held on ab^t North & N30W 1½M latter part extensive Marsh. We were then obliged to turn off at s80W to West, say 6M thro' almost continual Marsh but pretty well froze over – wherever the least green Woods were there the Horses broke through, & with difficulty were extricated. We camped at ½ past Noon along a grassy Swamp. Baptiste went off a hunting & to see how the Land lies before us, as we have had hard work to clear the Road & the appearance of the Country is against us. He returned in the Evening hav^g killed a Bull, thank Heaven.

Novr 10th [1810] **Saturday** Ther +14° Cold snowy cloudy Morn^g & Day, Wind a Gale at NW. At 8 ½ Am we set off & cleared the Road, in doing which we had much trouble from the closeness of the Woods. At 11 Am we came to the Bull, where we camped – ab^t 2 Hours after, the People arrived. Our Co may have been s80W 4M, a morass near end of Co which the Horses passed with Difficulty.

Novr 11th [1810] **Sunday** A cold snowy Day, wind a Gale at NNW. Hunters went off a hunt^g & to see how the Country is before us – Baptiste killed 2 Buck Moose & wounded a Doe; the others got nothing. Ther at 7 Am +12°, at 9 Pm +14°. Snowed all day.

Novr 12 [1810] **Monday** Ther +14° Cloudy snowy Day, Wind WNW. At 8:20 Am set off & held on to the place of the 2 Buck Moose, where we camped at 11:20 Am, & the People about Noon. Our Co may be ab^t s80W 7M, always by the Compass. Took the Meat of the Moose – we this Morn^g finished the Meat of the Bull – Baptiste killed a Bull & the Yellow Bird also a Bull. The latter part of Co we followed a small Rill of Water say 1 foot wide, at the farther end of which we camped. One of the Men, Canada, lost a Horse & all their Things on it.

Novr 13th [1810] **Tuesday** A fine mild cloudy Morn^g, fine afternoon Ther +16°. Sent for the Meat of the 2 Bulls, which was brought – also the Horse &c of yesterday was found & brought. At Noon Obs^d

for Lat^{de} Merid Alt^{des} of [sun's] LL Ther +22° [sun] Cloudy but will serve to correct the Courses Lat^{de} 53°:16':36" N Dec^n 17°:58':22" N. The Yellow Bird killed a good Cow.

Novr 14th [1810] **Wednesday** A very fine clear day Ther +4°. At 8:10 Am set off, cleared the Road which was mostly fine level ground & open Woods 'till 2 Pm, when we arrived at a small Meadow & camp[ed] for the Night – our Co may have been s80w 1M N70W 1M s70w 1M West 2M N80w 5M. We had gone about 3 Miles when we fell upon a bold Brook of 12 to 15 Y^{ds} wide, but at present shallow – since which we have followed all along the Brook to the Campment, cutting off the Points & descending the Current. Mr Henry & Kinville went for the Meat of the Cow.

Novr 15 [1810] **Thursday** Ther +4° A Shower of Snow in the Night, & clear & Snow at times for the Morn^g – fine cloudy Day. One of the NW Horses being lost I was obliged to send for him to the Campment we left – of course we must wait them. Weighed the Meat & found 1400 lbs which I had separated among the Men, each to carry his Share to prevent waste & dispute.

Novr 16th [1810] **Friday** Ther +10° A very snowy day with northerly wind. Finished the rough accounts & expences &c of the Summer & Fall. The snow before was only ab^t 2 In deep but it is now, say, 6 In deep.

Novr 17 [1810] **Saturday** Ther -14° A cold snowy day, Wind northerly & veering round to the west^d. Did not decamp on account of the bad weather. 9 Pm Ther -12°. Finished my rough Accounts with much trouble.

Novr 18 [1810] **Sunday** Ther -32° Very clear day & tho' cold, calm mostly & the cold bearable. At 9:10 Am set off & directly crossed the Brook which we think now sets off ab^t North & NNE. We went West 1$\frac{1}{4}$M to a Rill of Water in a great Morass with burnt Woods every where as usual, then s80w 1M to a Brook of 4 Y^{ds} running into the one we left this Morn^g, somewhere above where we camped. Went up this Brook N80w 2M West $\frac{1}{2}$M always running thro' a Morass – we then crossed it, & held on over a large Morass West or N80w 2M. We then came to a rising Ground, & in order to leave the Morass went off s60w 2M to 2 Pm, when we camped. The People came at 3 Pm & 2 of them at 7 Pm. Killed a Porcupine – the Hunters nothing. Ther -26°. Made Water of Snow.

Novr 19th [1810] Monday Ther -22° A cold but fine clear calm day. At 8$\frac{3}{4}$ Am set off – our Co thro' burnt Woods & Marshes as usual N85W 2M S80W 1$\frac{1}{4}$M we now come on the top of a Knowl from whence we have a fine View of the Country before us. Thomas pointed the Hill where he says there is a little House made by the Hunters &c – it bore s65w. A Part of the Rocky Mountains sse of us may be ab^t 50M from us – they appear low in proportion to those more to the south^d, & show only one range of snow clad Mountains. We have a hill in front of us all green Woods, to the left pt of which we bend our Co s65w ab^t 2$\frac{1}{2}$M – the first 1$\frac{1}{2}$M thro' mossy Wood & Morass, when we came upon a small Rill, down which we went 1M to it's Junction with a Brook of 50 y^{ds} wide where we camped at 1 Pm – the People at 2 Pm. Here are a few Buffalo & Moose, as there have been all along, but they are very thinly scattered – the Country every where appears to be impassable to heavy Animals in Summer. 4 Tents of Stone Indians have been here ab^t 2 Months ago. The Hunters nothing. 9 Pm Ther -30°.

Novr 20th [1810] Tuesday Ther -32° Tho' cold a very fine day & agreeable walking. At 8:40 Am set off – we held on down the Brook, Co ab^t N65W 3$\frac{1}{4}$M then ab^t N35W 5M or 6M to 2 Pm. In this last Co we crossed & re-crossed the Brook often as the burnt Woods & Ground form a bad Country, but being all bound in frost is passable everywhere. The Brook is now ab^t 6 y^{ds} wide but shoal – marks of a few Beaver Houses &c. Baptiste killed a young Buck Red Deer, half of which I took & the rest to the Men. Ther -24°.

Novr 21st [1810] Wednesday Ther -13° Thin Clouds, at Noon [Ther] −18° fine clear day & Calm. Obs^d for Lat^{de} Long^{de} & Time Lat^{de} 53°:25′:52″ N Long^{de} 116°:55′:50″ w. Staid all day to rest the Horses &c. Hunters found a few Animals, but killed nothing.

Novr 22nd [1810] Thursday A very fine day Ther +15°. At 8$\frac{1}{2}$ Am set off & walked smartly 'till $\frac{1}{2}$ past Noon when we stopped on the Banks of a Branch of the Athabaska River – the People came at 1 Pm to 2 Pm. Our Co was N80w 5M (set the Hill from whence we have

come first s67w) s80w 1M n65w 2M – here we crossed the Brook now
16 y^{ds} wide for the last time, it going off ab^t n20w. We held on
s65w 2M to the place of our campment, a small Plain of good Grass.
The River is ab^t 30 y^{ds} wide & is fast froze over with Snow on it
like the small Brooks; the Banks in the obtuse Angles of the River seem
to be of Grind Stone – of this I shall examine the Morrow. Ther
+25°. Hunters nothing.

Novr 23rd [1810] **Friday** A very fine day Ther +25° a thin haze which
hid the Moon. Baptiste & the other Hunters off a hunt^g. Stepped
the River: 66 Steps in the narrowest part, & ab^t 80 in the widest. There
are no Flats here – the Current moderately strong, 2 ft deep ab^t
10 y^{ds} from the Shore, 6 ft in the middle & the Rocks, Banks &c much
the same as those ab^t the RM House – much rude & fine Grind
Stone. McLeod's River: from the top of the Bank I hope to see the Place
of it's Sortie in the Mountains. Working my Observations. The
Hunters found nothing. Boussé slept out. Ther +2°.

Novr 24 [1810] **Saturday** Ther 0° A fine cloudy day, wind westerly.
At 8¼ Am set off, Co s15e ½M – we then crossed the River; after
going a little on it, we went up the Banks & turned to the w^{td}. Ab^t 1M
a fine Knowl presented itself – I went to the top of it & from it our
Camp^t bore ne 1½M or 1¼M. The Sortie of this, McLeod's River, bears
s10e ab^t 40 or 50M dist – it runs seemingly to the north^d. High
Lands appear: those on the left we suppose to be the Banks of the main
Athabaska River, the lower pt of which bears n10w ab^t 40M dist,
to the right of which there is an opening where I suppose McLeod's
River joins the Athabaska River, & to the right of which a ridge of
high Land runs – at the foot of which McLeod's River is supposed to
run for ab^t 10 or 15M. A Fork of this River is thought to come from
due South in the Mountains. The Place where the Ho is said to be by
Thomas bears s30w ab^t 60M. The green Hill of Nov 19th bears ab^t
n65e. We now held on s70w ½M – we then descended the River Banks
& held on ab^t 1M – we then went over a low Pt & in ab^t 1½M came
to the River, on which we went again ab^t 1¼M – in the mid of which
a Brook of ab^t 5 y^{ds} wide falls in on the left. We then held on over
Land – hav^g at times much fallen Wood & at times small Plains to the
River, which we again left & held on thro' thick Woods to a
Channel of the River – we went on this Channel to the River, which
has now the Air of the Kisiskatchewan near the RM House. We

went on ab^t $\frac{1}{2}$M when we came to a place where Boussé had killed a Bull,
highly acceptable to us as we have nothing to eat. At Noon camped
– the People at 1 Pm & 1$\frac{1}{2}$ Pm arrived. We came hard on & the course
from the Knowl may be ab^t s30w 9M. There are no Animals of any
Kind, tho' the Woods have never been burnt, except a few Porcupines
of which the Yellow Bird killed 3. Ab^t wnw of our Camp^t this
Morn^g there is a large Lake of ab^t 15M long, in a wnw direction & ab^t
6M from our Camp of this Morn^g. Ther 0°.

Novr 25th [1810] **Sunday** Ther − 5° A clear Morn^g, fine cloudy day.
At 8 Am set off & held on 'till $\frac{1}{2}$ Pm sharp walking, when we camped
in a small Meadow on the River Banks. Our Co may have been ab^t
South or s10w 6M, great part of which on the Ice of the River,
which has all the appearance of the Kisiskatchewan below the rm Ho
– the same Stone, kind of Herbs &c. We then turned to the west^d.
It may be remarked that the River winds very much, but it's windings
lie in general from s80w to sse – a Brook of 2 y^{ds} x from the right
near end of Co. There are several Isles & Flats [in] the River, & where
entirely free the Channel is not above 25 to 30 y^{ds} wide & has seemingly lost much of it's water, tho' I cannot tell how, as I have seen no
Brooks of any consequence fall into it. We held on & cut a large
Point; we then came on the River, within ab^t 1$\frac{1}{2}$M of our campment
– here I ascended a high Bank, from whence I had a good view of
the River above & below us, & it is from this the first Co is taken – otherwise I had supposed the Co to be ab^t sw. The latter part may be
Co s75w 5 or 6M, & the Co for the major part of the Morrow will be
the same. Ab^t 1M short of end of Co a large Brook by Flats comes
in from the right, nearly parallel to the River. Where Thomas shewed
us the sortie of the River, the Ho &c is seemingly wrong, & he
appears to me to be much mistaken. Ther + 4°.

Novr 26 [1810] **Monday** Ther + 12° A fine clear day – the Night was
cloudy. At 8$\frac{1}{4}$ Am set off & held on across Land – $\frac{1}{2}$M gone a kind
of a Brook, say 4 y^{ds} wide – $\frac{1}{3}$M farther a small Channel of the River
came into it. Held on over Flats &c for a small space of the Brook
to a Swamp & Pond of a Beaver Ho, & mostly this Kind of Ground 'till
9$\frac{3}{4}$ Am when we again saw the River & went a little way on it – then
cut a large Point on the left & crossed the River to the right, keeping
close along the River where we again came on it, & crossed
& smoked at 11 Am. The whole Co may be s80w 6M – the River is

tolerable straight & has Isles, but not spread out except in Places; a small Brook also from the right falls into the first Brook at $1\frac{1}{2}$M from Campment. We then went on about full s80w always on the Flats of the River 'till $\frac{1}{4}$ Pm when we camped, say s80w $2\frac{1}{4}$M – here there appears to be low Land going to the foot of a high Hill stretching oblique across our Road ab^t 10M dist. The River we have hitherto followed comes from due South by the Compass (as all the Courses are). Thomas describes our Route of the Morrow to be first ab^t West & then turning round to sw, to fall on the Athabaska River & avoid the Hill. We have now much burnt Woods in Places, but also much green Woods. Obs^d for Lat^{de} Ther $+22°$ Lat^{de} $53°:30':39''$ N Dec^n $20°:58':4''$ Ex^d Watch moved $20'$ forw^d.

Novr 27 [1810] **Tuesday** Ther $+16°$ A snowy Morn^g, Wind NNE to NW – a Gale. At 8:20 Am set off & walked 'till $40'$ Pm when we camped along the little River. Hearing 4 Shots fired close to us, it proved [to be] Baptiste who had killed a Bull – tho' alone, very good – sent 3 Men for Meat. The People arrived at near 2 Pm. Our Co has been ab^t N60W 1M to a Lake of $\frac{1}{3}$M wide – went on thro' a Morass N50W $\frac{1}{2}$M to another lake – Co on it s80w $\frac{3}{4}$M; we then held on over a Morass N60W $\frac{1}{2}$M to a long Lake – Co on it NW 2M. From this a Lake or Brook of 4 Y^{ds} wide but very little Water went out. We followed down the Current going from N70W to N40W 4M where we camped on the Banks of the Brook, which winds much – from hence, on climbing a Tree, we see the Athabaska River. Ther -16°.

Novr 28th [1810] **Wednesday** Ther -18°. Baptiste & Family arrived as also Brière &c. Boussé & the Seauteaux a hunt^g – the latter returned – nothing. Obs^d Merid Alt^{de} of [sun's] LL Ther $+22°$ Lat^{de} $53°:37':54''$ N Dec^n $21°:19':29''$ N.

Novr 29th [1810] **Thursday** A fine day, wind Ther 0°. At 9 Am set off, at $10\frac{1}{2}$ Am, thank Heaven, came on the Athabaska River – Co has been ab^t WNW 3M mostly along the Brook, which for the last $\frac{3}{4}$ Mile we left on our right, going off more northerly. The Athabaska River below bears N53E $1\frac{1}{2}$M turning to the north^d – Co up the River s53w $\frac{3}{4}$M, 11:20 Am Co $+$ $\frac{2}{3}$M end of Co on Islet on the right s22w $\frac{2}{3}$M mid of Co a Brook of ab^t 20 Y^{ds} wide falls in from the right in 2 Channels, the upper the largest. Co s55w $\frac{2}{3}$M here we went mostly thro' the Woods, on acc^t of open Water – end of Co on Isl^d of $\frac{1}{3}$M large

& rather on the right. Co sw $\frac{3}{4}$M first part Wood, the latter along
an open Rapid. Mounted a high Bank, saw the Co of the River s12w
$1\frac{1}{4}$M end of Co an Isl^d on the right $+$ $\frac{1}{4}$M an Islet on the right s12w
$1\frac{1}{4}$M. The Co finishes with an Isl^d of $\frac{3}{4}$M long & an Islet at its head, both
on the left, opposite which & at end of Co we camped at 2:20 Pm
– the People all arrived by 3 Pm. Always high Lands & Thick woods
of Pine & Cypress, mostly the former, but green. The Country
appears very rude & marshy, mossy & very uneven – no appearance
of either Animals or Plains. Ther $+12°$. Boussé & Du Nord did not
join us.

Novr 30th [1810] **Friday** Ther $+12°$ A fine cloudy Morn^g but clear
day. At $8\frac{1}{2}$ Am set off, Co s20e$\frac{3}{4}$M $-\frac{1}{3}$M gone an Isl^d nearly square,
but indented rather on the right, close above another rather long to the
end of Co. The lower part of the Isles divides the River into
3 Channels s10w $\frac{1}{2}$M to the [right], s17w$\frac{3}{4}$ Co s54w $\frac{1}{2}$M s26w $\frac{1}{2}$M
end of Co on Isl^d begins Co s15w $\frac{1}{2}$M – Isl^d all this Co – the [right]
Co se $\frac{1}{4}$M as all Co Isl^d on the right, very narrow & end close on the
[left]; we x the end of it. Co s5w $1\frac{1}{4}$M Co sw$\frac{2}{3}$M s18w $1\frac{1}{4}$M
passed a Brook of 2 y^{ds} wide on the [left] when $\frac{1}{4}$M gone along
open rapid. The Co goes to the [right] Pt but we follow along shore.
$\frac{1}{4}$M gone also a large Isl^d begins, which forces the River at its lower end
to run nearly perpend to the Co – the Isl^d is ab^t $\frac{3}{4}$M long. There is then
in a Line, but rather on the [right] 2 other Isl^{ds} to the end of Co.
Then Co s20w $\frac{2}{3}$M to right, then Co s32w$\frac{1}{2}$M $+$ $\frac{1}{2}$M. Co to the
[left] pt s60w $1\frac{1}{2}$M, beg^g of Co an Isle on the [left]. We now went
over Land, over a high Bank of burnt Woods, which are all consumed
to a mere trifle – the Ground is quite barren. We descended on the
River, where we have come by the River s10w 1M – Isles in the end of
the other Co & beg^g of this d^o. We crossed the River: Co up it s48e
$\frac{3}{4}$M – in this Co 3 Islands at nearly equal distances, rather on the [right],
especially the last. We now went thro' the woods, up a Bank & into
a willow Plain, where the Seauteaux killed a Bull, thank Heaven, which
we took the whole of it of which we stood much in need. This
delayed us a little, but it was $2\frac{1}{3}$ Pm when we stopped at the Bull,
walking always a steady pace & not much delayed. Our Co thro' the
Willow Plain from where we left the River is s19w 1M s44w $\frac{1}{5}$M s68w
$\frac{1}{5}$M – we camped at $3\frac{1}{4}$ Pm. One of the Horses knocked up & was left
but his load was brought. The River runs round a large Point & is
dist from our Road thro' the Willow Plain & from the camp^t ab^t 1M

– our Road over the barren Pt from end of s19w 1M – Co appears
to have been ab^t s32w, & from the end of the last Co on the River, it
appears to come from s18w 2 or 3M, then winds from the west^d
for ab^t 3M then appears to come from the South^d. The Place of its Sortie
is ab^t s18w from the nearest Mountains. In the Evening Boussé arrived,
hav^g killed a Cow. Obs^d for Long^{de} & Time Ther + 16° wrong star.

Decr 1st [1810] **Saturday** Ther + 21° A fine cloudy day, wind sw^{tly}.
Sent Men for the Meat of the Cow. Hunters off a hunt^g – rested
the Horses & brought the one that was knocked up yesterday, but he
is unfit for farther Service; considering the very bad slippery Road
that we have had for these 2 days past on the River Ice, we may be
thankful that several of the Horses are not killed – they have
received many & severe Falls. Ther + 21°. Obs^d for Long^{de}, Lat^{de}
& Time Ther + 22°.

December 2nd [1810] Sunday Ther + 12° A fine clear Morn^g but
cloudy afternoon. At 8 Am set off & held on over the Willow Plain
s22w 1M – we then went up the Bank on the [right] for 1M thro' Woods
& a Morass & Pond to a Brook of 4 Y^{ds} x. We then went 1$\frac{1}{4}$M farther
to another Brook of 10 Y^{ds} x in 2 Channels. The whole Co may be
ab^t s20w 2$\frac{1}{4}$M – on the Morass & Pond we went ab^t s45w, making
a turn on the right. 9$\frac{3}{4}$ Am we stopped a few Minutes – we then set
off & held on over 2 Plains & intermediate Woods. At the end of the
second Plain we camped at $\frac{1}{2}$ Pm, having walked very smartly – the
People did not arrive 'till 2$\frac{1}{4}$ Pm. The Co may be ab^t s20w 6M going
to the right in Curves. The River may be ab^t $\frac{1}{3}$M from us on the [left].
The Country is very scantily furnished with Grass – scarce any –
but is almost wholly covered with Chikarsepuk &c with a very short
Juniper & Pines, scrubby & branched to the very Root, full of sand
&c – on the high Bank, there is much Cypress &c, but no other Woods
save small birch Willows. Baptiste & Thomas did not join us & we
guided ourselves by their Tracks; Du Nord slept out. Ther + 33°.
Boussé killed 1 Cow & 1 Bull.

Decr 3rd [1810] **Monday** Ther + 34° A very stormy day from South^d.
The Sand brought by the Wind from the Trees & Flats covered the
Snow & was very distressing to us, filling our Eyes & Mouth. At 7$\frac{3}{4}$ Am
set off & held on ab^t s18w 2$\frac{1}{2}$M to a Brook of 3 Y^{ds} x; we then held on
ab^t s15w 2M thro' Woods to the Banks of the River – here the Co

ab^t s20w $\frac{1}{2}$M parallel with the River on the bare Banks. The River
below goes off ab^t N20E IM & turns to the north^d. Our Co s48w I$\frac{1}{2}$M
to the entrance of the Flats which appear like a Lake – here we met
the Hunters &c &c who waited me. The Iroquois insisted on our going
to an old Hut on the Lake – we went ab^t s30w I$\frac{1}{2}$M & camped there
at $\frac{1}{2}$ Pm in a most disagreeable Place: the Hut is small & very dirty, besides being without Windows, badly situated & no Grass for the
Horses. Ther +34°.

Decr 4th [1810] **Tuesday** Ther +36° A stormy Night from South
& Morn^g but soon moderated & fine, with fly^g Clouds. At 8 Am set
off & went on ab^t N8w 5M, thro' mostly clear fine Aspins & camped
near a small Fountain of Water among Pines & Aspins, with plenty
of Grass for the Horses. Sent Men for the Meat of the Cow & Bull –
they slept out. Ther +20°. Cloudy night.

Dec 5 [1810] **Wednesday** Ther -2° A fine day, mostly clear. Men began
a Hut for the Goods, & for a Meat Shed. Sent 3 Men
& 5 Horses with Bapt[iste Bruneau] & the Yellow Bird who go a hunt^g
to the north^d. B[aptiste] D'Eau & Thomas with myself looking for
Birch for Sleds & Snow Shoes – found I hope sufficient, but the Rind
is bad for Canoes, & the Birch is itself very scarce. Men with Meat
arrived – part of it was rather spoilt. Ther -4°. Obs^d for Long^{de} & Time.

Dec 6th [1810] **Thursday** Ther +12° A fine Cloudy Day 'till Noon,
then partly clear. Obs^d for Lat^{de} Merid Alt^{des} of [sun's] LL Ther
+18° Lat^{de} 53°:23':27" N Dec^n 22°:30':50° N. Working at the Sheds
for Meat & the Goods.

Decr 7th [1810] **Friday** Ther +21° A fine but very cloudy Day. Men
finished the Shed for the Goods. Sent off Boussé, B. D'Eau
& Battoche to the upper part of the River to examine the Country & kill
what Animals they can & lay them well up. Methode, Villiard
& Thomas with myself split out & squared Wood for 7 pair of round
Snow Shoes. Ther +21°.

Decr 8th [1810] **Saturday** Ther +17° Very heavy fall of Snow which
lasted 'till 3 Pm. Could do nothing for the bad Weather. In the
Evening the Hunters arrived with the Meat of I$\frac{1}{2}$ good Cows.
Ther -2°.

Dec[r] 9th [1810] **Sunday** A tolerable fine day but very cold & the Trees covered with Snow Ther +9°, 9 Pm Ther -9° Cloudy Night.

Dec[r] 10th [1810] **Monday** Ther +20°. A fine mild but cloudy Day. La Fontaine & L'Amoureux for the Meat of a Bull. Splitting Wood for Sleds & making Shoes &c. Ther +9°.

Dec[r] 11th [1810] **Tuesday** Ther +6° A fine day. Sent off the Hunters, 4 Men & 6 Horses for Meat. Splitting out wood for Sleds, Snow Shoes &c, & squaring it. 9 Pm Ther +11°.

Decr 12th [1810] **Wednesday** Ther +11° A tolerable mild fine day, but always more or less cloudy – but rarely any wind. Coté & La Course with half of a large Bull, enormous in height, full 6 feet when standing on the Ground, & fat. Writing Letters [ ] Boussé, B. D'Eau & Battoche arrived – they have seen very few Animals & have killed only a Bull.

Decr 13th [1810] **Thursday** Ther +11° A cloudy snowy Day. Sent off Coté & Pareil for Meat, the rest of the Bull. Writing Letters. Getting ready Woods for Sleds &c. Ther -6° Wind NW[tly].

Decr 14th [1810] **Friday** Ther -28° A clear sharp Morn[g], fine day. Sent off Boussé to guide La Fontaine, Mousseau, B. Delcour, Desjarlaix, La Course & Canada for the RM Ho, for Pemmican & the Goods left there, with Letters &c. Coté arrived with the rest of the Meat of the Bull. Began turning Snow Shoes &c. 9 Pm Ther -16°.

Decr 15 [1810] **Saturday** A very cold day Ther -30°. Men for Snow Shoe wood – working at Sleds &c. 9 Pm Ther -26°.

Decr 16th [1810] **Sunday** Ther -22° A cold cloudy day. The Hunters with the Men for Meat came in the Evening with the Meat of a Cow & a Bull. Ther -9°.

Dec[r] 17th [1810] **Monday** Ther -11° A day of NE wind & constant Snow, which is now increased to near Knee deep. Hunters drinking – Men at work – myself for snow shoes &c. Ther -28° Clear.

Dec[r] 18 [1810] **Tuesday** Ther -36° A fine clear Morn[g], 9 Pm Ther

-16° a very cold day. Hunters killed 1 Red Deer of 1 year old & a Fawn. Working as usual.

Decr 19th [1810] **Wednesday** Ther -18° A moderate fine day. Began netting Snow shoes &c &c. 9 Pm Ther -18°.

Decr 20th [1810] **Thursday** 7 Am Ther -20° A fine day. Enabled to write Letters &c. 9 Pm Ther -12°.

Decr 21st [1810] **Friday** 7 Am Ther -18° A fine day. Worked at our preparations for the Journey. Ther at 9 Pm -16°.

Decr 22nd [1810] **Saturday** 7 Am, Ther -25° A cold but fine day. Baptiste, the Yellow Bird & 2 Men with 5 Horses off to hunt. 9 Pm Ther -17°.

Decr 23rd [1810] **Sunday** Ther -18° A fine but cold day, wind blowing from NNE. Battoche & Pareil with part of the Meat of the Bull killed by Boussé. 9 Pm Ther -32°.

Decr 24 [1810] **Monday** 7 Am Ther -32°, 9 Pm Ther -22° Snowy day in the Morn^g, the rest cold as usual. Packing up &c, for our Voyage.

Decr 25 [1810] **Tuesday** Christmas Day. 7 Am Ther -30°, 9 Pm Ther -22° Cold hazy day.

Decr 26 [1810] **Wednesday** 7 Am Ther -34°, 9 Pm Ther -24°. Working hard at our arrangements for the voyage. The Ther rises at Noon no higher than -20°, & has been so these several days past.

Decr 27 [1810] **Thursday** 7 Am Ther -30° A cold hazy day, wind as usual NE 9 Pm Ther -32° – always very cold weather. We are packing up Goods & making all the little arrangements possible for our intended Journey. The Women & Iroquois cutting Line & netting Snow Shoes &c &c, but the Line for the Snow Shoes is very bad, from the awkwardness of the Women.

Decr 28th [1810] **Friday** 7 Am Ther -32°, 9 Pm Ther -35°. Baptiste & Man arrived with the Meat of a Bull & a Sheep. We finished our packing up & hope to set off the morrow Morning.

Decr 29th [1810] **Saturday** 7 Am Ther -31°, 9 Pm -28°. Gave the Men their Loads for the Sleds – each Sled that has 2 Dogs, B. D'Eau, Coté, Francois, & L'Amoureux have 120 lbs of Goods & Necessaries for the Journey, & Vallade, Battoche, Pareil & Du Nord each 1 Dog & Sled have 70 lbs per Sled. 4 Horses loaded with Meat, hav^g 208 lbs of Pemmican, 35 lbs of Grease & 60 lbs of Flour, also accompany us to ease the Dogs, under the care of Villiard & Vaudette – Thomas the Iroquois for Guide & Baptiste for Hunter. By 9 Am we were ready with the Dogs, but the Horses were late. With much Trouble the Dogs got to the Hut by 2½ Pm, but the Horses did not arrive till [sun] set so that we camped for the Night in the Hut. Our Co as before mentioned in the Journey hereto. Horses had fresh Meat, a Load.

Decr 30th [1810] **Sunday** 7 Am Ther -33° A fine clear Morn^g. Men breakfasted before setting off, which took place at 9¾ Am, held on over the Flats S18E 5M. The River then contracts, but is still full of small Flats & Isles Co S50W 2½M West ½M to an Isle where we put up at 1¾ Pm. We found the Meat that B. Le Tendre & Pareil had been sent to secure not only all destroyed by the Animals, but the very scaffold thrown down, so very carefully had they done this Business. We had only fresh Meat for Supper – & seeing fresh Buffalo Tracks we put up, as our Hunter was behind. Very cold blowy cloudy Afternoon.

Decr 31st [1810] **Monday** 7 Am Ther -25° A Gale NE with cloudy Weather. Baptiste went off a hunt^g & the Men breakfasted on the rest of the fresh Meat – in ab^t an Hour's time Bapt[iste] returned hav^g killed a good Cow, thank Heaven. At 10¼ Am we set off – soon came to the Cow, which we took on the Horses & held on, say S35W by the [sun] 6M. We camped at 4 Pm, the Dogs knocked up. Baptiste killed 2 Sheep. 1M gone of Co a bold Cut & River from SE; when ab^t 5M in the Defile there appears a Brook to come from SSW & one from the East^d – bad Road on the Points but the Snow is not deep, & the Dogs are very fat. 9 Pm Ther -24°.

Jan^{ry} 1st 1811 **Tuesday** A fine day 7 Am Ther -24°. Sent Men for the 2 Sheep killed by Baptiste. Finding our Dogs unable to move on at a common walk with the present Loads, I had a Hoard made & reduced them to each Sled with 2 Dogs to ab^t 80 lbs, & each Sled with only 1 Dog to 50 lbs each, except Vallade's Sled which has 70 lbs – this Business the Men did in 5 Hours. I never saw such an indolent Sett of Men, & in this Time they took care to cook & eat 2 large Kettles of Meat. At length at 1 Pm we got off – our Co s45 or 50w by the [sun] 5M – walked well on over a kind of a Lake, at the lower end of which a bold River from the NE^d comes in, described yesterday as parting in 2 Brooks. We fell on the Lake ab^t 1M full above where the River goes out – we then held on ab^t s15w by the [sun] 2M to 4¼ Pm when we camped, hav^g all along walked smartly. Bap[tiste] killed a good Sheep & 2 good young Bulls. 9 Pm Ther -22°.

Jan^{ry} 2nd [1811] **Wednesday** A very blowy Morn^g & Day with light Snow from NE 7 Am Ther -20°, 9 Pm -12°. Sent for the Meat of the 2 Bulls & made a Hoard – they did not bring the Meat 'till 2 Pm. Here we staid all Day, as I intended waiting the 2 Men who are behind; we split up a good part of the Meat, all the fleshy parts, to dry it & render it more portable for our voyage – my Men did not forget to destroy all the Marrow Bones, as if they were as many Wolves.

Jan^{ry} 3rd [1811] **Thursday** A tolerable fine day 7 Am Ther -19°, 9 Pm Ther -22°. Baptiste the Hunter & Villiard returned with 2 Horses & 3 Loads of Meat. Sent Caudette to meet & bring on the Men who are behind – thank Heaven they arrived at 2 Pm. We then made the final arrangements of the Goods & Dogs & lessened the Trains to 8, as 2 of the Dogs are very little worth & are much beat by the Men.

Jan^{ry} 4th [1811] **Friday** 7 Am Ther -26°, 9 Pm -22° A fine day. As usual the Morning spent in eating Meat. Put the Meat & Goods which we could not take with us in Hoard & shut it up, & by 11 Am set off with 8 Sleds loaded & 3 Horses d° with Provisions, having 208 lbs of Pemmican, 35 lbs of Grease, 60 lbs of Flour & 80 lbs of half dried Meat & a heavy Horse Load of fresh Meat. Co by the Compass s42w 7M to the Brook from the sbE^d, where the Hunters formerly made a Hut for the Winter – the Brook is ab^t 20 Y^{ds} wide, but shoal. Our Co then s2E 4M where we put up at 4:10 Pm hav^g gone pretty well for the Time – indeed most of our Road of today has been over Ice lately froze. The River is full of gravel Shoals, but rarely more than 500 Y^{ds} wide & the Channel 150 Y^{ds} d°. The Country from our entrance into the Mountains hereto has been tolerable good for such northerly mountainous Lands: there are very many low rocky Hills, with plenty of wild Sheep but saw no Goats, & the many Defiles in the Mountains & Brooks with the Isl^{ds} &c afford room

& rude pasturage for a few Buffalo, Red Deer & a chance Moose. The
Woods are always low branchy Pines almost unfit for any Thing,
& when on fire throw the live Coals out every moment, so as to burn
Holes in every thing we have that will burn – even the Aspin has
this Fault. No Juniper, a little Poplar & many Willows & Alder.
Opposite us at end of Co there is a bold Defile from whence comes
the main Channel: up this River is the Canoe Road to pass to the Canoe
River on the west Side the Mountains, & so down to the Kootanae
River. It is also by this Stream that is opposite us that the large Animal
so much spoken of as haunting about here was seen & supposed
to be the Mammoth. The Horses must also pass by this Branch, the
real Athabaska River, to carry the Goods to the Canoe River.
Latter part of the Day much Cypress.

Jan^{ry} 5 [1811] **Saturday** 7 Am Ther -28° A very fine day. As usual the
Men made a good Kettle of Meat to eat. At 9¾ Am set off & held
on S50E 9M – 1M gone the large River that comes in from the West^d,
the Road for the Canoes & Horses in the Summer. Held on ab^t ½M,
when we turned a bold rocky Point on the left & went ab^t 1½M along
Rapids – this Branch is ab^t 40 to 50 Y^{ds} wide & not deep, say 2½ feet
at a mean. Our Road was bad among large Stones, close to the water
Edge – we were obliged to have our Sleds always on our Hands to
prevent them sliding into the River. The Horses cut the Point within
& the Men with them said the Road was very bad from thick
Woods. We then came to where the River spreads out in Islets & Shoals,
& the Channel seemingly is ab^t 100 Y^{ds} wide, tho' the Stream is in
my opinion not above ½ of this. At 3¾ Pm put up among Aspin Woods
– much of this wood all along the River & at times small Aspins in
the Morning. The Mountains bear a strong resemblance to those along
the Kootanae River, & have few or no Sheep, tho' Tracks of a very
few Red Deer & Buffalo, with Moose – in places much Snow, tho' there
are other places that have but little. 9 Pm Ther -22°.

Jan^{ry} 6th [1811] **Sunday** 7 Am Ther -30° A fine tho' very cold day,
wind NE^{tly} with misty Snow. Having well filled their Bellies the
Men set off at 9 Am & held on S24W 10½M & put up at 4 Pm. The River
for to day has been ab^t 30 Y^{ds} wide, windings mostly on the right
Side, very few Isl^{ds} & mostly always in one Channel. The River
& Country has a rude barren appearance & seemingly no Grass for

large Animals – where we put up there are a few small Ponds & Marshes that bear long Grass. Here a Herd of Buffalo had been lately feeding; [the hunters] wounded a Bull but very slightly. Here we must leave the Horses, as the Road further is unfit for them & there is no food. 9 Pm Ther -28°.

Jan^ry 7th [1811] **Monday** Ther -20°. Sent off Thomas our Guide with Battoche & Vaudette to beat the Road, while we should follow after the best we could, as the Dogs ma[y] be said to swim in the fresh beat Road made by the Snow Shoes – the Snow is getting ab^t 2 feet deep. They got off at 9 Am, for as usual a good breakfast before setting out. L'Amoureux undertook, for the sake of 2 Horses to be given him on the other Side the Mountains, to haul 130 lbs of Provisions to the Hut on the Kootanae River. This made us short of a Sled – we made one for a single Dog, & set off at 50' Pm, having hung up the Horse Bags &c to be retaken by Vaudette & Thomas on their return. Our Co ab^t s24w 3м by the Compass – end of Co passed a Brook from wbN. We held on up a Rivulet which is insensibly losing it's Water & Size, ab^t South ½м & put up at 3¾ Pm – this last Co has been up a Stream shut in by Rocks & full of large Stones & seemingly unnavigable. I saw the Track of a large Animal – has 4 large Toes, ab^t 3 or 4 In long & a small Nail at the end of each; the Ball of his Foot sank ab^t 3 In deeper than his Toes; the hinder part of his Foot did not mark well. The whole is ab^t 14 In long by 8 In wide & very much resembles a large Bear's Track – it was on the Rivulet in ab^t 6 In Snow. A fine day & we went well on, & until this last Co many Tracks of Animals, mostly Moose. 9 Pm Ther -4°.

Jan^ry 8th [1811] **Tuesday** Ther +4° A fine day, partly Cloudy & partly Clear, wind se in the Evening, & Night a Gale. At 7¾ Am set off, Co s40e 4м then we entered a small Brook, but still seemingly the main Stream of the Waters we have lately followed up, but they have dwindled away imperceptibly to a mere small Brook – cut a small Point, very bad with Willows &c. Our Co for the rest of the day s22w 5м – mid of Co up another Point, but not so bad as the last. Camped at 4¼ Pm – we lost an Hour in mending a Sled, otherwise kept on continually. No Animals. Much Ice left in the Mountains & they are ab^t 1м ascender – but not above 2000 ft high, & the highest not exceeding 3000 ft. Broke my Snow Shoes. Du Nord beat a Dog senseless – & the Sled we made got broke & was with the Dog thrown aside. 9 Pm Ther +22°.

Jan^{ry} 9th [1811] Wednesday Ther +32° A SE Wind with heavy Snow all day. At 7$\frac{3}{4}$ Am set off up the Brook ab^t 1$\frac{1}{2}$M to a Portage on the left – took half Load. We then came on the Brook & held on 2$\frac{1}{2}$M to where we found the Men we had sent ahead camped – they waited us as the Weather was too bad, & here we camped at 2$\frac{1}{2}$ Pm. Very bad hauling: the Sleds I may say stuck to the Snow, which is here ab^t 7 ft deep, but the Snow Shoes ab^t 3 In in it, the Snow is so compact. The Trees are Pines – much mountain white Pine, & are all sizeable. The Snow thaws & drops on us from the heat of the Fire & mildness of the Weather. Here the Men finished the last of their dried Meat – they have eat at the rate of ab^t 8 lbs per day of pure Meat.

Jan^{ry} 10 [1811] Thursday Ther +16° A very snowy Day & South^{ly} Gale. At 8 Am set off – having held on ab^t 1M, we left half load, from the wetness of the Snow, the Road otherwise being good. Du Nord threw his Load aside, saying he would not haul it any more altho' he has only 80 lbs to 2 good Dogs. We then went 1M to the height of Land, where we descended ab^t 1$\frac{1}{4}$M & camped at 3$\frac{1}{2}$ Pm. Very bad hauling all day, as the Snow from the mildness of the weather is wet – we camped on the Snow, it being too deep to be cleared away. Fine Evening. Our Co s25w. I ordered Du Nord to return for his bad behaviour, but accusing himself I permitted him to continue, altho' in my opinion he is a poor spiritless wretch.

Jan^{ry} 11th [1811] Friday A very bad Night & cold snowy stormy Morn^g. At 8 Am set off & held on down the Brook ab^t 2M – we then left the Valley of the Brook & ascended a Bank with much Trouble, & directly for 2 Hours began a great descent on the west Side, when we came to a Brook down which we went ab^t 3M full, & came on the Flats of the junction of the 2 Brooks – we went ab^t $\frac{1}{4}$M & camped at 3$\frac{1}{4}$ Pm. Thomas killed 2 Buck Moose, for which he has 16 Skins value – thank Heaven for this supply. In the last 36 Hours the Men have eat 56 lbs of Pemmican, more than $\frac{1}{4}$ of our whole Stock; they are a set of the most improvident, thoughtless Men I ever saw. I shared the Men our Supper, at which they were discontented tho' they are sure of plenty the Morrow.

Jan^ry 12th [1811] **Saturday** A snowy Morn^g & Day. Early sent off Men
for the Meat of the Moose which they brought by Noon – we fed
the Dogs, & Thomas & Vallade split up all the fleshy parts to dry & take
with us. The Men rested themselves & fed heartily on the Bones &c.
As my Situation does not permit me to write to the Partners &c on
Paper, I wrote them & Mr Henry on Boards, to be copied by
Mr W[illia]m Henry & forwarded. The Course of yesterday I take to
be ab^t S10W 2M S20W 2M SE 3M S7W $\frac{1}{4}$M to where we are camped.
Ther + 10°.

Jan^ry 13th [1811] **Sunday** Ther + 14° A very snowy Morn^g & Day. By
daylight the Men set off to bring the half Load they left a little East^d
of the Height of Land – Du Nord to hunt – Thomas & Vaudette return
with Letters. Du Nord hav^g been ab^t 2 Hours absent returned,
& finding fault that no Meat was ready, was answered by Francois they
did not expect him so soon. What, said he, do you take me for a
Horse to go for so long without eating – such is this famous FDP Man.
Our Co for the Morrow is S7W. We dried Meat; in the Evening
those that went for the Goods returned, with every thing but 5 lbs of
Ball which the Wolverenes had carried off; it was in a leather Bag,
& some of the Men's things were also destroyed.

Jan^ry 14th [1811] **Monday** A snowy day & very mild Weather. Hung
up a Bottle & a Brick of Soap & at 8 Am set off, but the Dogs from
the mild weather could not haul their Loads. I therefore cleared the
Sleds of every thing that was not absolutely necessary & had it hung
up, hoping to be able to send Iroquois or my Men for it when in a fit
place – the Weight in all ab^t 1$\frac{1}{2}$ piece: My Tent, 25 lbs of Flour,
11$\frac{1}{2}$ lbs of Rice, 1 Belt, 2 Shirts, 2 fms of Strouds, 1 Leather Skin
&c &c. This took 3 Hours. We then held on over good level Road,
but wet with Water & soft Snow, 'till 4$\frac{1}{2}$ Pm when we camped on the
Rivulet Ice. Co S7W 3$\frac{1}{2}$M S35E 1M – the last Co in the Rivulet of
20 Y^ds wide; all the rest is wide Flats. The Courage of part of my Men
(those from FDP) is sinking fast. They see nothing in its proper
Colour – the soft Weather is a thing, it seems, they never felt before.
The Snow, now reduced to 3 & 3$\frac{1}{2}$ feet is beyond all thought, yet
they talk of 6 & 7 feet Snow at Montreal, but that was in Canada, where
there are a great many People. I told them it was no matter the
Snow was 20 ft deep, provided we went well over it, & had they been

with me last Spring they would have carried Packs & Canoes over much deeper – but when Men arrive in a strange Country, fear gathers on them from every Object.

Jan^{ry} 15th [1811] **Tuesday** A fine day, thank Heaven. At 7 Am set off & held on s35E 2M, the Rivulet is quite narrow & full of large Stones – for the last Mile very bad Road & sometimes dangerous Road; the Rivulet then spreads out on very extensive Flats. Co s25w 4½M we now see the Mountains on the other Side the Kootanae River – I set the Co s80w, making a Curve on the left. We went ab^t 5M & stopped at 2¾ Pm, but it was 5 Pm before the last of the Men arrived. As Du Nord went before, we took all his Provisions on Vallade's & Coté's Sleds, & he arrived before the others, but had not the heart to do anything. We camped on the Snow, as it is 3½ ft deep. Saw 4 Moose but did not go after them as we are loaded enough already. The Road was very good but [we] often got wet in passing the Channels of the River.

Jan^{ry} 16th [1811] **Wednesday** A very heavy fall of Snow all Night & Day with mild soft Weather. Made a Campment in which I lost a large Dish, a Spoon & Fork, being buried in the Snow. Sent Du Nord & B. D'Eau to see what kind of Country was before us – they went about 3M & returned, hav^g seen the open Ground of the Kootanae River. Vallade a hunt^g, but the Weather was too bad – dropping much on our Campment.

Jan^{ry} 17th [1811] **Thursday** Ther +30° A snowy Night & Morn^g, but ceased a little in the Day. At 9½ Am set off, hav^g had much to thaw & dry. Sent Du Nord a hunt^g as the Moose cannot move in the great depth of Snow every where. We held on 'till ¾ Pm thro' deep Snow & Water for ab^t 1½M then a chain of Rapids & Falls of Water, shut closely in by large Rocks & Stones 1M. For most of this the Men took half load – Vallade & me held on with all our Loads – we went ½M farther of good Road & camped on the Ice, but to do this cleared ab^t 3 ft of Snow away. Our Co has been s80E 1½M s60w 1½M. Ther +34° & early smart Rain.

Jan^{ry} 18th [1811] **Friday** A night of moderate Rain Ther +35°. The Dogs eat much of our Provisions. Early Du Nord came to us hav^g

killed 2 Buck Moose, for which thank Heaven. We dried ourselves a
little & set off & went ab^t 1M & camped in a Point of Cypress within
a short Mile of the Kootanae River. Part of the Men went off directly
for the Moose Meat, which they brought at 3$\frac{1}{2}$ Pm – Vallade split
most of it in order to dry & render it more portable. Made a Campment
– snow 2$\frac{1}{2}$ ft deep. The day mostly fine but the Snow is like Water.
9 Pm Ther +34°.

Jan^{ry} 19th [1811] **Saturday** A very rainy Night Ther +36° wind
always South^{ly}. The Snow has diminished much & is like Water to
the bottom – all the Trees are cleared of their enormous Loads of Snow.
Rained all day – the Snow sank 6 In.

Jan^{ry} 20th [1811] **Sunday** Ther +36° A very rainy Night & Morn^g.
At 9 Am the wind changed to NW with a Tempest of Wind & Rain
for 2 Hours, then moderated to mild & a steady Gale – the Afternoon
fine & Clear 9 Pm Ther +24° freezing. Lat^{de} 52°:8′:35″ N Dec^n
17°:18′:17″ N.

Jan^{ry} 21st [1811] **Monday** Ther -12° & Clear. At 7 Am set off with ab^t
150 lbs of dried Meat, 90 lbs of Pemmican & 25 lbs of Flour for our
Provisions. We rounded a Point going down the Current to the
Kootanae River – here, the River being open, we went across a
Point of open Woods & fell on the River, which tho' open has fine
Beaches. The Snow every where bore us up without Snow Shoes.
At 9 Am we were obliged to cross a short rocky Point of 300 Y^{ds} – we
then went ab^t 2M to along a sloping Beach of hard Snow, which
obliged the Men to haul with a Line at the tail of the Sleds up the Bank,
to prevent the Sleds sliding in the River which is every where open,
deep, with strong Current & many Rapids. Here we were obliged to
go up a high Pt of Land with 2 high Steep Banks, which took us a
long Time tho' not above 700 Y^{ds} in all. Here Francois broke his Sled,
which with the bad Road kept us 'till 1$\frac{1}{2}$ Pm. We then went ab^t $\frac{3}{4}$M
thro' partly good, partly very bad Woods & then down a steep Bank
to the River Side – here the very sloping steep Beaches made it
exceedingly tiresome & sometimes dangerous to the Men to keep the
Sleds from sliding into the River, & often took 2 Men to a Sled. At
5 Pm we camped, only Pareil, B. D'Eau & Du Nord in company – the
others camped ab^t $\frac{1}{2}$M behind us. The last hour has been employed

in passing a rocky Point, which obliged us to go up a steep Bank & then along steep high Beaches of hard Snow. Camped on the Snow. Our Co has been ab^t East 3$\frac{1}{2}$M.

Jan^{ry} 22nd [1811] **Tuesday** A fine day. At 9 Am the Men arrived. Two of our Sleds being much damaged we repaired them, which held us 'till 1 Pm. We then set off & held on ab^t 2M to a steep Bank of ab^t 10 Y^{ds} high with a bit of Woods – this tho' not 40 Y^{ds} held my dispirited Men 2$\frac{1}{2}$ Hours. Pareil made 4 Trips helping them. The [sun] being set we camped in a good low Point of fine Wood. I went to see how the Country was.

Jan^{ry} 23rd [1811] **Wednesday** A snowy Morn^g & strong east wind. At 8 Am set off & held on for ab^t 1M tolerable good to a bold Brook, then ab^t 1$\frac{1}{2}$M winding with at times steep snowy Banks, to a fine large low Point of Woods. Many large Cedars close beyond a steep Rock, not passable without imminent Danger even to a light Man – but the Water at its foot is calm & may be easily ferried by a Raft. Hav^g seen this & the Weather very bad, I returned into the Point & waited the Men, who arrived ab^t Noon & we camped, when I told them the Road before us, & the Means to pass it. Du Nord with the FDP men, having long been dispirited & useless as old Women, told me he would return, & as I was heartily tired of such worthless fellows & but poorly equipped for such a long Journey as still remained before me, & the Season so far advanced, I determined to re-turn to the Junction of the Rivers Flat Heart & Canoe River with the Kootanae River, & there wait for more Goods, Provisions &c, & build Canoes for the Journey. Very mild Weather.

Jan^{ry} 24th [1811] **Thursday** A day of very mild light snowy Weather. At 11$\frac{1}{2}$ Am got the Goods in a Hoard – we sat down at every $\frac{1}{2}$M, so very low & dispirited are the FDP Men. By 3$\frac{1}{4}$ Pm got back to our Campment of the 22nd Inst, where we put up for the Night.

Jan^{ry} 25th [1811] **Friday** A very mild snowy Morn^g, fine day. At 8 Am set off, & like yesterday the Men sat down every $\frac{1}{2}$M. My Montreal Men (Pareil & Coté) would come much faster on with B. D'Eau, but the others are lagging behind & scolding them for going so fast in saying they are fairly knocked up. The Bank of 2$\frac{1}{2}$ Hours now took

us only a few Minutes; we passed our Camp^t of the 21st Inst & held
on over the Pt of Woods, which we descended & camped at 3 Pm on
the Snow, ab^t 1$\frac{1}{2}$M below the Point. Part of the Things in the Hoard
are 3 fine Capots, 4 d^o Shirts, 12 lbs of Beads, Garden Seeds, 8 groce
of Rings, 3 Rolls of Ribbon, 6 groce of Bells, 3 Jockey Caps,
4 Cotton Shirts, 1 p^r of Cloth Trowsers DT, 3 doz Glasses, 6 Bott[les]
of Turlington, 1 Roll of Gart^g, 2 Bott[les] of Peppermint, 6 Worms,
6 Steels.

Jan^{ry} 26th [1811] **Saturday** A very mild light snowy Morn^g, fine Day.
At 8$\frac{1}{4}$ Am set off, passed the last Rock – very steep Bank – then
onwards to the Flat Heart Brook at 10$\frac{1}{2}$ Am. Here Du Nord, Bap[tiste]
Le Tendre & Bap[tiste] D'Eau deserted, Francois returned ill,
& Pareil & Coté I sent with Letters to Mr Henry & to bring more Goods.
Vallade & L'Amoureux stay here with me. I sat down on my Sled
& wrote Letters on Boards to Mr W[illia]m Henry & to the Partners,
then gave ab^t 45 lbs of Pemmican to the Men for their Provisions
– they went off. I looked out a campment to which we removed all our
things, & we camped for the Night – 3$\frac{1}{4}$ feet of Snow. We have ab^t
35 lbs of Pemmican, 25 lbs of Flour & a little of the other Provisions,
& trust in the Mercy of Kind Providence to preserve us & find us
Food. My design is, by remaining here, to oblige the Men to come here
also, & however Panic struck some of the others may be, by seeing
I think myself safe & well here to encourage them to think the same
also, & at the same time to search out Materials for Canoes, a shed
for the Goods & ourselves, & Provisions. Please Heaven to bless us.
Ther +24°.

The Lower Columbia

3 – 21 July 1811

Voyage to the Mouth of the Columbia by the Grace of God 1811 by
D. Thompson & 7 Men on the part of the NW Company

July 3ʳᵈ [1811] Wednesday After arranging several small affairs, we
in number 8 Men with 2 Simpoil Indians set off on a voyage down
the Columbia River, to explore this River, in order to open out a
Passage for the Interiour Trade with the Pacific Ocean. My Men
are Michel Bourdeaux, Pierre Pareil, Jos[eph] Coté, Michel Boulard,
Francois Gregoire, with Charles & Ignace, 2 Iroquois – with a small
assortment of Goods to buy in Provisions &c. Our Co down the River
from the Ilthkoyape Falls at $6\frac{1}{2}$ Am, Co [49 courses] the Spokane
River falls in on the left abᵗ 60 Yᵈˢ wide [15 courses] high Rocks on the
right & for several Cos passed; high Rocks on the left as by lofty
steps in perpend descent s70w $\frac{3}{4}$M N85w $1\frac{1}{4}$M a strong Rapid. Carried
full half of this the major part of the Cargo, run the Canoe with
the rest close on the left. From 3:5′ Pm to 4:5′ Pm, s85w 1M N80w
$1\frac{1}{2}$M turned & went up a Brook from the right to the camp of the
Simpoil Indians North $\frac{1}{2}$M & put ashore at $4\frac{3}{4}$ Pm, but finding the place
dirty, we went abᵗ $\frac{1}{4}$M farther to a good campment. The Courses
are not so correct as I could wish – the strength of the Current caused
many Eddies & small whirlpools, which generally bore the Canoe
from side to side so that the Compass was always vibrating – I hope
by the mercy of Heaven to take them much better on my return.
The country always wears a pleasing romantic View; the early part of
the day Hills, Vallies &c with partly wooded thinly & partly

Meadow, the latter most prominent from ab^t 11 Am to the Simpoil Camp. The River presented much steep Rock, often in step like Stairs of 20 to 30 ft perpend of black greyish Rock, reddened in places. The Current of the River is every where strong, with a few Rapids, but the water is exceeding high – when it lowers, I make no doubt but Canoes can very well make their way up it.

On our Arrival at the Simpoil Camp, we pitched our Tents. No one approached us 'till we sent for them to come & smoke – the Chief then made a speech & they (the Men) all followed him in File, & sat down round the Tent, bringing a Present of halfdried salmon with ab^t ½ Bushel of various Roots & Berries for food. The Chief again made a speech in a rude singing loud smart Tone – smoking with 4 Pipes – went on 'till all the Tobacco I had given for this purpose was done. During the last Pipes being smoked, one of the Simpoil Indians who had come with me related in a low voice all the News he had heard & seen, which the Chief in his Speech Tone told again to his People. At the end of every 3 or 4 Sentences then he made a Stop, which was answered by all the People calling in a loud drawling Voice – Oy. The Smoking being done & the news being all told, I then told the Chief what I had to say, of my Voyage to the Sea &c &c – each 6 or 7 Sentences I also made a Stop, which the Chief in his relation to his People punctually followed, & they also regularly answered as before. I took notice that good & bad News, Life & Death were always pronounced in the same Manner & that the answer was also the same. A few Pipes more were now lighted & they were told this was enough for the present – they gave a long thankful Oy, & went away. A few Minutes after a Man came asking permission for the Women to come & see us & make us a small Present; to this we consented, provided they brought us no Eetoowoy, as we found those roots to bring on the Cholic. They came, accompanied by all the Men, & altogether formed a circle round us – the Women placing themselves directly opposite us, half of them being on the right & left of a Man painted as if for War, with Black & Red & his head highly ornamented with Feathers – the rest of the Men extended from us to the Women on either hand. The Men brought their presents & placed them before me, which consisted wholly of the bitter, the white & Eetoowoy Roots, with a few Arrow Wood Berries. The Women had all painted themselves & tho' there were a few tolerable faces among them, yet from the paint &c not one could be pronounced bearable. The Men are all of a mid Size – well made, moderately muscular, well Combed

& of a tolerable good Mien. The Women, though, were all of rather small stature, clean made, & none of them seemed to labor under any bodily defect.

Having smoked a few pipes we said, the Visit is long enough; this was received as usual with a thoughtful Oy & they went away. As the Chief was going, my Men wished to see them dance – I told the Chief, who was highly pleased with the request. He instantly made a short Speech to them, & all of them young & old, Men, Women & Children began a Dance, to the sound of their own Voices only, having no Instruments of any kind whatever. The Song was a mild simple Music, the cadence measured, but the figure of the dance quite wild & irregular. On one side stood all the old People of both sexes – these formed groups of 4 to 10 who danced in time, hardly stirring out of the same spot; all the young & active formed a large group on the other Side, men women & children mixed, dancing first up as far as the line of old People extended, then turning round & dancing down to the same extent, each of this large group touching each other with closeness – this continued ab^t 8 Minutes, when the Song being finished, each Person sat directly down on the Ground, where on the Spot he happened to be when the Song was done. The Chief made a Speech of ab^t 1 or 2 Minutes long; as soon as this was ended the Song directly began, & each Person starting up fell to dancing the same figure as before. They observed no order in their places, but mingled as chance brought them together – we remarked a young active woman, who always danced out of the Crowd & kept a line close along us, & always left the others far behind – this [was] noticed by the Chief, who at length called her to order, & either to dance with the others or to take a Partner: she chose both, but still kept close to us, with her partner leading up the Dance. Having danced twice this way, the Chief told them to dance a third time, that we might be preserved in the strong Rapids we had to run down on our way to the Sea. This they seemingly performed with great good will. Having danced ab^t an Hour, they finished – we retired much sooner as the dust of their feet often fairly obscured the Dancers, tho' we stood only ab^t 4 feet from them, as they danced on a piece of dusty ground, in the open Air.

Their Huts are of slight Poles tied together, covered with Mats of slight rushes – a sufficient defence in this season. They were considered altogether as moderately cleanly tho' very poorly clothed,

especially the Men, as Animals are very scarce & they are too
poorly armed to be able to obtain any spoil of worth from the Chase.
They had a good Weir on the Brook of ab^t 15 Y^{ds} but only small
Salmon come up it, some very poor, others tolerable good. Cloudy Night.

July 4 [1811] Thursday A fine day. The Indians brought us 5 poor
Salmon – paid them. We staid inquiring of the State of the Country
&c ab^t us 'till near Noon, when I tried to get an Obs^n by the natural
Horizon, as my Watch is little worth to take one by 2 Alt^{des}, the
River presenting a tolerable Horizon of ab^t $\frac{2}{3}$ or $\frac{3}{4}$ of a Sea Mile dist –
the Rock on which I was obliged to stand to overlook the Willows
was ab^t 40 ft high. [sun's] Merid Alt^{de}, but I think the [sun] was past
the Merid. We then set off – Co to the River So $\frac{1}{3}$M, Co down the
Columbia [46 courses] we then went down the rest of it to another
strong Rapid on the right, the left good, it's Co s72w $\frac{3}{4}$M. We put
the Goods ashore & carried them ab^t 200 Y^{ds}, very bad with wet ground
& branches to an embarras of Wood. The Canoe was run down
hereto, but in doing this they run too close to a drift Tree on a Rock,
which tore part of the upper lath away, & struck Ignace out of the
Stem of the Canoe – altho' he had never swum in his Life he swam to
keep himself above the Waves, 'till they turned the Canoe round
& took him up. We then looked out for a better campment, as the place
was only rude Stones, but found none, the Banks coming down
steep to the River – put up at 7 Pm, hav^g lost ab^t 1 Hour in gathering
Wood to day, & looking for a campment, visiting of the Rapids
&c. I bled Ignace.
    All this day the Current has been very strong, with many Rapids
& Whirlpools, the first part the Land always fine, tho' high & many
fine prospects – latterly the Country tho' still meadow showed much
Rock & the few last Cos much isolated Rocks & large stones near
the water Edge & the Banks steep, of loose earth & Stones – dangerous,
as the least thing loosens them & they roll with impetuosity to the
River; there are no Woods but a chance Tree now & then, of straggling
Fir. The which may be said to be a vast low Mountain of Meadow
showing much Rock irrigated into Vallies, that come down to the River
– the bold Lands of the Mountain forming, as it were, so many
Promontories that drive the River now to the South^d, now to the
North^d & West^d, but always confining it within a very deep narrow
Channel, whose Waters thus contracted dash from Side to Side with

the violence of the Current, as the Water is very high, having lowered only ab^t 18 In as yet, or 2 ft yet, from the Trees brought down, say ab^t 3 Years ago. The Water must then have been full 10 ft higher than now, if not more. We split out Wood for 4 Paddles, as we have already broke 2. Killed 1 old & 1 young Goose.

July 5th [1811] Friday A rainy Morn^g. Hav^g made 2 Paddles, at 6$\frac{1}{4}$ Am we set off & went s50w $\frac{3}{4}$M s80w 1M run part of the 1st Co & carried the Goods on Horses, but by the Indians the rest of it – & part of the 2nd Co being all very strong Rapid & full of high waves & whirl-pools. Here we were met by a Chief & ab^t 60 Men with their Women & Children, who made us a Present of 5 Horses, 5 good roasted Salmon, ab^t a Bushel of Arrow Wood Berries & ab^t 2 Bushels of Bitter, White &c Roots – some of them I had never seen before. We declined the Eetoowoy, also 4 small dried fat Animals which I take to be the Marmot. Heavy Rain came on & we were obliged to send off the Indians, having paid them for the Present they brought us with 3 ft of Tobacco, 10 com & 4 Stone Rings, 18 Hawks Bells, 1 fm of Beads, 1$\frac{1}{2}$ fms of Gart^g, 4 papers of Paint, 4 Awls & 6 Buttons. Ab^t 2$\frac{1}{2}$ Pm the Indians returned singing us a Song of a mild Air – the Women had welcomed us with one also. Having smoked a few Pipes [we] discussed of the Country, which they described as a hilly Meadow with very few Trees of Fir from hence to the Occhenawga River. Of course there can be no Beaver; they have Bears & Rats, with a few Sheep & black-tailed Deer; Horses they have many & the Country appears good for them. We discussed of the River & People below us, after which they offered to dance for our good voyage & preservation to the Sea & back again, & that they might see us as well every way as at present.

We accepted their offer – they all both Men, Women & Children formed a Line in an Ellipsis; they danced with the [sun] in a mingled Manner. An old Man who did not dance set the Song & the others danced as it were as a Person running, but passing over a very small space of Ground, their Arms also keeping Time tho' hardly stirring from their Sides. Some few danced apart, but these were all old Women & seemed to dance much better than the others. Having danced 3 Setts, each beginning with a Speech from the Chief above, and ending with a kind of prayer for our safety, all turning their faces up the River & quickly lifting their hands high & striking the Palms together then letting them fall quickly, & bringing them to the same

action 'till the kind of Prayer was done, which lasted ab^t $1\frac{1}{2}$ Minute
or 2'. The Men are slightly ornamented with Shells &c but the Women
are more profusely, especially ab^t their Hair, & their Faces daubed
with Paint – some few of them have copper Ornaments hanging either
to their girdle or to the upper part of their Petticoat. The Women
appeared of all Sizes but none corpulent, none handsome but one
young woman. The Men tho' many quite ordinary, yet several
were well looking Men & almost all well made, tho' not one lusty. We
gave them a few pipes to smoke & they went to their Tents, having
brought us a good Salmon for which I paid them ab^t 6 In of Tob – with
what I have given & they have smoked, the amount is 5 ft of it.
[They tell me they now intend] to pull up a little of their own Tobacco
for smoking, tho' not yet ripe. The Land to us appears to be very
poor – white grey Earth of a kind of impalpable Powder mixed with
Stones, bearing Grass in Tufts of a round hard kind & two kinds
of strong scented Shrubs whose white Leaves proceed directly out from
the Stem or the Branch.

I may here remark that all their Dances are a kind of religious Prayer
for some end – they in their Dances never assume a gay joyous
countenance, but always a serious turn with often a trait of enthusiasm
– the step is also most always the semblance of running, as if People
pursuing & being pursued. Tho' a dialect of the Saleesh, my Interpreters
could not understand them, tho' they understood him – my
Simpoil, who spoke both dialects, here was of service, then at the end
of each Sentence of the Chief's Speech always called Oy, if possible
louder than the Simpoils. The Women were tolerable well clothed, the
Men rather slightly, their Blankets of Bear, Musk Rat & Black
tailed Deer Skins. Their Ornaments of Shells whether in Bracelets, Arm
Bands, [ ] their Hair or their Garments, or in fillets round the Head
always appear to advantage from their brilliant white. Ab^t 60 Men –
Women & Children in proportion.

July 6th [1811] Saturday A cloudy rainy Morning – could not embark
'till 6$\frac{1}{2}$ Am. Our Hosts found us early & notwithstanding the Rain
smoked several Pipes. We then set off, after giving to the Chief a Bag
of bitter Roots, one of white d^o & one of Eetoowoy to take care of
for us. Our Co [19 courses] these last Co^s fine view & see the high
woody Mountains of the Oochenawga River s78w $1\frac{1}{2}$M n65[w]
1M s55w 1M – this Co is over flats: when the water is low, we suppose
to be [ ] + $\frac{1}{4}$M s70w 2M fine Current s50w 1M sw $\frac{1}{4}$ s40w $1\frac{1}{2}$M.

Inspaelis is name of the Tribe we left this Morning, & the Name of those
we now arrived at is Smeeth howe – to where we came at 10 Am.
We put ashore; as we approached, they gave several loud thankful Oys.
I sent my Simpoil to invite them to smoke; the Chief received the
Message thankfully, & they began to collect a small Present – hav^g done
which I again invited them & they came forward & sat down in a
ring, & began smoking without any ceremony. The Women then
advanced all ornamented with fillets & small feathers, dancing in
a body to the tune of a mild Song which they sang. When close to the
Men, an old Man directed them to [sit] down all round the Men,
on the outside, with the Children &c. Thus pl[aced] they smoked with
the Men, only the Women were permitted no more than a single
Whiff of the Calumet, whilst the Men took from 3 to 6 Whiffs. Having
smoked a while I explained to the Chief by means of the S[impoil]
my intention of going to the Sea to open out a Road to bring
Merchandize &c to trade with them, which they thankfully
received & wished [us] a good voyage. They said the River was tolerable
from hence to an[o]ther Tribe & that they would inform me of
some dist^{ce} beyond th[at] again, as their Knowledge reached no farther.
Having accepted p[art] of the Present they brought, 3 roasted
Salmon & ab^t $\frac{1}{2}$ Bushel of Arrow Wood Berries, I made them a present
of 2 ft of Tob, 6 Rings, 1 fm of Ga[rt^g], 6 Hawks Bells, & 2 Awls
– & 4 In to the Chief.

    At Noon we left these friendly People, & went down s46e 2m – $\frac{1}{2}$m
gone put ashore on the right. The Indians lent us Horses, & the
Chief with 4 young Men came with them & brought part of our Goods
to the foot of the Rapid – the rest was run down in the Canoe on
the right for 1m: the Rapid is very strong, but good in the mid to near
the end, then on the right. Gave the Chief 2 In of Tob & each of the
young Men 1$\frac{1}{2}$ In for their trouble, & they thankfully left us. At 1:10 Pm
embarked – Co [13 courses] At 2:30 Pm saw the first sheep –
Michel went after it, but the wind had started it. At 2:52 Pm set off
– killed 2 Rattle Snakes – Co So 1m s20w 1m s56w 1m end of Co
sr and Isl^d good between the Isle & the left. Co s65w 1m s55w 2m the
Country is now very rude & mountainous, but bare of wood except
on some of the Heights n75w 1$\frac{1}{2}$m a very strong head Wind most of
the day. [11 courses] – at So 1m Co we see Mountains before us
whose tops have much Snow in places s33w 1$\frac{1}{2}$m s5w 1$\frac{1}{2}$m – $\frac{1}{2}$m of Co
gone put up at 6 Pm on the left among high rude Lands, steep on
the right. The early part of the day was strong Rapid – walked part

of [ ] up a high Bank &c, part fine Current – latter part again very strong R Current & strong Whirlpools. Obs^d for Lat^{de} Long^{de} &c.

July 7th [1811] **Sunday** A fine day but cloudy Morn^g. At 7 Am set off, Co S5E 1M + 1M [S]28E 2M + $\frac{1}{2}$M beg^g of Co to the SW^d see high rocky Mountains bending to the So^d – saw band of Horsemen from a Brook going downwards S35E $\frac{3}{4}$M S78E 1$\frac{1}{4}$M [R]C N82E 1M d^o rude Rock on an end East 1M SRC walked, embarked & [cro]ssed to 2 Horseman, staid ab^t $\frac{1}{2}$ Hour smoking – then Co S56E 1M to the Rapid [S50]E 1M. At mid of Co S65E 1M we came to a large Band of Indians at 10$\frac{1}{2}$ Am – smoked with them 'till 1$\frac{3}{4}$ Pm. They received us all dancing in their Huts, one of which was ab^t 80 Y^{ds} long & the other 20 Y^{ds} d^o – they were ab^t 120 families. I invited [the]m to smoke, & the 5 most respectable Men advanced & smoked a few Pipes. I asked them to invite the others, which they readily did, but it was 20' before [we] could get them all to sit down. They put down their little Presents of Berries, Roots &c, & then continually kept blessing us & wishing us all manner of good for visiting them, with clapping their Hands & extending them [to] the Skies. When any of us approached their Ranks they expressed their [goo]d will & thanks with outstretched Arms & Words followed by a strong [whi]stling aspiration of the Breath. I discoursed a while with them & they seemed thankful for the good I offered them of trading their superfluities [for] Articles they stood so much in need of.

A very old respectable Man [sa]t down by me, thankful to see us & smoke of our Tobacco before he died – he after felt my Shoes & Legs gently as if to know whether I was like [the]mselves. A Chief of the Countries below offered to accompany me; he understood the Language of the People below, which I gladly accepted & we embarked him, his Wife & Baggage. I paid them for the present made us of 2 Salmon, a few Berries & Roots – we took only part, being sufficient for our wants. We had much trouble to get away, as they very much wished to detain us all night, & when we went they all stretched out their Hands to Heaven, wishing us a good voyage & a safe return. At 1$\frac{3}{4}$ Pm I walked down the Rapid – the Canoe ran it close on the left with every thing. Many of these People like the others have Shells in their Noses. Their burying Grounds are all of the same fashion. They say the south Lands are bare of Animals, but the North Side have Chevreuil, Sheep, Goats &c, of the latter of which they make good Blankets. Tho' poor in Provisions, they were all hearty

in Health & tolerably well clothed for the Country – a few Buffalo
Robes &c.

The Country is wholly Meadow, with a few Rocks showing themselves along the River side & on the high Lands. Co S50E 1M Co
S1OE 1$\frac{1}{2}$M + 2M S1OE$\frac{1}{2}$M S56E$\frac{1}{2}$M steep fluted Rocks on the left Co
N68E 1$\frac{1}{4}$M see a vast wall of Rock bounding the River on the right,
also much of the same on the left. At 3:5′ Pm put ashore to boil Salmon
& at 4$\frac{1}{2}$ Pm set off. Saw one of their Winter Huts – the Ground is hollowed away for ab^t 1 foot deep. Co S70E $\frac{1}{2}$M S5E 2M S30E 1M S1OE 1M
S20W 1$\frac{1}{2}$M S8W 1M all steep Rock & fine low meadow Pts; it is curious
to see fine Meadow as it were springing out of the face of steep
Rocks & spreading along the River – at times fine Know[ls of] Sand
S40E 1$\frac{1}{4}$M +$\frac{1}{2}$M S22E 1$\frac{1}{2}$M a very long Reach + 1$\frac{1}{2}$M + 2M S1OE
2M S35E 1M S1OW 1M S55E 1$\frac{1}{2}$M S15E $\frac{1}{2}$ at end of Co at 7$\frac{1}{2}$ Pm put up.
I went up a Hill & remarked that the compass showed the last
Co S55E & the other next above S12W – on my return, please Heaven
I hope to take the Courses more exact, as the whirlpools keep the
Compass continually agitated. Co for the Morrow is S20W.

July 8th **[1811] Monday** Passed a bad Night with Musketoes & a high
Wind. To the Co^s of yesterday add S15E $\frac{1}{2}$M (done) to the Campment.
Prepared a Mast, Sail &c, & at 6:5 Am set off. Co S22W 1$\frac{1}{2}$M from our
campment & for a very long way upwards we have no occasion to
cross S8W $\frac{1}{2}$M So $\frac{1}{2}$M S8E $\frac{1}{2}$M all SRC S22E $\frac{1}{3}$ S33E 1M + $\frac{1}{2}$M SRC high
waves at end of Co the left – near the mid SE 1M came to 62 Men & their
Families. Thank Heaven, we were as usual well received; they
made us a present of 4 Salmon, much Berries &c of which we took only
part, also of 2 very small Salmon like those of the Oochenawga.
Here the Chief came to visit us on Horseback, then returned with word
to the Camp, as the Current drove us down $\frac{1}{2}$M below them. He returned with another, & with them an old white headed Man, with
the handle of a Tea Kettle for an ornament ab^t his Head; he showed
no Signs of Age except his Hair & a few Wrinkles on his face; he
was quite naked & ran nearly as fast as the Horses – we could not but
admire him. I invited the [Horsemen] to call all their People to
smoke, which they set off to do on a round Gallop, & the old Man on
foot ran after them & did not lose much ground. They all came
& sat down; we smoked & discoursed as usual – what I said the Chief
repeated to his People & another d^o repeated after him, both very
loud. The Women then advanced singing & dancing in their best dress,

with all of their Shells in their Noses – two of them naked, but no
way abashed. They danced all the time the men smoked, & like the rest
something of a religious nature. When done I paid them for their
Present of which I took only part, but the pounded Roots were made
in neat Cakes &c. They have very few Chevreuil. They are of the
Shawpatin Nation, & speak that tongue – here my last Guide showed
his Service, interpreting with an audible Voice, & seems a sensible
respectable Man. The Name of the Indians of yesterday is Sin kow arsin
– those we now leave, Skeem mooin – Skaem en a, of those close
below us.

Co N85E 1M N75E $\frac{3}{4}$ N68E 1 $\frac{1}{2}$M N52E 1$\frac{2}{3}$M N85E 1 $\frac{1}{3}$M these last 2 Cos
by the Watch, which is for the future to be my guide here, as the
low Pts are so dist that I cannot determine the dist^{ce} by them
[18 courses] sight the Shawpatin Mountains, seemingly low yet
many patches of Snow on them – s78E 1$\frac{1}{2}$M put ashore at 5:20 Pm
& camped, seeing a very large Camp close before us. 4 Horsemen came
ahead – they smoked & I sent them to invite all the Indians to come
& smoke also, which they did, bringing a Present of 4 Salmon – they
might be ab^t 150 Men with their Families. We discoursed much,
3 Chiefs repeating after each other what I said. They say that the Snow
falls only ab^t 1$\frac{1}{2}$ ft deep & soon again goes off, there are plenty of
Chevreuil & 2 Species of the small Deer, with small Trout & another small Fish in the Winter, which with the dried Salmon forms their
winter livelihood. They have no Berries &c whatever, nor did we
see any Roots. Salmon is plenty with them in the Seine &c; the Salmon
of this Morn^g & those now are fat a little – they give a little Oil in
the Kettle, the very first that have done so, & have a trout like taste.
When done smoking they gave us a Dance after the fashion of the
others. The Women & Men were more tolerable well clothed, but had
not so much shell ornament as the others: they have not the Sea
look, but much of the Plains features – they did not appear to make
so much use of the nose ornament as the others. The whole lasted
'till 9 Pm & they went away.

Obs^d for Lat^{de} Long^{de} & Time, but on the 9th I found my Instrument
had got shaken quite out of adjustment to the left, which makes
me doubt the use of either this or the other of Antares, as I do not know
when the Sextant got this shake. Promised them a House here.

July 9th [1811] Tuesday A stormy night & Morn^g, wind NW^{tly}. At
6:10 Am set off, Co s80E $\frac{1}{2}$M to the Junction of the Shawpatin River

with this, the Columbia. Here I erected a small Pole with a half sheet of Paper well tied about it, with these words on it: Know hereby that this Country is claimed by Great Britain as part of it's Territories and that the NW Company of Merchants from Canada, finding the Factory for this People inconvenient for them, do hereby intend to erect a Factory in this Place for the Commerce of the Country around. D. Thompson. Junction of the Shawpatin River with the Columbia, July 8th, 1811.

The Shawpatin River may be ab^t 500 Y^{ds} wide, troubled waters & strong Current – Indians say that when the water is low it is full of Rapids & bad. Co from it below SE 2$\frac{1}{2}$M, say, passed 20 Families Co S37E 1M + 1$\frac{1}{2}$M – at 8:5 Am put ashore & at$\frac{1}{4}$ Pm set off. Here I met the Principal Chief of all the Tribes of the Shawpatin Indians; he had an American medal of 1801 Tho[ma]s Jefferson & a small Flag of that Nation – he was a stately good looking Man of ab^t 40 years old, well dressed. His band was small as he had separated himself for fishing, but he had Cousins all round, & they all collected: he had his Soldier who, when 2 old respectable Chiefs approached, went & met them ab^t 100 Y^{ds} from where we were smok^g. I found him intelligent; he was also very friendly, & we discoursed a long time & settled on the Junction of the Shawpatin River for a House &c. When he had smoked a while with the others, he ordered all the women to dance, which they did as usual. He gave me 2 Salmon & I made him a present of 2 ft of Tob, hav^g smoked & given away with last Night full 2$\frac{1}{4}$ fms. Co S5W 1M S30W 2M S33W 1M SW 3M (say 3$\frac{1}{2}$M – see MM) S67W 1M. MM – the Co of SW 3M may be lengthened to full 3$\frac{1}{2}$M Co S82W 3M S65W 4M + 1M S82W 1$\frac{1}{4}$M N85W 1$\frac{3}{4}$ S60W 1$\frac{3}{4}$ S60W 2M + 1M see a conical Mountain right a head alone & very high, seemingly a Mass of Snow. Co + $\frac{1}{2}$M Co S70W 1$\frac{1}{2}$M a very strong head wind all day & camped at 6$\frac{1}{4}$ Pm – the Men could not advance without great fatigue. The Country is still a vast Plain & getting more & more sandy. The Indians inform us that from the Shawpatin River they go with Horses in a day to the foot of the Mountain, which is now low & dist, the next day to the Side the mount^n, & the third day among the Buffalo – but they fear the Straw Tent Snake Indians with whom they are at war. The Co they point out is ab^t East or EbS. Obs^d Merid Alt^{de} of Antares and Saturn Lat^{de} 45°:50′:45″ N. Passed in all ab^t 80 Families in small straggling Camps.

July 10 [1811] Wednesday A fine Morning, wind as usual a Gale ahead.
At 5:33 Am set off, Co s62w 2½M + 2½M sw 1½M + ½M s32w
1M end of Co put ashore & obs^d for Long^de & Time. Lat^de by Acc^t
45°:48':10" N, say the Errour now − 3':30" since the Shake the
Sextant had received, as it was found to be so all the succeeding Obs^ns
– found the Sextant out of adjustment to the left. Long^de
120°:49' w. At 9:51 Am set off, Co s60w ⅔M Co s70w 2M. At
10¼ Am set off hav^g been with Indians who behaved well, Co
s15w 2¼M. They were 82 Men with their families – measured a
Canoe of 36 ft long & 36 In wide, noticed also their Seines with large
Poles & dipping Nets on long Hoops for the Salmon. Co s40w ¼M
s60w 1½M put ashore at 11 Am & boiled Salmon & at 11:44 Am set
off, Co s60w 2M & 3½M to Indians. Set off at 55' Pm to 80 Men
& Families; at 3 Pm set off – 3 Salmon, 2 ft of Tobacco. Co s[6]8w 2M
s75w 1½M N75w 2¼M West ⅓M s75w 1½M Co s35w 1½M beg^g of
Co put ashore at 2 Men with a Seine & bought 2 Salmon at 5:26 Pm.
At 5:50 Pm put up with a very Storm of Wind; we have had a
strong head Gale all day but in the even^g it increased to a Storm – the
water was swept away like Snow. Co for the Morrow ab^t s40w.
In the last band of In[dians], one of them had his Nipple cauterized –
I saw no other. They danced in a regular manner & by much the
best I have seen: all the young of both Sexes in two curve[d] Lines,
backwards & forwards – the old formed the rank behind; they
made much use of their Arms & Hands. The Dance, Song & Step were
measured by an old Chief. Sometimes they sat down at the end of
3' sometimes at the end of 10', but never reposed more than ½' –
they gently sank down as it were, & rose up as regularly, the whole as
usual in a grand style. Obs^d Merid Alt^de of Saturn Lat^de
45°:44':54" N. Heard news of the American Ship's arrival.

July 11th [1811] Thursday A fine Morn^g – Wind a Breeze a head as
usual. At 5 Am set off, Co s40w 1M s22w ⅔M s40w 1M – at 5:55 Am
put ashore at 63 Men, staid 'till 6:48 Am then set off. Co s50w 1⅔M
s40w 1M put ashore at 7½ Am & obs^d for Long^de & Time. July 10th
Astronomical Day Lat^de by Acc^t 45°:41':1" N Long^de
121°:14' w. At 8½ Am embarked, Co s40w 1¼M to Indians; set off at
9:25 Am s68w ¾ & run part of a Rapid – the ignorance of our Guide
nearly occasioned the loss of our Canoe on the Rocks. Went down
on the left ab^t 10 y^ds with the Line, but all this is good out in the mid

& left SRC very many large Crickets SW $\frac{1}{2}$M S50W $\frac{1}{2}$M S68W $1\frac{1}{2}$M. At $\frac{1}{2}$
past Noon again left another large Band Co S56W $\frac{2}{3}$M to a strong
Rapid S60W $\frac{1}{4}$M S78W 1M S15W 2M to a series of strong Rapids. At 2 Pm
put ashore & carried ab^t 200 Y^{ds}, then camped with ab^t
300 Families who gave us as usual a rude Dance, but the respectable
Men among them had much Trouble to reduce them to order,
& they were the least regular in their way of behaviour of any we have
yet seen – at Night they cleared off with difficulty & left us to go
to sleep. A Gale as usual. Saw nothing of the reported bad Indians.

July 12 [1811] Friday A fine Morn^g but windy. Early got up & waited
the promised Horses to be lent us to carry the Things over the
Portage, but not coming, we carried them a full Mile to a small Bay Co
S12W 1M – here we saw many grey coloured Seals. At 8 Am set off
& went ab^t $\frac{1}{2}$M part paddle, part Line – fired a few Shots without
effect at the Seals. At mid of last Co put ashore & carried ab^t 100 Y^{ds}
– good. On an Isl^d on the left side of Channel boiled fish, gummed
the Canoe & obs^d for Lat^{de} Long^{de} &c. July 11th Astron[omical]
Day Lat^{de} by Acc^t 45°:37':53" N. Long^{de} 121°:48$\frac{3}{4}$' W. At 10 Am set
off, Co S68W $\frac{1}{2}$M S78W $\frac{1}{4}$M W $\frac{1}{4}$M N78W $\frac{1}{4}$ N60W $\frac{1}{4}$ N22W $1\frac{1}{4}$ N30E $\frac{1}{4}$M
N55W $\frac{3}{4}$ W^t $2\frac{1}{4}$ – at 11:19 Am put ashore to gum, at Noon set off
Co + 1M Co S80W $2\frac{1}{2}$M in this Co saw the first Ash &c. S56W $\frac{3}{4}$M
S75W 2M N88W $2\frac{1}{4}$M S70W $2\frac{3}{4}$M – $\frac{1}{2}$M gone, a Snow Mount rather
ahead, say 30M, another on right rather behind, say 25M. The
Country is now hilly & at end of Co the Hills high, rude with patches
of Snow on the Summit – much large Willow, with spots of Ash
&c. Co S60W 2M + 3M all Cos well wooded with red Fir, smooth
Poplar, Willows & a few Ash &c & Cedars, but full of Branches.
S82W $3\frac{1}{3}$M S65W 1M S55W 2M SW $\frac{3}{4}$M at end of Co at 5:50 Pm we
stopped for a Canoe of 2 Men, who came & smoked with us – we
made signs for them to take a bit of Tob to their People & tell them we·
were coming to smoke a pipe with them. We went ab^t 100 Y^{ds} thro'
Poplars – stopped at 5 Pm & camped for the Night at the desire of a
Chief: traded 2 good Salmon & he jabbered a few words of broken
english he had learnt from the Ships. Obs^d Saturn for Lat^{de}
45°:39':47" N. These People took us into their Houses which were
well arranged, very full of Salmon & so close as to be intolerably warm
– staid there ab^t 1 Hour, when I came to my People. They speak
a Language quite different from the others, are of a squat fat brawny
make, dark brown Hair, the Children light coloured d° – the

Women fat brawny & naked, as are also the Men – not so dirty as those at the Falls.

July 13 [1811] Saturday A fine day. The People on the right Side or North Side are called Waw thloo las – on the [South] Side We yark eek. Thloos: good; Kummen tacks: I understand, or know it; Knik me week no se ye: far off; Perhuk: bad. After much delay we were obliged to set off at 9:5′ Am – got across to the north Side with 9 We yark eek – Co say NW $\frac{2}{3}$M, then carried South 1M S70W 1M embarked [15 courses] at end of Co put ashore & boiled Salmon – here an Indian followed us, & gave us a Salmon. At 6$\frac{3}{4}$ Pm set off – we had before stopped ab^t $\frac{1}{2}$H to trade Salmon at 2 Houses S48W 5M So$\frac{2}{3}$M this Co crossed the River & camped at 8:5 Pm, a little above Point Vancouver.

July 14 [1811] Sunday A very fine Morn^g. At 3$\frac{1}{4}$ Am set off, Co [11 courses]. We lost ab^t 1H at their Houses & traded a few half dried Salmon. At 10$\frac{1}{4}$ Am put ashore to boil Salmon, at 11:35 set off, Co N40W 1$\frac{1}{2}$M a simple conical Mountain at end of Co bore N15E 30M, buried under Snow. Co [18 courses] put up in an ugly place of Rocks & an old Campment – left the Canoe in the Water. Obs^d Saturn for Lat^{de} 46°:10′:5″ N. Tide fell ab^t 2 ft in the Night.

July 15th [1811] Monday A very fine day, somewhat cloudy. Staid ′till 6:25 Am shaving & arranging ourselves, when we set off, Co N33W 1M N65W 2M N78W 1M S70W 1M S60W $\frac{1}{2}$M SW 1$\frac{1}{2}$M the Fog all along prevents me seeing well S34W 2M S22E $\frac{1}{2}$M So $\frac{1}{2}$M S50W $\frac{1}{5}$ w^t $\frac{1}{6}$ SW $\frac{1}{2}$ + $\frac{2}{3}$M S50W 2M + 1M N68W 1M + 1$\frac{1}{2}$M to Pt Tongue, but as the Wind was blowing from the Sea very hard, we made a Portage of ab^t 100 Y^{ds} over this Tongue & again embarked, Co to the Ho S50W 1$\frac{1}{2}$M. At 1 Pm, thank God for our safe arrival, we came to the House of Mr Astors Company – Messrs McDougall, Stuart & Stuart – who received me in the most polite Manner, & here we hope to stay a few days to refresh ourselves.

July 16th [1811] Tuesday A fine day. Obs^d for Lat^{de} Long^{de} & Time Lat^{de} 46°:13′:56″N by Acc^t Long^{de} 123°:48$\frac{1}{4}$′ w.

July 17th [1811] Wednesday A very fine day, if we except an appearance of Rain with a few Drops of d°. A steady Gale from Sea as usual.

July 18th [1811] Thursday A very hot calm Day. I went across to the
Indian Villages with Mr Stuart & my Men – after visiting the
Houses we went up a great Hill, where we gratified ourselves with an
extensive view of the Ocean & the Coast South^d. From hence I set
the Lands: Cape Disappointment s80w 4M, Pt Adams s25w 1½M
or 2M, Co a bold Pt s5E 13 or 12M, a Bay of 1½M deep to the
east^d which is almost met by a cut of fresh water & inundated Marshes
&c – the cut of water bears s17E 3M. A Flat at Pt Adams ab^t ¾M dist
bears towards Cape Disap[pointmen]t from that Pt, the Flat ab^t
300 Y^{ds} long. Lewis's River opposite Ft George bears s36E, running
from the sw Bay above. MM – the Pt & Bay: from the Ho set Cape
Disap[pointmen]t bears N78w 7M, the Pt above from whence I set the
above Courses N62w 3½M; the nearest Land across bears NW 2½M
& then forms a Bay; the little Pt close to the Ho lies nearly in the same
Line with the Cape Disap[pointmen]t dist ⅕M.

July 19th [1811] Friday A fine hot day. Obs^d for Lat^{de} by 2 Alt^{des} [cal-
culations crossed out] without the Rule.

July 20 & 21 [1811] Saturday & Sunday Fine weather.

Return Upstream

22 July – 23 September 1811

July 22 [1811] Monday A fine day. Arranged for setting off for the Interiour in company with Mr David Stuart & 8 of his Men in 3 Canoes. I pray kind Providence to send us a good Journey to my Family & Friends. At 1:24 Pm set off in company with Mr David Stuart & 8 of his Men; they are to build a Factory somewhere below the Falls of the Columbia at the lower Tribe of the Shawpatin Nation. Co from the Ho to Tongue Pt N35E 2M + $\frac{1}{4}$, a sail Wind & very high Waves – Co not very certain (N50E S80E dist pts) Co [S]10E $\frac{1}{4}$M S2W $\frac{1}{3}$ S55W $\frac{1}{5}$ – we stopped at the Isthmus for Mr Stuarts Canoes who carried all their Goods &c here. The Co from Tongue Pt to the great Pt on the right is S58E 6M, but hav^g gone into the Bay the Co from end of S55W $\frac{1}{5}$ Co is N84E 3M sailing – we run ab^t 3M & then turned N48E to the great Pt, say Co NE 2M + 1M + 2M N20E 1$\frac{1}{4}$M N77E $\frac{1}{2}$M + $\frac{1}{4}$M – at 6:30 Pm put up in a very awkward Place for the Night. 2 Indians came to us – we sent them for Salmon, of which they brought us a little.

July 23 [1811] Tuesday A fine cloudy Morn^g. At 4:21 Am set off, Co N75E $\frac{1}{2}$ end of Co 7 Ho^s on the [right] N80E$\frac{1}{3}$M S80E $\frac{1}{2}$M – the Nation on Pt Adams is named the Klatsup or Klatsap, the other on the north Side the Chinook. Co S70E 1M + $\frac{1}{4}$M S68E $\frac{1}{2}$M S72E $\frac{1}{4}$ S65E $\frac{1}{6}$ S42E 1M S80E$\frac{1}{2}$. At 7 Am put ashore to boil Meat & at 8:40 Am set off, Co S70E $\frac{1}{2}$M – $\frac{1}{8}$ Co gone the place where I Obs^d & camped going to the Sea, then Co S70E 1$\frac{1}{4}$ S80E $\frac{2}{3}$ N78E $\frac{1}{2}$M N73E 1M – from beg^g of Co the white conical Mount^n bears N70E (No 1) N72E 1M N58E 2$\frac{1}{2}$M end of Co an opening on the [right] bears S65E from which a River comes, perhaps the one passed a few Miles below. Co N58E $\frac{1}{4}$M N18E 2$\frac{1}{4}$M N26E $\frac{1}{2}$M N30E $\frac{3}{4}$ + $\frac{1}{6}$ NE $\frac{1}{5}$ N55E $\frac{1}{6}$ passed 2 Houses, Co to Pt of Isl^d N60E $\frac{1}{2}$M — we go on the South side of the Isl^d to avoid the large Village of ab^t 20 Houses. Co N75E $\frac{1}{4}$M N88E 1M + 1M + 1M S85E $\frac{3}{4}$ E^t $\frac{1}{2}$M S72E $\frac{1}{4}$ S65E $\frac{3}{4}$ S57E $\frac{1}{2}$M SE $\frac{1}{3}$M S35E $\frac{1}{4}$. At 7 Pm at the end of a line of steep Rocks on a very steep Shore we put up: with difficulty we could place the Goods & we slept as I may say standing, as all the lower Lands are overflowed & no campment can be found.

July 24 [1811] Wednesday A cloudy musketoe Morn^g. The white Mount^n bears ab^t N65E; our Co is N88E 1M; at 4$\frac{1}{2}$ Am E^t $\frac{1}{2}$ + $\frac{1}{4}$M S80E $\frac{2}{3}$ + $\frac{3}{4}$M + 1$\frac{1}{2}$M — at 6$\frac{3}{4}$ Am put ashore to gum & boil Salmon. At 8$\frac{3}{4}$ Am set off, Co S80E $\frac{1}{2}$M S75E $\frac{1}{4}$ S60E $\frac{1}{6}$ S50E $\frac{1}{2}$ SE $\frac{1}{4}$ S50E 1M S10E $\frac{1}{6}$ S36E $\frac{1}{2}$M 3 Ho on the [left] S30E $\frac{1}{6}$ S40E $\frac{1}{2}$ at end of this Co we crossed S20E $\frac{3}{4}$, but our straight Co to the [right] pt is S48E 3$\frac{1}{2}$M which we take S40E $\frac{1}{6}$ S25E 2$\frac{1}{2}$ + 1M. At end of this Mile a Gap on the [left] which seems to send out a large Brook. A Mount bears S86E + 1$\frac{1}{4}$M end of Co set the first conical Mountain N42E, another N56E, the 3rd S84E (perhaps the distances are too long here as the Sail is up & I go by the Watch) + $\frac{1}{2}$M S25E 1M S40E 1$\frac{1}{2}$M passed in the Woods 60 Y^{ds} & Co West $\frac{1}{4}$M to the Wil ar bet River; as it blows too hard then Co S15W $\frac{1}{2}$M, or which is best take the Co from the entrance of the River, which we see S8W 1$\frac{1}{2}$M & less on the S40E 1$\frac{1}{2}$M Co $\frac{1}{4}$M at end of Co we put up at 6$\frac{1}{4}$ Pm. A few Indians came to us — their Village is ab^t 1M below, & is seemingly a fine Place, say 12 Houses. Obs^d for Lat^{de} [by] Merid Alt^{de} of Saturn Lat^{de} 45°:49′:38″ N.

July 25 [1811] Thursday A Cloudy Morn^g. At 5:7′ Am set off up the Wil ar bet River Co [15 courses] — all along the River on both Sides the Country is inundated S5W $\frac{1}{2}$M S10E $\frac{1}{3}$ at end of Co the River cont^g to come from the Isl^d & ssw^d. We returned the last Co to paddle across the inundated Lands for the Columbia S70E $\frac{1}{4}$ NE $\frac{1}{6}$ NO $\frac{1}{8}$ SE $\frac{1}{8}$ S35E $\frac{2}{3}$ when we carried ab^t 60 Y^{ds} into the Columbia River again, Co in it S28E 1M which may also be the Co downwards for 3$\frac{1}{4}$M. Co + 1M — in this Co put ashore at 10 Houses; this is the place we traded Salmon & afterwards boiled d^o as we went to the Sea. S27E $\frac{1}{2}$M — $\frac{1}{4}$ gone to 5 Houses, boiled Salmon & dried a few Things of Mr Stuarts. S28E 1M Co S5E $\frac{1}{2}$M beg^g of Co set the Mount^n (No 2)

N24E 25M. S30E 1M we crossed the River in this Co & cannot as yet perceive any Channel going to the Wilarbet River, but the Ground is all overflowed; on looking back we see part of this Side an Isl^d as drawn. MM: when we left this River yester even, a bold Channel in the Isl^d on the [left] appears ab^t ½M above where we turned to the Wilarbet River – I did not draw it. Co S1OE ½M S30E ½M passed 8 Canoes seining of Salmon of which they killed 10 at a haul (the Seine is ab^t 30 fms long, exclusive of 10 fms of Cord at each end) but they are as unhospitable as most of these of their Nation – not a Salmon to be got from them, altho' there are plenty. S40E 1M SE ⅙ S70E ⅙ S80E 1½M + ½M S72E 1M S80E ¾ mid of Co turned NE½M to a good camp-ment at 7 Pm – fine Meadow Land below Pt Vancouver. Michel went a hunt^g & wounded a Chevreuil, of which the tracks are plenty here; we traded much split Salmon at a very dear rate for Rings, Bells, Buttons & Tobacco. A large snowy Mountain bears S88E 40M dist from Camp^t. Measured the Chevreuil. Obs^d Merid Alt^de of Saturn, Antares and Arcturus Lat^de 45°:38′:29″ N Long^de 122°:44′ W.

July 26th [1811] Friday A fine cloudy Morn^g. Michel killed a good fleshy Chevreuil, but not fat. Dimensions as follows: length 5 ft 5 In + 14 In for the Tail, height of the fore leg 3 ft 3½ In, hind d^o 3 ft 6 In, just at the Breast 3 ft 4 In – a fawn Colour, Throat Breast & Belly white, Legs a fawn Colour, upper part of the Tail d^o, lower part white, but not such fine long Hair in the Tail as the upper Country d^o – length of the Horns 19 In, 3 Branches, & 8 In between Tip & Tip. Made 2 Oars & arranged a Canoe of Mr Stuarts. At 7:55 Am set off, Co S88W 1M fine meadow Ground – at end of Co found ourselves shut in & obliged to carry ab^t 40 Y^ds to the River + ¼M S60E 1M + ½ S86E 2M beg^g of Co Snow Mount right ahead S85E 1M + ½M S88E 1M + 1½M N86E ½M N60E ½M N50E ¼ N68E ⅙ E^t ½M N8OE 1M + 1M + ¼M + ⅙ at end of Co put up at 5½ Pm. On the left a few Oaks & much of it all day, but only in a thin Ledge. Co for the Morrow S86E 3M. Traded a few Berries; our Salmon is almost all spoilt. The Mountain bears S81E 20M. Obs^d Merid Alt^des of Saturn, Antares and Arcturus Lat^de 45°:34′:22″N Long^de 122°:16½′ W, 122°:27¾′ W.

July 27th [1811] Saturday A fine but foggy Morn^g. At 5:47 Am set off, Co S86E 3M + ½M N73E 1M – from ¾M of Co on the opposite Side of the River ab^t $\frac{1}{4}$M below us, there is a remarkable isolated Rock like a Windmill of ab^t 90 ft height; a little above, abt 300 Y^{ds}, a rock covered with Sod resembling a Ho of 1 Story with a Door in the mid; from this place our Camp^t bears off going to the Sea s82E 1M. Co N73E $\frac{1}{2}$M N50E $\frac{1}{2}$M N48E 2$\frac{1}{4}$M Co N48E 1$\frac{1}{2}$M opposite end of Co a Brook falls ab^t 121 ft Co N55E 2$\frac{1}{2}$M (this last Co or from end of Co, looking back, appears s55w 2$\frac{1}{2}$M) Co + $\frac{1}{2}$M Co N35E$\frac{1}{4}$M beg^g of Co a Brook falls 40 ft on the [right]. At end of Co put ashore at the same place where we boiled Salmon going down; at 1:20 Pm set off, hav^g cooked Salmon &c & arranged our Arms. Co N46E 1M Co + N46E $\frac{1}{3}$M NE $\frac{1}{4}$ N5W $\frac{1}{8}$ — for these Co^s cannot see anything, but they are put down to bring up a Chart of the Isles. Co N45E $\frac{1}{6}$ N55E $\frac{2}{4}$ — I must now give over as I cannot see for the Sail; at the mouth of the little Channel took in Sail, & I took the Co^s, but from whence I left off to this place may be ab^t NE $\frac{3}{4}$ or so with an Isl^d on [right] Co NE $\frac{1}{3}$M N30E $\frac{1}{4}$ N25E $\frac{1}{4}$ N1OE $\frac{1}{2}$ R N6OE $\frac{1}{3}$ N18E $\frac{1}{2}$ at end of Co put up at 5$\frac{1}{2}$ Pm as we are close to the great Rapid & the Houses — pray good Providence to send me well up it. A Canoe with a blind good old Chief came to us & smoked, also 2 Canoes that passed & went to the Village — we requested them to bring us some Salmon which they promised, but not coming at all made me suspect some treachery & I had the Canoes loaded, ready for any occasion.

July 28 [1811] Sunday A fine blowy Morn^g. At 5:5′ Am set off, Co s55E $\frac{1}{4}$M + $\frac{1}{4}$M R here we met 4 Men with 7 Salmon — we put ashore & boiled d^o. They as well as the others enquired ab^t the Small Pox, of which a report had been raised that it was coming with the white Men & that 2 Men of enormous Size [were coming] to overturn the Ground &c. We assured them the whole was false, at which they were highly pleased, but had not the Kootanaes been under our immediate care she would have been killed for the lies she told on her way to the Sea. At 7$\frac{3}{4}$ Am set off, Co N78E$\frac{1}{2}$M SC we kept on by the Line & Paddle, several bad Places — one of the wood Canoes nearly filled — the Indians assisting with good will. Co to the Portage N70E 1M by 9:30 Am — here we waited Mr Stuarts Canoes till Noon & then set off. Mr Stuart employing a number of the Indians to aid in carrying the Goods, Canoes &c, we carried 20′ & then put down — when all was got forward to this place, we set off again & carried ab^t 400 Y^{ds} farther (the Co may be North 1M) by 2$\frac{1}{4}$ Pm. When Mr Stuart was to pay the Indians, they could not be known who had carried

from those who had not, & much Tobacco was given, yet the Indians
were highly discontented: they all appeared with their 2 pointed
Dag[gers] & surrounded us on the land Side, their appearance very
menacing. Mr Stuart set off with a few to get his Canoes brought,
which they refused to do 'till better paid – when gone I spoke to the
Chiefs of the hard usage they gave Mr Stuart, & reasoning with
them, they sent off all the young Men. We loaded & went up 3 strong
Points with the Line & Paddle Co N52W $\frac{1}{2}$M & put up close to end of
Co – here we went back & brought up Mr Stuarts Canoes, & thank
Heaven put up altogether tho' late. These people are a mixture of
Kindness & Treachery: they render any Service required, but
demand high payments & [are] ready to enforce their demands
Dag[ger] in hand; they steal all they can lay their Hands on, & from
every appearance only our Number & Arms prevented them from
cutting us all off – this was their plan as we were afterwards
informed, tho' not agreed to by all, & they perhaps only wait a better
opportunity.

July 29th **[1811] Monday** A fine Morn[g]. Went & fetched a light Canoe
of Mr Stuarts & at 6:5′ Am set off, Co [12 courses] – $\frac{1}{4}$M short of Co
crossed the River, as the appearance of 2 Canoes that followed us
was hostile, with their always shouting to show where we were, which
was answered by a Number on shore. As the Land was inundated
they could not approach us, but we were drawing near a Pt of Pine,
where the Land was dry & good for an Ambush – we accordingly
crossed North $\frac{3}{4}$M & put ashore to boil Salmon &c. At 10:40 Am
from hence – the [left] pt of the Rapid bears S22W & the Place where
we slept S26W 3$\frac{1}{2}$M – Co at $\frac{1}{2}$ Pm N70E $\frac{1}{6}$ N62E $\frac{1}{4}$ N58E $\frac{1}{5}$ N78E 2$\frac{1}{2}$M
S82E 1M + 1M N86E $\frac{1}{4}$ N78E 1M + $\frac{1}{4}$M N62E 1M + 1$\frac{1}{4}$M + 1$\frac{1}{2}$M to the
other side Co N67E – little of Co gone put up at 6$\frac{1}{2}$ Pm. Late 4 Indians
in a Canoe came & camped with us – they are going to buy Horses.

July 30 [1811] Tuesday A fine Morn[g] – head wind. At 5$\frac{1}{2}$ Am set
off, Co N67E 3M N70E 1M end of Co at 8:5 Am put ashore & boiled
Salmon. Plenty of Oak, but like all we have seen, stunted. Set off
& crossed the River N3W 1M to a Brook at 10$\frac{1}{4}$ Am, where we
smoked with a few Shawpatins. We sight a Mountain at the head of
the Brook, Nas ma neet, & from the mouth of this Brook set a
Mountain bears S3W 30M. At 10:40 Am set off, Co S72E 1$\frac{1}{2}$ + $\frac{1}{2}$M
S82E $\frac{1}{2}$ N85E 1M + $\frac{1}{4}$M N84E 1M N70E 1$\frac{1}{4}$ N72E $\frac{5}{6}$ at mid of Co

camped at $4\frac{3}{4}$ Pm to split out Oars, Poles &c &c, but found the
Wood bad &c.

July 31st [1811] Wednesday At 5:2′ Am set off, end Co then Co N72E
$1\frac{1}{4}$M beg^g of Co steep fluted Rocks like Pillars with quite perpend
Strata: some Pillars are loosened & broke & stand like Stumps − no
horizontal Strata − the rock is of a grey black. Co s86E $1\frac{1}{4}$ East $1\frac{1}{4}$M
SC N85E $\frac{2}{3}$ − all these Co^s are high steep perpend Rocks s84E 1M − these
Co^s are well taken but the dist^{ces} are not quite so as the Ground
is on fire & very smoky s75E $\frac{1}{2}$M s72E 1M. At 7:25 Am at beg^g of
Co where we gummed going to the Sea s43E $1\frac{1}{2}$M s24E $\frac{1}{2}$M; at end of
Co at $8\frac{1}{4}$ Am to the Portage Road, the Co continues $1\frac{1}{2}$M. I sent
our Interpreter Indian for Horses − he brought them, with Salmon; we
boiled d^o & set off at $1\frac{1}{2}$ Pm. By $3\frac{1}{4}$ Pm got all across: we walked
smartly − the dist^{ce} is full $4\frac{1}{2}$M. Here we had scarcely set down the
Things &c than Word was brought that one of the Chiefs was gathering
his Band to seize all our Arms from us; this brought on some sharp
words, which thank good Providence ended well for us. I asked for
Salmon [of] which they brought to [us] 13 − major part for
Mr Stuart. We passed a very bad Night with a Storm of Wind, drifting
Sand & Rogues walking ab^t us all Night to steal − they cut our Line
tho' fastened to the Ponces & got off with ab^t $2\frac{1}{2}$ fm of d^o.

Augst 1st [1811] Thursday A fine Morn^g. Had a little Trouble to get
our Indian Interpreter to come with us − at 5 Am set off, Co N18E
$1\frac{1}{4}$M N58E 1M passed an Isle with Houses for the Dead s75E$\frac{1}{3}$ to a
Village of ab^t 15 Men − smoked with them. Co s76E $1\frac{1}{2}$M part Line
s88E 2M SC to a Village of 20 Men − boiled Salmon N72E $2\frac{1}{2}$M − $\frac{1}{2}$M
gone a strong Rapid − the Line & handed, on to the Indians. The
Name of the great River in the great Bay opposite the great Isle is Wun
wow eve neer (Wun vow we). End of Co stopped 1 Hour with ab^t
120 Men then finished Co SC Co N78E $\frac{2}{3}$M N68E $\frac{1}{6}$ N55E $\frac{1}{5}$ N48E $\frac{5}{6}$ the
Rocks hereto have still the same perpend pillar like Strata, but
many much cracked horizontally N85E $\frac{1}{3}$ at end of Co carried ab^t
10 Y^{ds} the[n] Co N67E 1M to a Village of 15 Men − here we smoked
with them, then Co N58E $1\frac{3}{4}$ SC − Co + $\frac{1}{4}$M always steep rocky
Banks N56E $\frac{2}{3}$M N54E $1\frac{1}{4}$M + $\frac{1}{2}$M water has fallen ab^t 10 ft perpend
since we have passed. Co N55E 1M + $\frac{1}{4}$M − Note: this Co is almost
rubbed out & is perhaps N55E or 45E to the Camp of the Malade.

Stopped $\frac{3}{4}$H, then Co N53E 1$\frac{1}{2}$M N62E $\frac{2}{3}$ when we crossed S15E$\frac{1}{2}$M
& put up at 6$\frac{3}{4}$ Pm – a Gale aft, the Sand drifting, little Wood, but
very quiet. Where we crossed, the Current tho' moderate on the No
Side was very strong in the Mid, with shoal Rocks & swif[t] on the
Shore we [are] on – all the Land very sandy without any mixture of
Earth, & the Wood so scarce that all the bits we could gather was
barely sufficient to boil a Salmon – every thing is full of Sand.

Augst **2**nd **[1811] Friday** A fine blowy Morn^g. At 5:5' Am set off after
hav^g gummed, Co N25E 1$\frac{1}{6}$M SC Muscle Rapid – very many of those
Shells – at end of Co a Ho of 6 Men &c. On an Isl^d close below ab^t
50 Men in a small Village, opposite above ab^t 20 Men in a small
Village. We lined up end of Co, then N30E 1$\frac{1}{4}$M – $\frac{1}{2}$M of Co gone
opposite where we camped going to the Sea, & a River of 80 Y^{ds} wide
on this Side named Torks paez. Co N55E $\frac{1}{2}$M SR N55E 1M SR lined up.
Measured a Salmon of 4 ft 4 In long & 2–4 In circumference – he
is a fine large fish rather above the common Size. Still along the steep
rocky Strata, with rocky grassy Hills rising above & going off in
vast Plains, tho' very unequal; the first Strata may be 100 ft high of
the different Rocks, the others ab^t 800 ft. Boiled fish – we then set
off. 2 Men crossed among the rocky Rapids which [have] always been
since Morn^g in the mid of Channel – they seemed hurt that we did
not stop at their Villages & give them the News of our Voyage, of which
they are all very fond. Co rubbed out (N85E) dist^{ce} $\frac{1}{2}$M + $\frac{1}{4}$M East
$\frac{1}{6}$ S88E $\frac{1}{2}$M Co rubbed out N40E $\frac{2}{3}$M S52E 2M S56E $\frac{1}{2}$M smoked at a
Village of 20 Men & then held on, Co S56E 1$\frac{1}{2}$M nearly rubbed out.
Co (S56E 1$\frac{1}{2}$M S65E) 1$\frac{1}{2}$M end of Co a River of ab^t 60 Y^{ds} x named
Now wow ee. Co N82E $\frac{1}{2}$M passed 5 Ho^s on an Isl^d &c Co N75E$\frac{1}{2}$M
drawn to the South^d instead of the north^d + $\frac{3}{4}$M + 1M N70E$\frac{1}{2}$M
mid of Co a Village of 30 Men, from 1$\frac{1}{2}$ Pm to 3$\frac{1}{2}$ Pm Co N65E
2$\frac{1}{2}$M – no naked women in this last Dance; they were tolerably clothed
– to a Village of 15 Men, staid ab^t 1 Hour Co + 1M + 1M
+ $\frac{1}{4}$M Co N70E 1$\frac{1}{4}$M end of Co put up at 6:40 Pm with ab^t 12
Horsemen in company, among a number of their winter
Habitations. Obs^d for Long^{de} & Time by Antares and Arcturus Lat^{de}
by Acc^t 45°:42':52" N Long^{de} 120°:28$\frac{1}{2}$' W. It may be remarked here,
that all the Obs^{ns} made going to the Sea was with a com Watch that
went very badly, losing time – on my return also with a com Watch
that went tolerable well. The Wind always blowing a Gale.

Augst 3rd [1811] **Saturday** A fine Morn^g. At 4:24 Am set off, Co as yesterday N65E 1M N70E 1$\frac{1}{4}$M N76E 1M + 1M N50E$\frac{1}{6}$ N32E 1M N18E
2M N64E 1M [+] $\frac{1}{2}$M a Village of ab^t 100 Men at 7:20 Am; at
9:27 Am embarked, Co + 1M + 2M + $\frac{1}{4}$M N50E $\frac{1}{4}$M put ashore 1H to
gum Co at 11$\frac{3}{4}$ Am N55E $\frac{1}{2}$M N50E $\frac{1}{3}$ + 2$\frac{1}{2}$M – before this last Co
the last 4M only a line of Rock with large Pts &c: the Hills have retired,
especially on the So Side; the last 2M low meadow Banks & Shores,
bold in places but retiring – $\frac{3}{4}$M of the 2M gone a River opposite,
named A hoaks ha. Co + 1M + 1M + 1M N80E 1M N75E $\frac{1}{3}$ N62E
$\frac{1}{2}$ N63E 1$\frac{1}{2}$M + 1M NE 1$\frac{3}{4}$M N70E 1$\frac{1}{2}$M to a Village of 12 Men – stopped
40′. Co + 1M to our old campment going down Co + 1M N65E
$\frac{1}{3}$ N55E $\frac{1}{2}$ (something rubbed out) NE $\frac{2}{3}$ N50E $\frac{1}{2}$M N40E $\frac{1}{3}$ N30E $\frac{1}{2}$M + $\frac{1}{6}$ Co
N28E $\frac{2}{3}$ N27E 1M at end of Co camped at 7$\frac{1}{2}$ Pm. Strong sail Wind
in the evening. Many Indians in company from the last Villages & gave
us a Dance.

Augst 4th [1811] **Sunday** A fine Morn^g. Gummed – at 5:5′ Am set off,
Co N55E 1M N42E 1M + 1M N58E 1M – here I end the Co^s for the
present as it blows very hard & I cannot see on acc^t of the Sail. We
turned along the Land ab^t s70E for 1M – an Isl^d near the [right]
Shore, then along the Pt ab^t s80E 2M East, say 1M. Here the Wind became more fair; I again took the Co^s: Co N82E $\frac{2}{3}$M N56E 2M N75E 1$\frac{1}{4}$
N70E $\frac{1}{5}$ N68E $\frac{1}{2}$ N60E $\frac{2}{3}$ N50E $\frac{2}{3}$ + $\frac{1}{3}$ N68E 1M beg^g of Co Ho of 5 Men,
end of Co a Rapid – lined up, 20 Y^{ds} of steep Rocks & many
Rattlesnakes. Co N80E 2$\frac{1}{2}$M the Lands now heightened especially
on the [left], level on the [right], end of Co strong Rapid – lined 200 Y^{ds},
then N60E 2$\frac{1}{2}$M. From end of this Co the Pt of Rattle Snake Rock bears
s55W 4$\frac{1}{2}$M dist & mid of Co, the Line fairly clear – the Pt on the [right]
side & this ought to be the real Co: the others are not correct as the
2 Co^s ought to form a deep regular Bay. Co s85E $\frac{1}{2}$M N80E 1M
N75E $\frac{1}{2}$M N72E 1M beg^g of Co a Rapid & a remarkable Table Rock
isolated on the [right], also a Village of 30 Men on the Isl^d – smoked
with a few who crossed to us + $\frac{1}{4}$M Co N65E $\frac{1}{5}$ N60E $\frac{2}{3}$ + 1M N52E 2M.
At 6:40 Pm put up near end of Co – at 1$\frac{1}{2}$M gone obs^d for Long^{de}
& Time by Antares and Arcturus Lat^{de} by Acct 45°:54$\frac{1}{4}$′ N
Long^{de} 118°:49$\frac{3}{4}$′ W.

Augst 5th [1811] **Monday** A fine Morning. Again gummed – at
5:15 Am set off, all our Gum quite expended & no Woods what-

ever, so that we must go without that most necessary Article & our
Canoe is very leaky. Finished Co, then + 1M N43E $\frac{1}{3}$M N42E $\frac{1}{2}$M
N30E $\frac{1}{4}$ N33E $\frac{1}{3}$ N28E 2$\frac{3}{4}$M beg^g of Co boiled Salmon & shaved. Co
N42E 1M – we now see no Agate along Shore as below; these Lands
are wholly composed of Strata of Rock from 10 to 30 ft thick
& those on the upper Strata of ab^t 20 ft of pillar like Rock – this is often
like the flutes of an organ at a distance; its Strata seems perpend
& is often split in pieces. The pillars are split also in various directions
as if broken & cracked by a violent blow – this rests in a Strata of
black rude Rock, as p^r Specimens of both. These two different kinds
of Rock lie alternately one on another to the bed of the River,
which is mostly of the black Rock, tho' sometimes of the pillar Rock
– the black Rock appears always to have the thickest bed. The last
100 ft is covered with splinters of the upper Rocks, sometimes to a
good depth. The surface of the upper Rocks forms what is called
the Plains; this is covered with pure Sand, thro' which the Rocks appear
every where & bears scanty Grass, round, hard & in tufts with a few
Shrubs & Thistles of 1 to 5 ft high. Co N5E $\frac{1}{2}$M N5W $\frac{3}{4}$M – the whole is
ab^t 350 ft to 400 ft high – on the [right] these Rocks finish with this
Co, & are all of deep Strata as p^r the 2 specimens; the rasp or rude black
Rock often shows from 2 to 3 Lines in the Strata or Bed, the same
Strata almost always inclining to the West^d & sometimes descending
in a Curve, & then assuming a horizontal Line. This Strata is sometimes 40 ft deep, & many pieces stand isolated like Tables & Pillars
&c. The Pillar like Rock has always its Chasms perpend & split in
pieces as by accident, in every horizontal direction – it appears to be
one compact bed, having no Lines in it that are not perpend, & the
depth of its bed is as far as 30 ft. One must say that the finger of the
Deity has opened by immediate operation the passage of this River
thro' such solid Materials, as must for ever have resisted its action. The
Tops have mouldered away, & the fragments from the Beach
&c – there is no appearance of any Earth but in a few places where water
springs up, & the Grass &c have formed a vegetable Mould of no
depth, & even this is rarely found. Co N12W 1M N5W $\frac{1}{6}$ end of Co
a Village on the [right] of 25 Men; we have besides passed 3 d^o each
of ab^t the same Number of Men. C^o [22 courses] mid of Co set the
Pt of the Forks N20E $\frac{2}{3}$M to which we camped at 6:40 Pm with ab^t
200 Men at least, who gave us a Dance &c, & behaved very well – thank
Heaven for the favour we find among these numerous people.

Augst 6th [1811] **Tuesday** A fine cloudy Night & Morning. Traded a
Horse for our Guide & paid him as p^r Agreement. Wrote a Letter
to Jaco Finlay to send & meet us with Horses &c. At 7$\frac{1}{2}$ Am embarked, Co up the Shawpatin River N15E 1M + $\frac{1}{4}$M N32E $\frac{1}{2}$M
N35E $\frac{1}{4}$ N37E 1$\frac{3}{4}$M N40E $\frac{1}{3}$ N55E $\frac{1}{6}$ N60E 4$\frac{1}{2}$M NE $\frac{1}{6}$ N32E $\frac{1}{6}$ N23E 1M + $\frac{1}{3}$
all very strong Current from the Columbia N50E $\frac{1}{2}$M N32E 1$\frac{1}{2}$M
end of Co an Isl^d & Village of 15 Men; have also passed 4 Ho^s of each
6 Men – traded Salmon. [11 courses] near end of Co put up at
6$\frac{1}{2}$ Pm, with ab^t 22 Men who gave us a Dance. The River has been ab^t
regularly 300 Y^{ds} wide, with strong steady Currents: the Water is
very high, the tops of the Willows just appearing – when low, I should
think, full of Rapids. The Land very rude with Rock & Ravines –
Grass very scanty. The Men in passing the Ravines broke the Scurf of
the Soil; the Dust & Sand rushed down as free to the look as water,
pouring down for a considerable time & raising a dusty smoke not to
be seen thro'. The Road lies close along the River & ascends & descends continually – very rocky, by no means such a country as the
Columbia above. The Salmon small & very fine.

Augst 7 [1811] **Wednesday** A fine clear Morn^g – a little distThunder.
At 4:50 Am set off, Co N5E 1M N13E $\frac{1}{4}$ + $\frac{1}{2}$M N75E 1M + $\frac{2}{3}$M end of
Co stopped ab^t 2H at a Village of 15 Men, gummed & boiled
Salmon. Co [13 courses] mid of Co obs^d for Lat^{de}, N22W $\frac{2}{3}$M
N10E 1M (doubtful) N12W 1$\frac{1}{4}$ a Ho – nobody – Co N10W-$\frac{1}{6}$ N10W
$\frac{1}{2}$M N5E 1M all R N18E 1M part R + $\frac{1}{4}$M N25E $\frac{1}{6}$ N33E $\frac{4}{5}$ SE $\frac{1}{5}$ – Co
N8E 1$\frac{1}{2}$M including our crossing the River. We put up at end of Co in
company with 8 Horsemen. Co for the Morrow is N50E 1M. Obs^d
for Long^{de} & Time by Aldeb[aran], Aquila[e], Jupiter &c. Lat^{de} by Obs^n
at Noon 46°:25':23" N, by Acc^t 46°:33$\frac{3}{4}$' N Long^{de} 118°:20$\frac{3}{4}$' W.

Augst 8th [1811] **Thursday** A very fine Morn^g. At 5:5' Am set off, Co
[20 courses] – $\frac{3}{4}$M gone, obs^d for Lat^{de} & cooked Salmon. [Obs^d sun's]
Merid Alt^{de} 118°:51$\frac{3}{4}$' – VG Var^n 19° East – VG. Co + $\frac{1}{2}$M S70E $\frac{1}{5}$ S82E
$\frac{1}{5}$ N85E $\frac{1}{5}$ N66E $\frac{1}{8}$ N47E 1M S75E $\frac{2}{3}$ beg^g of Co see the blue
Mountains, between the Shawpatins & the Snake Indians, bearing S60E
40M. Co S72E $\frac{1}{3}$M S85E $\frac{1}{4}$ at end of Co put ashore at the mouth of
a small Brook & camped, as this is the Road to my first Post in the
Spokane Lands. Here is a Village of 50 Men – they had danced 'till
they were fairly tired & the Chiefs had bawled themselves hoarse – they

forced a present of 8 Horses on us with a War Garment. Obs^d for Long^{de}, Time &c by Aquila[e], Fomalhaut and Aldebaran Lat^{de} at Noon 46°:36′:26″ N Dec^n 16°:15′:53″ N Long^{de} 119°:21$\frac{1}{4}$′ w.

Augst 9th [1811] Friday A fine day – Wind a Gale south^d. Obs^d for Long^{de} Time & Lat^{de} this Augst 8 Astronom[ical] Day. Lat^{de} 46°:36′ N by 7°:56′ w Dec^n 15°:58′:48″ N Long^{de} 118°:44′ w. It was late before the Horses could be collected & I left one they could not find. They said the Chief below knew how to talk but not how to act; they declared they did not wish for any return for the present of Horses, but that they knew the nature of a Present – I gave each of them Notes for the Horses, to be paid when the Canoes arrive. At 5 Pm set off & held on up the Brook, cutting off the great Pts 'till 11$\frac{1}{2}$ Pm, when we camped. Co N5E 1$\frac{1}{2}$M n[ea]r Brook, at 1M crossed – end of Co went up the Banks Co N20E 14M, last 1M along the Brook. The Land very rocky & full of rocky Hills cut perpend wherever the Rocks show themselves, & exactly of the same kind of Rocks as along the Columbia, with much fragments in splinters &c, very bad for the Horses, & the Soil a sandy fine impalpable Powder which suffocated us with Dust & no water to drink to where we camped.

Augst 10th [1811] Saturday A fine cloudy blowy Day. At 7$\frac{1}{4}$ Am set off & held on ab^t N1OE 5M, then crossed a shoal Brook of 6 Y^{ds} wide from the East. Held on Co + 2$\frac{1}{2}$M & baited at 11$\frac{1}{2}$ Am; at 1 Pm set off & held on say North 2$\frac{1}{4}$M a Brook came in from the NE^d. Held on up the left Brook & put up at 6 Pm, say Co No 8M. The appearance of the Country is much the same tho' somewhat less rude, & there is often a few Aspins, Alders, with a very rare Fir along the Brook, much wild Cherry & 3 Sorts of Currants – one sweet & red, the others yellow acid, red light acid.

Augst 11 [1811] Sunday A very fine day, mostly cloudy. At 7$\frac{1}{4}$ Am set off, Co up the Brook N1OE 2$\frac{1}{2}$M when we crossed a Rill from the NW^d – we kept on along a Rill of Water in the Spring, now dry. North 9$\frac{1}{2}$M to a little water among some Poplars & Willows: it is a long time since we saw any – here we baited from $\frac{1}{2}$ Pm to 2:20 Pm. We then went off North 1M N20w 1$\frac{1}{2}$M to a kind of [ ] of wet Ground – hereabouts are Willow Bushes & see Woods before us. Held on

Co N15E 6½M – for the last 2M we had a kind of Brook or Ravine
on our left. Camped at a Pond at 6¼ Pm – killed a Duck. Our
Provisions being fairly done & fasting all day, not seeing the People who
were to have met us with Provisions & Horses, we were obliged to
kill a Mare for Food, as our Guide told us we had yet 3 days Journey
to go. The Country 'till 10 Am like the past, very rocky & barren,
since which it has much mended, & only stony when on wet low
Ground; the rest is tolerably well for Grass & the Soil appears
good, tho' parched up for want of Rain, which rarely or never falls
during the Summer Months. At the Camp^t the Firs are thinly
scattered along the kind of Ravine – all the rest is all wide Plain without
a Tree. A few Chevreuil Tracks & Dung.

Augst 12th [1811] Monday A fine Day. At 6:20 Am set off, held on
along a Line of Woods on our Co, ab^t North 1M to a Pond of some
size, then N50E 4M N30E 5M & stopped at 11½ Am to bait the
Horses among a few Ponds & good grassy Lands with their Woods. At
1 Pm set off & camped at a Rill at 6¾ Pm – say Co N30E 1M N10E 7M
across a large Plain without Water, to the Woods of a Brook: we
descended the Banks which are high & crossed it ab^t N10W 1M, then
along the Brook of 6 y^{ds} x N10W 1M – here it sank in the Ground,
& we went North 1½M & camped at a Rill to which we were
guided by a Spokane we met, from whom we got a little dried
Salmon.

Augst 13th [1811] Tuesday A very fine day. At 5½ Am set off & at
6½ Am arrived at the House – thank God for his Mercy to us on
this Journey. Found all safe, but Jaco was with the Horses sent to meet
me – late in the evening he arrived. Our Co was ab^t NW 3M; we
came faster but our Road was always down Hill.

Augst 14 [1811] Wednesday A fine day. Much Indian Business & arranging the Furrs &c for to take the acc^t of d^o. They catch but few
Salmon & those of a poor quality. Augst 13th [Astronomical Day] at
the Spokane House – Mean Lat^{de} 47°:47′:4″ N Mean Long^{de}
117°:27′:11″ W Var^n 21° East.

Augst 15 [1811] Thursday A fine day. Sent off Michel to the Saleesh
River. Several Kullyspells arrived – finished the acc^t of the Furrs

&c. Obs^d [sun's] LL Mean Lat^{de} 47°:47′:2″ N Dec^n 14°:11′:3″ N Mean Long^{de} 117°:27′:11″ W Var^n 21° East.

Augst 16 [1811] Friday A fine day. Many of the Indians, mostly Skeetshoo, went away. Put our Things in order to go off the Morrow & arranging many little Matters – Acc^t of the Goods &c &c.

Aug 17 [1811] Saturday A blowy cloudy day. Early began arranging, but it was 1$\frac{1}{4}$ Pm before the Men could get off, before the Horses could be found &c. Our Baggage &c is on 3 Horses. At 3$\frac{1}{2}$ Pm set off hav^g waited Michel. Co by the Compass down the Spokane River NW 8M to the place where we baited formerly in June – here we camped at 5$\frac{1}{3}$ Pm. Killed 2 Ducks & 1 Pigeon; we have with us 32 lbs of Salmon, dried.

Augst 18 [1811] Sunday A fine day. At 6$\frac{3}{4}$ Am set off & held on up the Banks & by 9 Am below the Banks at the Brook; Co by the [sun] N10W 4$\frac{1}{2}$M there is a plain. At 10 Am crossed a Brook of 2 Y^{ds} that goes to the Spokane River Co N30W 2M, then to Noon crossing a Ridge of Knowls to a Brook of 1 Y^d X that runs to the North^d Co N20W 4M baited the Horses. At 2:20 Pm set off, Co W $\frac{1}{4}$M up a Rill which comes from S30W 3M Co N10E 6$\frac{1}{2}$M to a Brook from W^t to NE + $\frac{1}{2}$M to a large Brook Co d° to NE^d 5 Y^{ds}. Co N15E 3M to a Brook at which we camped at 6$\frac{3}{4}$ Pm – the last 1M nearly down along the Brook. Michel joined us.

Augst 19 [1811] Monday A fine day (froze to Ice this Morn^g). At 7 Am set off, Co N30E 2$\frac{1}{2}$M a Rill, Co N20E 2$\frac{1}{4}$M to a Brook, Co North 6M to a Rill, baited at 11$\frac{1}{2}$ Am – the last 3M all have been along a considerable Brook. [At] 2 Pm set off, Co N10E 2M to a Rill from sw^d Co N10E 2M passed a Brook of 3 Y^{ds} Co North 3$\frac{1}{4}$M to where we crossed in a Canoe in June, Co North 6M & put up at 7 Pm, Bon Vieux in company. We keep on the So Side of the Brook.

Aug 20 [1811] Tuesday A fine day (froze to Ice this Morn^g). At 6$\frac{3}{4}$ Am set off, Co N10W 3M Co N40W 5M to where we crossed the Rock Brook – the crossing place is good & quite shoal, say 1 ft of water; in this Co is 2 Rills ab^t 1M + 1M beyond the crossing place, Co NW 2$\frac{1}{2}$M to the Ilthkoyape Falls on the Columbia at 1 Pm, thank

Heaven. The Ilthkoyape & Oochenawga Indians gave us a Dance
& made me a Present of Berries & dried Salmon, for which I laid down
Tob & other Things to the amount of 32 Skins.

Aug 21 [1811] **Wednesday** A fine day. Sent off Charles, Pareil & Coté
for Cedar Wood – in the evening Coté brought 24 Timbers; they
are of stiff wood. Hamelin arrived with Beaulieu, Bellaire & Michel
Allaire here; La Breche & another Saleesh Indian arrived – they
gave us the News of the War with the Meadow Indians &c.

Aug^st 22 [1811] **Thursday** A very fine day. Coté went off for Wood
& brought 8 boards & 2 Gunwale pieces – had the Timbers knifed
& a Trough made to heat them with hot water. Cartier with many
Kullyspels arrived – they smoked & made a Present of dried
Berries. Traded ab^t 2 Packs of Furrs from the Oochenawgas. Blowy
evening. Rivé arrived.

Aug^st 23rd [1811] **Friday** A fine day. Coté & Rivé went off with Horses
for Wood. Obs^d Merid Alt^de of [sun's] LL Lat^de 48°:38′:1″ N.
Could not turn the Timbers for want of Cords as all are sent with the
Men for Wood.

Aug^st 24th [1811] **Saturday** A fine day – cloudy Morn^g & Even^g.
Turned the major part of the Timbers & knifed the Bottom,
Gunwales, Thwarts &c.

Aug^st 25th [1811] **Sunday** A fine day – cloudy Morn & Even. Sent off
Le Bon Vieux to Jaco with a Letter for a few Articles – La Breche
also went off. Knifed several Boards & finished the Timbers, the Stern
& Stem for the Canoe &c. Coté has been very ill since yesterday. A
few Kullyspels went away.

Aug^st 26 [1811] **Monday** A fine day – cloudy Morn^g & Even^g. Knifed
Boards, arranged the Gunwales, fixed the Bottom of the Bed which
we also cut & laid. A quarrel among the Ilthkoyape Indians – 1 killed
& several wounded.

Aug^st 27th [1811] **Tuesday** A fine day. Cartier & the rest of the
Kullyspels went away. Got all ready for fixing the Timbers.

Mr Finan McDonald & 4 Men with 2 Indians arrived – they had been up a long way, but had returned short, hav^g seen nothing of the Men & Canoes.

Augst 28th [1811] **Wednesday** A rainy Morn^g & showers at times. Fixed the Timbers with a Line &c. Lolo arrived. Put a turn of Plank round the Canoe but did not sew the whole. Mr McDonald 1 poor Goose, 1 Salmon.

Augst 29th [1811] **Thursday** A cloudy cold Morn^g. Martin, Charles, Cha[rle]s Loyer & Cha[rle]s La Gassé with Rivé went off to the South^d, also Bellaire & Michel Allaire to the Oochenawga River. The Indians here still in dread of each other & do nothing – a few went away – gave a net to the Grand Picota for the Skins we owe him.

Augst 30th [1811] **Friday** A cold Morn^g, cloudy day. Men finished sewing the Canoe &c. 2 Salmon; killed 5 Ducks.

Aug 31st [1811] **Saturday** A fine cloudy cold day. Pegged up the Holes & gummed the first touch, 6 Seams – this was all. Killed 4 Teal Ducks & a Pheasant.

Septr 1st [1811] **Sunday** A fine but mostly cloudy day. Obs^d [sun's] Merid Alt^{de} – light, no shades – fly^g Clouds Lat^{de} 48°:38′:14″ N Dec^n 8°:25′:10″ N. Got ready to set off the Morrow; gummed the Canoe. In the evening Charles arrived. Got 5 Salmon & Trout from the Indians, many of whom are going up the River to hunt & fish &c.

Septr 2nd [1811] **Monday** A rainy day 'till Noon. Co down the River to where we embarked to go to the Sea is Co South 1M as p^r Map from end of small Isl^d. At 1 Pm set off: I pray God for a good Voyage & a happy meeting with my People & Canoes. Co N5W $\frac{1}{4}$M N2oW 1$\frac{1}{2}$M Co No $\frac{1}{8}$ N4oE $\frac{1}{5}$ N6oE 1$\frac{1}{2}$M NE $\frac{1}{7}$ N5oE $\frac{1}{6}$ + $\frac{1}{6}$ the River may be estimated at 450 Y^{ds} or 500 Y^{ds}, yet appears only 300 Y^{ds} X 'till we cross it – we then find it wide. Veins of that whiteish hard kind of Rock appear high up in the Bank, intermixed with light grey. N35E $\frac{1}{8}$M N24W $\frac{2}{3}$M N3oW $\frac{1}{3}$ N32W $\frac{1}{8}$ N4oW 1$\frac{1}{2}$M + 1M – $\frac{1}{2}$M short of Co put up at 5:20 Pm. Current always very strong & many Rocks in the Current, but generally good along shore – poled & paddled all the way. A Canoe is [ ], & beyond where we put up the old Chief & his Band. The Country very hilly with low narrow Pts, the Banks to which are ab^t 20 ft high on the Bay Side.

Septr 3rd [1811] **Tuesday** A cold cloudy Morn^g. At 5$\frac{1}{2}$ Am embarked Co done, then Co [18 courses] at end of Co arrived at the Portage on the right. Obs^d for Lat^{de} lower end Merid Alt^{de} of [sun's] LL Lat^{de} 48°:52':18" N Dec^n 7°:41':28" N. Co over the Portage N30E $\frac{1}{2}$M or 1100 Y^{ds}. The Water falls ab^t 2 ft perpend at the upper end in 3 Channels; the rest is strong deep eddy Current among Rocks & steep Banks of d^o on each Side, but good. At 1:55 Pm embarked Co N46E $\frac{2}{3}$M + $\frac{1}{3}$M N22E $\frac{1}{2}$ N25E $\frac{1}{2}$ + $\frac{3}{5}$ N15W $\frac{1}{7}$ N1OE $\frac{1}{8}$ N15E $\frac{1}{8}$ N22E $\frac{1}{5}$ N4OE $\frac{1}{2}$ all these Co^s vs Current + $\frac{1}{2}$M N15E $\frac{1}{2}$M d^o N55E $\frac{2}{3}$M end of Co camped at 6 Pm, very strong Current all day – for this 2M past see the Cut of the Saleesh River. The River more & more wooded & hilly, but still good.

Septr 4th [1811] **Wednesday** A foggy cold Morn^g – could not embark 'till 5:55 Am. Co N65E $\frac{3}{4}$ No $\frac{3}{4}$ N35E $\frac{1}{8}$ N4OE $\frac{1}{5}$ NE $\frac{1}{2}$ these 2 last Co^s small Cedars N25E $\frac{2}{5}$ + $\frac{1}{5}$ N4OE $\frac{1}{2}$M N25E $\frac{2}{3}$ No $\frac{1}{8}$ N12W $\frac{2}{3}$ the River is very narrow & deep strong Current, well wooded & the [left] Side seems good for Horses all along as yet. N30E 1M end of Co the Saleesh River in several Falls ab^t 200 Y^{ds} wide, very steep high Rocky Hills & slightly covered with Wood seems to come from the N30E^d, & the Country on the [right] appears much more rude than before. Co [21 courses] – on the [left] end of [last] Co a range of high Hills, woody & rocky, which form the height of 2 or 3000 ft, before only 8 or 1200 ft. N78W $\frac{1}{3}$ N75W $\frac{3}{5}$ N65W $\frac{1}{8}$ NW $\frac{1}{6}$ N4OW $\frac{1}{8}$ N35W $\frac{4}{5}$ N5W $\frac{1}{5}$ No 1 $\frac{1}{4}$M – ab^t $\frac{1}{3}$ of Co gone crossed & camped at 6:10 Pm at a Brook. The River here is not above 120 Y^{ds} wide & rarely exceeds 150 Y^{ds} – Current very strong, but the Canoe seems to go well. Lat^{de} 49°:2':7" N Dec^n 7°:19':24" N.

Septr 5th [1811] **Thursday** A fine Morn^g, a little misty. At 5:50 Am set off, finished Co + $\frac{1}{4}$M [11 courses] end of Co obs^d Merid Alt^{de} of [sun's] LL Lat^{de} 49°:17':5" N Dec^n 6°:57':13" N. [Co] N30W 1M N50W 1M N17W $\frac{1}{6}$ N5E $\frac{3}{5}$ – $\frac{1}{8}$M gone to McGillivray's River, Co up it N65E $\frac{2}{3}$M. At 1$\frac{1}{4}$ Pm we went up a little & crossed over & sent 2 young Men to spear fish, as we are unwell with eating dried Salmon

& Berries – they did not return 'till 5 Pm, when they gave us 1 poor
Salmon & 4 small Mullets. We set off & directly met 5 Men & 7 or
8 Women bringing me a small present of a Salmon & Berries, which
made us camp for the Night. This cost me a few of my small Articles,
with ab^t 4 ft of Tob in smoking &c, & payment for what we got from
the 8 Canoes who came up with us & who stay here, also ab^t 4 lbs of
Bears fat & a Side of Ribs half dried – they have Eetoowoy Roots.

Septr 6th [1811] **Friday** A misty Morn^g. At 5:40 Am set off, Co as yesterday, end of Co strong Rapid – handed. Co N55W $\frac{1}{3}$ end of this Co
a Cut & a Brook that is said leads by a short Road to McGillivray's
Lake, Co s70w $\frac{2}{5}$M + $\frac{2}{5}$ s84w 1M + $\frac{1}{4}$ s60w 1$\frac{1}{4}$M + $\frac{1}{4}$ s50w 1M
+ $\frac{3}{4}$M. From the Saleesh River the Hills have been close on the
River, especially on the [left] Side, but well wooded; those on the [right]
but thinly. Since McGillivray's River is mostly bare rock like a wall
of a hard dark grey & black, & much in Knowls & Gullies – say first rank
is 100, then ab^t 1200 for the 2nd; on the [left], hills of small Woods
sloping down to the Water, say 800 ft; on the [right], a narrow stripe
of level Land at the foot of the Hills, well wooded. Co + $\frac{2}{5}$M Co in a
narrow kind of Lake N[8]3w 1$\frac{2}{3}$M. At noon obs^d [sun's] Merid
Alt^{de} Lat^{de} 49°:21':19" N Dec^n 6°:34':54" N. Co N85w $\frac{1}{4}$ N80w 1M
+ 1M + 1M + $\frac{3}{4}$M + $\frac{1}{2}$M N85w $\frac{1}{4}$M beg^g of Co put up at 3$\frac{1}{4}$ Pm.
The Grounds on the [right] being fine for Animals & several Tracks of
the black tailed Chevreuil & Rein Deer in the Sand, sent Charles
& Hamelin a hunt^g – but they had no other Success than firing at a large
black Bear. Coxe very ill & most of us a little so.

Septr 7th [1811] **Saturday** A stormy Night with Lightning & a little
Rain. At 6 Am set off – head wind & high waves, finished Co, then
N60w $\frac{1}{2}$M N68w $\frac{1}{4}$ N45w $\frac{3}{4}$ N40w 3M near end of Co obs^d for Long^{de}
& Time – say $\frac{2}{5}$ in Co, Lat^{de} by Acc^t 49°:30$\frac{1}{3}$' N Mean Long^{de}
118°:51':15" w. Co + $\frac{2}{5}$, Co N35w $\frac{1}{2}$ N32w 2$\frac{1}{2}$M – ab^t $\frac{1}{5}$M short of
Co, obs^d [sun's] Merid Alt^{de} Lat^{de} 49°:35':30" N Dec^n 6°:12':30" N.
The Wind blew so hard that we remained on shore till 3:25 Pm;
when moderating a little, we set off, Co N25w 1M sight high Mountains
+ 1M + $\frac{1}{2}$M N18w $\frac{1}{2}$M + $\frac{1}{2}$ Co N13w + 2$\frac{1}{2}$M – 1M short of Co
camped at 6$\frac{1}{2}$ Pm. Fine evening. The Lake has not very high Hills,
say 400 to 800 ft, but very rude on the [left]; opposite end of Co, a Cut
with 2 Ravines from the West^d & deep low narrow Lands seeming

to be there. Obs^d a Comet this even^g: we had seen it these few nights past but hav^g a cloudy hilly horizon took it for a misty cloudy [ ] there – it's place is nearly in a right Line with the 2 guide Stars at 8:25 Pm, but below the 2nd Star at 4° or 5°, that is, below those Stars at that time. It's size is that of a Star of the 1st Mag, it's train of Light 2° long to the NE^d.

Septr 8th [1811] **Sunday** A fine mild Morn^g. At 5:38 Am set off, Co N1OW 1M [ ] N1 1E 2M N2OE 2$\frac{1}{2}$M – at 1M of Co obs^d for Long^{de} & Time, Co + $\frac{1}{2}$M, Lat^{de} 49°:58':24″ N Dec^n 5°:00':50″ N Mean Long^{de} 118°:43':45″ W (Septr 25th Ex^d the Errour of Sextant 3':30″). Co N55E 2$\frac{1}{2}$M – $\frac{3}{4}$M gone obs^d [sun's] LL; end of Co a little Snow on the [right], Rocks at 3000 ft N3OE $\frac{1}{3}$ NE $\frac{1}{5}$M N2OE $\frac{1}{3}$ N15E $\frac{3}{4}$ N22W $\frac{2}{3}$ + 2M. Remarks: the Lake we have passed has always Current in the Mid & very often from Side to Side – the last half has a Ledge of low Wood & Land with fine Shores on both Sides, the Mid steep ugly rocks, & the lower end rocky & good Shore by turns; it is said never to freeze over in Winter; the Land is all wet except towards the So end. At end of Co the Rocky Mountain bears N32W ab^t 40M with patches of Snow, quite white, running off to the WbS – they do not seem to exceed 4000 ft & are bare Rocks, the same of the head of the Brook we have just passed, where they seem to finish. Co N1OW 1$\frac{1}{2}$M N33W $\frac{1}{3}$ N33W $\frac{1}{3}$ N22W $\frac{1}{5}$ N1OW $\frac{1}{4}$ N65W $\frac{1}{5}$ No $\frac{1}{2}$M at end of Co put up at 5:25 Pm. We lost ab^t 40' at the Brook look^g for Trout, & ab^t 10' after a Duck I killed, besides my Observations.

Septr 9th [1811] **Monday** A fine Morn^g, a little Misty. At 5:40 Am set off, Co [13 courses] – the last 2$\frac{1}{4}$M in a Lake at 8$\frac{1}{2}$ Am, Co N22W 2$\frac{1}{2}$M the Brook from NE^d end of Co obs^d for Long^{de} & Time Lat^{de} by Acc^t 50°:15':43″ N Mean Long^{de} 118°:30':22″ W. Co NW 1M + 1M N5OW 1M + 1$\frac{3}{4}$M end of this Co obs^d Merid Alt^{de} of [sun's] LL Lat^{de} 50°:18':55″ N Dec^n 5°:27':23″ N. Co N5OW 2$\frac{1}{2}$M, Co N2[8]W 6$\frac{1}{2}$M N25W 3$\frac{1}{4}$M – at end of 1M gone, the Mountain that I set below bears N75W 5M end of Co put up at 5$\frac{1}{2}$ Pm.

Septr 10th [1811] **Tuesday** Water rose much – a cloudy Morn^g & soon heavy with Showers of Rain for most of the Day. At 5:15 Am set off, Co as yesterday N18W 3$\frac{1}{2}$M [a] River, Co N5W 4M NW 1$\frac{3}{4}$M we turned to the north^d to a Lodge of Indians, but they were away a hunt^g, when we were obliged to put up with smart Rain at 9 Am. At

11 Am set off, & went to the end of Co in the River Mouth – much
Wood stuck on an end in the Lake & both ends. Co [13 courses] near
end of [last] Co killed 3 Geese & put up at 6 Pm. Water rising.
Woods of fine Cedar, Fir Pine & other Pines – no Fir – much Willows
& low Lands with Isl^{ds} &c. Current very strong, but good poling
& pieces with the Line, except in places.

Septr 11th [1811] **Wednesday** A fine Morn^g. At 5:35 Am set off – water
rose full 1 ft per[pend]. Co [24 courses] at end of [last] Co put up
at 5:5′ Pm – it was here that Mr McDonald turned ab^t. Water fell 8 In.

Septr 12th [1811] **Thursday** A fine sharp Morn^g. At 6 Am set off, Co
N48E $\frac{1}{2}$M E^t $\frac{1}{8}$ N2OE $\frac{1}{5}$ N1OE – $\frac{1}{4}$ discharged at beg^g of Co, at the en-
trance of the Dalles at 200Y^{ds} gone, & carried most of the Cargoe.
North $\frac{1}{2}$M N5W $\frac{3}{4}$M N12W $\frac{3}{4}$ + $\frac{1}{4}$M at end of Co obs^d Merid Alt^{de} of
[sun's] LL Lat^{de} 51°:5′:13″ N Dec^n 4°:19′:00″ N. [Co] N3OW $\frac{1}{8}$M
N18W $\frac{3}{4}$ N5OW $\frac{1}{4}$ NW $\frac{1}{3}$ + $\frac{2}{5}$ N3OW $\frac{3}{4}$ NW 1M + $\frac{1}{6}$ + $\frac{2}{5}$ N3OW $\frac{2}{5}$ N3OW $\frac{1}{6}$
N2OW $\frac{1}{3}$ + $\frac{1}{2}$M N1OW $\frac{1}{2}$. From early Morn^g the Dalles very bad; all
the rest is very strong Current & Rapid – came up with the Line, latter
part by pieces. At 5$\frac{1}{4}$ Pm put up.

Septr 13th [1811] **Friday** A misty cold Morn^g. Water fell 2 In. At 6$\frac{1}{4}$ Am
set off, Co [14 courses] beg^g of [last] Co obs^d Merid Alt^{de} of [sun's]
LL Lat^{de} 51°:17′:0″ N Dec^n 4°:19′:00″ N. [Co] N65W $\frac{1}{2}$M + $\frac{1}{2}$M
from McGillivray's River there is Birch, Poplar, Aspin & Fir Pine with
the other Pines – Willows, Alders, small Plane & much Hazel below
– very fine Cedar below the Dalles to the Lake, none beyond or on the
Lake that appears to be good, but there are tolerable Box Trees.
Co [16 courses] end of Co at 5:50 Pm put up.

Septr 14 [1811] **Saturday** A misty Morn^g. At 7$\frac{1}{4}$ Am set off, Co
[11 courses] end of [last] Co say West 30 or 40M to the Oochenawga
Lake as seen by Indians from the tops of the Mountains, Co w^t $\frac{1}{4}$ NW
$\frac{1}{7}$ N18W $\frac{3}{4}$ N3OW 1M beg^g of Co where Mr McDonald turned ab^t on
foot & made a small Canoe NW $\frac{3}{4}$ – this Co is in a Narrow ab^t
60 Y^{ds} wide of steepish Rocks, but a small Beach except in the mid. 'Till
now much blue Clay & sometimes that hard white stone like Earth,
at times in the Banks with large low Pts NW 1M end of Co obs^d Merid
Alt^{de} of [sun's] LL Lat^{de} 51°:30′:1[4]″ N Dec^n 3°:32′:59″ N. Co
N78W $\frac{1}{4}$ N5OW $\frac{1}{8}$ N36W $\frac{2}{3}$ W^t $\frac{1}{8}$ N35W $\frac{1}{2}$ all bad N5OW $\frac{1}{8}$ N36W $\frac{2}{3}$ strong

rapid Current – lined on the [left], good to run. w^t $\frac{1}{8}$ SR discharged all the heavy Pieces & for 210 Y^{ds} carried – lined up the Canoe
on the left, hav^g crossed. N30W $\frac{1}{2}$M beg^g of Co a fall & rush of Water,
discharged all for 150 Y^{ds} & lined up quite light – very dangerous
to line down. The rest of Co strong rapid Current, lined the whole up
loaded. On the [left], end of Co a large rock between which & the
Shore lined & handed – here the Canoes going down ought to bring
up. N40W $\frac{3}{4}$ N10E $\frac{1}{6}$ SRC N30W $\frac{1}{4}$ N45W $\frac{3}{4}$ N35W $\frac{1}{4}$ N50W $\frac{1}{2}$ N60W $\frac{1}{4}$ N50W
$\frac{1}{2}$ – crossed over in mid of Co & camped at 5:50 Pm. Sight a large bold
Mountain on the [left], still much Snow on them. The River is very
strong Current; I suppose loaded Canoes must line down much of the
Dalles.

Septr 15th [1811] **Sunday** A fine Morn^g. At 5$\frac{1}{2}$ Am set off, Co
[29 courses] mid of [last] Co on the left put up with small Rain – see
the Mountains now turn to the right. The Current always rapid
& very strong, & lined up some dangerous rocky Pts. Woods as usual,
tho' apparently less fine Cedar & much small Pine, white d^o, Fir
Pine – no Fir since below the lower Dalles.

Septr 16th [1811] **Monday** A rainy Morn^g – Water rose ab^t 18 In. At
10 Am set off, Co as yesterday, then [15 courses] mid of [last] Co
camped, hav^g staid $\frac{1}{2}$H waiting the Rain to cease. At first to day
long strong Rapids, since more moderate.

Septr 17 [1811] **Tuesday** A fine Morn^g. At 6$\frac{1}{2}$ Am set off, Co
[35 courses] at end of [last] Co camped at 6$\frac{1}{2}$ Pm. The Current
always very strong, but always rapid; here the River bends to the east^d.
Many of the Mountains green & fit for Sheep & Goats, but there
are no Sheep, only Goats – the Snow is too deep in Winter.

Septr 18 [1811] **Wednesday** A misty Morn^g. Dried my Tent, gummed
the Canoe & at 7$\frac{1}{4}$ Am set off, Co [16 courses] to our old Hut, thank
Heaven. We searched about to see if anyone had been here, but
finding no Marks of any person, we set up a few Lines in Iroquois as
we supposed only those People would pass here. We staid ab^t $\frac{1}{2}$H
& then set off up the Canoe River in hopes of meeting my People. At
2:55 Pm N5W $\frac{1}{5}$ N30W $\frac{1}{5}$ N40W $\frac{1}{2}$ N5W $\frac{1}{2}$ S60W $\frac{1}{4}$ w^t $\frac{1}{7}$ N80W $\frac{1}{7}$ N50W $\frac{1}{8}$
finding this Channel blocked up with drift wood returned, Co
[16 courses]. At 5$\frac{1}{4}$ Pm camped, seeing marks of Beaver & Moose

Tracks. Very strong Current, like one continued Rapid, with much Wood.

Septr 19th [1811] **Thursday** A rainy Morn^g. Charles caught a very small Beaver – they cooked it, which took us till 8:10 Am. Co [47 courses] – camped in [last] Co at 5$\frac{3}{4}$ Pm – all day strong Rapids, especially where the Banks have slid down. The Country fine for Wood: Cedar, Pines & Cypress – no Firs – small Plane – no Box. A vast Glacier in the mid Fork of a Brook on the [left], the largest I have ever yet seen.

Septr 20th [1811] **Friday** A misty cloudy Morn^g. At 7$\frac{1}{4}$ Am set off N1OW $\frac{1}{4}$ SW $\frac{1}{8}$ N75W $\frac{1}{8}$ N35W $\frac{1}{7}$ N1OW $\frac{1}{6}$ N60W $\frac{1}{2}$ the River is nearly closed by Wood [19 courses] at end of [last] Co a Rapid: here the Water falls full 3 ft perpend in ab^t 40 Y^{ds} & there are very many like [25 courses] – at 5:50 Pm put up in Co. Much Beaver vestiges & has been all along, as well as Moose. Killed a fat Cormorant, the only one seen.

Septr 21 [1811] **Saturday** A very rainy day. Hamelin killed 4 Stock Ducks, poor. The weather is too bad for hunt^g, altho' plenty of Moose & Beaver. Lay by all day – made myself a winter Cap & a pair of Shoes. Snow Geese & Grey d^o passed for the first [time] this Season.

Septr 22 [1811] **Sunday** After a rainy Night, a misty Morn^g. At 7$\frac{1}{4}$ Am set off, Co N75W $\frac{1}{4}$ N22W $\frac{1}{8}$ N1OE $\frac{1}{2}$ NO $\frac{1}{6}$. The Snow that fell when it rained with us at the upper Dalles remained unthawed at 3000 ft & above; now the snow is only 1000 ft above us, below which rain. Leaves now turning yellow on the Birch only – Alders &c still green. N32W $\frac{1}{4}$ Cedar very rare N22W $\frac{1}{4}$ NW $\frac{1}{8}$ S55W $\frac{1}{4}$ N60W $\frac{1}{7}$ N35W $\frac{1}{8}$ N5E $\frac{2}{5}$ much Aspin, the River now good N20W$\frac{1}{8}$ NW 1/10 N75W $\frac{2}{5}$ S85W $\frac{2}{5}$. Here, hearing Charles call who was a hunt^g, we returned, he having thank good Providence killed a good doe Moose – we staid till 20' Pm, cooked Kettle &c of which we had much Need, & then went off to the end of Co^s, then [28 courses] – at 5$\frac{1}{2}$ Pm camped. Plenty of Moose – their roads are like those of the Buffalo, so well [are they] beat; they have not yet begun the rut – fired at a Buck [which] got off wounded. At night Joseph the Nipissing with Bap[tiste] Delcour in a small Canoe came up with us, with Word that the People,

Goods &c with Mr W[illia]m Henry had crossed the Mountains by the Flat Heart Brook & were at my d° Hut.

Septr 23rd [1811] Monday A rainy day. At $7\frac{1}{2}$ Am set off & ran down the Canoe River to the Columbia, where we turned to the Flat Heart Brook & found Mr W[illia]m Henry, & the Men, Goods & Horses &c, thank good Providence.

Notes to the Text

Journey to the Kootanaes

Source: AO journals 13

Four attempts were made to cross the Rocky Mountains in 1800–01 under the direction of Duncan McGillivray; Thompson participated in three of these, and he copied McGillivray's account of the fourth in AO journals 13. A summary in AO journals 75 states McGillivray's purpose, administrative provisions and preparation for this first attempt: "By arrangements made at Fort William, Mr Duncan McGillivray was to be early at the Rocky Mountain House, about the latter end of September 1800 to prepare for crossing the Mountains and proceeding to the Pacific Ocean the next year."

5 October 1800, "the Men" Thompson's position at this time was that of clerk – cf. Finan McDonald's duties (27 May 1807, 19 September 1807, 7 November 1808, 6 October 1809, 27 August 1811). Beauchamp, Morrin, and Pierre Daniel are not mentioned again. But La Gassé reappears several times in the Columbia journals, and Boulard, whom Thompson engaged year after year until he traded him for a Hawaiian (31 July 1811 note), becomes a familiar figure. McGillivray and Thompson later visited the He Dog at the Highwood River camp (24 November 1800). "He Dog" and "Old Bear" are probably English translations of Native names, as is "the Thunder" (30 August 1809); cf. French names given to other Native associates, which seem as often as not to be sobriquets (1 September 1807, 9 May 1808, 16 October 1808, 18 August 1811), not unlike the names assigned to horses (9 November 1808, 31 October 1810). Native hunters from eastern tribes were given Christian names (3 July 1811, 22 September 1811); exceptions are the Wolverene (13 May 1807) and Yellow Bird (29 October 1810).

5 October 1800, "a Pekenow Indian ... several Blood Indians" members of Peigan and Blood bands. Cf. 22 November 1800 and McGillivray's "Account": "The Blackfeet, Piegans & Blood Indians are unquestionably the same nation, as they speak the same language and have the same manners & customs. They consist of about Seven hundred tents or a thousand families. From the circumstance of their being placed near the frontier they are generally at war with their neighbours and even extend their warfare beyond the Rocky Mountains and far beyond the Mississouri. They are a brutish and stupid nation, have some peculiar regulations amongst them and are generally governed by their chiefs and great men" (67).

Cf. also Henry: "The Country which the Peagans call their own ... is along the foot of the Rocky Mountains, the Bow River and even as far as the Banks of the Missouri, to the Southward. It is the motion of the Buffalo which regulates their course throughout the year, over this vast extent of meadow Country, as they must always be near them, to obtain a supply of Provisions for their Families ... From the contempt they have of labour, [they] will not even kill a Beaver ... to enable them to purchase an Axe or other European utencil although Beaver are exceeding numerous ... they very frankly tell us, that War, Women and Horses are all they delight in. Liquour now begins to become one of their principal objects of desire. Many families are yet destitute of either a Kettle or an Axe" (NA MG19 A13, 1122–4/Coues, 723–4).

5 October 1800, "our Guide" Like other fur trade explorers, Thompson engaged local men as guides: cf. 9 October 1800, 17 November 1800, 6 June 1801, 22 June 1807, 3 October 1807, 19 and 24 May 1808, 29 October 1810, 9 January 1811.

5 October 1800, "crossed the River" – the North Saskatchewan River at Rocky Mountain House. Cf. Henry: "Our establishment at this place stands on a high Bank on the North Side of the River; the situation is well adapted for defense ... Our block Houses have a full command of the Fort for some distance ... above this establishment the Rapids are more frequently met with, and the navigation more tedious as the water becomes shoal and will not admit of Canoes passing with more than half a Cargo to the foot of the Mountains" (NA MG19 A13, 1096–7/Coues, 701–2).

5 October 1800, "Goods amounting to about 300 Skins" Merchandise was priced according to the value of a prime beaver pelt, although the trader could vary the rate of exchange if he wished to encourage new customers – cf. 7 August 1807, 19 May 1808, 13 September 1809, 6 October 1809, 5 and 6 July 1811, 14 and 29 August 1811, as well as 27 December 1810 note. Cf. also Laroque: "Took the Inventory, the Results of which is a Balance of Eighty-Four skins, on the side of the Book it ought to be" (Wood and Thiessen, 150). In 1808 Henry noted: "The Beaver and other Skins are paid according to their appearant value for the current Year. The prices put upon our Goods as heretofore been very inconsistent, seldom a year passes, but some alteration is made ... This occasions us in the interior some trouble and inconveniencies" (NA MG19 A13, 1155). The HBC "overplus" was a response to this problem – see Ray (63–5).

5 October 1800, "Our Co ... may be about SEbE 2½M" Distances were estimated by the time it took to cover them; directions were by the sun, as here (cf. 28 and 30 September 1809, 29 October 1810) or by compass (22 November 1800, 13 July 1807, 1, 2 and 12 November 1810). Sun readings were given as rough marine directions, the sixteen points of the wind rose. For compass readings, Thompson used a pocket directional compass made by Dollond and marked in quadrants of 90° each. HBC records note his purchase of compasses just before leaving the company (HBCA A16/III). Thompson was aware of compass variation, which was as much as 21° in the region of his explorations – cf. Robertson's *Elements of Navigation*, the manual of navigation used by Turnor, Fidler and Thompson: "The variation of the compass is the difference between the bearings of the true and magnetic north poles, and is measured by an arc of the horizons contained between the true and magnetic north points of it ... The variation is found by comparing the true and magnetic amplitudes or azimuths of celestial objects together" (242).

To chart his course, Thompson noted his distances and directions, estimated his route by dead reckoning, and from time to time corrected his position by astronomical observations. Turnor and his students translated the maritime model into terrestrial terms. Cf. Robertson's explanation of the method of dead reckoning and its limitations: "If an accurate account could be kept of the true courses which a ship has steered, as directed by the compass, and of the distance she has run, as measured by the log ... then both the latitude and longitude of the place where the ship is at any time, would be known on settling the ship's account to that time ... But as the ship's motion is liable to be disturbed from a variety of causes ... her place, assigned by these means, may justly be suspected to be erroneous" (289). See also Smyth (6–7, 11–12).

5 October 1800, "the crossing place of the Clear Water River ... the Bridge" Cf. 19 October 1800, 17 November 1800.

6 October 1800, "thro' a willow plain" – *Salix* sp.

6 October 1800, "saw a herd of Cows" – *Bison bison*, buffalo. Cf. AO journals 28: "The Bison in the Woods is much larger than in the plains, from superior pasture and water." Thompson's Columbia journals attest to the presence of buffalo not only massed on the prairies but frequently found in the mountains – cf. 24 and 30 November 1800, 27 October 1808, 4 and 6 January 1811.

6 October 1800, "Here we had a grand view" – Sundre, at the junction of the Red Deer and Little Red Deer rivers. Cf. 17 October 1800, 20 November 1800, 11 June 1801, 13 June 1801 note, 1 June 1807, and AO journals 71: "The east side of the Rocky Mountains from Latitude 32° N to Lat^{de} 57° N sends out no branches eastward, but has almost every where, as viewed from the vast plains, a most imposing and grand appearance, in a waving line, of a vast mountainous bulwark of Hills behind Hills in close succession, rising each high above the other to the centre ridge."

Fidler's first sight of the mountains was from the same place on 20 November 1792: "The Rocky Mountain ... appeared awfully grand, stretching from ssw to wbs p^r Compass, very much similar to dark rain like clouds rising up above the Horizon on a fine Summers evening – it does not appear of a regular height in all places but appears like 5 hills, being the highest parts; on account of the distance, the other parts that connect the whole are not visible here" (HBCA E3/2). Cf. also Bird, 20 September 1799: "The snowy summits of the Stony Mountain like vast heaps of white clouds appeared in view presenting to our sight (as the sun shone full upon it) the most grand and romantic views" (HBCA B60/a/5).

6 October 1800, "what a Quantity of Ground ..." The sentence is unfinished; it should probably read, "It is surprising what a quantity of ground was occupied by the river bed."

6 October 1800, "Let us ask the Cause of this" The cause was no doubt flash flooding, the most dramatic form of erosion in the Rockies' front ranges and foothills. Cf. Simpson: "Above high Water Mark the trunk of a large Tree is to be seen evidently left there by the Stream but when the Cognoscenti must determine; some of our Columbia Sages will have it that it was in the Days of Noah!" (Merk,

130). The importance accorded erosion in Hutton's *Theory of the Earth*, published in 1788, was slow to gain popular acceptance. For his part, Thompson still imagined that the earth in its present state was the result of rapid creation rather than slow evolutionary forces – cf. 30 November 1800 and 5 August 1811.

8 October 1800, "a jumping Deer ... the Red Deers River" Cf. 2 October 1807, 19 July 1807, 31 October 1810, 26 July 1811. *Odocoileus virginianus*, white-tailed deer, was called variously Virginian deer, jumping deer, or chevreuil, although "chevreuil" was also at times a generic term including *Odocoileus hemionus*, mule deer, and its sub-species the Columbian black-tailed deer. The red deer – *Cervus elaphus*, now commonly called elk – was always distinguished from the chevreuil. Cf. Ogden, who discriminated among the species: "The meat of one Elk and two Black Tail Deer were brought to Camp the latter are certainly of a larger size than the white tail and altho there is no defferance in the taste of their flesh still in their habits there is a wide differance" (Ogden, ed. Davies and Johnson, 62).

9 October 1800, "They are so jealous of the Kootanaes" Cf. 5, 10, and 23 October 1800, 22 November 1800, 28 July 1807, 27 August 1807, 8, 13, and 25 September 1807, 8 May 1808, 29 October 1811. Cf. also Fidler, 31 December 1792: "They [Kootenays] was never near any of the Trading Settlements altho they much wish it. But the Muddy River [Peigan], Blood, Black Feet & Southern [Cree] Indians always prevents them, they wishing to monopolize all their skins to themselves, which they do, giving the Poor [Kootenay] Indians only a meer trifle, for they scarce give them as much for 10 Skins as they can get for one at the Trading Settlements" (HBCA E3/2).

Henry saw Hidatsa opposition to trade with the Crow in the same light: "It was really disgusting to see how those impious vagabonds the Big Bellies keep those poor inoffensive Crow Indians in subjection ... The price once fixed by these scoundrels, they will permit you to give not more than they offer themselves. By this means they generally get into their hands the total of what ever is brought into their Villages, and then sell out again to strangers for double what it cost them" (Gough, 276/Coues, 399). By seeing "distant" tribes as victims of middlemen, traders were able to justify expansion of their own exploitive practices – cf. 20 October 1800, 30 September 1809, 7 July 1811.

9 October 1800, "At Noon Obs[erve]d Merid[ian] Alt[itu]de of [sun's] L[ower] L[imb]" In the journal MSS the sun is always indicated by a dotted circle. Robertson explains how to measure the sun's alti-tude: "To take the Sun's Altitude with Hadley's Quadrant [or a sextant] ... The face being turned towards the Sun, hold the quadrant by the braces or by either radius, as is found most convenient ... put the eye close to the left-hand hole in the vane; look at the horizon through the transparent part of the horizon glass; at the same time, move the index with the left-hand, until the image of the Sun, seen in the quicksilvered part, falls in with the line of the horizon, taking either the upper or under edge of the solar image. Swing your body gently from side to side, and if that edge of the Sun which is observed touch the horizon line like a tangent, without cutting it, the observa-tion is well made: and the degrees on the arch, reckoned from that end next your body, give the altitude of that edge of the Sun which was brought to the horizon. If the lower edge ["lower limb" or LL] was observed, then 16 minutes added to the said degrees, give the altitude of the Sun's center; but if the upper edge ["upper limb" or UL] was used, the 16 minutes must be subtracted" (250).

Thompson described his sextant in a letter to Sir Robert Hall, 26 March 1817 – cf. the draft of this letter in AO journals 31: "My instru-ment is a 10 In brass sextant of Dolland, my Companion for these 28 years past and is a good one, but its size allows division to only $\frac{1}{2}$ Min[ute] and the reading off to 15 [seconds]" – nevertheless accurate to Roberston's standard: "In a Hadley's quadrant of 15 inches radius, if the limb and Vernier's scale are well divided, the measure of an arc may be read to thirds or quarters of a minute, with the assistance of a magnifying glass" (Robertson, 299). Its normal error was $1'30''$ to $1'34''$ (26 April 1808 and 23 September 1809), but Thompson extended this to $3'30''$ on 10 July 1811 after the "instrument had got quite shaken out of adjustment" two days before.

9 October 1800, "Lat^{de} 51°:47':21" N Dec^n 6°:23':59" S." Robertson indicates the method of finding latitude: "Find the meridian altitude or zenith distance of the Sun or Star ... Apply the corrections for the dip of the horizon, the refraction ... and semi-diameter, if the object be the sun. Seek the Sun's or Star's declination ... in the Nautical Almanack, observing to correct the Sun's decl. for places more than 8° or 10° to the E. or W. of London" (261).

Bowditch gives a fuller explanation:"To find the Latitude of a Ship at Sea or Place on Shore, from the observed meridional Altitude of the Sun or a Star. RULE. To the observed altitude of the sun's lower limb add the difference between the sun's semidiameter and the dip of the horizon ... their sum will be the apparent altitude of the sun's centre ... From the apparent altitude of the sun's centre, subtract the refraction answering to that altitude ... the remainder is the sun's true altitude ... Subtract the sun's true altitude from 90; the remainder is the true zenith distance, which is north if the zenith be to the north of the sun ... Take the sun's declination ... from page 2 of the month in the Nautical Almanack, noting whether it is north or south ... Then if the zenith distance and declination be both north or both south, add them together; but if one be north and the other south, subtract the less from the greater, and the sum or difference will be the latitude" (141).

10 October 1800, "thick Woods of Pines with Spots of Aspins" – conifers, together with patches of *Populus tremuloides*, trembling aspen, which would be found in cloned groups on alluvial fans and beside streams. According to contemporary usage, "Pines" was a generic term – cf. Douglas, referring to mixed woods: "The greater part of the whole country as far as the eye can reach is closely covered with pine of several species" (103). Cf. also Henry in similar country, on his way to Howse Pass: "I observed here no less than seven different sorts of Pine, viz. épinette blanche, épinette rouge, sapin, cypress, Rocky Mountain pine, white pine, and prush; the two latter trees are peculiar to these mountains" (NA MG19 A13, 1069/Coues, 688). See later references to specific trees.

10 October 1800, "they purposely misrepresent the country" Cf. 28 September 1807, and Mackenzie's suspicious response to Native information: "It's very certain that those people know more about the Country than they chuse to tell me at least than what comes to my Ears. I am obliged to depend upon my Interpreter for all News." (214–15).

12 October 1800, "Long^{de} 114°:45' w" Robertson followed Halley and Maskelyne in recommending that the best method for finding longitude was by lunar distances. Ideally this method required an accurate watch and four observers: "1st. Let the watch be adjusted to true time, or its error found, a few hours before or after the observation. 2nd. Let three persons, each having a good Hadley's quadrant, make observations; one taking the apparent angular distance of the moon from the Sun or Star, another taking the altitude of the moon; and the third, taking the altitude of the Sun or Star. These observations are to be made at one and the same time, which another person is to note by the watch. 3rd. Let the observed altitudes be corrected for the centers of the objects [cf. 9 October 1800 note], and then the distance be corrected by parallax, &c, to have the true distance of the centrers. 4th. Find the time at Greenwich, when this true distance happened. 5th. The difference between the Greenwich time and the ship's time, is the difference of longitude" (Robertson, 307). To ensure greater accuracy, Robertson recommended several sets of observations for the same position (308), a recommendation that Thompson followed whenever possible (see AO journals, *passim*, calculations).

Thompson's biggest problem was his faulty watches, which lost time and often had to be reset by observation. He mentioned this matter frequently in his journals (see, for example, 4 June 1807, 26 November 1810, 4 July 1811, and 2 August 1811). Faced with this problem, the best Thompson could do was to keep track of the watches' rate of inaccuracy.

Robertson gives instructions for finding time by equal altitudes of the sun before and after noon: "The ship lying by, let the Sun's altitude be taken at any time in the forenoon ... set down that time and altitude. In the afternoon, wait until the Sun has the same altitude exactly (the index of the quadrant being already set to the morning altitude) and note down that time; then the half sum of these two times is the apparent time shewn by the clock or watch, when the sun was on the meridian of that place" (258).

The exactness of Thompson's observations and subsequent calculations has been questioned: cf. an anonymous note in the Selkirk Papers, dated 1 November 1816: "[The observations] lately published all rest on the authority of a Mr David Thompson of the NW Co whose survey on a large scale is hanging up in the great Hall of this Fort [Fort William]: nothing can be more rediculously incorrect than every part of it which we have had an opportunity of scrutinizing ... But the neat drawing, the minuteness & apparent care bestowed on his plans may well have deceived people into the belief of their accuracy, so long as there were no other surveys to compare with his." (NA MG19 E1, 7:2895–6). See Stewart (289–303) for more recent criticism. But cf. Tyrrell's introduction to the *Narrative*: "While my instruments may have been better than his, [Thompson's] surveys and observations were invariably found to have an accuracy that left little or nothing to be desired" (Tyrrell, xxxii). See also Tyrrell-RSC (233–4), and Whitrow (81) on the "personal equation." For a thorough description of Thompson's method of observing for longitude and a favourable judgment of his results, see Sebert (405–14).

12 October 1800, "over a high point of land" Parker Ridge.

12 October 1800, "Pekenow Indians ... were Eagle hunting" – *Haliacetus leuocephalus*, bald eagle. Cf. Douglas: "[Eagles] are caught as follows: A deep pit is dug in the ground, covered over with small sticks, straw, grass and a thin covering of earth, in which the hunter takes his seat; a large piece of flesh is placed above, having a string tied to it, the other end held in the hand of the person below. The bird on eyeing the prey instantly descends, and while his talons are fastened to the flesh, the hunter pulls bird and flesh into the pit" (269).

12 October 1800, "a rough Sketch of the Appearance of the Mountains" See Thompson's drawings of the mountains near Kootanae House in Tyrrell's edition of the *Narrative* (flyleaves). This sketch of the *appearance* of the mountains should not be confused with Thompson's small rough maps (20 April 1808), which probably resembled those of Fidler and William Clark. See HBCA E3/1–3, Moulton, *Atlas,* and Thwaites, *passim.*

12 October 1800, "Fisher ... Wolverenes ... Moose ... and Grisled Bears but too many" – Martes pennanti, Gulo gulo, Alces alces and Ursus arctos. Cf. 21 October 1800: the Kootenays' trade is in these furs. See Ordway (Quaife, 204, 210, 212, 227, 241) for evidence of numerous grizzlies in the foothills and on the western plains.

13 October 1800, "Pekenow young Men ... have stolen two fine Mares" Introduced from California to the Pacific Northwest after the Spanish conquest, horses were herded, traded and stolen until they reached the Saskatchewan watershed by the mid-eighteenth century. Some ran wild (6 June 1807, 20 August 1807). Horse thieving was great sport and a cause of intertribal skirmishes – cf. 15 October 1800, 24 and 27 November 1800, 1 September 1807, 8 May 1808, and 16 October note.

13 October 1800, "the Kootanaes would be on the Heights of the Mountain" On 31 December 1792, Fidler "accompanied [a group of Peigans] on purpose to see these Indians, who has never seen a European before ... The [Peigan] Chief used every method in his power except force to persuade me to return, as he said the road was very bad, also a great distance & perhaps the Cottonahaws might hurt me ... however I strongly insisted in going forward to see the Country and the Ind[s] ... the Cottonahaw Chief met us alone, and saluted us in his manner all with a Kiss" (HBCA E3/2). Judging from the Peigan chief's opposition to Fidler's meeting, the HBC approach to trading with the Kootenays was doomed to failure – cf. Bird, 4 October 1799: "Made the Muddy River Indian [Peigan] Chief some small presents and promised him larger in case he can succeed in bringing the Cottanaho Indians to this place with beaver; he promised to do everything in his power but whether he will succeed or not time only can determine" (HBCA B60/a/5). By contrast the NW Co sent Thompson out to meet the Kootenays.

The pencilled draught of a letter found in AO journals 19 indicates Thompson's hopes for trade across the divide: "All the Indians are desirous of opening out a Trade with us, and look on our arrival as a Blessing. How far I may be able to improve this good Disposition Time alone will tell." Cf. Bird: "Beaver are said to be numerous in the country of the Cotta na ha's, and nothing will prevent the Canadians getting part of them; the hopes of immediate gain is a strong encouragement to them; they have every requisite for undertakings of this kind, plenty of goods, canoes, and able men ready to second all their enterprises however dangerous or laborious" (Johnson, 219).

14 October 1800, "West 22 Miles to the Foot of the high Cliffs" – near the junction of the Red Deer and Panther rivers.

14 October 1800, "a few Furrs in Beaver & Bears ... a Red Fox skin" *Castor canadensis, Ursus americanus* and *Vulpes vulpes.*

14 October 1800, "a Present of his Bow & Quiver of Arrows" Cf. a note on the front flyleaf of the VPL journal: "Mr Thompson's bow & six arrows" among goods "taken down by Hughes, June 26th, 1801." Cf. also 14 May 1808, and Henry: "These People make by far the handsomest Bows I have ever seen and they are always preferred by other Indians. I have seen a Peagan pay a Gun or a horse for one" (NA MG19 A13, 112/Coues, 713–14).

14 October 1800, "to reward him for the Present" The Kootenay chief was paid for his handsome gift in the form of a return present of trade goods – cf. 5 July 1811, 8 and 9 August 1811, 5 September 1811 for the conventions and expectations of this rough barter system. The HBC and HW Co traders always adhered to it, paying Natives for whatever they accepted. The Lewis and Clark expedition was more demanding – cf. Lewis: "As these people had been liberal with us with rispect to provision I directed the men not to croud their lodge [in] surch of food in the manner hunger has compelled them to do at most lodges we have passed, and which [one chief] had informed me was disagreeable to the natives. but their previous want of hospitality had induced us to consult their enclinations but little and suffer our men to obtain provision from them on the best terms they could" (Thwaites, 5:16).

14 October 1800, "I cut a fathom of tobacco ... among them" Cf. Hearne: "Every one of any note, who joined us, expected to be treated with a few pipes, and on some occasions it was scarcely possible to get off without presenting a few inches to them ... The tobacco ... is twisted into the form of a rope, of near an inch in diameter, and then wound into a large roll: from which it is taken by measures of length, for the natives" (99).

14 October 1800, "Bogs" – watery flats and sloughs that could be crossed without sinking into them only when they were frozen – cf. 18 November 1800, 19 and 20 May 1807, 29–31 October 1810, 8 November 1810, and Kane: "Nere sundown we got into a large swamp about 14 miles acros ... put up my tent and eat my supper of dride Buffalo meete lade down in the swamp muscitose in millions could not sleepe [n]ext morning I had to wade up to my middle in water to cetch they Horses ... I got on and tried to fors my Hors thru he sank up to his belley and would go no further ... after a grate dele of trubble I got out" (MacLaren, 28).

14 October 1800, "those high Craigs ... were inaccessible to human feet" Cf. 30 November 1800, 12 and 13 June 1801, 17 May 1807, 25 June 1807, 19 November 1810.

16 October 1800, "In the Morn ... assembling the horses" Since the foothills and mountains offered sparse forage, horses were allowed to wander freely overnight in order to feed, and considerable time each morning was spent in rounding them up (cf. 19 May 1807, 6 June 1807). Occasionally they would be hobbled or picketed – cf. 8 November 1808, and Laroque: "When it was dark we tied our horses, with long Cords to pickets fix'd in the ground, In order that they might not go at a distance from us during the night" (Wood and Thiessen 135–6). But most of the time the horse thief's job was easy – cf. Henry: "You are not sure of your horse except upon his back" (NA MG19 A13, 25).

16–19 October 1800, "the Water Campment" Cf. 5 October 1800; *"the Plain of the grand View"* – cf. 6 October 1800; *"the Bridge"* – cf. 5 October 1800.

17 October 1800, "a Gambling Match" Cf. 6, 18, and 19 September 1807. The contestants probably played a version of the hand or stick game – cf. Ordway (Quaife, 276, 344), and Cox: "Their common game is a simple kind of hazard. One man takes a small stone which he changes for some time from hand to hand, all the while humming a slow monotonous air. The bet is then made; and according as his adversary succeeds in guessing the hand in which the stone is concealed, he wins or loses. They seldom cheat, and submit to their losses with the most philosophical resignation" (177–8). The outcome of one session at Kootanae House is given in AO journals 19 for 6 February 1808: "After a good long gambling Match, our Kootanae has gained nearly the whole. His gains are 17 Red Deer Skins, 24 Chevreuil, 1 Gun, 3 Axes, 10 Knives, 350 Balls, 7 lbs of Powder, 6 Horses & Saddles, Saddle Stuff &c, 1 Robe, 1 Blanket & many small Articles, besides 2 good Tents. The others have only their Wives, Children & old leather clothing left. 2 Family Men have only 1 p[ai]r of Leggins and 1 leather Shirt between them."

20 October 1800, "an Old Man ... went to the English" – to Acton House, the HBC post under James Bird's direction which was located next to Rocky Mountain House. Both posts were built in 1799. Cf. Bird to Joseph Howse, 18 September 1799: "We have been under the necessity of Settling such a number of new Howses that we find ourselves much at a loss for men to Oppose our new opponents with that vigour it will require. I however hope we shall be able to prevent their Making Fortunes this year but am absolutely affraid to look forward to the next ... Merely to bring a quantity of goods inland is no longer all that is necessary; men are now required to dispose of it, or it will infallibly remain on hand or must be given for such Furs as others cannot find their interest in taking" (HBCA B60/a/5). Anthony Henday, Matthew Cocking, and others had been making the same point to their HBC superiors for almost fifty years. Cf. also Hearne: "For Sertin, the Canadians goods in most of the Prinsaple articals are nowise inferior to the Companys and all the Differance it makes to an Indian is in the Prise" (Tyrrell-HTF, 160).

20 October 1800, "made them a present of near half a keg of Rum" Cf. 22 November 1800, 5 September 1807, and *Narrative*: "I had made it a law to myself, that no alcohol should pass the Mountains in my company, and thus be clear of the sad sight of drunkenness, and it's many evils" (Tyrrell, 396/Glover, 287). Cox affirms that the sale of alcohol was prohibited in the Columbia department even after Thompson left the Northwest: "We never brought ardent spirits amongst [the Natives] for the purposes of barter, and therefore cannot say how far an abundance of it would have seduced them to its intemperate use" (266).

Meanwhile the brandy trade was brisk in other departments: cf. the NW Co minutes for 1810, which record the partners' response to Wilberforce's prohibitionist legislation: "The Consumption of Liquor in all the Trade carried on by the North West Company was next examined (at present estimated at 10,000 Gallons – including Spirits), in order to ascertain the least possible quantity that might be made to Answer should *the Saints in Parliament* – in their mistaken notions of Philanthropy – persist in the Intention of abolishing the use of that Article wholely in the Trade – and it is the general opinion that even one Half of the above quantity or 5,000 gallons if restricted to that small quantity, might still serve the Trade was it found advisable to make any offer of that kind to Parliament, in order to prevent its total prohibition" (Wallace, 268–9).

21 October 1800, "Conversed much with them about … their Country" Thompson informed himself of the geography as well as possibilities for trade – cf. 24 November 1800, 19 July 1807, 16, 17, 28, and 30 September 1807, 18 May 1808, 4 July 1811. He usually received detailed information, although the knowledge of those questioned was at times limited by a natural barrier to travel (2 October 1809, 6 July 1811). Cf. also Mackenzie, who was asked why he made such inquiries: "I replied, that we certainly were acquainted with the principal circumstances of every part of the world; that I knew where the sea is, and where I myself then was, but that I did not exactly understand what obstacles might interrupt me in getting to it … Thus I fortunately preserved the impression in their minds, of the superiority of white people over themselves" (323).

21 October 1800, "fitted La Gassé and Le Blanc to winter with them" Thompson had wintered with Peigans in 1787–88 (Glover, 48–51), Fidler with Chipewyans in 1791–92 and with a Peigan band the following year. In April 1872 Fidler summed up his first winter's experience: "Being absent from all European intercourse & alone with the Jepewyans ever since the 4ᵗʰ September last, having acquired a sufficiency of their language to transact any business with them, upon the whole this has been rather an agreeable winter than otherwise" (HBCA E3/1).

Fidler noted the NW Co wintering among the Kootenays in a postscript to his 31 December 1792 entry: "In the fall of 1800, 28 Cotton na haw men with 2 Women came into Acton House, our uppermost settlement in the Saskatchewan river, with a few furrs – this is the first time they have ever seen a House. After remaining here for a few days (no other Indians being near the House) 2 Canadians accompanied them to their Country to examine it & learn whether or not any Beaver in any quantity was to be found there – but as these 2 men could neither read nor write, what remarks they made was merely verbal … They arrived at the House … on the 23rd of May 1801" (HBCA E3/2). Such infiltration of "distant" tribes produced results: by the time Thompson established a transmontane post in 1807, the Kootenays were already organized to provide hunters and guides – cf. 12, 16, and 20 July 1807, 2 and 15 August 1807.

23 October 1800, "the Route the Kootanaes took" Cf. confused references to the Kootenays' route in Fidler's postscript and the irritation of John McDonald of Garth, Thompson's superior at Rocky Mountain House. Fidler, postscript to 31 December 1792: "In going out [La Gassé and Le Blanc] crossed over the Mountain near the Source of the Saskatchewan in an oblique direction the latter place was more easy to pass than the former across the Mountain. Beyond the Mountain opposite to the head of the Saskatchewan a thick woody country – they passed thro' it along an old Track formerly cut by the Cottonahaws, being the Northern most track they have; it was now very troublesome to pass thro' it on account of the long time they have not passed that way, being much encumbred with Wind fall wood &c" (HBCA E3/2). McDonald of Garth: "Mr Thompson had not done as I expected. During the winter, I took three good men with dogs, &c, and went up the river myself, a journey of a week, going and returning, and found the gap in the mountain not to be exactly as Mr Thompson represented it" (NA MG19 A17, 15r/Masson, 2:26). The Kootenays appear to have returned west across the divide by Howse Pass. Thompson attempted to trace their route in June 1801, and succeeded in June 1807.

23 October 1800, "found Mr McGillivray" Cf. AO journals 75: "On my arrival [at Rocky Mountain House] saw Mr Duncan McGillivray on the other side the River just arrived from Fort William a Month later than he intended. Crossed to him. He was very anxious to see the Kootanae Indians, but they were too far advanced. Mr D. McGillivray remained quiet, when from my account of the Country to the Southward he wished to see it."

Two weeks later McGillivray and Thompson rode south to the Bow and Highwood rivers.

If Thompson rode from Rocky Mtn house he did not retrace Fidler's route

Journey to the Bow River

Source: AO journals 13

This journey retraces the route Peter Fidler travelled with a Peigan band in late 1792. In 1800–01 Fidler was posted at Manchester House downstream from Rocky Mountain House and recorded news of Thompson's attempts to cross the Rocky Mountains. Since he and Thompson knew each other well, Fidler may have provided information about the Bow River region despite Thompson's defection from the HBC. Certainly Thompson's Bow River journal provides many parallels with Fidler's: not only the same route, but also verbal echos such as Fidler's "hommock" in place of Thompson's usual "knowl" (27 November 1800), and evidence of a running survey (28 November 1800).

17 November 1800, "we set off – Mr Duncan McGillivray, Boulard, Charron, Dumond, Bapt[iste] Regnie and myself" Of the men, Boulard's name appears again; Thompson was still a clerk, assisting McGillivray.

17–19 November 1800, "a Brook ... increased to a Rivulet ... a small River on our right" – Stauffer Creek, the Raven River, and James River. In Thompson's notation of watercourses, the main distinctions are "rill" (very small), "stream" and "brook" (small, unnavigable), "rivulet" (somewhat larger, seasonally navigable), and "river" (navigable).

19 November 1800, "Swamps with much Larch ... no Woods ... fit for Tent Poles" – Larix laricina, tamarack; and Pinus contorta, lodgepole pine.

19 November 1800, "called by the French Tate des Femmes"
Thompson's spelling indicates his men's Canadian pronunciation.
Cf. *Narrative* (Tyrrell, 435/Glover, 41, 313), and AO journals 74:
"The education of the Canadians ought to be wholly in the English
language, Books &c. At present it is wholly in French, & the Women
are the most instructed; they govern the Men, & the Priests govern the
Women." In spite of the partners' avowed preference for their native
English, the North West Company operated from day to day in
French. McDonald of Garth, appraising an associate, called him "a
very good fellow, but no trader: he never could learn to speak French"
(NA MG19 A17, 2r/Masson 2:13). Harmon confessed, "Now I am as it
were alone, there being not a person here able to speak a word of
English" (43–4). Fidler remarked of an acquaintance, "This Canadian
cannot speak any English – consequently can have but little conversation together but what we carry on in the Indian Tongue" (HBCA
E3/1); according to Douglas, the same could be said of Jaco Finlay,
Thompson's associate from 1807 to 1812, and his son, brought up in
the fur trade milieu (171). From time to time Thompson's journals
echo the language he spoke daily with his men – cf. 22 June 1807,
20 April 1808, 25 May 1808, 7 June 1808, 29 October 1808,
25 August 1809, 8 September 1809.

*20 November 1800, "the Bow Hills in sight ... we go in a line parallel
to the Mountain"* – south of Carstairs – cf. Fidler, 10 December 1792:
"These Hills run in a parallel direction with the Rocky Mountain from
their Northern termination near the Devils head & their South end ter-
minates at the banks of this [Bow] river – they are high & run in
Parallels with the mountain, they are covered with Pine & Fir & very
deep vallies between each parallel ridge" (HBCA E3/2).

*20 November 1800, "the Rocky Mountain ... whose tops pierce the
clouds"* "Mountain" was often used as a collective noun, indicating a
range or "chain" of peaks, as opposed to a "detached mountain" –
cf. 8 and 9 June 1801, 17 May 1807, 25 April 1808, and Fidler to the
HBC London Committee, 10 July 1802: "The mountain appears like a
Stupendous & steep wall across the greater part of the North American
continent ... in several places there are very high peaks ... These single
detached mountains towards the NW & N are more numerous, than
they are toward the W & SW" (HBCA A10/1). In Thompson's MS the original verb "touch" is crossed out and "pierce" written above it; occasionally Thompson's laconic style suffers from such conventional
reaching for effect – cf. 30 November 1800, 8, 10, and 13 June 1801,
7 June 1807.

20 November 1800, "on our left, before & behind us, a verdant Ocean" Cf. Butler's famous paean of the plains: "[On] old maps ... the centre of America was represented as a vast inland sea ... an ocean there is, and an ocean through which men seek the treasures of Cathay, even in our own times. But the ocean is one of grass, and the shores are the crests of mountain ranges, and the dark pine forests of sub-Arctic regions ... In winter, [this sea is] a dazzling surface of purest snow; in early summer, a vast expanse of grass and pale pink roses; in autumn too often a sea of raging fire. No ocean of water can vie with its gorgeous sunsets; no solitude can equal the loneliness of a night-shadowed prairie; one feels the stillness, and hears the silence" (199–200).

20 November 1800, "Ran a Bull Buffalo" Cf. McGillivray's *Journal*: "Hunting is the only amusement which this country affords ... In our vacations from business we fly to it with impatience to pass a few agreable hours and when we are successful it gives us satisfaction, to think that we have united pleasure and profit together ... besides from the nature of the country & quantity of animal food we devour, I am persuaded that violent exercise is very necessary for the preservation of the consitution" (67).

Herds of buffalo were numerous at this time – cf. Fidler by the Red Deer River, 13 February 1793: "I am sure there was some millions in sight, as no ground could be seen for them in that compleat Semicircle & extending at least 10 Miles" (HBCA E3/2). Fidler saw Peigan youths running buffalo, "shooting them with arrows – they are so expert at this business, that they will ride along side of the Cow they mean to kill & while at full gallop will shoot an arrow into her heart & kill her upon the spot – sometimes when they happen to miss their proper aim (which is very seldom) they will ride close up to the Buffalo while at full Gallop & draw the arrow out & again shoot with it" (HBCA E3/2: 25 December 1792). Cf. also McDonald of Garth: "It was a grand sight to see such a Grand River [Saskatchewan River], the innumerable herds of Buffaloes & Deers & many Grizle Bears on its Banks, feeding & crossing, in such numbers that we often got our Canoes amongst them & I shot hundreds without need" (NA MG19 A17, 35/Masson, 2:18). In 1846 Kane still saw vast herds and took part in a hunt with Métis from the Red River Colony: "We ware behind a small rise of ground so that they bffalo could not see us ... we started on a wak for about 200 yards whin they buffalo saw us for the first time we now put our Horses to the gallop and in 20 minutes ware in the midts of them thare ware at least 4000 all Bulls and now comenced the sloter the bulls flying in everay derection ...

this evening I wus verry tired and sare from my days exersion"
(MacLaren 25–7).

21 November 1800, "we found the Marks of Indians" "Marks" could
be simply signs of passage (26 April 1808) or messages (28 April 1808,
18 September 1811).

*22 November 1800, "We then descended the banks of the Bow River
and crossed it"* The ford is now within the city of Calgary. Cf. Fidler,
10 December 1792: "Arrived upon the banks of the Bad [Bow] river,
by the Southern Indians [Cree] called As kow seepee, & by the Muddy
river Indians [Peigan] Na ma kay sis sa ta or the Bow hills river ... at
present little or no Ice in it, being quite open – what a difference between this river, & the Saskatchewan which was very full of Ice ...
more than one month ago, and here scarse any to be seen" (HBCA
E3/2). A dotted line on Thompson's PRO (1) map shows his route
south of the Bow River, which is called "Na ma Sahti."

*22 November 1800, "the Spitchee River ... which we crossed & came
to a Camp of 7 Lodges of Pikenows"* – Highwood River. Cf. Fidler's
account of the same meeting place eight years before, 14 December
1792: "Arrived at the Spitcheyee river at Noon, & found nearly
150 Tents of Muddy river Indians [Peigan] that had been here many
Days. When near the Enemies Country they are always found in large
bands, that they may be the more able to resist any enemies that may
dare to attack them, which is generally either the Snake [Shoshoni],
Flat heads [Interior Salish] or Crow Mountain Indians" (HBCA E3/2).

22 November 1800, "Sac o tow wow" Cf. *Narrative* (Tyrrell, 381–4/
Glover, 277–9): "the foolish Saktow" is unfavorably compared to
Peigan the war chief Kootanae Appee, whom Thompson calls "my
steady friend" for having opposed a plan to prevent transmontane
trade. Thompson's opinion of Natives was based on their degree of
compliance with his own commercial and geographical objectives –
cf. 27 August 1807, 1 and 13 September 1807, 3–9 July 1811.

*22 November 1800, "introducing a Number of Iroquois & Seauteaux
into this Country"* Thompson engaged several Iroquois and Ojibwa
men who had drifted west in the wake of the fur trade (29 June 1807,
2 and 12 July 1807, 4 October 1808, 2 and 6 November 1808, 3 July
1811, 18 and 22 September 1811). By mid-century the western tribes
were facing the same predicament – cf. James Hector of the Palliser
Expedition, who visited a Stoney camp on the Highwood River in

1859: "I had a long talk with the chiefs about what was likely to become of them and the other Indian tribes. They said that every year they find it more difficult to keep from starving, and that even the buffalo cannot be depended on as before" (Spry, 432).

24 November 1800, "to the Missisouri River" – Milk River, a tributary of the Missouri. The present name is Lewis's: "Perhaps this river ... might furnish a practicable and advantageous communication with the Saskashiwan River ... the water of this river possesses a peculiar whiteness, being about the colour of a cup of tea with the admixture of a tablespoonfull of milk" (Thwaites, 2:9–10).

24 November 1800, "they warned us ... to beware of the Flat Heads" – Salish who lived along the Clark Fork and Kootenai rivers.

25 November 1800, "At Night I Obs^d Doub Merid Alt^de of Rigel" Cf. 1 and 3 May 1808, 28 September 1809, 4 October 1809, 26 July 1811, 6 and 8 August 1811; see also Tyrrell's comments (Tyrrell-RSC, 233–4). For night observations Thompson relied on the usual navigational stars, together with the planets Saturn and Jupiter. Most of these stars are in constellations near the ecliptic and all are very bright, of 0–1 magnitude.

27 November 1800, "a Rivulet" – Sheep River, called "I ton kai ou" on the PRO (1) map and labelled "very rapid."

28 November 1800, "The nearest part of the Mountain bears now from me s38w 25M" Like Fidler (HBCA E3/2:4 and 7–8 December 1792), Thompson made a running survey along the eastern edge of the mountains, using prominent peaks to take his bearings. Cf. also 22–5 April 1808.

28 November 1800, "to a Gully" – across the Elbow River to a point west of Jumping Pound Creek.

29 November 1800, "running after the Goats" – *Ovis canadensis*, bighorn sheep. At first Thompson seems to have confused sheep and goats (cf. 9 and 12 June 1801), but in later years he specified "white goats" – *Oreamnos americanus*, mountain goat – and clearly distinguished between the two animals (25 June 1807, 22 and 25 October 1808, 4 January 1811); cf. also 20 July 1807 note. Like Thompson, Lewis was amazed at the agility of these sheep: "Saw a large herd of the Bighorned anamals on the immencely high and nearly perpendicular clift opposite to us; on the fase of this clift they walked about and bounded from rock to rock with apparent unconcern where it appared to me that no quadrupud could have stood" (Thwaites, 2:243). Ordway gives a concise description: "Capt Clark ... killed a female Ibex or big hornd animal of a blackish colour or dark duskey colour over the body. they have great resemblance to the deer kind, especially the leggs, but the head & huffs resemble a sheep. they are verry active & keep frequently on the Sides of Steep bluffs & places where wolves & bears cannot hurt them" (Quaife, 218). Douglas viewed Clark's stuffed specimen in Philadephia, and after crossing Athabaska Pass in 1827 was treated to "a shoulder of *Mouton gris*, which I found very fine" (172, 260).

29 November 1800, "many strong rapids with several falls ... the River everywhere navigable for large Canoes" – Morley rapids and Horseshoe Falls (Seebe); the falls are now dammed. Thompson always assessed the trading potential of areas he visited, and judged his routes according to their usefulness as transportation corridors – cf. 13 June 1801, 12 and 14 May 1807, 3 June 1807, 27 April 1808, 5 May 1808, 4 January 1811, 6 July 1811.

29 November 1800, "Canoes, loaded with 20 Pieces" – packs or bales weighing 90 lbs each – cf. the minutes of the annual meeting of NW Co partners at Fort William, 7 July 1808: "It is supposed that an average loading of a Canoe is about twenty packs – But that making allowance for Proprietors, Clerks and other Incumbrances, we reduce their number again to fifteen" (HBCA F1/1). Like "skin" (5 October 1800) and "pipe" (17 May 1808), the object was often abstracted to become a measure.

29–30 November 1800, "Its Banks ... are composed of a black slaty Rock, not extremely hard" – black shale; *"The Rock of the Mountain ... produces ... a strong disagreeable Smell"* – limestone.

30 November 1800, "Our View from the Heights" – Loder Peak. Thompson recalled this view in AO journals 71: "The primitive Mountains of every part of the Globe bear resemblance to each other ... every where presenting scenes of ruin and desolation ... as on the verge of chaos ... Often, sitting on an elevated rock, the awful assemblage appeared to me as the mighty waves of part of an immense ocean duly arrested and consolidated in their wild forms ... A more comprehensive view of the mountains prove[s] them to be the well ordered work of a divine Being, all powerful, wise and most benevolent to mankind, in thus creating and forming for their use these stupendous heights ... for the detention of the vapours, forming them into vast stores of snow and ice, to be gradually thawed for supplying the Rivers, so necessary to the fertility of the earth, the health, convenience and comfort of mankind." Cf. Hector's very different impression of the Bow Valley from the same viewpoint: "The scene from the summit was very remarkable, the great distinctness with which the eye was able to follow the gigantic and complex plications giving it more the look of a magnified geological model than a natural view" (Spry, 435).

Like Thompson, Saussure imagined the Alps as "une Mer subitement congelée dans l'instant même ou les aquillons soulevoient leurs flots" (1:viii) and assigned them a role in a constant and beneficent nature – "ces proportions admirables que la Nature a établies entre les forces génératrices & les forces déstructrices" (1:461). But like Hector, Saussure was interested in the pattern of geological forces which a view of mountains revealed: "Il semble que, dominant au dessus de ce Globe, [le naturaliste] découvre les ressorts qui le font mouvoir, & qu'il reconnoît au moins les principaux agens qui opérent ses révolutions" (1:iv). Looking down at the Alps from the summit of Mont Blanc, "je saisissois leurs rapports, leur liaison, leur structure, & un seul regard levoit des doutes que des années de travail n'avoient pu éclaircir" (4:147).

30 November 1800, "low shrubs of Fir & Canadian Pine" – stunted *Picea engelmanni*, Engelmann spruce, and *Pinus contorta*, lodgepole pine.

1 December 1800, "to our Gully" Cf. 28 November 1800; *"Bow Rivulet"* – Ghost River; *"Co along the Bow Hills in he Plains"* – north to the Little Red Deer River, near Cremona.

2 December 1800, "our old campment" Cf. 19 November 1800; *"at the same Place"* – cf. 6 October 1800.

Thompson spent the winter of 1800–01 at Rocky Mountain House. Early in June 1801, he and James Hughes made a further attempt to carry out Duncan McGillivray's plan of extending trade across the continental divide.

Journey to the Rocky Mountain

Source: VPL journal

This report, based on a journal that is now lost, exists in two very similar versions. In this case rough and fair copies can be identified – the VPL journal and NA report, respectively. Phrases of the VPL journal version not included in NA 1801 are indicated by angled brackets in the text.

6 June 1801, "⟨1800⟩" Thompson wrote "6 June 1801" at the head of both accounts. In the VPL journal the year has been overwritten (title and first entry) to read "1800," no doubt to correspond with the date "1800" written in Thompson's shaky *Narrative* hand at the end of the 10 June entry. But the days and dates accord for 1801.

6 June 1801, "Mr Hughes, nine men & myself" – NA report: "Mr James Hughes." Duncan McGillivray was to be the leader of this expedition but could not set out because of poor health – cf. 30 June 1801, and McDonald of Garth: "1802. Mr McGillivray being unwell left the country for Montreal & there died [in April 1808] – as fine a fellow as ever lived" (NA MG19 A17, 76/Masson, 2:23). James Hughes, characterized in the Selkirk Papers as "enterprising but careless" (NA MG19 E1, 1:186), and Thompson were left to carry on. Of the nine men, only three are named: Meillet, LaRamme, and Gladu.

6 June 1801, "a Nahathaway Indian" Cf. NA 1801: "a Cree Indian." Previously a Kootenay guide had been engaged, who had been murdered – cf. 30 June 1801. Apparently the Cree man had crossed the mountains before (cf. 13 June 1801) but did not clearly remember the route he had followed.

6 June 1801, "carrying with us Birch Rind sufficient to make a Canoe" – *Betula papyrifera*, paper birch. Good bark could not be found west of the divide. At one point Thompson seems to have thought it could – cf. RCSL report: "The information we had received ab^t the Birch Rind, Cedar &c proved to be quite false, & I was obliged to search the Islands [sand bars in the Columbia River] before I could find the materials for a Canoe." Experience confirmed the lack of good birch bark in the Columbia watershed (16 July 1807, 8–9 August 1807, 1 and 6–7–8 September 1807, 22 August 1809, 5 December 1810), although cf. Douglas, writing of the west side of Athabaska Pass: "*Betula*, sp., a tree 40 to 60 feet high, 18 inches to $2\frac{1}{2}$ feet diameter, in the moist parts of the woods; of this the canoes are made" (257).

For a description of "raising" bark, cf. Graham on the Cree who traded at Hudson Bay, from whom the HBC, including Thompson, learned to make canoes: "[They] have two ways of decorticating the birch. Sometimes they ascend a tree, and loosening the bark at the top keep a continual afflux of hot water which destroys the cohesion. It is then cut in a perpendicular direction and taken off in a large sheet. At other times the tree is fallen and a fire made near it, and of the same length; the heat loosening the rind, it is removed by cutting it open as in the preceding method ... They are so curious, that observing the bark to be thicker on one side of the tree than on the other, they make the incision down the thinnest side, reserving the strongest part for the bottom of the canoe, where it is most wanted" (190).

6 June 1801, "we loaded our Horses and set out" Tyrrell's itinerary in the *Narrative* says only that "twenty-eight miles above Rocky Mountain House ... [Thompson] left the main river and struck southward up the valley of Sheep [Ram] River to its source" (Tyrrell, lxxxi/ Glover, lxxxvii). Howay claims that this source was Onion Lake; another suggestion has been the small unnamed lake NE of Whiterabbit Creek. A dotted line on the PRO (2) map indicates Thompson's route from the Saskatchewan River along a southern tributary, terminating at a lake; the tributary seems to have been the North Ram River. Falls would have blocked access to the upper Ram River, so a route along the north branch, up to the unnamed lake, is more likely than a route ending at Onion Lake. But Howay still has the last word: "It is difficult if not impossible to trace exactly the route followed by Thompson under the blind direction of his ignorant and craven guide" (336).

7 June 1801, "Fortunately La Ramme could swim" Cf. Ignace, 4 July 1811.

8 June 1801, "we now held on for the Mountains West 1 Mile WSW 4M sbw ½ Mile wbs 3 Miles sw 2 Miles" Cf. NA 1801: "West 1M WSW 4½M sbw ¾M wbs 3½M sw 2½M." This discrepancy in the distances is exceptional; multiple versions of the 1807 and 1808 journals show consistent figures for distances.

8 June 1801, "we saw 10 or 12 Beaver Houses" Cf. Hearne, who admired beaver dams "as the most curious piece of workmanship that is performed by the beaver; not so much for the neatness of the work, as for its strength and real service; and at the same time it discovers [reveals] such a degree of sagacity and foresight in the animal, of approaching evils, as is little inferior to that of the human species, and is certainly peculiar to those animals" (227).

9 June 1801, "[Tuesday]" Thompson wrote "Thursday" in both the VPL journal and NA 1801.

9–10 June 1801, "the first chain of Mountains" – Brazeau Range; *"the South Branch of the Saskatchewan"* – Ram River, as marked on the PRO maps.

10 June 1801, "The Thunder ... added Horrour to the Darkness" The VPL journal romanticizes – cf. the plainer prose of NA 1801: "The Thunder ... darkned the Night."

11 June 1801, "one of our men exclaimed with indignation to our Guide" Dialogue is rare in fur trade journals – cf. Du Nord, 13 January 1811.

11 June 1801, "so savage an Action" – The Europeans' "utter Abhorrence" is odd given the common medical practice of bleeding (cf. 4 July 1811) and the familiar eucharistic symbolism of Christ's blood. Equally odd is the guide's assertion that "all our Nation do this," given the Crees' utter abhorrence of cannibalism – cf. Nelson: "There is a kind of disease (or distemper rather, and of the mind I am fully persuaded) peculiar to the Crees and Sauteux's, and of which they have the greatest dread and horor ... They term this Win-di-go" (85). But cf. Keith to Roderic Mackenzie, 28 February 1810: "Letting blood, even in the proper vein, with an awl, pointed knife, pointed white iron &c is common to many of them" (NA MG19 CI, vol. 51).

13 June 1801, "great Banks of Snow … had come shelving down"
Cf. 7 June 1807.

13 June 1801, "up to our middles in Snow, we went along the lower Bank of the Lake" Cf. NA 1801: "… the lower Bank of the western Side of the Lake."

13 June 1801, "Meillet joined us, who it seems had become ashamed of staying behind" Cf. Du Nord, 10 January 1811.

16 June 1801, "at a Place … where … the Nahathaway Indians had made a War Tent" – beside the North Saskatchewan River, downstream from its junction with the Ram River, Henry's "Bas fond of the Loge de Medicine" (NA MG19 A13, 1050/Coues, 677) – cf. 19 May 1807, 10 October 1808. This was the "upper War Tent"; cf. 17 May 1807: the "lower War Tent." Both "tents" seem to have been sweat lodges used in preparation for skirmishes against Peigans or Kootenays, or both.

17–26 June 1801, "We now set to work to build a Canoe" Thompson describes the construction in detail in AO journals 18 – cf. 6–7–8 July 1807 note; see Roberts and Shackleton (156–63) for photographs and explanations. A large canoe for transporting goods took several days to build, unlike small fording canoes which were put together in a few hours – cf. 5 and 8 June 1808. After the canoe frame was shaped, the pieces of bark were, according to Graham, "sewed up with strong fibrous roots, the juncture being afterwards covered with turpentine boiled to the consistence of pitch, which prevents the water from gaining admittance" (190). *Picea glauca*, white spruce, provided both the roots and the sap. During a voyage, pitch or gum had to be reapplied almost daily in order to prevent the canoe from leaking – cf. 13 and 29 July 1807, 9 and 10 September 1807, 25 April 1808, 2 and 3 November 1808, 5 August 1811.

26 June 1801, "by the Line or the Pole we should be able to stem the Current" Long poles were used for punting upstream in shallow currents when paddling became too laborious (25 April 1808, 2 and 10 September 1811). Cf. Kane: "The men thrue a way thare poales to Day with a loud shout as they ware of no further use and took to thare paddles" (MacLaren, 23). The canoe could also be "lined" or "tracked" while some or all of the contents were removed and carried along the bank (27 August 1809, 5 and 11 July 1811, 14 September 1811). Cf. also Fidler, 15 September 1792: "Tracked … two men at one time at the line hauling & the other steers the canoe, & they relieve one another at the end of every two hours. But when a young hand is in a Canoe ... he tracks constantly as not being qualified to steer the Canoe his Spell – so that on this account ... several are quite rendered useless for some time by the constant walking & great fatigue they undergo" (HBCA E3/1) In the case of very dangerous rapids, the canoe itself could be carried or "portaged" (21 April 1808, 16 May 1808), but Thompson almost always lined it, upstream and down (4, 11–12, and 29 July 1811, 12 and 14 September 1811). If there were overhanging branches, the canoe could also be "handed" upstream, as here and on 13 July 1807. See Morse (5–11, 28, 82) for photographs and explanations.

29 June 1801, "nearly passing the first great Chain of Mountains" – the upper end of the Kootenay Plains – cf. 25 May 1807.

29 June 1801, "Here then for the Present was my last Hopes destroyed" Cf. 17 and 21 May 1808, 23 and 24 January 1811.

29 June 1801, "the Nature of the River" Cf. 16 May 1807, 31 May 1808, 5 and 15 January 1811, 23 July 1811, 5 September 1811 note, 10 September 1811 note.

30 June 1801, "this Journey ... has taught us" Thompson followed these suggestions to the letter in 1807, when he finally crossed the divide: he took fewer men, he combined horses and canoes for transportation, and he set out from Rocky Mountain House a month earlier.

30 June 1801, "Modes of Conveyance" Cf. a pencilled draft letter in AO journals 19: "our Horses, now Animals as necessary in the Mountains, as the Canoes in the water." The object of the 1801 expedition was to find a route across the divide for horses *or* canoes. The crossing in May 1807 showed that both "Modes of Conveyance" were necessary – cf. Henry: "Above [Rocky Mountain House] the Rapids are more frequently met with, and the navigation more tedious, as the water becomes shoal and will not admit of Canoes passing with more than half a Cargo to the foot of the Mountains, although they can proceed with the same load over to the Kootenoes Plains ... Canoes have also reached the Forks in the Summer season when the water was high, but it has always been found more expeditious to take the property on horse back, at the lower end of the

Kootanoes Plain, where we generally lay up our Canoes for the Winter" (NA MG19 A13, 1096–7/Coues, 701–2).

30 June 1801, "I have been so tedious in detailing trifling Occurrences" Cf. Thompson's summary account of this journey in AO journals 75: "[Mr Duncan McGillivray] ordered Mr Hughes and myself with 6 Men to cross the mountains and discover the Columbia River, but arrangements were such that I saw plainly the whole was hopeless. Mr Hughes engaged a Nahathaway Indian Guide who conducted thro' defiles which at length had no outlet, and we returned and thus ended the business of 1801. After which the whole was an affair entirely forgotten or ridiculed until the expedition of Captains Lewis and Clarke."

In a letter to Sir James Alexander, 9 May 1845, Thompson confused this 1801 trip with two expeditions across the divide, in June 1807 and January 1811: "In 1801 the northwest company determined to extend their Fur Trade to the west side of the Rocky Mountains, and if possible to the Pacific Ocean; this expedition was intrusted to me, and I crossed the Mountains to the head waters of McGillivray's River; but an overwhelming force of eastern Indians obliged me to retreat a most desperate retreat of six days for they dreaded the western Indians being furnished with Arms and Ammunition. The report of my attempt and defeat soon reached Washington and in 1804 the Executive of the U. States organised a plan of discovery, to be conducted by Captains Lewis and Clarke." Alexander forwarded this letter to the Foreign Office with the following endorsement: "Inclosing a letter from Mr David Thompson shewing that he had reached the River McGillivray on the Western side of the Rocky Mountains previous to the journey of Lewis and Clarke" (PRO letters FO5/441).

Cf. also Fidler's strangely garbled account of this journey in his postscript to 31 December 1792: "On the 6th of June 1801 Mr David Thompson, Hughes & 9 Canadians with the Crow a Southern Indian [Cree] as guide – these intended to cross the Mountain near the Source of the Saskatchewan, but after being away about 3 Weeks the Guide refused to go any farther for fear of the Cottonahaws killing him. They had entered the Mountain several days but made very small progress – in the day they found the current so exceedingly strong that they could not stem it, also deep, & in the morning not a drop of water was to be seen – this is understood after they left the main channel which took a northern direction, more northerly than they wished to follow" (HBCA E3/2)

In 1801–02 Thompson again wintered at Rocky Mountain House. He then spent two years in the Peace River district of the Athabaska department (1802–04), and two more in the "Rat Country" southwest of Hudson Bay (1804–06). He returned to Rocky Mountain House in the fall of 1806, wintered there, and in May 1807 set out once more to cross the mountains. This time he succeeded.

Across the Mountains

Source: AO journals 20

Unlike the earlier probes of 1800 and 1801, the "expedition" of 1807 succeeded because of careful preparation. This time Thompson was informed in detail of the route he was to take across the mountains (22 June 1807); as well, he sent Jaco Finlay ahead to clear a path and to leave canoes ready at the Columbia River (27 and 30 June 1807). Cf. Bird to John McNab, 23 December 1806: "Mr David Thompson is making preparations for another attempt to cross the Mountains, pass through [the Kootenays'] Country and follow the Columbia River to the Sea ... the object of his enterprise is said to be to ascertain positively whether a Trade can be formed with that Country valuable enough to be worth pursuing thro' the difficulties with which it must be attended, and if it should, the uniting of the Commerce of the two Seas [Atlantic and Pacific]" (HBCA B60/a/6).

10 May 1807, "sent off Mr Finan McDonald & 5 Men ... sent off 2 Men ... set off with Bercier" Thompson was now in command, having been made a partner of the NW Co in 1804 (Wallace, 502). Cf. RCSL report: "I now reckon myself at 6 voyaging Men, 1 Man to take care of the Horses at the Kootanae Plain for the Portage, 1 Clerk & 1 Summer Man & myself for where necessary." The "voyaging Men" are named here and there in the text: Boulard again, Bercier, Clément, Boisverd, Buché, and Beaulieu. Finan McDonald was the clerk — cf. RCSL report: "I had for a second Mr Finan McDonald, who, however well intentioned was by far too unexperienced to act alone in the present unfavorable situation." Judging from letters that he wrote to John George McTavish (1815–21), McDonald lacked enterprise and was barely literate, despite his clerk's status (HBCA F3/2). Jaco Finlay was the "Summer Man" – cf. 16 and 29 May 1807 and 30 June 1807. Finlay reappears in later journals as a "freeman" (28 August 1809, 21 September 1809) and as a clerk (6 and 14 August 1811). See also Douglas, who met "Mr. Jacques Raphael Finlay, a Canadian Sauteur," at Spokane House in 1826 (169, 203).

10 May 1807, "we arrived at the Horse Tent" – a guarded horse pasture at some distance from the fort – cf. the "Lodge du Paille" (6 June 1808).

10 May 1807, "thick Woods very much fallen down" Cf. Henry, who travelled up the same valley in 1811 and remarked on the "continual dreary waste of Country that has been destroyed by fire some years ago. The Ground is now covered by immense piles of wood and fallen Trees, laying across each other which gives a gloomy appearance to the Country around, while towering summits of the Mountains tends to strike [the mind] with awe" (NA MG19 A13, 1050/Coues, 678).

10 May 1807, "at the brook of my former Journey" – Ram River – cf. 6 June 1801.

16–19 May 1807, "came to Jaco's Brook ... the north Brook" – Shunda Creek – cf. 16 October 1808. *"The Mountain between us & the Saskatchewan"* – Brazeau Range. Coues (650) maintained that "Jaco's Brook" was named after Jaco Cardinal but gave no reason or authority for this claim. Jaco Finlay is a more obvious candidate.

19 May 1807, "Many Porcupine ... a few Geese & Ducks" – Erethizon dorsatum – cf. 6–7–8 July 1807. Two species of geese migrate through this area – *Branta canadensis*, Canada goose, and *Chen caerulescens*, snow goose – as well as over thirty species of ducks.

21 May 1807, "the Lake ... there are Loons in it" – Gavia immer in one of several small lakes west of Nordegg.

25 May 1807, "where the Goods of the Winter were put in Hoard" Cf. 22 August 1809, 1 and 4 January 1811, and Lewis: "A place being fixed on for a cash [cache], a circle of ab[o]ut 20 inches in diameter is first discribed, the terf or sod of this circle is carefully removed, being taken out as entire as possible in order that it may be replaced in the same situation when the chash is filled and secured. this circular hole is then sunk perpendicularly to the debth of one foot, if the ground be not firm somewhat deeper. they then begin to work it out wider as they proceed downwards untill they get it about six or seven feet deep giving it nearly the shape of the kettle or lower part of a large still. it's bottom is also somewhat sunk in the center. the dementions of the cash is in proportion to the quantity of articles intended to be deposited ... in this manner dryed skins or merchandize will keep perfectly sound for several years" (Thwaites, 1:136–7).

25–27 May 1807: "From this plain" – the junction of the Bighorn and Saskatchewan Rivers; *"at the Kootanae Plains"* – above the junction of the Cline and North Saskatchewan Rivers. The Kootenay Plains are now flooded by Lake Abraham, reservoir of the Bighorn Dam – cf. 29 June 1801, 27 May 1807, 3 and 22 June 1807, and Southesk: "This so-called plain is merely an inconsiderable enlargement of the valley, – a space of some fifty acres, bare of trees, and covered with short prairie grasses" (235). Henry explained the name: "I observed ... the remains of an Old Kootonoes Camp, where the Wood of their Tent [was] still standing ... Formerly that nation used to frequent this place for the purpose of making dried provisions" (NA MG19 A13, 1067/Coues, 687).

1–3 June 1807, "Put up at the Muleton Plains" – at the junction of the Cline and North Saskatchewan rivers; *"Muleton Rivulet"* – Cline River; *"a bold Rivulet from the sw^d"* – Whiterabbit Creek – cf. 13 June 1801.

6 June 1807, "a very bold rapid Brook" – Mistaya River; *"end of Co the Forks"* – the junction of the North Saskatchewan and Howse rivers.

7 June 1807: "the rushing of the snows" Cf. Henry: "[On] perpendicular summits, so steep that no human being could ascend them ... I observed an emmense depth of snow, where a part seems lately to have seperated and fell down the Mountain ... The noise occasioned by the fall of such a great body of Snow will cause an explosion equal to loud Thunder, as it sweeps away every thing that is moveable in it[s] course to the vallies below" (NA MG19 A13, 1072–3/Coues, 689). Deluc was the first to distinguish, in 1772, between winter and spring avalanches and to explain how the latter occurred: "L'humidité, la fonte des neiges au printemps, occasionnent une seconde espèce d'avalanche. La neige fond plutôt en dessous qu'en dessus; ayant perdu ses points de contacts, si elle est sur un plan incliné, elle glisse, entraîne avec elle celle qui est au-dessous de proche en proche; la vitesse s'accélère par la pente, la force avec le poids ... Les arbres les plus forts sont rompus, brisés et transportés; les plus grosses masses de rochers, entraînées" (Broc, 184).

9 June 1807, "up the mid Rivulet ... to a Lake" – up the Howse River to Glacier Lake. Cf. Hector: "Up this river there is said to be a pass direct to the Columbia, which was the first one used by trappers in the time of the North West Company, as far as I could make out from the accounts of the Indians" (Spry, 444). Thompson named the pass in honour of Joseph Howse of the HBC – cf. 29 October 1810 note.

9 June 1807, "a Fir Pine" – *Tsuga heterophylla*, western hemlock. Cf. 10 August 1807, 30 September 1809, and AO journals 19 for 21 July 1807: "This wood, the Hemlock or Pruche: of all woods I have ever built with, this is the worst and heaviest." Henry noted, "The prush has an extraordinary thick heavy Bark, and some of those trees grow to a great size" (NA MG19 A13, 1070/Coues, 688). Cf. also Hector: "The 'Prushe' of the voyageurs ... is so named by them from its general resemblance to the hemlock spruce (*Abies canadensis* [*Abies grandis*?]). It is, however, a very distinct tree" (23).

16 June 1807, "Measured the Height of 3 Peaks" Cf. 25 June 1807, 8 and 9 January 1811, 8 and 22 September 1811, and Fidler to the HBC London Committee, 10 July 1802: "I measured the height of [a mountain near the Oldman River] by means of the Sextant & found it to be in that place 3520 feet perpendicular above the *level of its base*. I am unacquainted with the method of finding the Altitude of mountains above the level of the Sea – probably other instruments are requisite to ascertain that point" (HBCA A10/1).

Although Thompson's knowledge of measuring elevations was no greater than Fidler's, he made extravagant claims – cf. RCSL report: "Considering their elevated Situation on the Globe, they fall little short of the most celebrated in Height above the level of the Ocean"; cf. also AO journals 71: "By the Athabaska Passage across the mountains, on the height of this passage by the point of boiling water, it is 11,000 feet above the Pacific, yet the summits of the mountains appear fully 7000 feet above us, making 18,000 feet ... The height of these Mountains above the level of the Ocean, as far as my information extends, is not yet well known ... I twice procured a barometer to be sent to me but the person who was entrusted with them [McDonald of Garth] by his negligence allowed them to be broken." Both Cox (291) and Simpson (Merk, 35) repeated Thompson's figures.

Thompson's erroneous estimate of these elevations should be seen in its contemporary context: the height of major peaks in the Alps were not measured until the 1770s, and then only by employing an elaborate procedure of simultaneous barometric readings – cf. Saussure: "J'ai enfin calculé la hauteur du Mont-Blanc, par une combinaison d'observations barométriques et trigonométriques, dont je regarde le résultat comme approchant assez près de la vérité" (1:491). Thompson's experiment with boiling water was ultimately based on "les belles & profondes recherches de Mr Deluc sur ce sujet"; in Saussure's opinion, "leur précision & leur exactitude semblent ne laisser aucun doute sur les résultats" (2:563), but here Saussure was in error.

In 1858, using a barometer, Hector reduced the height of the Rocky Mountains by one-third, but he still overestimated: "The average altitude of the highest part of the Rocky Mountains is 12,000 feet; but they never rise into marked peaks, and their cliff-like structure still further detracts from the grandeur of their appearance" (4).

21 June 1807, "visiting the Portage" – Howse Pass, called a "Portage" because goods had to be carried between the North Saskatchewan and Columbia Rivers – cf. 16 and 31 October 1808, 7 and 9 January 1811.

21 June 1807, "Matter ... its state of preservation ... a state of decay" Such "decay" is mainly the effect of spalling, glaciation, frost-wedging and avalanches; lightning can also split rock but is a minor and incidental agent. Of the two eighteenth-century geological schools, the Neptunists, who argued for the formative power of water, and the Vulcanists, who imagined the creation of the world as a fiery convulsion, Thompson belonged to the latter; he did not see the Rockies as sedimentary formations – cf. Saussure: "Relativement à la théorie de la terre, ce qui rend intéressante la question de savoir, si une montagne est ou n'est pas *stratifiée*, ou composée de couches; c'est que l'on suppose que les montagnes stratifiées ont été formées par des dépôts successifs de matières auparavant suspendues dans une fluide, tandis que celles qui ne montrent aucun indice de couche, peuvent être supposées devoir leur origine à une création simultanée" (4:487).

22 June 1807, "a Rill ... whose Current descends to the Pacific Ocean" – Blaeberry River, in later entries called the "Portage River" (29 and 30 June 1807; cf. 29 October 1808). Cf. also AO journals 71: "[On] the west side ... the Mountains are more steep, and consist of fewer ridges and are irregular in direction, throwing out very many Branches and Spurs ... several seem to extend to the low chain of Mountains which border the whole coast of the Pacific Ocean, especially north of the 49th parallel of Latitude. The vallies between these

Branches and Spurs have each its Rivulet watering a space of a few hundred yards to five miles in width, gradually lowering into the great valley of the Columbia River."

22 June 1807, "May God in his Mercy" To judge from the prayers and exclamations of traders like Harmon, Ogden and Ross, as well as naval officers like Franklin, Thompson was not exceptionally pious.

22 June 1807, "we found no Snow whatever ... & all the appearance of Spring" Cf. 30 October 1808, 9 January 1811, and AO journals 82: "The western sides of all Continents, and even of large Islands, have a greater and more uniform degree of heat, that is, are much warmer than the east side of Continents, large Islands, &c. But what is the limit of heat on the west side and the beginning of the descending scale of heat to the east side ... is a problem not yet solved."

Hind explains the difference in climate: "The influence of the warm westerly winds from the Pacific Ocean, in connection with the prevailing northeast wind ... is one of the established physical phenomena of this part of British America. It would appear, at first sight, that the snow-capped ridges of the Cascade, Blue and Rocky Mountains would abstract so much heat from the warm westerly winds coming from the Pacific Ocean, as to neutralize their influence upon the winter and spring temperature of a large part of the country drained by the Saskatchewan. Such, however, is not the case" (124).

26 June 1807, "Gave the Men a large Dog of which they made a hearty meal" "Dog Camp[t]" is marked on the PRO (2) map. Cf. 6–7–8 July 1807, 8 June 1808, and Clark: "While at dinner an indian fellow verry impertinently threw a poor half starved puppy nearly into my plait by way of derision for our eating dogs ... I caught the puppy and th[r]ew it with great violence at him and struk him in the breast and face, seized my tomahawk and shewed him by signs if he repeated his insolence I would tommahawk him, the fellow withdrew apparently much mortifyed and I continued my repast *on dog* without further molestation" (Thwaites, 4:358). Townsend was more tender-hearted: "I am always unwilling, unless when suffering absolute want, to take the life of so noble and faithful an animal. Our hungry oarsmen, however, appeared to have no such scruples. The Indian called his dog and he came to him, *wagging his tail*! ... I turned away my head to avoid the sight, but I heard the dull, *sodden* sound of the blow" (246).

26–7 June 1807, "Pines, much of two unknown Species ... willow vine... much of a very sharp prickly shrub ... the first Cedars ... white-fir Pine" The pines are unidentified; *Salix* sp.; the prickly shrub is *Oplopanax horridum*, devil's club; *Thuja plicata*, western red cedar; *Tsuga heterophylla*, hemlock.

27 June 1807, "the Horses were continually bucking ... the loads" Cf. 23 October 1808, also 20 October 1800, 5 September 1807, and the *Narrative*: "[The partners] insisted upon alcohol being the most profitable article that could be taken for the indian trade. In this I knew they had miscalculated; accordingly when we came to the defiles of the Mountains, I placed the two Kegs of Alcohol on a vicious horse; and by noon the Kegs were empty, and in pieces, the Horse rubbing his load against the Rocks to get rid of it; I wrote to my partners what I had done; and that I would do the same to every Keg of Alcohol ... no further attempt was made to introduce spiritous Liquors" (396).

27 June 1807, "the Road is so very narrow & bad" Cf. AO journals 18 for 28 June 1807: "By this vast Trouble we have had, it may be seen how Jaco, McM[as]ter & two Men with them have earned their Wages. Those of Jaco ought certainly to be forfeited as he has done next to nothing." Cf. also the RCSL report: "From what has been said of the Road on the Portage, it is clearly seen that Jaco Finlay with the Men engaged last Summer to clear the Portage Road, has done a mere nothing – the Road was nowhere cleared any more than just to permit Jaco & his Family, to squeeze thro' it with their light Baggage and it is the opinion of every man with me, as well as mine that Jaco ought to lose at least half his wages for having so much neglected the Duty for which he was so expressly engaged at £150 p^r year, besides a Piece of Tobacco & Sugar, & a Clerk's equipment." Thompson's impatience with Jaco Finlay is generalized in AO journals 22 for this day: "Indians are too lazy to cut even a small Tree out of their Road, they prefer making a turn round it ... even among hilly Rocks, [just as they prefer] risking their necks and the Lives of their Families rather than give 2 Strokes of an Oar." Cf. 2 October 1809 note, 4 July 1811 note.

30 June 1807, "to the Kootanae River" – Columbia River, at its junction with the Blaeberry River. At first Thompson was unsure whether this river which flowed northwest was the Columbia or the Kootenay River; in the spring of 1808 he figured out the southward course of "McGillivray's" (Kootenay/Kootenai) River, but at times he still called the Columbia the "Kootanae River" (15 and 16 January 1811).

3–4 July, "getting materials for the large Canoe" Cf. 6 June 1801.

6–7–8 July 1807, "Working at a large Canoe" Cf. 17–26 June 1801, and AO journals 18 for 6–11 July 1807: "6: Working at Canoe Wood a while, then ... went & looked out Birch Rind – rose abt 10 fm but all brittle ... 7: Knifed the Gunwales – finished – split out & worked 22 Timbers & laid the Birch Rind for the Bottom of the Canoe &c. Worked hard ... 8: Began the Canoe – working Timbers, &c – got the Bottom sewed, & the Side Seams &c. 9: Finished sewing the Gunwales Bars &c &c & split out all the Splinters, & put the last of the Timbers to soak – tried to turn a few, but they were still too brittle. 10: finished the sewing. 11: Timbered up the Canoe with very much Difficulty, from the badness of the Wood."

6–7–8 July 1807, "he sent for me" Cf. 5 September 1807 and 4 July 1811. The leader of the party was expected to have some medical skill – cf. Mackenzie: "This circumstance now obliged me to be their physician and surgeon, as a woman with a swelled breast ... presented herself to my attention ... by cleanliness, poultices, and healing salve, I succeeded in producing a cure. One of my people also ... was attacked with a sudden pain ... He was in a raving state throughout the night ... the propriety of taking some blood from him now occurred to me, and I ventured, from absolute necessity, to perform that operation for the first time" (244).

Clark was relatively skilled in medicine – for example, "I dressed the sores of the principal Chief ... his wife who I found to be a sulky Bitch ... was somewhat efflicted with pains in her back. this I thought a good oppertunity to get her on my side giveing her something for her back" (Thwaites 4:298). However, Clark was not above offering useless cures in exchange for food – cf. Lewis: "My friend Capt. C. is their favorite phisician and has already received many applications [from the Nez Perces]. in our present situation I think it pardonable to continue this deseption for they will not give us any provision without compensation in merchandize and our stock is now reduced to a mere handfull. We take care to give them no article which can possibly injure them" (Thwaites, 4:358).

12 July 1807, "Agreed with Boulard" A similar sort of brief, specific arrangement was made with L'Amoureux (7 January 1811) – for Boulard's formal engagement, cf. 11 September 1807; "FDP" – Fort des Prairies, the administrative centre of the NW Co's Saskatchewan River department, at this time Fort Augustus next to the HBC's Fort Edmonton. "FDP Men" were not usually engaged to cross the divide (22 October 1808), hence Thompson's characterization of them as fearful and "useless" (13 and 23 January 1811).

13 July 1807, "the Rapid River" – Kicking Horse River.

13 July 1807, "fine Willow, especially of Arrow Wood & Choak Cherry" Like "pines," Thompson sometimes used "willow" generically, to describe bushes or small trees: "Arrow Wood" has been variously identified as *Cornus stolonifera*, arrowwood; *Sagittaria latifolia*, arrowhead; and *Amelanchier alnifolia*, saskatoon. *Prunus virginiana* is chokecherry.

13 July 1807, "Swans ... mullets ... partridge nests" – *Cygnus columbianus*, tundra or whistling swan; a species of trout – *Salvelinus confluentus*, bull trout, *Salmo gairdneri*, rainbow/steelhead trout, or *Salmo clarki*, cutthroat trout; *Perdix perdix*, grey partridge – cf. Douglas: "[Near Spokane] I killed seven black partridges ... In the ovary of the females thirteen to seventeen eggs; found one nest with seven eggs about the size of common pigeon's egg, bright brownish-dun colour, with large and small red spots. Blew one egg as a specimen and cooked the others" (170–1).

15 July 1807, "Gooseberry Hill" Cf. AO journals 18 for this day: "Co s68E 8M to nearly past the high stony Hill on the right, a lake for nearly half way, strong current latter part ... At $7\frac{1}{2}$ Pm put up. Found a few Gooseberries [*Ribes oxyacanthoides*]."

16 July 1807, "we were in the River that comes from the NW^{d}" – Spillimacheen River.

18 July 1807, "the River of the Lakes" – Toby Creek.

Building Kootanae House

Source: AO journals 20

19 July 1807, "*this bad turn of hav^g all our Horses left behind*"
Cf. 18 July 1807.

19 July 1807, "*we hope ... we shall be able to penetrate farther*"
Cf. 18 and 29 September 1807, 2–6 October 1807, and RCSL report:
"What a fine Opportunity was here lost of going to the Flat Bow
Country, from the embarrassed Situation of my Affairs ... I hoped still
to have Time enough between my Departure & the 15th Sept^r (the day
when the People must go off for the Goods from Kam[inistiquia, at the
head of Lake Superior]) to explore at least the Flat Bow Country, & by
the Course of the large River, determine whether it is the Columbia or
not" (13).

19 July 1807, "*Found no fit Place ... 200 Y^ds above the Level of the
Lake*" Thompson shifted the location of his fort when it was partially
built – cf. 28 July 1807, 2 October 1807. The first location was on the
northern shore of Lake Windermere, the second on Toby Creek.

19 July 1807, "*the Country is extremely poor in Provisions ... & we
are in all 17 Mouths to feed*" Cf. 8 May 1808, 24 August 1809, and
AO journals 19 for 22 July 1807, which gives the count as "13 Men
& Women besides 6 Children." In command were Thompson, proprietor, and McDonald, clerk. The five men already mentioned as partic-
ipants in the journey across the mountains (10 May 1807 note) were
joined by Le Camble and Lussier. The other eight to ten "mouths"
were wives and children.

The problem of an adequate food supply did not take Thompson by
surprise; La Gassé and Le Blanc, who wintered with Kootenays in

1800–01, experienced hardship, according to Fidler's postscript to 31 December 1792: "In their own country [the Kootenays'] principal subsistence is upon the Jumping Deer a small animal they are numerous but not easily approached to kill them ... at times they was much reduced for Provisions, however they was very kind & generous to these 2 Men" (HBCA E3/2). Thompson informed the senior partners in his RCSL report that he had experienced the same conditions – cf. McGillivray's "Account": "From recent discoveries beyond the Rocky Mountains by the N.W. Co. on the waters of the Columbia, it appears that the natives are numerous and susceptible of improvement, their country is mild, but they find great difficulty to subsist owing to the scarcity of Animals, which are principally of the Deer kind" (67).

Ogden faced a similar problem in 1824 when he ventured into the "Snake Country" south of the Columbia River: "On my last years travels I met with so many reverces and the men constantly grumbling and discontented that I am in a manner prepared for them at the same time can afford them no relief ... so far as we can judge from appearances we cannot entertain great hopes of escaping [from starvation] may God preserve us" (Ogden, ed. Rich, 108).

20 July 1807, "the Lake and Saleesh Indians" – members of Kootenay and Salish bands; cf. the designation of AO journals 19 for this day: "Flat Bows and Flat Heads." Cf. also Henry, whose descriptions of transmontane tribes, written at Rocky Mountain House in 1811, were almost certainly based on Thompson's information: "Of the several different Tribes of Indians to the Southward and Westward of the Kootonaes, we are but only just beginning to be acquainted ... The Flat Bow or as some call them the Lake Indians, dwell on the boarders of a large Lake [Kootenay Lake], into which McGillivray's [Kootenay/ Kootenai] river empties in its course to the Columbia ... The Saleesh or Flat Head Indians, are numerous, and dwell ... along the Saleesh [Pend Oreille] River where the country is open and admits of their using horses of which they have great numbers ... they frequent [the plains] at particular seasons to make provisions. It is generally there where they encounter the Peagans and fight most desperately when they are attacked" (NA MG19 A13, 1104–6/Coues, 709–10).

20 July 1807, "Early traded with a few Kootanaes" Cf. AO journals 19 for this day: "They brought ab^t $\frac{1}{3}$ of a Pack of Beaver with 4 White Goat Skins in the Wool"; also RCSL report: "The Kootanaes traded ... the Skins of 4 white Goats, with the wool of 4 others. I traded them to send to Montreal that their value might be known

& if worth taking." Thompson gives the sequel to this experiment in his *Narrative*: "Some of the ignorant self sufficient partners of the Company ridiculed such an article for the London market; there they went and sold at first sight for a guinea a skin ... These same partners then wrote to me to procure as many as possible ... for their ignorant ridicule I would send no more, and I kept my word" (Tyrrell, 380/ Glover, 277). Cf. Simpson: "I have directed a few Skins to be ... sent home next Season and if the Manufacturers could afford a tolerable price say 10/- or 15/- p^r Skin nett they might become an object of Trade worthy our attention" (Merk, 33).

20 July 1807, "Beat Meat" Cf. 9 and 11 January 1811, and Franklin: "The meat is dried by the Indians in the sun, or over a fire, and pounded by beating it with stones when spread on a skin. In this state it is brought to the forts, where the admixture of hair is partially sifted out, and a third part of melted fat incorporated with it ... the pemmican is then firmly pressed into leathern bags, each capable of containing eighty-five pounds, and being placed in an airy place to cool, is fit for use. It keeps in this state, if not allowed to get wet, very well for one year, and with great care it may be preserved good for two" (117).

22 July 1807, "Began to build..." AO journals 18 includes a plan of Kootanae House: a "Dwelling House," two smaller houses, a "Magazine," a "Shop," and a "Hangard." Each building was made by setting up vertical posts ("needles") at the corners and by filling in the walls between the needles with horizontal logs. The relocated fort was finished on 27 October 1807 – cf. AO journals 19 for this day: "Sawed Boards for the Gate & made it &c – thank Heaven we have now fully enclosed ourselves." Construction of Kullyspel House was faster (12–26 September 1809) but followed the same order of tasks. Cf. Hearne, building Cumberland House in 1774: "Most of the People complain'd of the great hardship it ware to work the whole Day ... but ... finding it Necessary for the good of the Expedition I commanded them to work from 6 till 6, and shall keep them at such hours tell the house is compleat" (Tyrrell-HTF, 142).

22 July 1807, "Shared all the Meat equally among us" Thompson took charge of whatever food was available and distributed it each day; he, his clerk and their families ate separately from the men – cf. 16 August 1807, 4 and 6 November 1808, 15 and 20 November 1810, 11 January 1811, and RCSL report: "The Men were now so weak, that however willing, they actually had not strength to work, & some of them told me that two or three days more of Famine would bring them to the Ground. I deeply felt for their Situation & my own, but was determined still to wait a few Days before I could consent that any should return ... a dram of H[igh] Wines had often done us much good, but our Keg, what with leaking & with expenditure, was nearly finished" (16).

Hearne also depended on equal shares to minimize his men's dissatisfaction: "The very scanty allowance of Provisions that we have ben put to for some time past, has accationd many grumblings amongs some of the men, but as from the first of the scarce times ... I stipolated myself to the very same allowance in every artical, I told them they had no right to complain, knowing it ware not in my Power to Redress them" (Tyrrell–HTF, 136). For his part, Ogden reminded his men how the Shoshoni behaved in times of even greater need: "Reduced to one meal a day how loudly and grievously do we complain, but in truth how unjustly and without cause when I consider the Snakes suffrings compared to ours many a day they pass without food and still without a complaint or murmer and in this wretched manner do they pass their *lives*" (Ogden, ed. Davies and Johnson, 21).

25 July 1807, "the Fire that is burning the Country" Cf. 11 September 1807, 20 August 1807, and AO journals 19 for 26 July 1807: "The Ground was set on fire by the Kootanaes 8 days ago below, & the Fire now fast approaches us." Cf. also Fidler, 18 December 1792: "Grass is now burning with great fury ... it drives along with amazing swiftness – indeed several Inds I have heard being burnt in this manner, to death ... The Lightning in the Spring & Fall frequently lights the Grass – & in the winter it is done by Indians" (HBCA E3/2).

28 July 1807, "Men working at the Weir" Cf. 13 August 1807, 3 and 10 July 1811; and Mackenzie: "To take [salmon] with more facility, [the natives] had, with great labour, formed an embankment or weir across the river ... The stream is stopped nearly two thirds by it. It is constructed by fixing small trees in the bed of the river in a slanting position (which could be practicable only when the water is much lower than I saw it) with the thick part downwards; over these is laid a bed of gravel on which is placed a range of lesser trees, and so on alternately till the work is brought to its proper height. Beneath it the machines are placed, into which the salmon fall when they attempt to leap over" (361).

28 July 1807, "close on the Banks of a rapid Stream" – Toby Creek. In the RCSL report Thompson acknowledges the advice of visiting Kootenays: "After some Conversation they told me plainly that the

Situation of the Building was bad, as it was far from water, & open to the insult of the Peagans ... I had long thought this myself ... at last found an eligible Spot on the Kootanae River, in a commanding Situation, the water quite near" (16–17).

29 July 1807, "Load of Goods Lumber &c &c" – load of merchandise and personal effects – cf. 5 and 8 September 1809.

4 August 1807, "Went round Kootanae Lake & a little way up the mid Rivulet" – around Windermere and upstream towards Columbia Lake. Cf. 2 October 1807, 5 June 1808, and RCSL report: "Here it may not be amiss to state the nature of the Country. This of the Kootanaes is a Valley of from 6 to 12 Miles wide, if we compute from Mountain to Mountain, but if only the level space, it will seldom exceed 2 Miles, being the Ground occupied by the River, it's Islands, small Lakes & Marshes ... As one approaches the Lakes, the Woods of this almost impenetrable Forest, become gradually less close ... & soon ... open clear Ground for Horses ... a fine Meadow of Hill & valley & Gullies, with Hemlock planted upon it as it were for Shelter against the Heat & bad weather" (13–14).

10 August 1807, "Buché began a Wood Canoe" Cf. 12 September 1809, 21 August – 1 September 1811, as well as AO journals 25 (3 pp.) and 27 (5 pp.) for details of construction. Thompson did not have much success building either birch bark or pine bark canoes west of the divide. The wood canoe was his invention, made after the pattern of a bark canoe; it consisted of a frame to which boards were sewn with spruce roots. Buché's was the prototype of Thompson's Columbia canoes built at Boat Encampment and Kettle Falls. These became in turn the models for company boats on the Columbia River – cf. Stuart: "This Canoe is the same with those made use of by the North West Company on this [west] side of the rocky mountains, it is composed of Cedar boards $\frac{1}{4}$ of an inch thick, its only support within are a few braces or knees of the same material, $\frac{3}{8}$ of an inch, to which the boards are secured with sturgeon twine, and the space which is caulked in Boats is here filled up with gum; Thus you have a vessel to answer the purpose of a bark Canoe, so far as regards facility of transportation, but in every other respect so much its inferior that no attempt at comparison can with justice be made; even in strength the latter is far superior, for the bark will bend and give way to pressure (without material injury) which would split the Cedar one and send her to the bottom" (Spaulding, 52). For a photograph and

Thompson's insistence on a wood canoe for boundary surveying in 1837, see Roberts and Shackleton (235–6).

13 August 1807, "the Death of the Old Chief's son" – a consequence of the Peigan-Salish war that summer – cf. 20 July 1807 note, 17 and 25 September 1807, 21 August 1811, and AO journals 27: "An Indian thinks the Revenge of Murder belongs only to the kin of the Murdered, & this, because they have lost a Good, a something desirable; Society has nothing to do with it. Those not of the Kin say, it was a foolish Action, & there the Matter stands. But a foreigner, or one of another Tribe to kill another Indian, is to call the injured Tribe into the quarrel, if they are strong enough, but otherwise they let the matter pass, as what cannot be helped."Cf. also McGillivray's *Journal*: "Tho' the numbers that compose a tribe live seldom in harmony among themselves, yet they never fail to unite against a common enemy, and when an opportunity offers of annoying a neighbouring nation, without incurring much danger, they generally embrace it, whether the provocation be recent or not" (62).

13 August 1807, "they also added" Cf. 10 July 1811, and RCSL report: "They also informed me that about 3 weeks ago the Americans to the number of 42 arrived to settle a military Post, at the confluence of the two most southern and considerable Branches of the Columbia & that they were preparing to make a small advance Post lower down the River ... This establishment of the Americans will give a new Turn to our so long delayed settling of this Country, on which we have entered it seems too late; but, in my opinion the most valuable part of the Country still remains to us, and we have nothing to obstruct us, but the difficulty of getting Goods from Fort des Prairies, & the still more formidable poverty of the Country in Animals. Time & Perseverance will show what we can do, & if worth our Expence & Trouble" (43).

20 August 1807, "saw a fine Herd of wild Horses" Cf. AO journals 19 for 8 December 1807: "Saw several Marrons" – here Thompson uses the Hispano-Franco-American term for freed slaves.

27 August 1807, "Peagan ... I had expected to see them long ago" Cf. AO journals 19 for this day: "We expected all along that this Nation would be displeased with a Settlement here. They say they are contented, & that as soon as Kootanae appe the Kootanae [*sic*] Chief heard of our being here, he sent them off to see the truth of the matter. What their future Intentions are Heaven knows – we hope for the best, as it is in their Power to be very troublesome to us." Cf. also 29 October 1810, 15 August 1811 note, and *Narrative* (Tyrrell, 380–4/Glover, 277–9).

27 August 1807, "Several Salmon seen" – *Oncorhynchus tshawytscha*, chinook salmon, which swam the entire length of the Columbia River to spawn. Cf. 29 and 31 August 1807, 5 September 1807, and Simpson: "Those Fish ascend the Stream from the Sea in immense shoals in the month of July for the purpose of Spawning and find their way to the foot of the mountain penetrating every little Creek; they however never get back to their native element as towards the Fall they become lean exhausted and diseased and are cast ashore in large quantities or found in nearly an inanimate state on the surface of the Water; they are even in this putrid condition acceptable to the Natives who dry them for Winter stock" (Merk, 40). Salmon runs to the upper Columbia ended with the proliferation of dams on the lower reaches of the river (1915–40).

Thompson's party caught salmon with spears; Finan McDonald was the most adept, but not equal to Native fishermen whom Douglas observed along the lower Columbia: "Not once out of twelve will they miss bringing a fish to the surface on the barb. The spear is pointed with bone and laced tight to a pointed piece of wood a foot long and at pleasure locks on the staff and comes out of the socket when the fish is struck; it is fastened to the staff by a cord. Fifteen hundred and sometimes two thousand are taken in the course of the day" (203).

2 September 1807, "the Camp is very sick" Cf. AO journals 19 for this day: the entry adds, "it seems, by the Hooping Cough" – cf. 25 and 28 September 1807, 30 September 1809, 28 July 1811. Western tribes were no strangers to epidemics; the worst, a wave of smallpox in 1781, was transmitted just like this "Hooping Cough," in garments and blankets as well as by direct contact. In the *Narrative* Thompson recalls an old trader's account of the smallpox epidemic: "None of us had the least idea of the desolation this dreadful disease had done, until we ... looked into the tents, in many of which they were all dead, and the stench was horrid; Those that remained ... were in such a state of despair and despondence that they could hardly converse with us ... From what we could learn, three fifths had died under this disease" (Tyrrell, 321–2/Glover, 236).

5 September 1807, "Gave Turlington to those afflicted" Turlington's Balsam (compound tincture of benzoin) was the traders' patent medicine, and fur trade proprietors were expected to dispense it – cf.

27 December 1810 note, Hearne (28), Mackenzie (368), Harmon (182), and Fraser (119).

11 September 1807, "Only 1 Carp in the Nets" – probably *Catostomus machrocheilus*, large sucker.

11 September 1807, "engaged Boulard at 400 livres – no Equipment" Cf. AO journals 25 for 4 May 1811: Thompson's engagement of the Grand Nipissing as hunter, and Louis as steersman: "Each have 600 Livres & an equipment for their Summer's Work & 3 Skins for every large Animal they kill on the east Side the Mountains & 6 Skins for every dº on the west Side the Mountains, the small Animals in proportion." By comparison Boulard's value was not high. Although Thompson repeatedly engaged him, he willingly traded Boulard for a Hawaiian (31 July 1811).

The conditions of engagement are spelled out in the NW Co's usual printed contracts (HBCA F5/1) and in Thompson's draft of a contract with François Desjarlaix, found in AO journals 23: "Convention faite entre Monsʳ James Hughes un des Representants de la Compagnie du Nord Ouest d'un part et Francois Dejarlaix de l'autre part – le dit Francois Dejarlaix confesse et reconnoit n'étre libre que a son retour a Ft William et s'oblige pendant le Tems qu'il restera dans le Nord en Vertue de ces conventions de travailler les Castors et toute peltrie qui il pourra tuer ou amasser et oblige de livre tout entier a la Societé du Nord Ouest sans avoir la permission de donner la moindre partie au Gens oppose aux Interest de la dite compagnie ni de leur donner aucune aide, ni assistance, soit en traitant avec eux ou en leur donnant de l'Information ou lumiere sur aucune chose. Fait et passé au Ft Auguste, L'An Mille huit Cent Neuf, le 20 de Juliet, et les Parties ont signé a l'Exception du dit F Dejarlaix qui ayant declare ne le savoir ecrire a faite sa marque afin lecture faite Temoins."

12 September 1807, "I shall send them across the Mountains to fetch Goods" – to meet the supply brigade from Rainy Lake – cf. 23 September 1807, 3 October 1807, 7 June 1808, 7 November 1808, 2 October 1809, 18 and 22 September 1811. Cf. also the ruling of the partners' meeting at Fort William in July 1809, "that the trade hereafter to be carried on, to the district beyond the Rocky Mountains, known by the name of Columbia, shall be precisely on the same footing as the Trade to Athabaska – that is – that the Canoes for that quarter with the Returns shall come annually to Lac La Pluye, and there take the Outfit, as otherwise it would be attended with too great an Expence to the Compy" (Wallace, 262).

In 1801 Mackenzie described the transcontinental supply route to the Athabaska department; the same would later be true of the Columbia department: "The immense length of the voyage [even to Rainy Lake], and other concurring circumstances, is a most severe trial of patience and perseverance: there [the men] do not remain a sufficient time for ordinary repose, when they take a load of goods in exchange, and proceed on their return, in a great measure, day and night ... Such is the life which these people lead; and is continued with unremitting exertion, till their strength is lost in premature old age" (247). A letter written by Jules Quesnel to J.M. Lamothe, sent from New Caledonia on 1 May 1809, is evidence of Mackenzie's assertion: "Les Hommes les Plus Robuste qui ont été 3 Ans dans ce Pays ici sont déjas apeine capable de faire leurs Devoir, et malgré que je suis d'un bouillant tempérament je m'apperçois dejas que ma santé Décline" (Fraser, 262).

13 September 1807, "I spoke to those who loitered behind" Cf. RCSL report: "I told them we were well prepared for the worst that could happen, & if any Trouble was given us, it was a very easy thing to build far out of their Power, & where they would never get a pipe of Tobacco from us, but that all their Efforts would never make us relinquish the Trade this Side of the Mountains. They again repeated they had no wish for a rupture & were glad we were here to get a pipe of Tobacco in the Summer & thus we parted" (23–4). Thompson's warning was made in earnest – cf. AO journals 19 for 26 October 1807: "Held a Council with the Kootanaes concerning the Blood & Blackfoot Indians who are said to meditate an attack on us, & we agreed to join them Battle the moment they appear, & for the Success of which we pray the mercy of the Supreme Being, Arbiter of Life & Death."

17 September 1807, "Bercier ... from the band of Kootanaes" Cf. AO journals 19 for this day: "Bercier from the great Band arrived; he says they are so ill that they cannot decamp but by very small campments. The Kootanae Chief is bent on revenging the Death of his Son on the Peagans, & means to take the very first opportunity of killing some of those People. As Bercier was returning here yesterday he met with two Peagan young Men going there, whom he brought back again to their camp. The Peagans kindly received him, & when he told them of the Kootanaes hav^g thrown the Tob they sent them to the Dogs, they were at a loss how to proceed. Bercier advised them instantly to cross the Mountains, as the Old Chief meant to strengthen himself with the Flat Bows, & then to follow them. Bercier thus parted with them. This News again brings me up, & I must wait the event of this Business

& see these strange Indians. They will, in all probability, not be in under 8 or 10 days hence, so that I must send & trade Horses from them for the Portage."

17 September 1807, "They speak well of their Country" Cf. AO journals 19 for this day: "They drew me out a Sketch of their Country, & to near the Sea, which they say I may go to from hence & be back in a month's hence [*sic*], were it Summer Time." Thompson's inquiries elicited another map on 30 September 1809. Native maps were drawn with charcoal on skin or bark, or with a stick on the ground; if Thompson made paper copies of these maps, they have not survived. Cf. RCSL "Indian Chart," Clark's transcriptions of Native maps (Moulton, Atlas, and Thwaites, *passim*), as well as Fidler's copies of five Blackfoot maps (HBCA E3/2, B39/a/2, and G1/25), and his comment, 10 July 1802: "Th[ese] Indian map[s] convey much information where European documents fail; and on some occasions are of much use, especially as they shew [where] such & such rivers & other remarkable places are, tho' they are utterly unacquainted with any proportion in drawing them" (HBCA A10/1). Cf. also Laroque, who met with Crow and Shoshoni in 1805: "A few of them assembled and draughted on a dressed skin, I believe a very good map of their Country, and they showed me the place where at different seasons they were to be found" (Wood and Thiessen, 182).

18 September 1807, "the junction of McGillivray's River with the Kootanae d^o" – Kootenay and Columbia Rivers – not a junction but a portage over Canal Flats.

18 September 1807, "Ugly Head, their Chief" Cf. AO journals 19 for 25 September 1807: "The Old Chief [of the Kootenays] with Ugly Head of the Flat Bows" – "so named from his hair curling": *Narrative* (Tyrrell, 390/Glover, 283). Ugly Head guided Thompson from Windermere to Canal Flats (2–3 October 1807), organized a trade rendezvous (12–14 May 1808), and later guided Thompson along the Moyie River to Canal Flats (24 May – 5 June 1808). Thompson commended the Kootenay chief's "manly exertions, Perseverance & Attention" (5 June 1808).

18 September 1807, "we had paid no attention ... thinking it the Effect of Superstition" Cf. Mackenzie: "These people [on the Bella Coola River] indulge an extreme superstition respecting their fish, as it is apparently their only animal food. Flesh they never taste, and one of their dogs having picked and swallowed part of a bone which we had left, was beaten by his master till he disgorged it" (362). Thompson had read Mackenzie's *Voyages*.

23 September 1807, "a Gun ought to be double the value" Cf. 30 September 1809 and a ruling of the partners' meeting at Fort William in July 1808: "Outfits made in the Interior to distant posts such as Mackenzies River, New Caledonia from Athabaska and the Columbia from Fort de Prairies, requiring new Setts of Men and Incurring additional Expences, ought to be valued accordingly" (Wallace, 251). Cf. also Cox: "A good gun was not to be had [at Spokane in 1812] under twenty beaver skins; a few short ones we gave for fifteen; and some idea of the profit may be formed, when I state that the wholesale price of a gun is about one pound seven shillings, while the average value of twenty beaver skins is about twenty-five pounds! Two yards of cloth, which originally cost twelve shillings, would generally bring six or eight beavers, value eight or ten pounds! and so on in proportion for the other articles" (115).

25 September 1807, "Shawpatin Indians" – Nez Perces, also called Green Wood Indians – cf. 24 September 1809 and 3 October 1809.

25 September 1807, "the Blackfeet had plundered Fort Augustus" Cf. AO journals 19 for this day: "The Old Chief with Ugly Head of the Flat Bows & 21 Kootanae Men & Lads arrived – gave them to smoke. They informed [me] that by the accounts of the Peagans 2 or 3 Months ago, the Brother of the Old White Swan, a Blackfoot Chief, had with his Band, a party of Blood Indians & a few Fall Indians [Atsina], pillaged Fort Augustus & left the Men without even cloathing on their Backs, but whether they murdered the Men or not, they [the Kootenays] do not know, any more than whether they pillaged both Forts or only one; but that they were possessed of many Guns, much Ammunition & Tob with various other Articles, & finding themselves thus rich, they were gone to war on the Crow Mountain Indians."

In opposing the traders, the Blackfoot risked cutting off supplies which were increasingly regarded as essential – cf. Bird, 7 April 1807: "A few Blackfeet arrived, among them was their principal Chief, a man who has long been remarkable for his attachment to white Men, & his friendship for the Crees. This Man tells us that his Country Men all wish sincerely for Peace, that having been long accustomed to be supplied with Brandy Tobacco &c, these articles are become objects of primary necessity to them" (HBCA B60/a/6). Cf. also Franklin: "The Indians spoke of killing all the white people in that vicinity ... [to which an old Cree replied], A pretty state we shall then be in without the goods you bring us" (117–18).

28 September 1807, "some Animal of their Nurses Fables" Thompson's scientific scepticism concerning this report was to be sorely tested – cf. 4 and 7 January 1811.

29 September 1811, "Meadow Indians" – Peigan, Blood and Blackfoot.

29 September 1807, "by personally examining that Country I may be able to form a judgment" Thompson's commercial and geographical interests are combined in this rare statement of purpose – cf. 3 and 10 July 1811.

29 September 1807, "the large River ... which I name McGillivray's River" – Kootenay/Kootenai River – cf. 30 June 1807, 5 September 1811, and Henry, who provides several names as well as describing the river's course (traced by Thompson in 1809): "The land the Kootenays now inhabit ... is on the upper part of the Columbia, and on Ram River, a little s. of it, now called McGillivray's River, but formerly termed by the natives Flat Bow River, from a tribe of Indians who then inhabited the lower part of it. This river, after making a great bend s.e., returns and empties into the Columbia, far above the place where the latter receives the river down which Captains Lewis and Clark proceeded on their way to the Pacific" (Coues, 705–6). Ogden deplored "the arbitrary mode of naming places, without reference to the aboriginal nomenclature, by which alone they ought to be distinguished" [Ogden], 35). Cf. PRO (1) and (2): Thompson's careful record of Native names in the Bow Valley and along the lower Columbia is combined with fur trade names and those bestowed by other explorers such as Lewis, Clark and Vancouver.

2 October 1807, "McGillivray's Portage" – Canal Flats – cf. 21 April 1808, 4 June 1808, 20 August 1809.

2 October 1807, "the Road takes along" Part of the phrase has been omitted – it should read "The Road takes [its course] along."

2 October 1807, "Red Fir Trees ... Mountain Larch ... a Kind of Cypress" – *Pseudotsuga menziesii*, Douglas fir; *Larix occidentalis*, western larch; *Juniperus scopulorum*, Rocky Mountain juniper, which has cedarlike bark.

3 October 1807, "those Meadows about Fort George" – a NW Co post east of Elk Point on the North Saskatchewan River – cf. AO journals 13: "Journey from Rocky Mountain House to Fort George" and "Journey from Fort Augustus to Fort George by Land." Both trips were made in 1800.

3 October 1807, "me & my guide converse together partly by signs and partly by words" Cf. Ferris: "The Indians … cannot be induced to convey their ideas in any other tongue except their own. This custom would in a great measure prevent a proper understanding in many instances, were it not for their numerous signs, which constitute a kind of universal communication, not to say language, at once understood by all the various Indians in the mountains. These signs are made with their hands or fingers, in different positions, with rapidity; and are so extremely simple, that a person entirely unacquainted with them, will readily conceive a great portion of what may be expressed by them" (323–4).

3 October 1807, "I shall therefore proceed no farther on this Route" Cf. AO journals 19 for this day: "So much time, to see a Road utterly useless to me, was what I could not spare in such circumstances as the present, especially from the News I had learnt concerning the Plunder of the Fort Augustus by the Blackfoots; I therefore told my Guide I would return the morrow towards the house, as I had seen the River, & was satisfied it was quite navigable for Canoes."

3 October 1807, "the Torrent Rivulet" – St Mary's River – cf. 31 May 1808, 2 June 1808, 22 August 1809.

Thompson spent the winter of 1807–08 at Kootanae House, trading with Kootenays and always wary of a Peigan attack. In the spring of 1808 he carried out his plan to explore "McGillivray's" River.

Journey to the Lake Indian Country

Source: AO journals 21

Accounts of this journey are found in AO journals 19 as well as 21. The version in AO journals 21 is slightly fuller, so it has been used here as the base text. Passages not included in AO journals 19 are indicated by angled brackets. Small differences (single words and phrasing) are not noted, but significant variants are given below.

20 April 1808, "Co down the Kootanae River" – down Toby Creek; *"Kootanae Lake"* – Windermere; *"the Rivulet"* – between Windermere and Columbia Lake.

20 April 1808, "left off draw^g" – a rough sketch map of the river channels – cf. AO journals 25 for 13 May 1811: "I do not draw the River off as the Channel is small, mostly only one."

20 April 1808, "an Embarras ... plenty of Beaver; the mid part, full of embarras" – obstructions – cf. 30 May 1808, 8 June 1808, Fidler (HBCA E3/1:4 April 1792), and Douglas: "I felt no little embarrassment in making my way through the thicket" (219). Cf. also Fidler, 8 June 1791: "Very easy current & a good number of Beaver Dams which in great measure facilitated our progress by their stopping the Water, & keeping in sufficient water to float the Canoes" (HBCA E3/1).

21 April 1808, "At 10 Am put the Goods ashore & began to carry" – across "McGillivray's Portage" (Canal Flats), called in AO journals 19 "the Kootanae Flat Bow River Portage."

21 April 1808, "Clement & Bercier ... to Kootanae House" The other men named are Lussier, Beaulieu, Mousseau, and Le Camble.

21 April 1808, "obs^d for Lat^de by 2 Alt^des of [sun's] UL" – the sun's upper limb, its edge above the centre. Thompson almost always observed the lower limb.

22 April 1808, "a remarkable high Mountain" – Teepee Mountain, southeast of Skookumchuk.

22 April 1808, "many Ducks, but mostly of the whistling kind. A few Wolves" – possibly *Anas americana*, American wigeon; *Canis lupus*, grey wolf.

22 April 1808, "a Garden for Herbs" Cf. 24 August 1809 and the pencilled draft of a letter (addressee indecipherable) in AO journals 19: "The Lake Indian country is very central for Trade, but this is the only advantage it possesses, as the Place is extremely bare of Animals. Our living must be in what we can raise from the Ground – for the purpose I shall try & get a few Potatoes and trust you to send me ab^t 1 Bushel of good Indian Corn parched, with a little Barley, Rice, Pease & Beans for the same purpose: otherwise we must abandon this Country & take to Places where we may live better, but lose the Trade of the Indians who cannot cross Mountains."

Cf. Simpson, sizing up the Columbia department in 1824: "I mean to send some Garden and Field Seed across next Season to be tried at Spokane House and I feel confident that they will thrive, *Indian Corn cannot fail* ... some of our Factors and Traders ... would be more usefully employed on this side [west of the divide] in the peacable safe and easy occupation of Farming than in Councilling Dealing with Indians or exploring new countries for which many of them are totally unfit but it unfortunately happens that in these savage regions Gentlemen ... are not satisfied unless they have a posse of Clerks Guides Interpreters & supernumeraries at their disposal while they look on with a pair of Gloves on their hands" (Merk, 49–50).

22–3 April 1808, "Pines, but of the swampy kind ... Large Poplars ... small wild Onions" – *Picea mariana*, black spruce; *Populus trichocarpa*, black cottonwood; *Allium cernuum*, nodding onion or *Allium schoenoprasum*, wild chive.

24 April 1808, "the Torrent Rivulet from which I returned last October" Cf. 3 October 1807 and 31 May 1808.

24 April 1808, "I set 2 Steel Traps" Cf. 30 September 1809. At this time the usual way of catching beaver was by breaking open their lodges; some tribes had not hunted them at all before trading with Europeans – cf. Fidler, 27 November 1792: "These Indians [Peigan] are very little acquainted with killing Beaver in their houses. What few they have to trade are generally shott by them when the rivers are open Spring Fall & Summer. Several of them are so full of superstition as even not to touch one; and a great many of them will neither eat of them or suffer them to be brought into their Tents" (HBCA E3/2). Canadian, Iroquois and Ojibwa hunters had no such scruples – cf. Bird, 4 February 1808: "I am apprehensive that in a very few Years a Beaver will be nearly as great a curiosity here as in London; 'tis the free Canadians & Iroquoys with their Steel Traps that have so totally destroyed them" (HBCA B60/a/7).

25 April 1808, "passed the bad Rivulet" – Moyie River, which Thompson later called "McDonald's River"; *"fine bold River"* – Bull River; *"Stag River"* – Elk River.

25–6 April 1808, "Beautiful Meadows on both Hands … the Tobacco Meadows … Fine Meadow Rivulet" – Tobacco Plains, now partially flooded by Lake Koocanusa, the reservoir of the Libby Dam; Tobacco River. Native tobacco was *Nicotiana quadrivalvus*; when smoked, it was often mixed with *Arctostaphylos uva-ursi*, kinnikinnik.

27 April 1808, "we set Beaulieu & Lussier ashore to follow the indian Road" A Native trail followed the Kootenai River down from the Stillwater River to the Fisher River, where two trails then continued south to camas meadows along the Clark Fork River. Dotted lines indicate these trails on the PRO (2) map.

29 April 1808, "banks of Rock on both Sides" – the Kootenai River between the Stillwater and Fisher Rivers.

30 April 1808, "am so lame of the Knee" This injury is again mentioned on 22 May 1808 and may have contributed to the rather querulous tone of the rest of this account.

30 April 1808, "our subsistence this day was a Dram of Rum & half a Partridge p^r Man" In AO journals 19 this phrase is first written under 29 April 1808, then crossed out and repeated in this day's entry. Cf. 4 November 1810, and Fidler, 5 January 1792: "It never rains but it powers: sometimes a Single Partridge or a Beaver's Tail has been all we had for a day's allowance amongst 10 of us – now at present the times are different & the Indians are now wallowing up to the Eyes in good Meat – I [shall] wish ere long that they had ... thought ... to have provided against any future want" (HBCA E3/1).

2 May 1808, "did not observe for want of Candles" Cf. *Narrative*: "By too much attention to calculations in the night with no other light than a small candle my right eye became so inflamed that I lost its sight" (Glover, 55).

3 May 1808, "a species of Tiger" – *Felix concolor*, a young cougar – cf. Hector: "Suddenly my horse shyed at a bush, and immediately out sprang a splendid panther ... of a browny red colour, and I had only time to remark the great width of his face, and the length of his tail. This is the only one I have seen in the mountains, although in some localities his easily distinguished track is not unfrequent" (Spry, 331).

3 May 1808, "Two of us ... had a violent head Ache for a few hours" AO journals 19 substitutes a completely different statement: "We have lost 2 Horses of the Co^y – they crossed the River & got far out of our reach."

3 May 1808, "Many small Plane Trees" – *Acer glabrum*, Douglas maple.

5 May 1808, "returned back close above the Rock River" – Fisher River.

5 May 1808, "to shave & wash ourselves &c" – a ceremony reserved for approaches to forts and meetings with "strange Indians"; it was always worth a mention in journals – cf. 29 September 1809 and 15 July 1811, as well as Mackenzie (359), Fraser (75, 156), and Franklin (101). Fidler's entry for 12 December 1792 shows that Natives insisted on this custom of sprucing up to meet strangers: "[The Peigan chief] wished us to strip all our old clothing off & put on our very best one, that we might cut a more respectable appearance to the Snake Indian [Shoshoni visitor] ... Several times since I have reflected that Our Indians did right in wishing us to appear in our Sundays clothes before the Stranger: to impress a proper opinion of our surprising qualifications, as Our Indians was pleased to term it" (HBCA E3/2). But Fidler also reveals that washing was sometimes a simple necessity: "26 December [1791] ... Put on a clean Shirt, never shifted myself since I left the House 4th Septr having at first only 2 Shirts & no Soap or Kettle to wash one with" (HBCA E3/1).

5 May 1808, "alders" – *Alnus tenuifolia*, thinleaf alder.

6 May 1808, "the Portage & Fall" – Kootenai Falls.

7 May 1808, "I have taken half the timbers out to lighten it" Cf.
1 November 1808 and Landemann: "Four poles, three or four inches
at their thickest ends ... were laid side by side in the middle of the bottom of the canoe. On these poles, the cargo was carefully arranged so
that all the weight rested on them, and none allowed to press against
the bare and unprotected sides of the canoe" (Davidson, 216–17).

8 May 1808, "a kind of Bread made of Moss from the Trees" – made
of *Bryoria*, hair lichen. Jaco Finlay gave Douglas his first taste of moss
bread, together with the recipe: "The manner of preparing [moss for
bread] is as follows: It is gathered from the trees and all the small dead
twigs taken out of it, and then immersed in water until it becomes perfectly flexible, and afterwards placed on a heap of heated stones ... and
allowed to remain until cooked, which generally takes a night. Then
before it cools it is compressed into thin cakes and is fit for use"
(Douglas, 171). Cf. Thompson's comment in the *Narrative*: "[It is] acceptable to the hungry, and in hard times, of great service to the
Indians. I never could relish it" (Tyrrell, 388–9/Glover, 282).

8 May 1808, "I wait Boulard for a more circumstantial account"
Cf. AO journals 19 for this day: "They tell me their Poverty is owing
to a war broke out between them & the Peagans, the latter hav[g] wished
to follow after the Men I sent to the Kootanaes to encourage them to
kill beaver. The Kootanaes followed them: this brought on words & a
scuffle, in which 1 Peagan was killed & another his Arm broke – on the
Kootanae Side the Old Chief was shot thro' the Thigh, & his Horse
wounded. The Peagans hid themselves & shortly after stole 35 Horses,
with which they got off."

8 May 1808, "the River here is ... edged with Thorn ... small elder"
– *Crataegus douglasii*, black hawthorn, and *Sambucus racemosa*, red
elderberry.

12 May 1808, "Backed a Sturgeon Net" – to catch *Acipenser trans-
montanus*, white sturgeon.

12 May 1808, "I propose to examine this River down to the Lake" –
to Kootenay Lake, home of the "Lake" or "Flat Bow" Kootenays.

14 May 1808, "for Mr Duncan McGillivray" Unknown to Thompson, McGillivray had died a few weeks before, in Montreal.

15 May 1808, "a Lake, but when the water is low, a Meadow" – Leach Lake. Playfair explained this phenomenon: "A lake is but a temporary and accidental condition of a river, which is every day approaching to its termination; and the truth of this is attested, not only by the lakes that have existed, but also by those that continue to exist. Where any considerable stream enters a lake, a flat meadow is usually observed increasing from year to year" (357–8).

17 May 1808, "paddled a good Pipe" Cf. 26 November 1810 and Landemann: "These Canadian voyageurs ... smoke almost incessantly, and sing peculiar songs ... marked by the movement of their paddles. They rest from five to ten minutes every two hours when they refill their pipes: it is more common for them to describe distances by so many pipes than in any other way" (Davidson, 218–19). Morse estimates "trois pipes" as 15 to 20 miles (12); one "good pipe" would have been 7 or 8 miles.

17 May 1808, "To our old Campment" Cf. 13 May 1808.

17 May 1808, "received the disagreeable News" Cf. the pencilled draft letter in AO journals 19: "The Flat Heads &c &c were only 12 day's March from us last Winter & the Lake Indians only 6 days & yet both [are] as completely shut up by Mountains as if they were on the other Side ... & the Waters rising in the Summer have nearly the same effect ... We are too few to separate ourselves – last Winter I had only 7 Men & it is not likely I shall have more this Winter ... I labour under many disadvantages which only Time and a generous assistance can overcome." Cf. also Fraser's letter to the NW Co senior partners, written at Stuart Lake in August 1806: "To form establishments this summer certainly depends upon us – but to render them productive, will depend on the attention you Gentlemen pay them ... tho few of you can imagine what it costs to feed the people in this quarter, there are none of you but know that exploring new countries and seeing strange Indians is expensive was it only to procure a welcome reception" (Fraser, 233).

19 May 1808, "got ready to set off" Thompson and his men left the Kootenai River and crossed to "McDonald's River" (Moyie River), following a Native trail to the junction of the Moyie and Kootenay rivers. This trail was partially flooded and apparently impossible to retrace without a guide – cf. 23–8 May 1808. A dotted line on the PRO (2) map indicates the route; cf. also 29 August 1809.

20–5 May 1808, "We found the Brook so deep & rapid ... Beaulieu's Brook" – Yaak River.

21 May 1808, "Here we found our Guide, who ... was about to desert" Cf. Mackenzie, one of whose guides was "so averse to continuing with us, that I was under the very disagreeable necessity of ordering the men to carry him into the canoe; and this was the first act during my voyage, that had the semblance of violent dealing" (330–1). Mackenzie prevented the escape of another guide by sleeping next to him: "My companion's hair being greased with fish-oil, and his body smeared with red earth, my sense of smelling, as well as that of feeling, threatened to interrupt my rest; but these inconveniences yielded to my fatigue, and I passed a night of sound repose" (342).

27 May 1808, "a family of Lake Indians" Cf. AO journals 19 for this day: "a family of Mountain Indians."

29 May 1808, "the Lake ... another Lake" – Moyie Lake, actually two lakes linked by a mile-long channel.

30 May 1808, "a Parcel ... was totally lost" Cf. the pencilled draft letter in AO journals 19: "In Nelson's Mountains, McDonald's River, I lost the best part of a pack of fine Beaver with 2 fine Bears, one of them I think the finest this Country would have produced this year. You will see the Quality of the Beaver: you will please take note that the Furrs have been wetted 15 or 20 Times – I have nothing to cover them with to FDP but my Tent & Cloak."

31 May 1808, "direct on the War Road" Cf. 3 June 1808 and AO journals 19 for 17 June 1808: "Anxious for the Men & Horses to a high degree – are they destroyed; has some war party followed them and cut them off – such was our thoughts all day."

31 May – 3 June 1808, "Nelson's Mountains ... Skirmish Brook ... Lussier's Rivulet" – Purcell Range, Wild Horse River, and Lussier River.

6 June 1808, "Lodge du Paille" – horse camp – cf. 29 October 1808.

After a summer trip to Rainy Lake, the new depot for the Athabaska and Columbia departments, Thompson returned up the Saskatchewan River to Boggy Hall on his way to Kootanae House.

From Boggy Hall
to Kootanae House

Source: AO journals 23

This journal is a sample of Thompson's accounts of travel over routes previously explored. The pace is faster, description is minimal, and local names such as "Baptiste's Brook" and "Mr Pangman's Tree" are in evidence.

4 October 1808, "the Seauteaux" – Thompson's Ojibwa hunter – cf. 29 October 1810, 28 and 30 November 1810: this hunter and Yellow Bird might be the same person, but the identity should not be assumed. The men named who took part in this journey were Ignace Parizeau, Brière, La Gassé, Méthode, Mousseau, Buché, Crépeau, Le Camble, Clément and Dupré; of these, the last three were "FDP Men" who were not contracted to cross the divide. As well, two clerks accompanied Thompson: Finan McDonald and James McMillan, the latter described in Simpson's "Character Book" as "a very steady plain blunt man ... who has gone through a vast deal of severe duty and is fit for any Service requiring physical strength firmness of mind and good Management provided he has no occasion to meddle with Pen & Ink ... An excellent Trader, speaks several Indian languages ... a good practical man" (Williams, 183–4).

7 October 1808, "Baptiste's Brook" – Baptiste River.

8 October 1808, "Boggy Hall" – a NW Co post situated on the west bank of the North Saskatchewan River, a little above Blue Rapids. Cf. Henry's description, written in 1811: "At this place we had an Establishment a few years ago ... but Beaver getting scarce we abandoned the place in the Fall of the Year 1808, the remains of the building stand ... about half a Mile from the River, through a thick Woods which must have made it very tedious getting water at this post in the Winter season. The situation of the House is very pleasant, having a beautiful Meadow on one side, sufficiently large for a horse race, the whole is bound in by tall Poplars, Aspen and pine" (NA MG19 A13, 1179–80/Couet, 738). Cf. 29 October 1810.

8 October 1808, "the old Fort" – Rocky Mountain House. A fur trade post was considered "old" after its first season, but "old" did not necessarily mean abandoned – cf. 6 June 1808, 22 October 1808 and note, 10 November 1808, 29 October 1810, 18 September 1811. Patterns of trade accounted in part for the transient nature of these posts, but even more important was the exhaustion of immediate resources – animals for food and furs, trees for fires and beds. Thompson did not even like camping where others had camped before him (3 December 1810, 14 July 1811).

9 October 1808, "Mr Pangman's marked tree" – a lobstick three miles upstream from Rocky Mountain House. Henry described the "rising ground ... where Mr Pangman cut his name on a pine in 1790. This spot was then the utmost extent of discoveries on the Saskatchewan toward the Rocky mountains." (NA MG19 A13, 1039–40/Coues, 662).

10 October 1808, "brought to the Canoes the Meat of the Cow" Cf. McDonald of Garth: "It was usual ... to send good Horses ... to await the Canoes at a certain place, in order to follow the Brigade on their way up the River to provide fresh provisions – the Partners & Clerks rode for this purpose with the Hunters. This was thought the most pleasant part of our lives, riding a swift Horse in the fine Valley of the Saskatchiwan, abounding Buffalos & Deers & all Game. We rode all day following the Progress of the Brigade against a currant of 4 Knots" (NA MG19 A17, 58/Masson, 2:22).

12 October 1808, "Making socks, Mittens, Capots, &c" These articles supplemented the men's "equipments." Cf. AO journals 19 for a list of such "equipments," of which one man's may be taken as an example: "1 broad Ceinture, 1 black Handk, 1 fine Cotton Shirt, 1 Capot of fine Cloth, 1 pr of fine Cord Trowsers, 1 Vest (red striped), 2 lbs of Soap"; also "Equipments to Canadian Steersmen, Bowsmen & Middlemen" (HBCA B239/z/1). Winter clothing was made from stroud, a woollen blanket fabric manufactured for the North American trade – cf. 8 November 1808, 27 December 1810 note, 21 September 1811, and Fidler, 28 October 1791: "I being in such a very poor situation, having neither Shoes, Socks, Mittens, nor anything to make them off, I offered to trade a small blanket & a moose skin." Sewing animal hides was more difficult than sewing cloth – cf. Fidler, 16 December 1791: "On account of the very wretched condition I am in for want of Trowsers (Having nothing of the Kind), the Man I am with cut a skin out of the bottom of his Tent to make a pair ... broke all my needles in making them, the leather being so stiff & hard, & went to work in the Indian manner with an Awl & sinews before I compleated them." On the other hand, hides were more versatile than cloth, as Fidler's journal also records, 18 November 1791: "Very poor times – we were under the necessity of roasting a piece of Buffalo Skin ... that had served to lye upon this long while past, having nothing else to eat" (HBCA E3/1).

16 October 1808, "Jaco's Brook" From Jaco's Brook westward, the route now travelled is the same as in May–June 1807; *"passed the Beau Parler's Tent"* – cf. McDonald of Garth: "1794 ... Our fort was in charge of one Jacob Finlay, an Indian half brother of Mr James Finlay, a man of courage. He had also an Indian chief of the Cree tribe called 'Beau Parleur,' in the fort, and a fine speaker he certainly was" (NA MG19 A17, 8v/Masson 2:21).

20 October 1808, "they were all well, but had suffered much from the extreme bad weather" Cf. conditions described in the RCSL report: "The greatest hardship of the People lay in being continually wet up to the waist, exposed to cold high winds, & the water, coming direct from the Snows on the Mountains, was always so excessively cold as to deprive them of all feeling in their Limbs" (2). Cf. also Kane: "It was so could that the water frose on they poles they men thad to wade in the water sumtimes up to thare middle one sliped off a log over his hed and was nerley dround his close frose stiff I asked him if he was not could his ansur was that his coat was but he was not" (MacLaren, 33).

22 October 1808, "Sent off Le Camble, Clement and Dupré" In 1808 Fort Augustus was still "Fort des Prairies," the administrative centre of the NW Co's Saskatchewan River department. But in the summer of 1810 Alexander Henry moved up the North Saskatchewan River and built Terre Blanche House, which became the new FDP; here Thompson engaged several men (29 October 1810).

1 November 1808, "employed myself in writing" Thompson "wrote off" his journal a few days at a time – cf. 21 August 1809, 29 September 1809, 12–13 and 20 December 1810. Cf. also Douglas: "The position I am now in is lying on the grass with my gun beside me, writing by the light of my 'Columbia candle,' a piece of wood containing rosin" (231); and Kane: "I rite this part of my jurnal over a blasing fire ... and my 6 painted warers [warriors] sleeping in front of my with their hidieous fases shineing in the fire lite" (24).

3 November 1808, "the made Gum is too brittle" Each canoe carried a supply of birch bark, pitch and spruce roots for occasional repairs. Fidler's journal, 4 October 1791, notes a cold-weather substitute for gum: "Rubbed all the Seams of our Canoes over with fatt as the late severe weather has cracked all the Pitch & made them very leaky – the fat in cold weather is preferable to pitch, but it soon rubs off on touching the least thing" (HBCA E3/1).

4 November 1808, "Killed 6 teal Ducks" – *Anas crecca*, green-winged teal, or *Anas discors*, blue-winged teal – cf. Clark: "For the first time for three weeks past I had a good dinner of Blue wing Teel" (Thwaites, 3:115).

8 November 1808, "Buché 1 ss Jacket, 1 Milled Cap" Cf. 27 December 1810 note: these items are listed as trade goods. As here, AO journals 18 occasionally notes credit or payment: for example, 19 June 1807: "Paid $\frac{1}{2}$ fm of Tob to Boisverd, gave Bercier & Buché each a foot & opened a Roll, of which this is a part"; and 26 June 1807: "Gave my Cream Coloured Horse to Boisverd for Services rendered to the Society – as washing for the Clerks &c &c." See Davidson (234–5) on the NW Co partners' preference to pay in trade goods rather than cash.

Thompson spent a second winter at Kootanae House and in June 1809 crossed the mountains to Fort Augustus, where he sent his furs east and picked up his goods. After returning to the Columbia River, he pushed south to establish both Kullyspel House and Saleesh House in the fall of 1809.

Along the Saleesh River

Source: AO journals 23 and 22

This account of Thompson's most adventurous and productive year as a trader is a single text, written to the end of one memorandum book (AO journals 23, to 26 September 1809) and continued in another (AO journals 22, beginning at 27 September 1809). Like the journey from Boggy Hall to Kootanae House in the fall of 1808, the first part of this account tells of Thompson's travel over a familiar route, as far as the southernmost bend of the Kootenai River. From there he continued south to explore the Clark Fork and Pend Oreille rivers.

20 August 1809, "set off and held on" Those of Thompson's men who are named are Beaulieu, Bostonan, Boulard, Buché, Mousseau and the Seauteaux hunter, together with Finan McDonald as clerk and the Thunder, another hunter. Jaco Finlay and his family were going in the same direction, but at Jaco's pace; Finlay's status appears to have always been that of associate rather than "engagé."

20 August 1809, "the Lake ... the Portage" – Columbia Lake and Canal Flats; *"the campment of last spring"* – cf. 20 April 1808. From here as far as Bonner's Ferry, Thompson followed the Kootenay/ Kootenai River, as he had done in the spring of 1808.

22 August 1809, "The ground Raisins ripe & good, but very tart" – *Vaccinium scoparium*, grouseberry.

24 August 1809, "how the garden Seeds have thriven" Cf. 22 April 1808.

29 August 1809, "we arrived at the Great Road of the Flat Heads" –

a Native trail which extended from the Kootenai River to Pend Oreille Lake. The present road between Bonner's Ferry and Sandpoint follows the original Native path, indicated by a dotted line on the PRO (2) map and called the "Lake Indian Road."

29 August 1809, "killed 1 Cormorant" – *Phalacrocorax penicillatus*, double-crested cormorant.

30 August 1809, "the Grand River Flat Heads" – Salish from the Clark Fork River – cf. 20 July 1807 note.

6 September 1809, "our old Campment of last year" Cf. 13 May 1808.

8 September 1809, "Co S20E ½M to a Brook" – Pack River.

8 September 1809, "Beaulieu 1 Crane" – *Grus canadensis*, sandhill crane.

8–9 September 1809, "to the Lake ... embarked ... arrived ... at the mouth of the River" – to Pend Oreille Lake and the Clark Fork River – cf. Lewis: "I have ... named it in honour of my worthy friend and fellow traveller Capt. Clark. for this stream we know no indian name and no white man but ourselves was ever on it's principal branches" (Thwaites, 4:363). Thompson called both the Clark Fork and Pend Oreille rivers the "Saleesh River."

9 September 1809, "23 Pointed Hearts" – members of the Coeur d'Alene tribe, whom Thompson also called "Skeetshoos." Cf. Cox: "We found them uniformly honest in their traffic, but they did not evince the same warmth of friendship for us as the Spokans, and expressed no desire for the establishment of a trading post among them. They are in many respects more savage than their neighbours, and I have seen some of them often eat ... meat raw. They also ... beat their wives cruelly" (262).

10 September 1809, "a place to build a House on" – Kullyspel House, near the mouth of the Clark Fork River. This post was built in less time but in much the same way as Kootanae House in 1807. The same can be said of Saleesh House, built in October-November 1809 near the junction of the Thompson and Clark Fork rivers. These posts are a reminder that Thompson's work as NW Co "Astronomer" took second place to trade.

23 September 1809, "15 strange Indians arrived from the west^d" – probably members of the Spokane tribe – cf. 4 October 1809, 14–27 August 1811, and Henry: "The Spokanes are a tribe of the Flat Heads, speaking nearly the same Language, they dwell along the Spokane River, but seldom or ever go to the Meadows in search of Buffalo ... Red and fallow deer are their principal food, with a variety of Roots which are peculiar to the Country" (NA MG19 A13, 1108/Coues, 711).

24 September 1809, "5 Rats" – *Ondatra zibethicus*, muskrat.

27 September 1809, "we may if possible change our route" – in order to avoid harrassment from the Peigans – cf. 29 October 1810.

28 September 1809, "to the Head of the River" – Pend Oreille River, where it flows out of Pend Oreille Lake.

28 September 1809, "I observ^d the Merid Alt^{de} of Aquilae" – Altair, the brightest star of the constellation Aquila.

30 September 1809, "the Woods" Cf. the list that Douglas made at the mouth of the Pend Oreille River: "one *Pinus larix* [*Larix occidentalis*, western larch] of small growth and a species of scrub pine ... *P. taxifolia* [*Pseudotsuga menziesii*, Douglas fir] and *P. resinosa* [possibly *Picea glauca*, white spruce] smaller, on the latter more of the eatable moss. *Pinus strobus* [*Pinus monticola*, western white pine] abounds and although very lofty I have not seen one exceed 2 feet in diameter ... On the moist grounds in the valleys and shore of the river, birch [*Betula occidentalis*, water birch or, since it is large, *B. papyrifera*, paper birch] is seen of larger dimensions than any that has yet come under my notice. The *Populus* is *P. tremula* [*P. tremuloides*, trembling aspen]" (248).

30 September 1809, "much gummy white Fir" – *Tsuga mertensiana*, mountain hemlock; *"wide marshy Ground"* – Cusick.

30 September 1809, "2 Cakes of Root Bread ... 12 lb of Roots" *Camassia quamash, Camassia esculenta*, and *C. leichtlinii*, three species of camas – cf. the "eetowoy roots" which Thompson later refused (5 July 1811). The PRO (2) map labels this area "Eet too woy Plains." Douglas described how root bread was made: "[The roots] are prepared as follows: a hole is scraped in the ground, in which are placed a number of flat stones on which the fire is placed and kept burning until sufficiently warm, when it is taken away. The cakes, which are formed by cutting or bruising the roots and then compressing into small bricks, are placed on the stones and covered with leaves, moss, or dry grass, with a layer of earth on the outside, and left until baked or roasted, which takes generally a night. They are moist when newly taken off the stones, and are hung up to dry. Then they are placed on shelves or boxes for winter use. When warm they taste much like a baked pear. It is not improbable that a very palatable beverage might be made from them" (105–6). Cf. also Clark, who was given "some dried Salmon beries & roots in different States, Some round and much like an onion ... also ... the bread made of this root all of which we eate hartily ... I find myself verry unwell all the evening from eateing the fish & roots too freely" (Thwaites, 3:78–9).

30 September 1809, "they were very thankful ... having neither Axe nor Chissel among them" Cf. 7 July 1811, and the *Narrative*: "The goods taken [into the western countries] were of small value in money but of great utility to the Indians; everything is carried on by barter profitable to both parties but more so to the Indians than to us. We took from them furrs of no use to them and which had to pass through an immense distance of freight and risques before they could be sold in the market of London. See the wife of an Indian sewing their leather clothing with a pointed brittle bone or a sharp thorn and the time and trouble it takes. Show them an awl or a strong needle and they will gladly give the finest Beaver or Wolf skin they have to purchase it" (Glover, 45).

But cf. McGillivray's *Journal*: "Rum is their first inducement to industry ... Tobacco is another article of as great demand as it is unnecessary ... As for ammunition, it is rendered valuable by the great advantage it gives them over their enemies ... The rest of our commodities are indeed usefull to the Natives, when they can afford to purchase them, but if they had hitherto lived unacquainted with European productions it would not, I beleive, diminish their felicity" (31–2). Cf. also Henry: "A most striking example is to be see[n] throughout the North West Country of the depravity of manner and wretched state of the Natives. As you advance into the interior parts, vice and debauchery become less frequent. Happy [are] those who have the least connection with us, as the greater portion of their depraved manners of life at this day can be easily traced to have originated from their intercourse with the Whites ... To the fatal introduction of that subtle poison [Spiritous Liquors] among the Savage Tribes, may be attributed their miserable and wretched condition" (NA MG19 A13, 1108–9/Coues, 710–11).

1 October 1809, "as we descend, the width is contracted" – Box canyon above Metaline Falls – cf. 4 September 1811.

2 October 1809, "I asked our Guide if we were near the Falls" – Metaline Falls, now flooded by the Box Canyon Dam. Cf. AO journals 22 for 27 April 1810: "My new Guide who had once been here pointed out the Country to us. Ab^t 3M below us was ... a high steep Fall ... he told us they left their Canoes a little dist^{ce} this Side of the Fall & by Hands & Feet got along the steep rocks to the Fall, beyond which no Indians ever penetrate except a few to gather Red Ochre, which is very fine & in plenty among the Mountains. ... he assured us ... [that] beyond the Great Fall ... is little else but terrible Cataracts bounded on each Side by high Crags & is quite unnavigable."

2 October 1809, "We found that we had no Time" Thompson was obliged to turn back in order to meet the supply canoes at Canal Flats – cf. AO journals 75: "1809. The Partners of the Co^y allow of no further discoveries but only trading Posts on a small scale, and I have means for nothing else."

3 October 1809, "the Green Wood Indians" – Nez Perces, whom Thompson called elsewhere "Shawpatins": cf 24 September 1809, and Henry: "a numerous, distinct tribe, having a peculiar language of their own. They dwell ... along the [Snake] river ... These people are well provided with horses, like all their neighbors, and frequently resort to the plains in search of buffalo" (NA MG19 A13, 1109/Coues, 712). Cox explained their name: "As French is the language in general use among traders in this country, owing to the most part of their working men being Canadians, we commonly call them *les Nez Percés* ... They are clean, active, and smart-looking, good hunters, and excellent horsement" (88). Cf. also Simpson: "The Nez Perces tribe is by far the most powerful and Warlike of the Columbia and may be said to hold the Key of the River as they possess and are Masters of the country from Okenagan down to the Chutes [Dalles]" (Merk, 55).

5 October 1809, "to the Rivulet" – Priest River; *"the Skeetshoo Road"* – a Native trail from the Pend Oreille River south to the Spokane River; this trail is marked with a dotted line on the PRO(2) map.

Finan McDonald was left in charge of Kullyspel House while Thompson built Saleesh House and wintered there. In the spring Thompson once more crossed Howse Pass, and reached Rainy Lake on 22 July

1810. The celebrated "missing journal" (23 July – 28 October 1810) presumably accounted for his return trip west; the extant record begins again at Boggy Hall on 29 October 1810.

Athabaska Pass

Source: AO journals 25

This journal recounts the best known episode of Thompson's explorations, an emphasis imposed by the *Narrative*'s autobiographical hindsight and further enhanced by historical controversy. The account is nevertheless consistent with geographical and commercial aims reflected in the other Columbia journals, and may thus be seen as a steady continuation of Thompson's long-term enterprise rather than as a dramatic, "historic" moment.

29 October 1810, "Horses 24 in Number ... each loaded with the weight of 180 to 240 lbs" Thompson did not set out to cross the mountains lightly loaded or exceptionally late; Athabaska Pass was the detour route of a regular trading expedition – cf. 27 December 1810 note for a list of the goods to be transported. Cf. Bird, 31 October 1810: "Mr Thompson it appears ... set of[f] privately with twenty Men & Horses conveying a few Goods, to go by another way towards his last years abode near the Columbia. The N.W. Co^y appear now to pursue their trade to that Quarter with an avidity which can be created by prospects of great benefit only. They amuse us with Stories of their intention to send a Ship round to the mouth of the Columbia in pursuit of this trade, they tell us likewise that they are to hold a third part of the stock of a large American Company (Aster & Co^y) which is formed at New York to undertake a trade up the Missourey & by that River to the Pacific Ocean" (HBCA B60/a/9). Cf. 10 and 15 July 1811.

29 October 1810, "We in all 24 Men including myself" All of these men are named in the text: Battoche, Bercier, Boussé, Baptiste Bruneau, Canada, Côté, Baptiste D'Eau, Baptiste Delcour, François

Desjarlaix, Du Nord, Kinville, La Course, La Fontaine, L'Amoureux, Baptiste Le Tendre, Méthode, Mousseau, Pierre Pareil, Pichette, Thomas the Iroquois (guide), Vallade, Vaudette and Yellow Bird the Seauteaux (hunter). Le Tendre and D'Eau are the two FDP men who, together with Du Nord, deserted in January 1811.

29 October 1810, "the Athabaska River, for which place we now bend our course" Cf. AO journals 75: "I had often requested permission to change the route across the Mountains, as we must sooner, or later, be cut off by the Peagan Indians, but the great Partners assured me there was no danger. But this year when near the Mountains ... I left the Canoes for a day or two to get Provisions. ... Finding the Canoes did not come I sent Mr W[illia]m Henry and an Indian to learn the cause, and to beware of the Enemies. They returned at night having seen a strong camp of Peagans which [had] driven the Canoes down ... at dawn of day we had to ride for our lives; they followed us most of the day, but Snow coming on covered our tracks. I had now to find the Canoes and men, and with Horses cross to the Athabaska River."

McDonald of Garth, one of the "great Partners," learned of the Peigan blockade by the Fort William winter express. McDonald rushed west and found his advance party hiding out at the Kootenay Plains. "A halt was made my companions (shame upon them) thought that consequently we should return [to] the Rocky Mountain House full tilt, Canoes & all – I thought otherwise ... much debating took place all night amongst the Men – but they saw that nothing would make us return" (NA MG19 A17, 126/Masson, 2:39). By his own report, McDonald arrived at the Columbia River but did not descend it, and so did not find or assist Thompson.

Joseph Howse, leading an HBC expedition to Flathead Lake, was allowed past the Peigans on condition that he not try again – cf. Bird, 13 May 1811: "The Muddy River Indians [Peigan] have promised not to molest Mr Howse ... but declared that, if they ever again met with a white Man going to supply their Enemies, they would not only plunder & kill him, but that they would make dry Meat of his body. This threat they are sufficiently brutal to fulfill to its utmost extent" (HBCA B60/a/9).

Thompson's new Athabaska route ensured the continuation of NW Co trade west of the divide. By contrast, Howse's 1810–11 winter at Flathead Lake was the last HBC venture across the mountains until the companies merged in 1821 – cf. Bird, 30 May 1811: "[Mr Howse] has thought it too Dangerous, till a safer Road, than that by which he went, is examined, further to pursue a Trade so advantageously begun" (HBCA B60/a/9).

29 October 1810, "the Road on the whole tolerable" Thompson followed a Native trail called the "Stone Indian Road" after Assiniboin who had moved west – cf. 19 November 1810. The journal states that this trail linked the Saskatchewan and Pembina rivers (7 November 1810), but the trail is not marked on either of the PRO maps.

31 October 1810, "the Tail is not so large nor so long haired as those of the Columbias" Cf. 5 and 26 July 1811. Reference is to the Columbia black-tailed deer, a sub-species of *Odocoileus hemionus*, mule deer – cf. Clark: "The Deer of this [Pacific] Coast differ materially from our Common deer in as muech as they are much darker, deeper bodied, Shorter ledged horns equally branched from the beem the top of the tail black from the rute to the end. Eyes larger and do not lope but jump" (Thwaites, 3:237).

1 November 1810, "Wrote a letter to Mr A. Henry" – to distinguish Alexander Henry the Younger (the journal writer) from his cousin William Henry, who joined Thompson's party some time after it set out and acted as clerk to the expedition from the base camp on the Athabaska River. Alexander Henry recorded his reception of Thompson's 1 November letter six days later at Rocky Mountain House, on 7 November 1810: "At 11 o'clock arrived Pichette and Pierre with three Horses from Mr Thompson's camp. He was then upon the Panbina River with all his property, on his way to the Waters of the Columbia, cutting his road through a wretched thick Woody country, over Mountains and gloomy Maskagues and nearly starving with Hunger, Animals being very scarce in that quarter, and his hunter, B[aptis]te Prunoe [Bruneau], can only find a chance Wood Buffalo, upon which they subsist; when that fails they have recourse to what flour, and other douceurs Mr Thompson has along with them – in fact, their case is pitiful" (NA MG19 A13, 1038–9/Coues, 661–2).

6–7 November 1810, "Old Fort Peles ... Buffalo Dung Lake" The fort is unidentified – it was probably a small subsidiary post like Boggy Hall; Chip Lake.

18 November 1810, "Ther −32° ... the cold bearable" Ordway recorded the sufferings of the Corps of Discovery as they crossed the divide: "We set out at Sunrise and proceeded on with our big coats on and our fingers acked with the cold" (Quaife, 274); cf. Lewis's "Sketch" in the VPL journal: "I have not leisure at this moment to state all those difficulties which we encountered in our Passage over these Mountains — suffice it to say we suffered everything Cold, Hunger & Fatigue could impart, or the keenest Anxiety excited for the fate of [an] Expedition in which our whole Souls were embarked." The Lewis and Clark expedition crossed Lemhi Pass in August 1805, that is, far south of Athabaska Pass and in summer. By contrast, Bird commented to Fidler, 12 May 1811, on "the unexampled Depth of Snow and severity of the Winter" of 1810–11 (HBCA B60/a/9). Cf. also Henry: "I have always observed when travelling in this Country in the winter season, we feel the cold most severe, between day break & Sun rise" (NA MG19 A13, 1093/Coues, 699).

18 November 1810, "always running thro' a morass" Cf. Milton and Cheadle: "No one but a Hudson's Bay voyageur would dream of taking horses into such a region" (207).

22 November 1810, "a Branch of the Athabaska River" – McLeod River; *"the Banks ... seem to be of Grind Stone"* – sandstone.

23 November 1810, "Working my Observations" Thompson must have had great powers of concentration – cf. Douglas: "Intended to have arranged a few words of the Chenook language, but was molested out of my life by the men singing their boat-songs" (249).

23 November 1810, "Boussé slept out" Failure to move ahead as a group, slowness at performing simple tasks, eating breakfast before setting out, and repeated lightening of their loads are all signs of the men's reluctance to proceed. Thompson may be regarded as a poor leader, or a patient one.

24 November 1810, "a fine Knowl presented itself" Cf. Southesk, who had at about the same place "an unexpected, far-distant view of two grand peaks of the Rocky Mountains ... It was but an imperfect view, but so marvellous was the contrast between the damp, confined darkness of our track through the dripping fir-trees, and the sudden freedom of an open sky bounded by magnificent mountain-forms, that for a moment I was quite overwhelmed" (178).

24 November 1810, "where I suppose McLeod's River joins the Athabaska River" The junction is in fact farther to the northeast, at Whitecourt.

30 November 1810, "our Co through the Willow Plain" – following Maskuta Creek to the south end of Brûlé Lake.

2 December 1810, "Chikarsepuk" – *Arctostaphylos uva-ursi*, kinni-kinnik – cf. Isham: "Jac'kashepuck, so call'd by the natives, is a leaf Like unto a box Leaf, itt Grow's about 2 foot high, and Run's in long branches spreading itself upon the Ground … this Leaf they Dry and pound mixing itt with their tobacco when they smoak" (132–3).

3 December 1810, "the River below goes off" Cf. AO journals 52: "The Athabaska River, like all the Rivers that descend from the east side of the Mountains, has many channels, generally shoal, with gravel flats and sand"; cf. also Milton and Cheadle: "This river is called by the Indians [Cree] Mistahay Shakow Seepee, or the 'Great River of the Woods,' in distinction to the Saskatchewan, the Mistahay Paskow Seepee, or 'Great River of the Plains'" (228).

10 December 1810, "splitting Wood for Sleds" Cf. Franklin: "Sledges are made of two or three flat boards, curving upwards in front, and fastened together by transverse pieces of wood above. They are so thin that, if heavily laden, they bend with the inequalities of the surface over which they pass. The ordinary dog-sledges are eight or ten feet long and very narrow, but the lading is secured by a lacing round the edges … When the Snow is hard frozen or the track well trodden, the rate of travelling is about two and a half miles an hour, including rests, or about fifteen miles a day. If the snow be loose, the speed is necessarily much less and the fatigue greater" (95–6).

14 December 1810, "Sent off [seven men] for the RM Ho" Cf. Henry, 30 December 1810: "At 5 p.m. seven men arrived from Mr Thompson … It is 17 days since they left Mr Thompson on Athabaska river at the foot of the mountains. On their way here they ate an old horse and five dogs, but had been some time without food and were worn out with fatigue and hunger. They met this morning the two H.B. men who left yesterday, and got from them a mouthful of provisions, which enabled them to reach this place. These people came for provisions, dogs and horses, all of which they were entirely destitute. We have no more meat in store than will answer for eight days' rations, and of other provisions not a mouthful. Our hunters are lazy; and when we shall see an Indian to bring a supply, God knows" (Coues, 667–8). Henry could not or did not help Thompson; as William McGillivray was to observe to John George McTavish, 17 July 1814, "Mr Henry has not acted with decision indeed it is not in his character" (HBCA F3/2).

20 December 1810, "Enabled me to write letters &c" One of these letters was addressed to Alexander Fraser, a retired partner; the original is now lost, but a copy is included in McDonald of Garth's memoirs: "The following letter from Mr D. Thompson to Alex Fraser, of Rivière du Loup, is not without interest, as it gives an idea of the risks and sufferings this distinguished geographer had to undergo during his many years of exploration in the North West and in the Rocky Mountains. The original is in the possession of Mr Alphonse Pouliot, advocate and Professor of Laval University in Quebec." Masson printed the letter as a footnote (NA MG19 A17, 25r/Masson, 2:41–2):

21 Dec. 1810, Athabaska River,
foot of the Mountains

My dear Fraser,

I received your esteemed favor the 9th Sept. and am obliged to you for the traits of civilized life and the information of my daughter. She costs me £62 10s. at present, and I think £50 a year would do her all the good that the present sum costs me. It is my wish to give all my children an equal and good education: my conscience obliges me to it, and it is for this I am now working in this country.

I intended to have paid you a visit at Montreal this last summer, but the critical situation of our affairs in the Columbia obliged me to return. The Americans, it seems, were as usual ... determined to be beforehand with us in the Columbia in ship navigation. As the Peagans killed an officer and 8 soldiers out of a tribe of 12 d°, if this accident has not drove them back, they will probably get the start of me.

My canoes were also driven back by the Peagans, but no lives or property lost and I have changed our route from [blank in ms] to the Athabaska River and am now preparing in this hard season to cross the mountains and gain my first post near the head of the Missisouri, a march of about 34 days, and a part of it over a dangerous country for war. I hope good Providence will take care of us and bring me safe back again.

I am always in such distant expeditions that I cannot [write] to my friends regularly. They think I slight them, but they are mistaken. It is my situation that prevents me and not negligence. I shall, after this apology, be glad to correspond with you as usual, if you have time to spare.

If all goes well and it pleases good Providence to take care of me I hope to see you and a civilized world in the autumn of 1812. I am getting tired of such constant hard journeys; for the last 20 months I have spent only barely two months under the shelter of a hut, all the rest has been in my tent, and there is little likelihood the next 12 months will be much otherwise.

I hope you are better at your ease and that you now enjoy that society you merit, tho' I suppose you now and then cast a thought to your old friends the Chipewyans who still talk of you.

Your humble servant,
DAVID THOMPSON

27 December 1810, "We are packing up Goods" Cf. AO journals 25, "List of Goods, 29 Dec. 1810, Athabaska R.": listed are figures for "outfit, 1st Hoard, 2nd d°, brought to Columbia, by Coté & Pareil, total" (included below are only the items and the total).

Awls, Indian	Doz	12
Axes, half		5
small		10
Arm Bands	Pr	1
Blankets, green, 4pts	No	1
flowered		1
Brandy, french	Gall	2
Beads, small	lbs	$20\frac{1}{4}$
Belts, d°	No	4
Bells, hawk	Groce	$7\frac{1}{4}$
Books, blank	No	1
MM		2
Bayonets		4
Balls	lbs	93
Boxes, Japan'd	No	1
Brimstone	oz	1
Buttons, Coat	Groce	$5\frac{7}{12}$
Vest		$\frac{5}{12}$
Coats, Chiefs	No	1
Capots, fine		3
Ratteen		3
Molton		1
Caps, milled		2
Jockey		6
Calicoe, fine	fms	4
Cotton, checked		2
Chocolate	lbs	1
Files, of 8 In	No	6
handsaw		2
x cut d°		1
pit d°		1
Flints, Gun		416
Feathers, Cock		10
small fox tail		9
Flour	lbs	65
Ferreting	Pieces	$1\frac{1}{2}$
Flannel	fms	3
Gartering	Pieces	12
Glasses, look[g]	No	72

Guns, NW		8
Gun Powder	lbs	$93\frac{1}{2}$
Gimblets	No	2
Handk, China		19
Cotton		9
Pocket		5
Hatts		2
Hooks, Kirby		49
Horse belting	fms	2
Ink Powder	Paper	1
Jackets, fine Cloth	No	2
Kettles, Tin		11
Knives, large	Doz	6
small		$1\frac{1}{6}$
fine	No	5
crooked		-
& Forks		2
Lines, Cod		1
Linnen, white	fms	$2\frac{1}{4}$
Lavendar	Bott	1
Moultlets, Cal com	No	1
Nails		50
Needles, small		235
Paper, fools cap	Quire	3
Purses	No	6
Pepper	lbs	1
Peppermint	Bott	6
Quills	C	$\frac{1}{2}$
Razors & Strap	Case	1
Rings	Groce	12
Ribbon, 90	Pieces	3
160		3
Strouds, HB blue	fms	6
Red		6
Cloth, 2nd green		1
Scarlet		$\frac{1}{2}$
Shirts, Men's Cotton	No	15
fine dº		6
dº Calico		3
Sponges		2
Shot, Beaver & Pigeon	lbs	37
Spoons, Pewter	No	2
Steels, fine		12

Seeds. garden	Parcel	1
Soap, common	lbs	3
Salves, drawing	Box	1
Scissors	Pr	5
Stockings, worsted		3
Shoes		2
Spirits	Gall	2
Sheeting, Russia	fms	$3\frac{1}{2}$
Traps, steel	No	2
Tents, of 20 Ells		1
Trowsers, fine Cloth	Pr	3
Thread, sewing	lbs	$\frac{1}{2}$
Tobacco, Albany		141
Turlington	Bott	9
Vermillion	lbs	$\frac{1}{3}$
Vomits	No	10
Vitriol, blue	oz	$\frac{1}{4}$
Wick, Cotton	Balls	2
Worms, Gun	No	44
Wire, snaring	lbs	$\frac{1}{2}$

See also the NW Co's "Montreal Inventory 1812" (HBCA F4/3), lists of goods making up partners' adventures (HBCA F4/7), and cf. [Atcheson], 14:

The principal articles exported from Great Britain, for the Indian trade by the North West Company, are:

Blankets, manufactured at Whitney, Oxfordshire
Woollens ditto in Yorkshire, namely: Strouds, Coatings, Moltons, Serges, and Flannels, common Blue and Scarlet Cloths
Cotton Manufactures, from Manchester: striped Cottons, Dimities, Janes, Fustians, Printed British Cottons Shawls and Handkerchiefs, Gartering and Ferretting
Hardware, in large quantities
Irish Linens, Scotch Sheetings, Osnaburgs and Linens
Nets, Twine, Birdlime, Threads, Worsted Yarn, large quantities
Brass, Copper and Tin Kettles
Indian Fusils, Pistols, Powder, Ball, Shot, and Flints
Painters' colors, Vermillion, &c
Stationery, Beads, Drugs, and Large parcels of all kinds of Birmingham manufacture, with other articles of British manufacture.

27 December 1810, "from the awkwardness of the Women" Cf.

Hearne: according to his guide, Matonabbee, "women ... were made for labour; one of them can carry, or haul, as much as two men can do. They also pitch our tents, make and mend our clothing, keep us warm at night; and, in fact, there is no such thing as travelling any considerable distance, or for any length of time, in this country, without their assistance" (55). Fidler learned the same lesson while wintering with a Peigan band: "The Indian Men generally goes first pitching along; the Women children Horses & Dogs all loaded more or less – & by the time we think the Women have put up the Tent, Fires made &c, we contrive to arrive at that time & not before" (HBCA E3/2: 18 December 1792).

29 December 1810, "Our Co as before mentioned" Cf. 3 December 1810.

1 January 1811, "a kind of a Lake ... the Lake" – wide shoals between Brûlé Lake and Jasper Lake; Jasper Lake.

4 January 1811, "the Brook from the sbE^{d}" – Maligne River.

4 January 1811, "Up this River is the Canoe Road" Thompson already saw the long-term advantages of the Athabaska route over that of Howse Pass – cf. AO journals 25: "Navigation of the Athabaska River: ... from the sortie of [the Pembina] River to McLeod's Fort is ab^{t} 100 Miles, for the greater part of this way fine easy Navigation – the latter part very strong Current, but good poling along the gravel Flats: this 100 Miles is the ordinary March it is said of 4 days (say 5 days). Hence Fort Augustus to Pembina River 3 days + 4 days to Athabaska River + 5 days to McLeod's Fort + 13 days to the Mountain Port^{ge} = 25 days + 4 days to the Columbia = 29 days. This is only 2 days more than the other Route & avoids much of that tedious & expensive business of Horses, which can never be brought within strict Calculation, being liable to too many Accidents." Cf. also the summary statement in AO journals 77: "Whatever Route requires the fewer hands, and has the shortest distance will have a decided advantage."

4 January 1811, "the Canoe Road to pass to the Canoe River" Cf. 5 January 1811: "the large River ... the Road for Canoes & Horses in the Summer." The "Canoe Road to pass to the Canoe River" is in part the route Thompson followed, up the Athabaska River to the Whirlpool River. But his guide did not follow the main branch of the Whirlpool River over to Hugh Allan Creek and down to the Canoe River: the Canoe River was full of falls and rapids, as Thompson later discovered (18–22 September 1811). Instead the party was led over a "Portage on the left" (9 January 1811) to the Wood River. One factor in Thompson's confusion may have been the orientation of Athabaska Pass: as with Howse Pass, westbound travellers had to turn southeast to cross it from east to west. At the same time Thompson assigned a puzzling role to the "large River from the West^d," the Miette River, since this River leads to the Yellowhead Pass and over to the Fraser River – a route of no use to Thompson, whose aim was to reach the Columbia. Cf. 7 and 9–10 January 1811.

4 January 1811, "the large Animal so much spoken of" "Nurses Fables" (28 September 1807) had prepared Thompson and his men for the shock they experienced on seeing "the Track of a large Animal" three days later (7 January 1811) – cf. AO journals 52: "There were four Indians with me and we examined [the prints] ... One of them said, what can our balls do against such an animal ... I was anxious to see him, but did not think proper to go alone, and we agreed by tacit consent to let be ... Besides the four Indians there were seven Canadians with me, but I mention the Indians as being judges of the tracks of animals." Cf. also Cox: "One man [a Cree] has asserted that his grandfather told him he saw one of those animals in a mountain pass, where he was hunting and that on hearing its roar, which he compared to loud thunder, the sight almost left his eyes, and his heart became as small as an infant's" (290). Thompson later commented in the *Narrative*: "I never appeared to give credence [to] these reports, [for they] appeared to arise from that fondness for the marvellous so common to mankind; but the sight of the track of that large beast staggered me, and I often thought of it, yet never could bring myself to believe such an animal existed, but thought it might be the track of some monster Bear" (Tyrrell, 537/Glover, 383).

5 January 1811, "At 9¾ Am set off" Cf. Thompson's impatience with the "FDP men" and the aristocratic pace of the Rockies' first tourists – Cheadle: "Can't get up as early as I wish; men don't back up well, & Milton's laziness a great drawback" (154), and Southesk: "The Saskatchewan men have not added to the workability of the party, though good enough men in themselves. Last Saturday I had to find fault decidedly, because, in order to keep up with the freemen, McKay hurried over breakfast and started the men before I was ready. He took my reproof admirably" (188).

7 January 1811, "We held on up a Rivulet" – Whirlpool River, of which the smaller left branch leads to Athabaska Pass. Cf. Simpson: "As we proceed the Road gets worse and the Mountains rise perpendicular to a prodigious height; the scenery wild and Majestic beyond description; the track is in many places nearly impassable and it appears extraordinary how any human being should have stumbled on a pass through such a formidable barrier as we are now scaling" (Merk, 33).

8 January 1811, "Du Nord beat a dog senseless" Cf. Henry, on his "jaunt" to Howse Pass in February 1811: "I awoke my men to prepare for their departure ... the fatigue of the day was still heavy upon them ... but what grieved them most was that we have had nothing to eat before our starting. This put them in a surly humour; they first quarreled among themselves and then gave full vent to their ill nature upon the Poor Dogs, which they beat most cruelly" (NA MG19 A13, 1092/Coues, 699).

9 January 1811, "a Portage on the left" – as indicated by Thompson's guide, Thomas the Iroquois. Although Thompson's choice of this route transformed Athabaska Pass into a fur trade highway, others had preceded him – cf. Henry: "This affair of his Canoes being stopped by the Peagans, has induced [Thompson] to alter his route, and endeavour to open a new road ... by which a party of Nepissangues and Freemen passed a few years ago" (NA MG19 A13, 1021/Coues, 652).

10 January 1811, "Du Nord threw his Load aside ... I ordered Du Nord to return" Cf. AO journals 25 for 25 April 1811: "Had a few words with [Pareil] which I hope will do him good."

10 January 1811, "we camped on the Snow, it being too deep to be cleared away" Cf. 15 and 25–6 January 1811, also 14 and 17 January 1811 when they camped on the ice, and AO journals 25 for 20 April 1811: "As we are camped on 6 ft of Snow, we are sadly off." The habit of sleeping close to a fire in all seasons made this a hardship – cf. Franklin: "Preparation [of the encampment] consists only in clearing away the snow to the ground, and covering that space with pine branches, over which the party spread their blankets and coats, and sleep in warmth and comfort, by keeping a good fire at their feet, without any other canopy than the heaven, even though the temperature should be far below zero" (97).

10 January 1811, "Fine evening" In the *Narrative* Thompson transformed this brief journal comment into the climax of his popular work: "My men were not at their ease, yet when night came, they admired the brilliancy of the Stars ... Many reflections came on my mind; a new world was in a manner before me" (Tyrrell, 447–8/Glover 321–2). Cf. Cox: "The sun ... threw a chilling brightness over the chaotic mass of rocks, ice and snow, by which we were surrounded ... One of our rough-spun unsophisticated Canadians, after gazing upwards for some time in silent wonder, exclaimed with much vehemence, I'll take my oath, my dear friends, that God Almighty never made such a place!" (282–3). Cf. also Lewis, who built this climax into his journal: "The pleasure I now felt in having tryumphed over the rockey Mountains and decending once more to a level and fertile country where there was every rational hope of finding a comfortable subsistence for myself and party can be more readily conceived than expressed, nor was the flattering prospect of the final success of the expedition less pleasing" (Thwaites, 3:83).

11 January 1811, "began a great descent on the west Side" This is Simpson's "Grande Côte, where our descent could not be less than 40 feet p^r minute ... after making a fair allowance for time lost in falls breathing &c ... this is the lowest pass in the mountain behind which and on each side thereof are immence masses of mountain piled upon and overlooking each other" (Merk, 35). Kane followed the same route in reverse many years later: "Was up one our before day ascended the Grand Coat the snow getting deper as we ascended ... pased the Punch Bowl (rather coald Punch at present) though sun is shining vrry bright" (MacLaren, 50). The Committee's Punch Bowl was Simpson's name for the small lake which straddles the pass.

11 January 1811, "the Men have eat 56 lbs of Pemmican" Cf. Mackenzie (209) and "Treatment of Canadians on their Arrival at York Factory" (n.d.): "Each Man during his stay, is to receive as his ration of Provisions 2$\frac{1}{2}$ [lb] of Pemican P[er] Day" (HBCA B239/z/1). Cf. also Garry: "Two Pound of Pemican a Day is considered a fair Allowance. It requires 5 or 6 lb. of Meat to make 1 Pound." But Garry found that his brigade could live on less: "By an omission at Fort William no Provisions were put in the canoe for them and they had actually, in this Country of Portages and difficult Marching, nothing to subsist on but hard Indian Corn ... Not a Word of Discontent was uttered but they continued polite, obliging, singing their animating lively Songs to the last. We had fortunately Plenty of Provisions with us for ourselves" (120).

13 January 1811, "5 lbs of Ball, which the Wolverines had carried off" Cf. Cautley: "In August, 1921, [a member of the Provincial

Boundary Commission] discovered a somewhat scattered cache of 114 deeply corroded musket balls just north of the summit of the Pass ... there is very little room to doubt that the 'Ball' discovered in 1921 were the same which Thompson lost" (158–62).

23 January 1811, "many large Cedars" Henry remarked that west of the divide "Red Cedars are to be found of which the Soil produces and many other natural productions of nature, for which I am not calculated to examine into. I shall say nothing. The summer season would be by far the most preferable to visit those Mountains where a person adequate to the task would find an infinate field for amusement and Philosophical researches" (NA MG19 A13, 1082). The first adequate person was Douglas: "Around the camp on the point the woods are *Pinus taxifolia* [*Pseudotsuga menziesii*, Douglas fir], *P. canadensis* [*Picea glauca*, white spruce and/or *Picea engelmanni*, Engelmann spruce], *Thuya occidentalis* [*Thuja plicata*, western red cedar], *Populus*, sp. [*P. balsamifera*, balsam poplar and *P. tremuloides*, trembling aspen], all of large growth. The underwood, *Cornus* [*C. canadensis*, bunchberry], *Corylus* [*C. stolonifera*, red-osier dogwood], *Juniperus* [*J. scopulorum*, Rocky Mountain juniper], and two species of *Salix* [willow] ... *Linnea borealis* [twinflower] ... and on the highest mountains a species of *Lillium* [lily]" (254). Douglas named Mount Brown and Mount Hooker, peaks on either side of Athabaska Pass, in honour of illustrious botanists (72).

23 January 1811, "the Junction of the Rivers Flat Heart & Canoe River with the Kootanae River" – the junction of the Wood, Canoe, and Columbia rivers, long known as Boat Encampment and now the submerged midpoint of McNaughton Lake, the reservoir of the Mica Dam. Cf. 22 September 1811, and Cox: "We set off on foot along the banks of Canoe River, which winds its way through a wide and cheerless valley. We had not proceeded far when we found it impossible, from the great rise of the water, to pass the ordinary fords. It appeared like a lake, and completely set at nought the topographical knowledge of our guide" (280). Cf. also AO journals 27, flyleaf: the Wood River is called "Deserters' Brook." In the *Narrative* Thompson preserves the name "Flat Heart Brook" given in the text: "The upper Stream which forms the defile by which we came to the Columbia I named the Flat Heart, from the Men being dispirited; it had nothing in particular" (Tyrrell, 451/Glover, 324).

26 January 1811, "My design is ... to oblige the Men to come here also" Cf. AO journals 25 for 17 February 1811: "Pareil & Coté

& Villiard arrived from the Athabaska River where Mr W[illia]m Henry is in care of the Goods – they have 78 lbs of Fat, 42½ lbs of Powder, 1 tin Kettle of 5½ lbs, 1 fm of HB Blue Strouds & ab^t 20 lbs of Lead, with Provisions to make a Bag of Pemmican, I think. Thank Heaven for their safe arrival."

Thompson spent the rest of the winter at the "junction of the Rivers," where he built a wood canoe. In April 1811 he embarked with three men in the ice-choked Columbia and made his way upstream, then followed his 1809–10 route to Saleesh House. After visiting Spokane House, which Jaco Finlay had built in the summer of 1810, he built another wood canoe at "Ilthkoyape" (Kettle) Falls, in order to descend the Columbia River to its mouth.

The Lower Columbia

Source: AO journals 27

Thompson was well aware that Lewis and Clark had travelled and mapped the lower Columbia River, as well as some of its tributaries. He was also aware that John Jacob Astor intended to connect the Missouri fur trade with a maritime supply route to the Columbia's mouth. Thompson pursued his own ambitions within these circumstances and constraints. The meticulous detail of AO journals 27 is evidence of his project to map northwestern America, from Hudson Bay to the Pacific Ocean. His original contribution would be a picture of the Columbia River from source to mouth, together with most of its tributaries. His other project was to ensure that the NW Co department he had established could continue to trade in the Columbia watershed.

3 July 1811, "we ... set off on a voyage down the Columbia River" Cf. Mackenzie's "darling project" (267–8, 282–3, 303, 326, 328, 333), and Lewis: "Enterta[in]ing as I do, the most confident hope of succeeding in a voyage which had formed a darling project of mine for the last ten years, I could but esteem this moment of my departure as among the most happy of my life" (Thwaites, 1:285).

3 July 1811, "My Men ..." – engaged at various times – cf. AO journals 22 flyleaf: "Men on the Columbia 1810," and *Narrative* (Tyrrell, 455, 457, 460/Glover, 327–8, 330): Boulard, Pareil, and Côté ("Montreal Men") had accompanied Thompson from Boggy Hall in October 1810; Charles and Ignace (Iroquois) joined him on his way to Saleesh House in May 1811; Grégoire was engaged at Saleesh House, Bourdeaux at Kettle Falls. See also "List of People on the Columbia for Winter 1813/14" (HBCA F4/61): this list includes the names of fourteen clerks, engagés, and freemen formerly associated with Thompson.

3 July 1811, "with a small assortment of Goods to buy in Provisions &c" The flyleaf of AO journals 27 also notes "Furrs taken by D. Thompson as an adventure to the Mouth of the Columbia, July 2nd, 1811 ... 49 Beaver, 15 Black Bear, 5 grisled d^o, 5 yellow d^o, 3 brown bears, 1 Otter, 12 Cats." This note is evidence that Thompson expected to find a post already established at the river mouth.

3 July 1811, "Our Co down the River from the Ilthkoyape Falls ... 1$\frac{1}{4}$M a strong Rapid" From Kettle Falls to the Grand Coulee, Thompson's route is now flooded by Franklin D. Roosevelt Lake, the reservoir of the Grand Coulee Dam. Douglas named the first rapids below Kettle Falls: "I called it Thompson's Rapids, after the first person who ever descended the whole chain of the river from its source to the ocean" (165). Elliott, who edited this journal in 1914, remarked that Arrowsmith adopted this name but that locally they became known as the Grand or Rickey rapids (43). In 1940 the rapids themselves disappeared, together with their various names.

3 July 1811, "The country always wears a pleasing romantic View" Cf. Kane's published *Wanderings of an Artist*: "I pressed forward ... and saw the mighty [Columbia] river flowing at least 500 feet below us ... This river exceeds in grandeur any other perhaps in the world, not so much from its volume of water, although that is immense, as from the romantic wildness of its stupendous and ever-varying surrounding scenery, now towering into snow-capped mountains thousands of feet high, and now sinking in undulating terraces to the level of its pellucid waters" (210–11); in Kane's MS journal sublime prospects are mentioned in passing, but the hard travel to reach them is emphasized: "Continiude along the shore untill we came to sum perpandickelar rock ... asended to the top thrue a wilde and pictureck cuntree after a long sircut we made the Columbia again ... all day nothing but mountains to gow up and down made a long day" (MacLaren, 42).

3 July 1811, "on our arrival at the Simpoil camp" – on the Sanpoil River, now submerged under Roosevelt Lake. Cf. Douglas: "We embarked [near Kettle Falls] at seven precisely ... on getting into the current the boats passed along like an arrow from the bow ... Reached the junction of the Spokane River twenty minutes after three o'clock of the same day, having in the short space of eight hours made a distance of ninety miles, which may give some idea of the current [in June]" (179–80). Thompson went about 25 miles farther before stopping at the Sanpoil camp.

3 July 1811, "my Men wished to see them dance" Cf. Lewis: "We then requested the Indians to dance which they very cheerfully complyed with; they continued their dance untill 10 at night ... they were much gratifyed with seeing some of our party join them in their dance" (Thwaites, 4:332). Cf. also Stuart (Spaulding, 39), and Douglas: "In the evening about 300 men danced the war dance and sang several death songs. The description would occupy too much time" (138).

3 July 1811, "They were considered moderately cleanly tho' very poorly clothed" Cf. Cox: "The Sinapoils ... occupy a district on the northern banks of the Columbia, between the Spokan and Oakinagan rivers. They subsist principally on salmon and cammas, and sometimes small deer. Beaver is scarce; and they are consequently poorer than the neighbouring tribes ... They are dirty and slothful, and, from their habits of dishonesty, are regarded by the other natives with the utmost contempt. From the poverty of their territory no trading post has been hitherto established amongst them" (260).

4 July 1811, "I tried to get an Obs^n by the natural Horizon" Normally Thompson would use an artificial horizon of mercury. Cf. Robertson: "Into a wooden, or iron, circular box, of about $2\frac{1}{2}$ or 3 inches diameter, and about $\frac{1}{2}$ inch deep, pour about a pound or more of quicksilver; and on this lay a metal speculum, or piece of plain glass, the diameter of which is about $\frac{1}{3}$ of an inch less than that of the box; this will float in the quicksilver, and shew the image of the Sun very steady" (253).

5 July 1811, "Bitter, White &c Roots ... Marmot" As well as *Camassia* – camas roots called here "eetowoy" – Thompson was probably offered *Lewisia rediviva*, bitterroot, and *Perideridia gairdneri*, yampah; *Marmota flaviventris*, yellow-bellied marmot.

5 July 1811, [They tell me they now intend] The MS page is now torn off; the words in parenthesis are taken from Elliott's transcription of this journal.

5 July 1811, "two kinds of strong scented Shrubs" – species of sage. Cf. Lewis: "This plain as usual is covered with arromatic shrubs hurbatious plants and a short grass" (Thwaites, 4:341); cf. also Douglas: "This part of the country is barren, sandy soils and very parched ... the brushwood ... consists principally of *Purshia tridentata* [antelope brush] and *Artemisia arborea* [?]" (62).

5 July 1811, "all their Dances are a kind of religious Prayer" Cf. *Narrative*: "So far as I have seen the people on the west side of the Mountains, their Religion appears simple and rational, without sacrifices or superstition, and offers a most extensive and hopeful field for the labors of Missionaries to bring them to the knowledge of the heavenly Redeemer of Mankind" (Tyrrell, 479–80/Glover, 344). Simpson was of the same mind: "I do not know any part of North America where the Natives could be civilized and instructed in morality and Religion at such a moderate expence" (Merk, 106). Cf. also the view of the American Board of Commissioners for Foreign Missions, which sponsored Jonathan Green's tour of the Oregon Territory in 1829: "How desirable ... that the natives of this wilderness should hear the Gospel, before they are prejudiced against it by the fraud, injustice, and dissolute lives of men, who give up the blessings of Christianity, that they may not be troubled with its restraints ... In a word, thus may be sent forth another Plymouth colony, which shall extend its beneficent influences over millions of intelligent, enlightened and happy men, through successive ages, to the end of the world" (Green, 18–19).

5 July 1811, "a trait of enthusiasm" – in the eighteenth-century sense – a touch of fanatical excitement. Cf. AO journals 52: "The Performers bearing a part, and having an end to obtain, feel an Interest, the Passions are aroused, they become animated even to Enthusiasm and this is kindled & kept up, as by reflection one to another, 'till the whole is one glow of animated and passionate Action. This was the case with the Ancients, is so with the Indians, and probably most unpolished Nations. The Moderns are mere Spectators for amusement, have no other Interest than merely to be pleased, or beguile an hour of Ennui."

6 July 1811, "Mountains of the Ochenawga River ... we put ashore ... we see Mountains before us" Thompson passed the mouth of the Okanogan River and put ashore at the Methow Rapids; ahead were the Wenatchee Mountains. From this point to the mouth of the Wenatchee River, the Columbia River has been flooded to form Lake Entiat, the reservoir of the Rocky Reach Dam. Cf. the *Narrative*: "My reason for putting ashore and smoking with the Natives, is to make friends with them, against my return, for in descending the current of a large River, we might pass on without much attention to them; but in returning against the current, our progress will be slow and close along the shore, and consequently very much in their power" (Tyrrell, 480/Glover, 344). Cf. also Clark: "I smoked, with those about me who chose to smoke which was but fiew, this being a custom those people are but little accustomed to and only Smok thro: form" (Thwaites, 3:125).

6 July 1811, "Killed 2 Rattle Snakes" – *Crotalus viridis oreganus*, northern Pacific rattler. Cf. 4 August 1811, and *Narrative*: "That hateful reptile the Black Rattle Snake continues to be very numerous. What they feed on I cannot imagine ... of all Snakes they are supposed to be the most poisonous, and we dread them accordingly. On going ashore our custom always is, to throw part of our paddles on the grassy ground ... by doing so we are almost sure to start one of these Snakes that we did not see" (Tyrrell, 521–2/Glover, 372–3). Cf. also Ogden: "In our travels this day I saw two Rattlesnakes ... both we killed and miserably poor in this respect they are on a par with the Natives" (Ogden, ed. Davies and Johnson, 107–8).

7 July 1811, "we came to a large Band of Indians", Cf. AO journals 26: "Number of Indians on the Columbia River":

Ilthkoyape Village		150 Men	1 050
July 4th Simpoil Village		78	546
5th	60 Men + 60 Men	120	840
6th	45 Men 7th 120	165	1 155
8th	62 Men + 150	212	1 484
9th	20 + 60	80	560
10th	82 Men + 80 + 2	164	1 120
11th	63 Men + 45		
	+ 122 + 300	530	3 710
12–15 say to the Sea		450	3 150
			13 615 Souls

Cf. also Simpson: "The population on the banks of the Columbia River is much greater than in any other part of North America that I have visited ... it may be said that the shores are actually lined with Indian Lodges; this I account for by the River affording an abundant provision at little trouble for a great part of the year and as they do not turn their attention to Hunting the whole of the Interior population flock to its banks at the Fishing Season" (Merk, 94).

7 July 1811, "he after felt my Shoes & Legs gently as if to know whether I was like [the]mselves" Cf. Fidler's meeting with the Sho-shoni guest of the Peigans, 12 December 1792: "The Snake Ind. Reviewed us from head to foot & from foot to head – with the greatest attention felt at our skin in places & expressed great astonishment at us – particularly at our having a different coulered hair from any Indian ... We was the first Europeans he had ever seen before" (HBCA E3/2).

7 July 1811, "A Chief of the Countries below ... understood the Language of the People below" Cf. 8 July 1811. The Dalles marked the frontier between two major Native groups divided by race, customs and language. Natives above Celilo Falls were related to Plateau tribes such as the Nez Perces (Sahaptin linguistic group), while those below were connected with coastal tribes (Chinookan linguistic group). Like Lewis and Clark, Thompson was intrigued by the sudden and complete transition from one group to the other, and already, sev-eral days' journey above the falls, he was attentive to their differences. Cf. Clark: "Our two old chiefs expressed a desire to return to their band from this place [below Celilo Falls], Saying that they could be of no further Service to us, as their nation extended no further down the river than those falls, (they could no longer understand the language of those below the falls, till then not much difference in the vocabs)" (Thwaites 3:152–3).

7 July 1811, "I walked down the Rapid – the Canoe ran it close on the left with everything" – Rock Island Rapids, now submerged by the Rock Island Dam.

8 July 1811, "Prepared a Mast, Sail &c" Cf. 9 July 1811. Winds could be so strong that it was possible to sail upstream as well – cf. 27 July 1811, 3 August 1811, and Kane: "They boats ran up the rappeds under sale oure boat had the water curling over her bows and would have filled her if we had not taken in sale" (MacLaren, 39).

8 July 1811, "S[trong] R[apid] C[urrent] high waves at end of Co the left" – Priest Rapids, now submerged by the Priest Rapids Dam.

8 July 1811, "the handle of a Tea Kettle for an ornament" Cf. Mackenzie (341, 369), Gass (267), and Clark: "I cannot lern certainly as to the traffick those Inds carry on below, if white people or the in-dians who trade with the whites who are either settled or visit the mouth of this river. I believe mostly with the latter as their knowledge of the white people appears to be verry imperfect, and the articles which they appear to trade mostly i.e. Pounded fish, Beargrass, and roots; cannot be an object of comerce with furin merchants. however they git in return for those articles Blue and white *beeds* copper Kettles, brass arm bands, some scarlet and blue robes and a fiew articles of old clothes" (Thwaites, 3:185).

8 July 1811, "he showed no Signs of Age ... we could not but admire him" Cf. Stuart: "[Natives along the lower Columbia] are never troubled with epidemic or contagious diseases, except the small pox, which from nation to nation, has found its way across the Rocky mountains ... it is generally supposed that life is longer in places where there are few opportunities of luxury, but I found few or no instances among them of extraordinary longivety, *an indian grows old over his smoked salmon, just like a citizen over a turtle feast*: instances of long life are often related here, which (it appears to me) those who hear them are more willing to credit than to examine" (Spaulding, 41–2).

8 July 1811, "Shawpatin Mountains" – Blue Mountains – cf. 8 August 1811 and the RCSL "Remarks on ... the rough Chart": "On the south Side of the Columbia, at the dist^{ce} of ab^t 60M or 70M lies a ridge of blue Hills, well wooded, sending out many Brooks and Rivulets and 2 or 3 bold Rivers – they extend from the Hills of the Sea to the Rocky Mountains – it requires ab^t 1 day's march to cross them." Douglas botanized in these mountains in 1826: "I set out with my gun and a small quantity of paper under my arm to gain the summit ... [and] placed my foot on the highest peak of those untrodden regions where never European was before me" (191).

8 July 1811, "The Women & Men ... have not the Sea look, but much of the Plains features" Cf. 12 July 1811 and a note on the PRO (1) map: "The Indians of the Sea Coast, and a short Distance into the interior, are a different race of People, from those eastward of the Dalles. They are a strong, brawny, muscular heavy race of People, divided into Clans and classed into Nobility, Commonality & Slaves, governed by hereditary Chiefs." Thompson did not comment in his journals on the most remarkable feature of the Columbia "Sea look," the practice of head-flattening – see Townsend (193–4) for details.

Clark had noted that "those women [of the coastal tribes] are more inclined to Copulency than any we have yet Seen, with low Stature broad faces, heads flatened ... [They wear] large blue & white beeds, either pendant from their ears or incircling their necks, wrists & arms. they also ware bracelets of Brass, Copper & horn, and trinkets of

Shells, fish bones and curious feathers" (Thwaites, 3:125–6). Clark's passage echoes point by point Mackenzie's description of "a native of the sea coast, which was not a very great distance from us. This woman was more inclined to corpulency than any we had yet seen, was of low stature, with an oblong face, grey eyes, and a flattish nose. She was decorated with ornaments of various kinds, such as large blue beads, either pendant from her ears, encircling her neck, or braided in her hair: she also wore bracelets of brass, copper and horn" (343).

8 July 1811, "I do not know when the Sextant got this shake" Cf. 28 May 1807 note, and in AO journals 31, a draft letter to Sir Robert Hall, 24 March 1817: "I wish to suggest that to enable the Sextant to endure carriage without injury, it may be placed in a deal Box about 4 In every way too large for the Sextant & Can, and this space filled up with coarse Wool, Oakum &c &c."

9 July 1811, "to the Junction of the Shawpatin River" – at the junction of the Snake and Columbia rivers. The Snake River is called "Kamoenim River" on both PRO maps. Cf. AO journals 27: "Patrick Gass. MM ... The Junction of the Shawpatin River with the Columbia: Columbia is 860 Y^{ds} wide, Shawpatin 475 Y^{ds} at the Pt Captn Lewis Obs^d Lat^{de} 46°:15′:44″N." Cf. the passage in Gass's journal to which Thompson refers: "The small river, which we called the Flathead and afterwards Clarke's river, is a branch of the Great Columbia, and running a northwest course, falls into it a considerable distance above this place: we therefore never passed the mouth of that river. The Columbia here is 860 yards wide and the Ki-moo-ee-nem (called Lewis's river from its junction with the Koos-koos-ke) 475 yards ... Here the Columbia turns to the east of south" (181). Cf. 9 September 1809 and 5 August 1811.

9 July 1811, "Here I erected a small Pole with a half sheet of Paper well tied about it" Cf. McGillivray's "Account": "The integrity of British North America, is in the hands of the traders; and will continue so, while the present system of traffic, organized and regulated as it is, is not materially changed, not withstanding the labours of the ascendent party in America, to weaken and divide it. Embassies, bribes promises and experiments, have all been rendered abortive by the vigilance of the British traders whose interest is inseperable from that of the government in relation to the Indians" (64). Thompson's pole and paper were still in place when Alexander Ross arrived at the spot in mid-August. Ross, an employee of Astor's Pacific Fur Company, was indignant: "That he [Thompson] should have attempted to incite the Indians against us, in our helpless and almost forlorn state, was conduct which the world must condemn" (129).

9 July 1811, "I met the Principal Chief of all the Tribes of the Shawpatin Indians" When Thompson met him, Yelleppit still sported one of the medals and a flag which Lewis and Clark had given him – cf. Clark: "The great chief *Yel-lep-pit* two other chiefs, and a chief of [a] Band below presented themselves to us verry early this morning. we Smoked with them, enformed them as we had all others above as well as we could by signs of our friendly intentions towards our red children perticelar those who opened their ears to our Councils. we gave a Medal, a Handkercheif & a String of Wompom to *Yelleppit* and a string of Wompom to each of the others. *Yelleppit* is a bold handsom Indian, with a dignified countenance about 35 years of age, about 5 feet 8 inches high and well perpotiond" (Thwaites, 3:134 and 4:328).

In 1806 Henry met "Big Bellies" (Hidatsa) who had been similarly favoured by Lewis and Clark: "They pretended to say that those ornaments had conveyed bad Medicine to them and their children, for it must be observed they are exceeding superstitious and therefore supposed they could not dispose of these articles to better advantage than by giving them to other natives with whom they are frequently engaged in War, in hopes the ill luck would be conveyed to them. They were all much disgusted at the high sounding language the American Captains bestowed upon themselves and their own nation, wishing to impress the Indians with an Idea of their great power as Warriors, and a powerful people, that if once exasperated could instantly crush into atoms all the nations of the earth &c. This manner of proceeding did not agree with those haughty Savages. They have too high an opinion of themselves" (Gough, 238/Coues, 349–50).

9 July 1811, "a conical Mountain right a head alone & very high" – Mount Adams.

9 July 1811, "they fear the Straw Tent Snake Indians with whom they are at war" – Shoshoni. Cf. Clark: "Those Indians are mild in their disposition, appear Sincere in their friendship, punctial and decid-ed[ly] kind with what they have, to spare. They are excessive pore, nothing but horses there Enemies which are noumerous on account of there horses & Defenceless Situation, have deprived them of tents and all the Small Conveniences of life" (Thwaites, 3:9). Ogden, who spent two years exploiting the "Snake Country" south of the Columbia

River, was of much the same opinion – cf. 19 July 1807 note. Henry condemned them: "The Snake Indians are a miserable and defenseless nation that ever venture abroad. The Peagans still compare them to old women who they can kill with sticks and stones" (NA MG19 A13, 1129/Coues, 726). "Snakes" could be found on both sides of the mountains, from the Saskatchewan River to the lower Columbia – cf. Fidler's meeting with a member of this tribe who had ventured abroad as far north as the Highwood River, on 12 December 1792: "This is a man about 25 Years of age, well made & very neat & clean, & his clothing nearly resembles our Indians [Peigan]. The only peculiarity was his hair which dragged on the ground when he walked – but our Indians say that it is chiefly Buffalo hair woven with his own: it is plaited in 6 thongs nearly a finger-thick each" (HBCA E3/2).

10 July 1811, "their Seines with large Poles & dipping Nets on long Hoops for the Salmon" These were the uppermost fisheries of the Dalles – cf. Stuart: "[The Natives] erect stages or scaffolds to project some distance from the bank ... The places chosen are always a point where the water is strongest, and if possible a mass of rock near the projection between which and the shore the Salmon are sure to pass ... I call it speaking within bounds when I say that [in June and July] an experienced hand would by assiduity catch at least 500 daily" (Stuart, 52). Douglas described how the fish were caught here: "Before the water rises on the approach of summer, small channels are made among the stones and rocks ... over which is placed a platform for the person to stand ... [He] places his net at the top of the channel, which is always made to fit it exactly, and it is carried down with the current. The poor salmon, coming up his smooth and agreeable road as he conceives it to be, thrusts himself into the net and is immediately thrown onto the stage" (128).

10 July 1811, "news of the American Ship's arrival" Cf. 15 July 1811, and AO journals 75: "Mr Astor having engaged some of the Clerks of the N W Co^y formed a Company and sent a vessel [the *Tonquin*] around Cape Horn to the Columbia ... I was ... obliged to take 4 Canoes, and to proceed to the mouth of the Columbia to oppose them." The Canadian traders' rivalry with Astor was acrimonious and even endured beyond the NW Co takeover of Astoria. But both companies realized that more could be gained by cooperation than by opposition – cf. a letter from Mackenzie to McTavish, Frobisher & Co from New York, 30 January 1798: "While he's polite to me I shall be to him" (HBCA F3/1); and cf. William McGillivray to John George

McTavish, 19 June 1815: "Was it not that Mr Astor has it more in his Power to annoy us in the Indian Trade than any other man, I should prefer an arrangement with any other Person, for he is a most unpleasant Partner to deal with. We must however act from expediency" (HBCA F3/2). The Astorians were on their guard; McDougall recorded rumours of NW Co building along the Columbia and suspected a Native visitor of being a spy (Rosenbach AMS 1293/11: 30 April 1811, 16 June 1811).

In July 1810, while he was at Rainy Lake, Thompson learned of the NW Co wintering partners' decision to purchase stock in Astor's Pacific Fur Company and to agree on a joint Pacific venture. What Thompson did not know was that the NW Co's negotiations with Astor had faltered by the time the *Tonquin* set sail from New York. Thus Thompson was ignorant, and the Astorians uncertain, of their companies' positions when they met on 15 July 1811. See Ronda (232–5).

11 July 1811, "July 10th Astronomical Day ... Lat^{de} by Acc^{t}" Ship's time was calculated from noon to noon, to correspond with daily observations of the sun's meridian altitude. Latitude by account was an estimated position: the last observed latitude was moved ahead according to dead reckoning.

11 July 1811, "run part of a Rapid ... SRC very many large Crickets ... a series of strong Rapids" – Celilo Falls at high water, with many haystacks; the upper Dalles. These falls and rapids are now flooded by Lake Celilo, the reservoir of the Dalles Dam.

11 July 1811, "saw nothing of the reported bad Indians" Cf. 28 July 1811 – as reported in Gass's journal and a summary account by Lewis, both of which Thompson had read. Gass concluded that "all the Indians from the Rocky Mountains to the falls of the Columbia, are an honest, ingenious and well-disposed people; but from the falls to the seacoast, and along it, they are a rascally, thieving set" (254). In AO journals 19 for 11 December 1807, Thompson noted that he had "transcribed Captn Lewis's acc^{t} of his journey to the Pacific Ocean." The VPL journal contains the transcription: "On this portion of our Route we found the Natives extremely numerous & generally friendly, tho' we have on several occasions owed our Lives & consequently the final success of the Expedition to our number which consisted of 31 Men." See Jackson (336–43) for another version of this report.

12 July 1811, "the Portage" – past the lower Dalles, or Long Narrows, also submerged by the Dalles Dam. Thompson carried past the Dalles in July; Clark had amazed local villagers by running them both in October: "At this place the water of this great river is compressed into a chanel between two rocks not exceeding *forty five* yards wide and continues for a $\frac{1}{4}$ of a mile when it again widens to about 200 yards and continues this width for about 2 miles when it is again intersepted by rocks ... by good Stearing we could pass down Safe, accordingly I deturmined to pass through this place notwithstanding the horrid appearance of this agitated gut swelling, boiling & whorling in every direction, which from the top of the rock did not appear as bad as when I was in it" (Thwaites, 3:153–4).

Others were not so lucky – cf. Kane, who listed 68 "Axedunce" in rapids of the Columbia (MacLaren, 37), and Ogden, who vividly recalled one of them: "The men put forth, and began steering ... across the stream in order to avoid a string of whirlpools ... as the boat shot majestically onwards, I half repented my resolution of walking ... Suddenly, however, the way of the boat was checked ... Is it surprising that I grew dizzy and faint as I gazed, until at length one wild, long cry warned me that all was over" ([Ogden], 82). Thompson retold this story twice in the *Narrative* and concluded: "Imagination can hardly form an idea of the working of this immense body of water under such a compression, raging and hissing, as if alive" (Tyrrell, 496–7, 386/Glover, 355, 280–1).

12 July 1811, "here we saw many grey coloured Seals" – *Phoca vitulina*, harbour seal. Cf. Lewis: "Great numbers of *Sea Otters* in the river below the falls, I shot one in the narrow chanel to day which I could not get" (Thwaites, 3:150).

12 July 1811, "saw the first Ash" – *Fraxinus latifolia*, Oregon ash.

12 July 1811, "a Snow Mount, rather ahead ... another on right, rather behind" – Mount Hood and Mount Adams. Cf. *Narrative*: "With a powerful achromatic Telescope I examined [Mount Hood] ... from six thousand feet and upwards [it is] one immense mass of pure snow; what is below the limit of perpetual Snow, appears to be continually renewed by fresh falls of Snow, its many Streamlets form Rivers, one of which the Wilarmet [Willamette River], a noble River through a fine country falls into the Columbia River" (Tyrrell, 493/Glover, 353). Clark was more impressed by Mount St Helens – cf. 14 July 1811.

12 July 1811, "a Chief ... jabbered a few words ... he had learnt from the Ships" – "some of them not the best," added Thompson in the

Narrative (Tyrrell, 499/Glover, 357). Lewis noted some examples in his journal: "musquit, powder, shot, [k]nife, file, damned rascal, sun of a bitch, &c" (Thwaites, 3:327).

13 July 1811, "Kummen tacks" Like the Chief, Thompson came away jabbering a few words – "very good Chinook," comments Elliott (62). Cf. Ross: "The language spoken by these people is gutteral, very difficult for a foreigner to learn, and equally hard to pronounce. To speak the Chinook dialect, you must be a Chinook" (101). Cf. also Douglas: when Chinooks stole his tobacco "in their own tongue I gave them a furious reprimand, calling them all the low names used to each other among themselves. I told them they saw me only one *blanket man* [just a trader] but I was more than that, I was the *grass man* [botanist], and was not afraid. I could not recover [the tobacco]" (210–11). Douglas probably spoke the traders' pidgin Chinook, not the native Chinook language.

13 July 1811, "carried South 1M" – past the Cascades, now submerged by the Bonneville Dam. Cf. Clark: "One of the men shot a goose above this Great Shute, which was floating into the Shute, when an Indian observed it, plunged! into the water & swam to the Goose and brought i[t] on shore, at the end of the Suck [narrows] ... as this Indian richly earned the goose I suffered him to keep it which he about half picked and Spited it up with the guts in it to roste" (Thwaites, 3:180).

14 July 1811, "a simple conical Mountain ... buried under snow" – Mount St Helens. Cf. Vancouver: "The clearness of the atmosphere enabled us to see the high round snowy mountain ... to the southward of mount Rainier ... This I have distinguished by the name of *Mount St Helens*, in honor of his Britannic Majesty's ambassador at the court of Madrid" (421–2). Clark conjectured that "Mount Hellen [is] ... perhaps the highest pinecal from the common leavel in America" (Thwaites, 3:195–6), although Mounts Hood and Adams, which Clark had also sighted, are both considerably higher.

14 July 1811, "an ugly place of Rocks & an old Campment" Cf. Gass: "We ... put too at a branch of fresh water, under high cliffs of rocks ... Here we scarcely had room to lie between the rocks and water; but we made shift to do it among some drift wood that had been beat up by the tide. It rained hard all night and was very disagreeable" (195).

14 July 1811, "Tide fell ab^t 2 ft in the Night": Mackenzie's journal indicates his arrival at the Arctic Ocean in the same quiet, prosaic way: "I was surprized to observe the water had come under our Baggage ... We were all of Opinion that it was the Tide" (203). Cf. Clark's jubilant announcement: "Great joy in camp – we are in *view* of the *Ocian* ... this great Pacific Octean which we have been so long anxious to See. and the roreing or noise made by the waves brakeing on the rockey Shores (as I suppose) may be heard distictly" (Thwaites, 3:210).

15 July 1811, "over this Tongue" Here Thompson wrote to Duncan McDougall, David Stuart, and his nephew Robert Stuart of the Pacific Fur Company, proprietors at Astoria, (Bridgwater, 52):
Gentlemen:
Permit me to congratulate you on your safe arrival & building in the mouth of the Columbia River: Your situation is such as to enable you with the aid of good Providence to command an extensive commerce & humanize numerous Indians in which I wish you success.
With pleasure I acquaint you that the Wintering Partners have acceded to the offer of Mr Astor, accepting one third share of the business you are engaged in, their share of Capital not to exceed £10,000 without further permission – I have only to hope that the respective parties at Montreal may finally settle the arrangements between the two Companies which in my opinion will be to our mutual Interest.
Accept of my best wishes for your health & that of the Young Gentlemen with you.
I am with Esteem, Your Hu: Servt.
DAVID THOMPSON

15 July 1811, "we came to the House" Cf. McDougall, 15 July 1811: "Mr Thomson of the N.W. Co. in *Canada* arrived about 1 P.M. in a Cedar Canoe (made after the manner of a bark Canoe) manned by eight Men" (Rosenbach AMs 1293/11). Franchère provided more details: "Nous appercumes un grand Canot qui doubloit la pointe ... portant un pavillon ... Britannique, et l'equipage se montait à neuf personnes. Un homme assez bien mis, et qui paroissait commander, sauta à terre et nous abordant sans façon, nous dit qu'il s'appelloit David Thompson, qu'il étoit propriétaire dans la Compagnie du Nord Ouest, &c. ... Apres les civilités ordinaires, il nous informa ... que les Proprietaires hyvernants étoient d'avis d'abandonner les Postes qu'ils avaient établi à l'ouest des montagnes plutôt que d'entrer en concurrence avec nous – moyennant que nous ne les troublerions pas dans leurs commerce a l'Est" (240–1).

15 July 1811, "the House of Mr Astors Company" Cf. *Narrative*: "four low Log Huts, the far famed Fort Astoria of the United States"

(Tyrrell, 501/Glover, 358). Under NW Co administration, Astoria (renamed Fort George) took on, in Simpson's words, "an air or appearance of Grandeur and consequence which does not become and is not at all suitable to an Indian Trading Post" (Merk, 65).

15 July 1811, "Messrs McDougall Stuart & Stuart received me" Cf. Ross: "McDougall received him like a brother; nothing was too good for Mr Thompson; he had access everywhere, saw and examined everything; and whatever he asked for he got, as if he had been one of ourselves ... His own visit had evidently no other object but to discourage us – a manoeuvre of the NorthWest policy to extend their own trade at the expense of ours; but he failed" (85). McDougall, Stuart, and Stuart replied to Thompson's Tongue Point letter the next day (16 July 1811), while he was their guest at Fort Astoria (Bridgwater, 53):

David Thompson, Esqr.
Sir,
   We have the pleasure to acknowledge the receipt of your Note of yesterday, communicating the pleasant intelligence of the Wintering Partners of the North West Company having accepted of Mr Astor's offer, of one third share of the Business we are engaged in, and with you sincerely wish that final arrangements may take place to the mutual satisfaction of both parties, which would inevitably secure to us every advantage that can possibly be drawn from the Business ...
   We beg leave to congratulate you on your safe arrival here and accomplishing so arduous an undertaking in the midst of dangers & privations that must have attended so unusual a route, we shall therefore esteem ourselves happy in affording you any assistance that may be in our power while you may remain here, or in returning to your establishments.

We remain with regard, Sir,
Your mo: Hu: Serv'ts
DUNC: MCDOUGALL
DAVID STUART
ROBERT STUART

18 July 1811, "I went across to the Indian Villages" Cf. McDougall, 19 July 1811: "In the morning Messrs Thomson & D. Stuart went over to visit the Tshinook village, and in order that the former might have a view of the sea, they returned in the afternoon but were not fortunate enough to see either of the Chiefs" (Rosenbach AMS 1293/11). Cf. also Henry, who "visited a small encampment of Chinook Indians ...

these people all appeared to be a Savage and very filthy Race, they were surrounded with Fish Offles and their own excrements to such a degree as to demand our utmost circumspection and precaution in the selection of our steps. While here we saw one of their Largest Sea Canoes, coming across the River ... The Canoe was Paddled by Six men, one of whom stood at each end, while two of the remaining four, stood on each side, and all of whom kept regular time, in the use of their Paddles ... The Chief brought over about a hundred fresh Salmon weighing from five to eighteen pounds each" (NA MG19 A13, 1291–2/Coues, 749–50).

18 July 1811, "we went up a great Hill, where we gratified ourselves with an extensive view" Gass noted: "We are now at the end of our Voyage ... notwithstanding the difficulties, privations and dangers, which we had to encounter, endure and surmount" (199). Cf. also Clark: "I assended a high seperate bald hill covered with long corse grass ... men appear much Satisfied with their trip beholding with estonishment the high waves dashing against the rocks & this emence Ocian" (Thwaites, 3:231, 234). In the *Narrative* Thompson compressed the journal entries of several days into one moment of arrival, making much of the difference between his own scientific knowledge and his men's naive wonder: "On the 15th near noon we arrived at Tongue Point ... to a full view of the Pacific Ocean; which to me was a great pleasure, but my Men seemed disappointed; they had been accustomed to the boundless horizon of the great Lakes of Canada ... from the Ocean they expected a more boundless view ... and my informing them, that directly opposite to us, at the distance of five thousand miles was the Empire of Japan added nothing to their Ideas, but a Map would" (Tyrrell, 501/Glover, 358).

18 July 1811, "from hence I set the Lands" Cf. Broughton's report in the VPL journal transcription of Vancouver's *Voyage of Discovery*: "The Navigation of the Channel or Sound leading to the Entrance of the River is represented as very intricate & difficult, the Breakers in many places extending almost across from one Side to the other ... The northern Side of this Inlet is formed by Cape Disappointment & the south Side by Point Adams. Round Point Adams is a Bay inclosed at the other end by Point George ... A few miles above Gray's Bay commences a Chain of sandy Islets ... this appears to be what ought to be considered the Entrance of the River."

Return Upstream

Source: AO journals 27

Somewhat late in the day, the NW Co decided to respect once more Thompson's title of "Astronomer" and to support his project of exploring the Columbia River, just as the company had sponsored his early survey between the Saskatchewan and Missouri rivers. At the partners' annual meeting in July 1811, it was moved that a second wintering partner "be appointed to the superintendency of the Expedition [trading on the Columbia] ... intending by this arrangement that Mr David Thompson should be left to prosecute his plans of discovery on the west side of the Rocky mountains towards the Pacific" (Wallace, 266).

22 July 1811, "in company with Mr David Stuart" Cf. McDougall's journal for this day: "Mess[rs] Thompson & Stuart took their departure about 1 P.M. the former (who came across the rocky Mountains in the months of Dec[r] & Jan[y] last) is to proceed direct for Montreal; he told us that no doubt remained with him, but ere now a coalition of the two companies had taken place, regarding which he wrote us on his arrival and also handed us an extract from a Letter (on the same subject) addressed to Mr McGillivray of Montreal, by the Wintering Partners, the following day (say 16th ins[t]) we returned him an answer" (Rosenbach AMs 1293/11).

Cf. also Bird, 30 January 1812: "My Neighbour *says* that, conformably to Orders he had received from their Agents, Mr David Thompson proceeded (July last) down the Columbia to the Sea, on approaching which he found a Party of Americans, in the service of Aster & Co New York ... already building a House ... that on Mr Thompsons return up the Columbia four Canoes of the Americans actually accompanied him and are now settled near to Mr Thompsons principal post, where they so much undersell the NW^t Co Traders that they entirely ingross the Trade of that Quarter ... It is also reported that another Party is landed ... in the neighbourhood of that place where Sir Alex^r McKenzie arrived at the Sea ... It is impossible for me to ascertain the Truth of the above statements, the story has been related by several of the NW^t Co Clerks, at several places, and with a great deal of Consistency; and I have been shown passages of Letters from Mr Thompson, and Party, which confirm apparently the oral Information we had received on the Subject; but this amounts to no more than a proof that the story has not been fabricated on this side the Mountain; and I know the proprietors of the NW^t Co, in general, to be, so artful, so shameless, and so earnest in their Wishes to exclude us from a Participation in the Trade of that Quarter as to render it impossible for me to place much Belief in a Report of this Nature that is not supported by infallible Confirmations of its Truth" (HBCA B60/2/10).

23 July 1811, "we slept as I might say standing, as all the lower Lands are overflowed" Cf. Stuart, who travelled past this point in July 1812: "The river has fallen very considerably, but not as yet sufficiently to admit of our encamping in the bottoms, indeed from hill to hill the country has no very different appearance from an immense swamp, our days marches are therefore very irregular, being either compelled to stop often at an early hour, or sleep in our boats, without the possibility of finding a sufficiency of land wherein to kindle a fire for culinary purposes" (Spaulding, 44).

24 July 1811, "the first conical Mountain N42E, another N56E, the 3rd S84E ... Co West $\frac{1}{4}$M to the Wil ar bet River" – Mount St Helens, Mount Adams, Mount Hood; Willamette River.

25 July 1811, "the place we traded Salmon ... an Isl^d as drawn" – Sauvie Island – cf. 13 July 1811; *"fine Meadow Land below Pt Vancouver"* – cf. Thompson to Sir Charles Bagot, 22 February 1842: "Whoever settles in this fine Climate and Country has no wish to return" (NA MG19 A8, letters).

27 July 1811, "N48E 2$\frac{1}{4}$M Co N48E 1$\frac{1}{2}$M" – an exact transcription (the course direction is repeated); *"close to the Great Rapid and Houses"* – below the Cascades.

28 July 1811, "They ... enquired ab^t the Small Pox": These people had reason to be afraid. Cf. the information which Clark obtained from villagers at the mouth of the Willamette River: "I indeavored to obtain from those people of the situation of their nation, if scattered or what had become of the nativs who must have peopled this great town. an old man ... brought forward a woman who was badly marked with the Small Pox and made signs that they all died with the disorder which marked her face ... this Distructive disorder I judge must have been about 28 or 30 years past, and about the time the Clatsops inform us that this disorder raged in their towns and distroyed their nation" (Thwaites, 4:240–1).

The traders turned this fear to their advantage – cf. Cox (170) and Leonard: "Mr McDougal had recourse to a stratagem by which to avail himself of the ignorance and credulity of the savages, which does credit to his ingenuity ... He called together several of the chiefs ... The white men among you, said he, are few in number, it is true, but mighty in medicine. See here, continued he, drawing forth a small bottle and holding it before their eyes, in this bottle I hold the small-pox, safely corked up; I have but to draw the cork, and let loose the pestilence, to sweep man, woman and child from the face of the earth. The assembly was struck with horror and alarm" (130–1).

28 July 1811, "she would have been killed for the lies she told" This woman was the former wife of Boisverd, one of Thompson's men; the explorer had seen her the previous summer at Rainy Lake and met her again, disguised as a man, at Astoria – cf. *Narrative* (Tyrrell, 437, 512–3/Glover 314, 366–7) and Ross: "Mr Thompson at once recognized the two strange Indians, and gave us to understand that they were both females" (85).

28 July 1811, "the Indians ... surrounded us ... very menacing" Cf. Ross, who was a member of David Stuart's party: "We had no sooner commenced transporting our goods than [the Indians] tried to annoy us in every kind of way – to break our canoes, pilfer our property, and even to threaten ourselves ... We were not, however, in a situation to hazard a quarrel with them, unless in the utmost extremity; and it was certainly with great difficulty, and by forebearance on our part, that we got so well off as we did" (112).

Lewis and Clark reported hostile villagers here in 1806 (Thwaites, 4:266–7), as did Ogden (ed. Davies and Johnson, 3) and Douglas (158–9). On his first trip to the Columbia Simpson noted, somewhat high-handedly, "Surrounded by Indians all Day who assisted us on the Portage and conducted themselves with great propriety ... if any serious evil or difference arises hereafter with them it will be our own fault as notwithstanding the bad character they bear I should not hesitate to pass up or down the River with merely the Crew of my Single Canoe"

(Merk, 125). But in 1829 Simpson "likewise saw a great many Indians who were disposed to be troublesome" (Rich, 117).

30 July 1811, "the Brook, Nar ma neet" – Klickitat River.

31 July 1811, "steep fluted Rocks like Pillars" – columnar basalt – cf. 5 August 1811, and *Narrative*: "I am aware that geologists give an igneous origen to basalt; this is a theory I could never bring myself to believe; what is of igneous origen must have been in a fluid state, and could never have been cooled down in isolated fluted columns ... there is not the least vestige of volcanic action, no hot springs are known, nor salts of any kind ... every where they have the same indestructible appearance, neither heat nor frost, weather, or water seem to act upon them, what is broken, or shivered, does not decay, nor form rounded debris" (Tyrrell, 519, 529/Glover, 371, 377–8). But cf. Lyell: "The compactness of these rocks, and their different aspect from that of ordinary lava, [Hutton] attributed to their having cooled down under the pressure of the Sea, and in order to remove objections started against this theory, his friend Sir James Hall instituted a most curious and instructive series of chemical experiments, illustrating the crystalline arrangement and texture assumed by melted matter cooled down under high pressure" (61–2).

31 July 1811, "major part for Mr Stuart" There is no mention in the text of where and when Thompson parted company with David Stuart – cf. Ross: "On the 31st, after breakfast, Mr Thompson and party left us to prosecute their journey, and Mr Stuart, in one of our canoes, accompanied him as far as the long narrows ... On Mr Thompson's departure, Mr Stuart gave him one of our Sandwich Islanders, a bold and trustworthy fellow, named Cox, for one of his men, a Canadian, called Boulard" (113–4). Coxe is first mentioned in the entry for 6 September 1811.

1 August 1811, "passed an Isle with Houses for the Dead" Cf. Clark: "On the upper part of this Island we discovered an Indian Vault ... in it I observed great numbers of humane bones of every description perticularly in a pile near the centre of the vault, on the East End 21 Scul bones forming a circle on Mats; in the westerley part of the Vault appeared to be appropriated for those of more resent death" (Thwaites, 3:139).

1 August 1811, "the Name of the great River" – Deschutes River, marked on the PRO maps as "Wunwowe River," near the "Snake Indian Road" which Ogden followed in 1826: "Altho all [the men] appear happy still when I reflect on my last years privations and sufferings I *must* confess my sensations on leaving the Columbia are far different God grant we reach it again in safety and our exertions crowned with success ... Course from the Columbia South East" (Ogden, ed. Davies and Johnson, 4).

1 August 1811, "this Co is almost rubbed out" Thompson noted the courses in lead pencil while travelling, then copied them (in ink) into his journals.

1 August 1811, "every thing is full of Sand" Cf. Stuart (Spaulding, 67) and Kane's *Wanderings*: "The drifting of the sand is a frightful feature in this barren waste. Great numbers of the Indians lose their sight ... The salmon, while in the process of drying, also become filled with sand to such an extent as to wear away the teeth of the Indians, and an Indian is seldom met with over forty years of age whose teeth are not worn quite to the gums" (190).

2 August 1811, "a river ... named Torks Paez" – John Day River, renamed after a member of the Astorians' 1812 expedition; *"rocky grassy hills rising above & going off in vast Plains"* – cf. a note on the PRO maps: "Both Sides of the Columbia on this sheet, very bold rocky Land covered with short Grass, mostly bare of Woods."

3 August 1811, "a River opposite, named A hoaks pa" – Willow Creek; *"Co + 1M to our old campment going down"* – cf. 10 July 1811.

5 August 1811, "the finger of the Deity" Cf. Hearne: "The banks [of the Coppermine River] are in general a solid rock, both sides of which correspond so exactly with each other, as to leave no doubt that the channel of the river has been caused by some terrible convulsion of nature" (165). Thompson adhered to this creationist view despite Hutton's suggestion that river channels were the effect of gradual erosion – cf. Playfair: "In the times that are past, whatever may have been the irregularities of the surface at its first emerging from the sea, or whatever irregularities may have been produced in it by subsequent convulsions, the slow action of the streams would not fail in time to create or renew a system of valleys ... Water, in all circumstances, would find its way to the lowest point; though, where the surface was quite irregular, it would not do so till after being dammed up in a thousand lakes, or dashed in cataracts over a thousand precipices" (354). At the same time, without denying the effect of slow and continuous force, Paley pointed out that "the truth is, generation [or erosion] is not a principle, but a *process*. We might as well call ... spinning and weaving principles: and then, referring to the texture of cloths ... pretend to dispense with intention, thought and contrivance on the part of the artist; or to dispense, indeed, with the necessity of any artist at all" (335–42). Paley's artist was, of course, the Deity.

5 August 1811, "thank Heaven for the favour we find among these numerous people" These are the Natives who called Thompson Koo koo sint, "the man who looks at the stars" (Ross, 128) – cf. Thompson's "Saleesh and Kullyspel Vocabulary" in AO journals 23: "koo koo sim" is listed as the word for star. Such knowledge lent the explorers an aura of power – cf. Mackenzie (367) and Fidler, 12 December 1792 and 17 January 1793: "They have many whimsical notions concerning me and the Instruments – they had such a dread of the Sextant that none of them would touch it – had they been requested. They imagine that I could see all over the Country with it & know what & where other Indians was doing ... I never filled their heads with any thing that I could tell more than what they themselves knew, as had any accident happened to them, they would with very great probability have imagined that myself & Instruments had been the sole occasion of such accidents, as they are full of superstition" (HBCA E3/2). Clark used his instruments to frighten and "passif[y]" Natives from whom he demanded food (Thwaites, 4:237).

6 August 1811, "Wrote a Letter to Jaco Finlay" – at Spokane House. From the "Shawpatin River" (Snake River), Thompson travelled up the Palouse River and then overland to Spokane House by a Native trail marked on the PRO maps as "Shawpatin and Pilloosees Road."

6 August 1811, "The Road ... ascends & descends continually" Cf. Cox: "In some places the path wound along the almost perpendicular declivities of high hills on the backs of the river, and was barely wide enough for one horse at a time. Yet along these dangerous roads the Indians galloped with the utmost composure; while one false step would have hurled them down a precipice of three hundred feet into the torrent below. Even walking along these dangerous declivities, leading my horse, I experienced an indescribable sensation of dread on looking down the frightful abyss" (89).

9 August 1811, "the Land very rocky ... & the Soil a sandy fine impalpable power" – basalt and volcanic ash – cf. Douglas: "The whole country [is] covered with shattered stones, and I would advise those who derive pleasure from macadamised roads to come here, ... they will find it done by Nature" (208).

10 August 1811, "3 Sorts of Currants" – *ribes aureum*, golden currant.

14 August 1811, "Much Indian Business & arranging the Furrs" Cf. Henry: "This day was as troublesome as usual, our houses continually crowded with Indians going and coming. Trading and Begging" (NA MG19 A13, 838/Coues, 544). Meanwhile, according to Bird's journal for this day, "A Mr McDonald, a Proprietor of the NWt Company with two Clerks, and thirty-five Men in five Canoes, passed by us [at Edmonton House], bound, as he tells me, for the Country West of the Rocky Mountain ... the magnitude of the present Outfit sufficiently demonstrates that the NW Co consider the Country bordering on the Sources of the Columbia of no mean Value: they will now have upwards of fifty Men there" (NBCA B60/a/10). This was John McDonald, assigned to the Columbia department so that Thompson would have some time to pursue his explorations (Wallace, 269).

15 August 1811, "Sent off Michel to the Saleesh River" Cf. 21 August 1811. The *Narrative* explains that Finan McDonald was to have made ammunition available in case of war between the Peigans and Salish; it also includes a description of this war, in which Bourdeaux and Kinville were killed: "They were the last of those free hunters. I deeply regretted them" (Tyrrell, 546–552/Glover, 389–93). Cf. Townsend: "[There are extremely few] Indians who do not fear the power, and who refuse to acknowledge the superiority of the white man ... It must be acknowledged, however, that this determined hostility does not originate solely in savage malignity ... it is fomented and kept alive from year to year by incessant provocations on the part of white hunters, trappers, and traders, who are at best but intruders on the rightful domains of the red man of the wilderness" (104–5).

17 August 1811, "to where we baited formerly in June" Cf. AO journals 25 for 14 June 1811: Thompson had built a cedar canoe near "Ilthkoyape Falls" (Kettle Falls) for his journey to Astoria, and at the same place built another canoe to go upstream – cf. 21–31 August 1811.

17 August 1811, "Killed ... 1 Pigeon" – *Zenaida macroura*, mourning dove.

21 August 1811, "Hamelin arrived ... Bellaire & Michel Allaire here"
These are freemen, like Bourdeaux and Rivé. Cf. Ogden: "The life of
a Trapper altho at times he has some idle hours which however does
not often happen is certainly a most laborious one and one [which] in
four years makes a young man look almost as if he had reached the
advanced age of sixty of this many convincing proofs are now
amongst my party the cold water which more or less they are wading
in two thirds of the day aded to the cold and sleeping often without
fire and wet to the skin conduces to ruin their constitutions well do
they earn their 10 Shillings per Beaver a convict in Botany Bay is a
Gent living at his ease compared to them still they are happy and
amidst all their sufferings and privations if they take Beaver all is well
... a roving life pleases them and with nearly all it would be viewed
more as a punishment than a favour to send them to Canada" (Ogden,
ed. Davies and Johnson, 94).

27 August 1811, "Cartier" – chief of the Pend Oreille tribe.

*27 August 1811, "they had been up a long way, but had returned
short"* Finan McDonald had gone up the Columbia River beyond the
Arrow Lakes in hopes of meeting supply canoes from Athabaska Pass.
Cf. 11 and 14 September 1811.

28 August 1811, Thompson wrote a letter to Daniel Harmon, who
received it just over seven months later – cf. Harmon, 6 April 1812:
"Six Indians arrived from Frasers Lake and delivered me a Letter
wrote by Mr David Thompson, dated August 28th, 1811, Ilk-koy-ope
Falls Columbia River – which informs me that he accompanied by
Seven Canadians last Spring descended the above mentioned River to
where it empties itself into the Pacific Ocean, and where they arrived
on the 16th of July and found a number of people building a large
Fort for the American Company or rather Aster & Co. and that
Mr Alexander McKay &c. (one of the Partners but formerly for the
North West Co.) had gone to the Northward, in the vessel that
brought them out, on a coasting-trade. Mr Thompson writes that after
having remained Seven Days with the American People he set off to
return to his Establishments which are nigh the source of the Columbia
River and from whence he wrote the above mentioned letter, and
delivered it to an Indian to bring it to the next Tribe, that they might
forward it to the next and so on till it reached this place [Stuart Lake],
which manner of conveyance accounts for the great length of time it
has been on its way, for the distance is not so great but that People
might come from there in a Months time at most" (151–2).

2 September 1811, "Veins of that whiteish hard kind of Rock" –
quartz.

4 September 1811, "end of Co the Saleesh River" Cf. 2 October 1809,
and Thompson's conclusion in AO journals 22 for 27 April 1810:
"Attentively surveying the Country & considering all the mass of
Information I had collected from a variety of Indians, I concluded that
we must abandon all thoughts of this way & return, please Heaven, by
our old Road till future opportunity shall point out some more eligible, which I very much doubt." Cf. also Gass "... Flathead (called
Clarke's) river a beautiful river ... but there is no fish of any consequence in it; and according to the Indian account, there are falls on it
... six or seven hundred feet high; and which probably prevent the fish
coming up" (280–1).
 Thompson had read Gass's journal. But Simpson, as usual, preferred to ignore Thompson's discoveries and conclusions: "The Flat
Head or Ponderais [Pend Oreille] River from the South ... appeared a
large Stream but I understand is full of dangerous rapids; it has never
been explored which appears extraordinary considering the short distance between it and Spokane House and the length of time the place
has been established; I shall take care that it be examined next Season"
(Merk, 41).

5 September 1811, "McGillivray's River Co up it N65E ⅔M" Cf.
29 September 1809 note and the PRO maps: "7 to 11 Carrying Places
according as the Water is high or low but so bad as to be next to
unnavigable."

6 September 1811, "several Tracks of ... Rein Deer" – *Rangifer taran-
dus*, woodland caribou.

6 September 1811, "Coxe" – engaged on the lower Columbia River,
31 July 1811. Coxe probably numbered among the 12 "Insulaires"
which the Pacific Fur Company had hired during the *Tonquin*'s visit to
Hawaii – cf. Franchère: "Ces gens ... parurent fort empressés de
s'offrir a nous, et nous aurions pu en emener un plus grand nombre"
(227–8). Cf. also McDonald of Garth, who sailed from London for
Astoria in 1813: "We had on board half a dozen good Canadian
voyageurs, with a Sandwich Islander and four clerks: the voyageurs to
make and man a canoe, the Islander to guide us into the river
Columbia, where he had been before" (NA MG19 A17, 149/ Masson,
2:44).

7–8 September 1811, "the Lake ... the Lake ... with fine Shores" – Arrow Lakes, of which the level is now raised by the Hugh Keenleyside Dam.

10 September 1811, "Current very strong" Thompson was passing from the upper Arrow Lake into the river again. Cf. Simpson: "The current is so strong that at first sight one would scarcely suppose it possible to stem it even with the Towline but on more attentive observation it is found that in every reach there is a strong back current or Eddy which renders it easy of ascent and this appears to be occasioned by the Serpentine course of the River running with great strength against the Points which force the water up in shore" (Merk, 39).

12 September 1811, "the Dalles very bad" – later known as the "little Dalles," just north of Revelstoke, and now flooded by the Revelstoke Dam. Cf. Douglas: "A very dangerous rapid, where the water falls 9 feet over large stones, to pass which took all our united strength: two in the boat guiding her and seven on the line. Carried all my articles, lest evil should overtake them ... This night from exertion I can hardly write" (252).

13 September 1811, "small Plane & much Hazel ... tolerable Box Trees" – *Acer glabrum*, Douglas maple; *Corylus cornuta*, hazel; *Acer negundo*, boxelder.

14 September 1811, "Co say West 30 or 40 miles to the Oochenawga Lake" Okanagan Lake lies southwest of Thompson's position.

14 September 1811, "discharged ... lined" – the upper Dalles, later known as the Dalles des Morts. For explanations of the name, cf. Cox (278–9), Douglas (252), and Kane: "Past the dall de more an rapped of deth. thare was 2 men cilled and eatein here from starvation thare cenew haveing ben lost and thare parvishions run out one cilled 2 of his companions and the forth one ascaped" (MacLaren, 36). On his return Kane told the story again, including details of cannibalism – see MacLaren (46–8), and the published *Wanderings* (230–2).

14 September 1811, "very dangerous to line down" Cf. AO journals 27 for 23 October 1811: "We set off [downstream] – pray God for a good Voyage, for the Road appears terrible, the Snow is so deep ... at the Dalles Portage lost $\frac{1}{4}$H in visiting – at $2\frac{1}{2}$ Pm thank Heaven below the Dalles: we carried ab^t 200 Y^{ds} of $\frac{2}{3}$ Cargoe, & run the rest, all the fresh Meat &c – the Rapid very high Waves but run down in fine order." The Revelstoke Dam has flooded these narrows as well.

18 September 1811, "our old Hut" Cf. 23 January 1811, and Franchère: "Nous quittames la riviére Columbia, et entrames ... la petite riviére au Canot, et nous la remontames jusque sur le soir, l'orsqu'etant arrivé à l'endroit ou elle cèsse d'etre naviguable, nous campames à l'endroit ou hyverna Mr Thompson en 1811" (296). Cf. also Cox: "This gloomy valley ... appeared never to have been trodden by the foot of man, until the enterprising spirit of British commerce, after having forced its way over the everlasting snows of the Rocky Mountains, penetrated into this anti-social glen" (281).

18 September 1811, "a few Lines in Iroquois" Cf. Ferris's description of an Iroquois freeman, formerly a NW Co engagé: "He could read and write in his own language" (185). The written form of the language was probably derived from missionary translations.

19 September 1811, "a vast Glacier" – on Hallam Peak, at the head of Foster Creek.

After wintering at Saleesh House, Thompson explored farther up the Clark Fork River, and then repeated the journey of August–September 1811 from Spokane House to Boat Encampment. He crossed Athabaska Pass for the second and last time, and went east to Rainy Lake, Fort William and the Great Lakes–Ottawa River route to Montreal. Thompson established himself at Terrebonne in the fall of 1812 and began work on the huge maps that are now kept in the Archives of Ontario and the Public Record Office. Cf. minutes of the annual meeting of NW Co partners at Fort William, July 1812: "That Mr David Thompson now going down on Rotation shall be allowed his full Share for three years after the outfit and one Hund[re]d Pounds besides – that he is to finish his Charts, Maps &c and deliver them to the Agents in that time ... the Hund[re]d p[ounds] p[ér] an[nu]m is meant for compensation for making use of his own Instruments &c &c and for furnishing him with implements for drawing, writing &c" (Wallace, 272).

Maps

Maps

After completing his work for the International Boundary Commission under the Treaty of Ghent, David Thompson petitioned Canadian and British government officials to obtain a pension, or further employment, based on his years of surveying experience.[1] Reasonably enough, Thompson thought that his personal knowledge of the Oregon Territory might be useful in the final boundary negotiations between Britain and the United States.

As proof of his knowledge, Thompson offered the Foreign Office two manuscript maps of western North America, the first from 84°w to the Pacific Ocean, the second from 110°w. He described these maps as follows: "My survey of the Rivers &c of those western countries are to the one tenth of a mile connected by numerous astronomical observations for Latitude and Longitude & for five successive years; of all which I have accurate Maps in my possession, on the scale of three inches, and of six inches, to one degree of Longitude." Since these two maps had been drawn on the basis of revised calculations, they were better than his "hasty, rough map ... made for the north west company" in 1813–14 or even a second, corrected map drawn the same year and now in the Archives of Ontario.

Thompson had probably drawn the two maps sent to the Foreign Office between 1814 and 1817.[2] He offered his maps to the British

1. Cf. introduction for an outline of Thompson's life.
2. The *terminus a quo* is based on Thompson's statement that he revised his calculations after drawing the two 1814 maps; the *terminus ad quem* is Thompson's appointment to the International Boundary Commission. Dating is made easier by the progressive deterioration of Thompson's handwriting;

government first in 1826 and later in 1843, during negotiations between Britain and the United States for possession of the Oregon Territory. On the first occasion they were returned to him; the British government was confident that it had obtained enough information from the Hudson's Bay Company. In 1843 the Earl of Aberdeen, then foreign secretary, kept the maps but refused to grant a pension or any remuneration, claiming that Thompson had already been paid £150 for information used to update Arrowsmith's *Map Exhibiting all the New Discoveries in the Interior Parts of North America*. Thompson's post-1814 maps of northwest America are still in London, catalogued with Foreign Office documents at the Public Record Office.[3] In 1845 Thompson also submitted a memoir which reiterated the pro-British arguments of the North West Company *Notice Respecting the Boundary between His Majesty's Possessions in North America and the United States*, published in 1817. If Thompson's cartographic information had been used and his views heeded, they might have made a difference: his work was the most exact mapping to date of the Pacific Northwest, and he had gauged with cynical accuracy the United States' determination to annex the whole Oregon Territory. Like his *Narrative*, to which he turned in the face of bureaucratic indifference, Thompson's latter-day correspondence with the colonial and British governments demonstrates that his western surveys were the principal work of his long life, and his preoccupation even into old age.[4]

The seven maps included in this section trace European knowlege of the western interior from 1800, when Thompson first attempted to cross the continental divide, to 1818, when some of Thompson's toponyms appeared on Arrowsmith's *Map Exhibiting all the New Discoveries ...* These seven maps furnish a context for the journals which record Thompson's exploration of the Pacific Northwest.

---

the PRO maps are drawn in an early firm hand, while shading and a few notes were added much later, probably in 1843. The PRO catalogue entry for these maps (PRO FO925/4622) gives 1843 as the year of reception and 1816 as the year in which they were probably drawn.

3. PRO letters FO5/402, 418, 421, 415: Thompson to the Earl of Aberdeen, 26 August 1843, 29 November 1843, 10 September 1844, 2 December 1844. Another of Thompson's maps, entitled "Map of the Oregon Territory" and apparently drawn at the same time as the two PRO maps, is in the British Library (BL Add. MS 27363 A–D).

4. PRO Letters FO5/441: Thompson to J.E. Alexander, 9 May 1845.

"Indian Chart Rocky Mountains." [1801]
Royal Commonwealth Society Library (Cambridge) CN 2807

This sketch shows the limit of European knowledge of northwest America at the beginning of the nineteenth century. The handwriting on this map may be William McGillivray's; if so, the information was probably forwarded to him by his brother, Duncan McGillivray, who directed attempts to cross the continental divide in 1800 and 1801. Another version of the same map, found in the Selkirk Papers (NA MG19 E1 1:192), retains more clearly the cartographic conventions of what must have been a Native original.

Aaron Arrowsmith, *A Map Exhibiting all the New Discoveries in the Interior Parts of North America*. 1795.
Additions to 1802 (second version of this year).
National Archives of Canada (Ottawa) NMC 19687

For the 1802 state of the western portion of this map, Arrowsmith's main source of information was Peter Fidler's report to the Hudson's Bay Company, written at Oxford House on 10 July of the same year. In this report Fidler described his journey along the Rocky Mountain foothills in 1792–93, and included copies of Blackfoot maps depicting the tributaries of the upper Missouri River. The 1802 state also shows Mackenzie's route to the Pacific which Arrowsmith had mapped for the explorer's *Voyages from Montreal* (1801); a dotted line connects Mackenzie's "Tacouche Tesse River" with Broughton's "River Oregan." In 1808 Fraser and Thompson were to realize that this single hypothetical river was actually two, the Fraser and Columbia rivers.

Aaron Arrowsmith, *A Map Exhibiting all the New Discoveries in the Interior Parts of North America*. 1795.
Additions to 1814.
National Archives of Canada (Ottawa) NMC 48909

The 1811 update of Arrowsmith's map showed no change from the 1802 state in its depiction of territory west of the continental divide. In 1814, however, Arrowsmith was able to incorporate the discoveries of Lewis and Clark, as published on a map in the John Allen/Nicholas Biddle edition of their journals. On the 1814 state of Arrowsmith's map, the lower Columbia is traced in detail together with "Lewis's River" (Snake River) and the "Flathead River" (Pend Oreille River). The upper Columbia is shown as a stylized line and the Arrow

Lakes as a single large "Ear bobs Lake," but three of Thompson's key discoveries are included: the source of the Columbia in two small lakes, its "big bend" northwest and then south, and the equally complex course of the Kootenay/Kootenai River. Arrowsmith may have obtained this information not from Thompson but from Joseph Howse, whose map of the upper Columbia, drawn in 1812, is now lost – it may have been discarded after its information was engraved on a published map.

David Thompson, "Map of the North-West Territory of the Province of Canada, 1792–1812." 1814.
Archives of Ontario (Toronto) R-C

Thompson worked on several maps of western North America after his retirement from the fur trade in 1812. His first map of the territory between Hudson Bay and the Columbia River, entitled "A Map made for the North West Company in 1813 and 1814 and delivered to the Hon[ble] William McGillivray then Agent," may have been the map which was displayed at Fort William. Thompson called this a "hasty, rough map"; certainly there was room for correction. This map has not been located, but a memoir which accompanied it, now in the Royal Commonwealth Society Library (RCSL Remarks), mentions a mysterious "Caledonia River" flowing southwest into Puget Sound. This "Caledonia River" found its way onto a map illustrating the North West Company *Notice Respecting the Boundary between His Majesty's Possessions in North America and the United States* (1817). This map frontispiece is a revised state of the plate which Arrowsmith had used for the original edition of Mackenzie's *Voyages from Montreal*. Within months of producing his "hasty, rough map" Thompson drew a second, corrected map which omitted the "Caledonia River." One of Thompson's sons sold this second map to the Ontario government in 1857, the year of Thompson's death.

Aaron Arrowsmith, *A Map Exhibiting all the New Discoveries in the Interior Parts of North America.* 1795.
Additions to 1818.
William L. Clements Library (Ann Arbor) 1-1-2

In contrast to his collaboration with Mackenzie and the Hudson's Bay Company, Arrowsmith did not have easy access to Thompson's cartographical information. For the 1818 state, Arrowsmith redrew the upper Columbia River, replacing "Ear bobs Lake" with two smaller

lakes (Arrow Lakes); he also drew in the Fraser River and added the
"Caledonia River." Several of Thompson's placenames were adopted
and the locations of North West Company posts were shown. These
details would seem to indicate Arrowsmith's access to Thompson's
"hasty, rough map" drawn in 1814. But the course of the upper
Columbia as shown on the 1818 and subsequent states does not follow any of Thompson's extant maps, the Arrow Lakes are still too
large, the positions of Howse and Athabaska passes are inaccurate,
and "McGillivray's River" (Kootenay River) joins the Columbia at the
forty-ninth parallel. This last error, perpetuated in later states of the
map, was an important reference point in the final round of negotiations concerning the Oregon Territory. Given the number and importance of such discrepancies, the transaction between Arrowsmith and
Thompson remains unclear: if Thompson was indeed paid for information about the Columbia watershed, Arrowsmith did not reproduce
this information. Moreover, Thompson's printed appeal for subscrib-
ers (NA MG19 A) is evidence that he wanted to compete, not collabo-
rate, with the London cartographer.

David Thompson, "Maps of North America from 84° West and
110° West to the Pacific Ocean." [1816.]
Public Record Office (London) FO925/4622

The two PRO maps are Thompson's final cartographic image of the
territory he explored. Thompson's maps are essentially river surveys;
relief is crudely represented by hatching and "caterpillars" according
to the cartographic conventions of the period. But rapids, portages,
isolated mountains, forts, and Native trails are precisely indicated.
Many of the landmarks described in Thompson's journals and drawn
on these maps have since disappeared, often under water. Since
twentieth-century reference points (towns, roads, political boundaries)
are of little help in locating Thompson's landmarks and are themselves
subject to rapid change, few modern references are given in the notes.
Thompson's maps and journals should be read together with topographical sheets published by the Canada Centre for Mapping (Department of Energy, Mines and Resources) and by the United States
Geological Survey.

Also included in this section are two documents which reveal the
process and purpose of Thompson's cartographic work:

"Observations according to the Order in which they were taken."
AO Journals 24

This list shows Thompson's reliance on observed positions as key points to which he adjusted his compass directions and estimated distances. The observations of this list should be compared with the journal entries for the dates given, and the PRO (1) and (2) map details which follow in this section. Explanations of the techniques for finding latitude and longitude, as well as identification of landmarks (where possible), are given in the notes to the text.

"Remarks on the Oregon Territory."
Public Record Office (London) FO5/441

This memoir, forwarded to the Foreign Office in 1845, was Thompson's last attempt to influence the boundary negotiations between Britain and the United States. The arguments employed in these "Remarks" repeat, decades later, the North West Company's position during the first diplomatic exchange over the Oregon Territory.

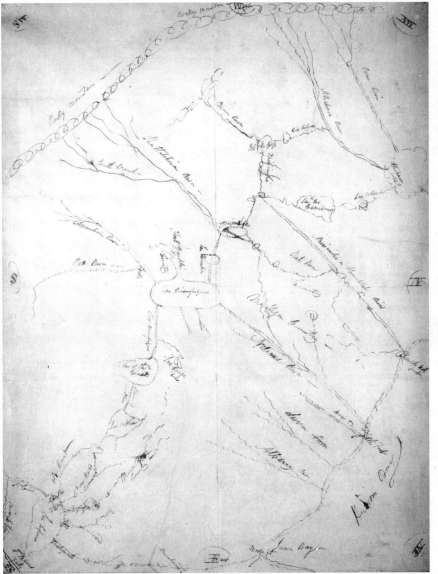

"Indian Chart Rocky Mountains" [1801] Royal Commonwealth Society Library (Cambridge) CN 2807

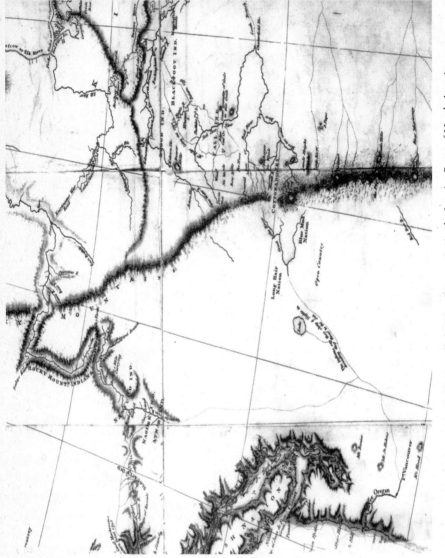

Aaron Arrowsmith, *A Map Exhibiting all the New Discoveries in the Interior Parts of North America.* 1795. Additions to 1802 (second version of this year). National Archives of Canada (Ottawa) NMC 19687 [detail]

Aaron Arrowsmith, *A Map Exhibiting all the New Discoveries in the Interior Parts of North America.* 1795. Additions to 1814. National Archives of Canada (Ottawa) NMC 48909 [detail]

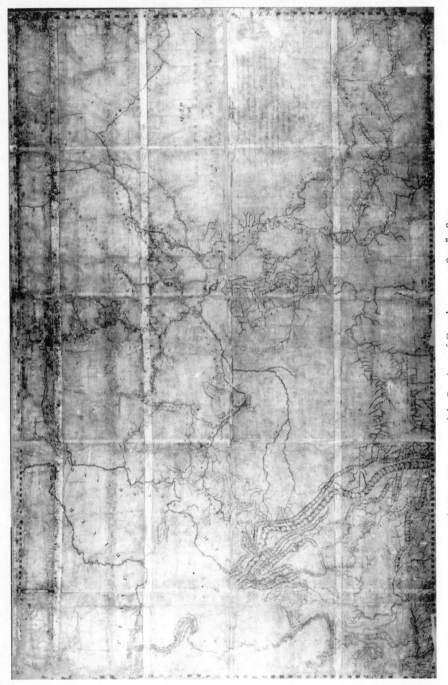

David Thompson, "Map of the North-West Territory of the Province of Canada, 1792–1812." 1814.
Archives of Ontario (Toronto) R-C

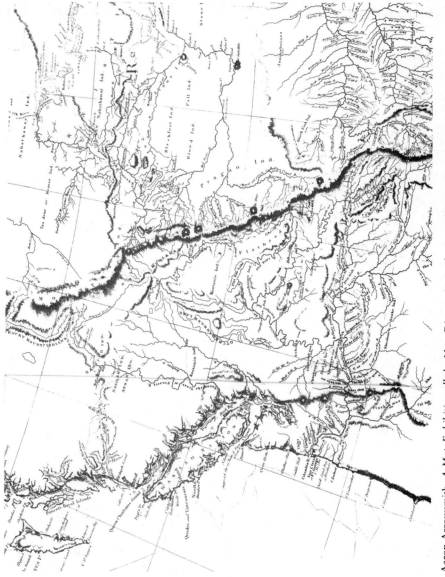

Aaron Arrowsmith, *A Map Exhibiting all the New Discoveries in the Interior Parts of North America.* 1795. Additions to 1818. William L. Clements Library (Ann Arbor) 1-1-2 [detail]

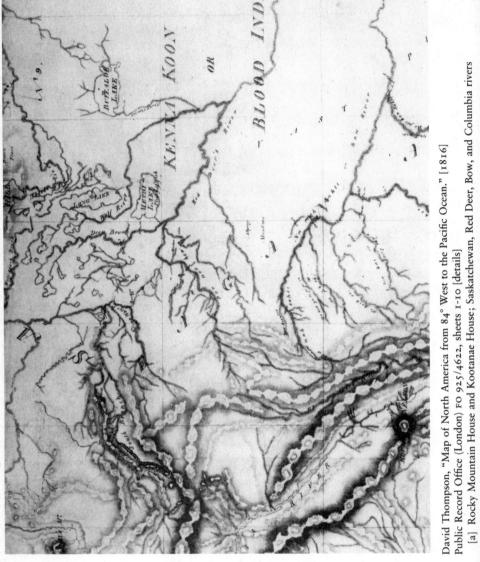

David Thompson, "Map of North America from 84° West to the Pacific Ocean." [1816]
Public Record Office (London) FO 925/4622, sheets 1-10 [details]
[a] Rocky Mountain House and Kootanae House; Saskatchewan, Red Deer, Bow, and Columbia rivers

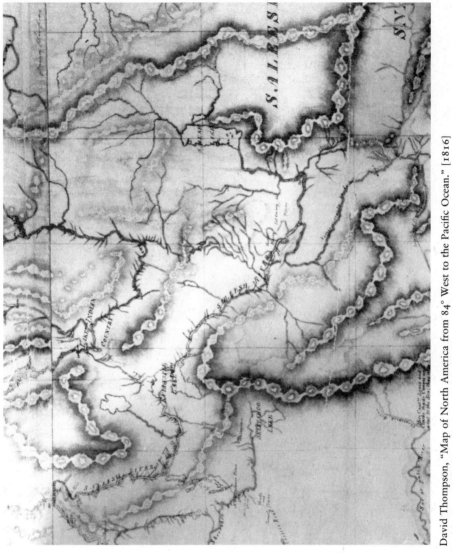

David Thompson, "Map of North America from 84° West to the Pacific Ocean." [1816]
Public Record Office (London) FO 925/4622, sheets 1–10 [details]
[b] Kullyspel House, Saleesh House, and Spokane House; Kootenai, Clark Fork, Pend Oreille, and Spokane rivers

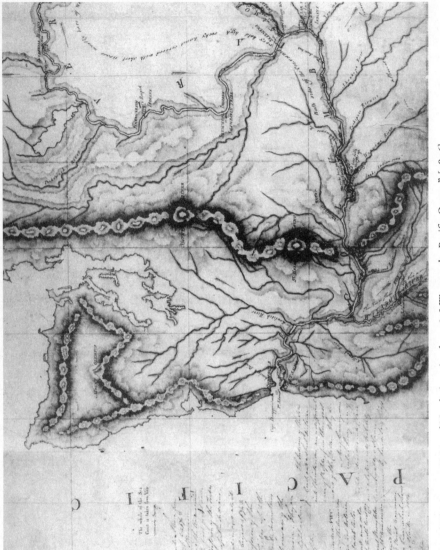

David Thompson, "Map of North America from 84° West to the Pacific Ocean." [1816]
Public Record Office (London) FO 925/4622, sheets 1-10 [details]
[c] Astoria; lower Columbia River

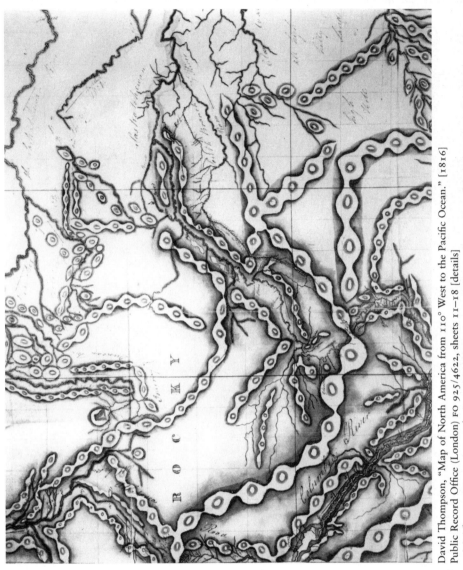

David Thompson, "Map of North America from 110° West to the Pacific Ocean." [1816]
Public Record Office (London) FO 925/4622, sheets 11–18 [details]

[a] Thompson's routes up the Ram River (1801), across Howse Pass (1807–10), and across Athabaska Pass (1810–12)

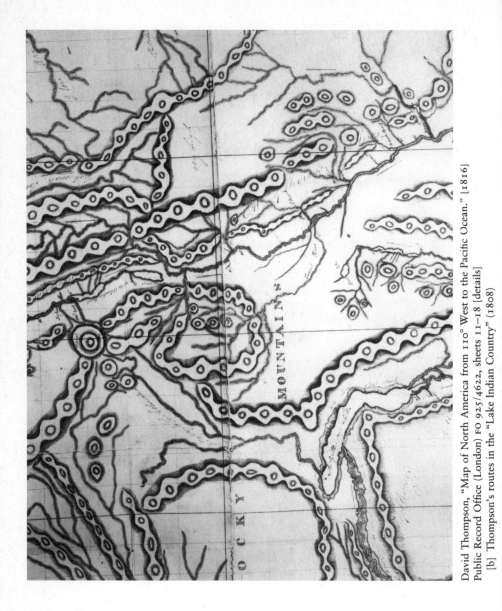

David Thompson, "Map of North America from 110° West to the Pacific Ocean." [1816]
Public Record Office (London) FO 925/4622, sheets 11–18 [details]
[b] Thompson's routes in the "Lake Indian Country" (1808)

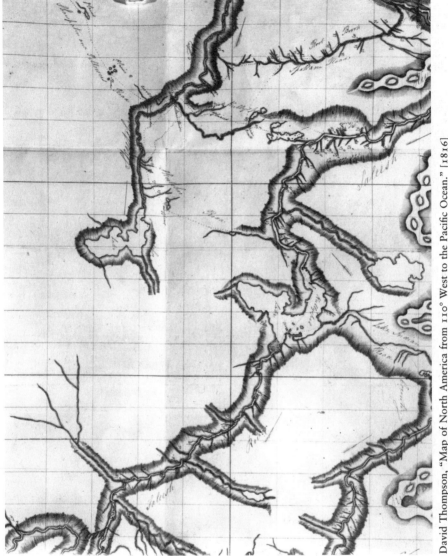

David Thompson, "Map of North America from 110° West to the Pacific Ocean." [1816] Public Record Office (London) FO 925/4622, sheets 11–18 [details]

[c] Thompson's routes to Pend Oreille Lake (1809), and to Spokane House (1811–12)

Observations according to the order in which they were taken

Date		Place	Latitude (N)	Longitude (W)
1807				
May	11	Round Plain	52°:24′:13″	
	12	Long Plain	52°:31′:32″	
	20	head of Jaco's Brook	52°:35′:56″	115°:42′:41″
	23	at a Brook, the River S60E 1M	52°:24′:17″	
	25	– d° –	52°:24′:17″	
	30	at the little Lake, killed a Cow	52°:20′:39″	
June	4	Kootanae Plain	52°:2′:6″	
	16	my Campment in the Mountains	51°:50′:31″	
	24	– d° –	51°:59′:49″	
	25	the Height of Land	51°:48′:25″	
	26	the Dog's Campment	51°:20′:21″	
July	1	Kootanae River, end of the Mountain Portage		116°:52′:45″
	21	head of the Kootanae River, sortie of the Lake	50°:31′:28″	115°:58′

Date		Place	Latitude (N)	Longitude (W)
Augst	10	Kootanae House	50°:32':15"	115°:51':40"
1808				
Feb^{ry}	9	– d° –		115°:29'
	11	– d° –	50°:32':12"	
	21	– d° –		115°:56':15"
March	31	– d° –		116°:18':15"
April	5	– d° –		115°:26'
	21	McGillivray's Portage	50°:8':12" 50°:15':28"	
	22	McGillivray's River, at the fine Plains on the North Side	49°:54':15"	
	25	McGillivray's River, a little above the Stag River	49°:12':42"	
	26	Tobacco Plains (sun hazy)	48°:55':54"	
	27	Junction of Fine Meadow River	48°:54':15"	
May	1	McGillivray's River (as p^r Journal)	48°:51':44"	114°:59'
	3–4	Tiger Campment	48°:45':50"	114°:50':22"
	5	North End of Kootanae Road	48°:22':24"	
	8–9	Lake Indian Portage	48°:42':44"	116°:0':8"
	14	South End of Akorkanookoo	49°:17':44"	

No more Observations in 1808, having been obliged to leave my Sextant when I crossed Nelson's Mountains.

1809				
April	30	at the Horn Plains, Kootanae River	50°:41':42"	
May	3	at the old Hoard	50°:53':34"	
Sept^r	2	McGillivray's River, South Side, at the Lake Indian Portage		116°:22':52"
	23	Kullyspel House	48°:12':14"	

Date		Place	Latitude (N)	Longitude (W)
	28	Saleesh House by Aquilae	48°:9':4"	
		[sun's] LL	47°:51':22"	
Oct^r	6	Kullyspel Lake	48°:16':55"	
	14	at the Spring below Saleesh House	47°:39':42"	114°:56½' 115°:3¼'
	15	beyond the High Rock on the Saleesh River	47°:32':8"	
		at the Brook entrance of the Horse Plains		114°:22':30" 114°:27':30"
	16	at the Spring where we first sighted the Rocky Mountains	47°:29':6"	
	17	at the Junction of 2 Brooks where we had lost the Road	47°:50':20"	
1810 Feb^{ry}		Saleesh House (mean of 5 Observations)	47°:34':35"	115°:22':51"
	25	Entrance of the Root Plains	47°:28':55"	
March	11	Saleesh River, where we built a Canoe (Saleesh Campment)	47°:21':14"	114°:3':15"
April	20	Saleesh River	47°:5':2"	
	23	Kullyspel House	48°:12':38"	
	24	West End of Kullyspel Lake,		116°:58':15"
		Sandy Point		117°:1':30"
	25	Saleesh River, lower part	48°:11':36"	117°:34':15"
				117°:34':30"
	27	Saleesh River, a little above (say 7M above) where the River is unnavigable	48°:42':22"	

Date		Place	Latitude (N)	Longitude (W)
	28	Saleesh River, on my Return	48°:19':56"	117°:35½'
July	23	Rainy Lake House	48°:36':57"	
Oct^r	23	Boggy Hall	53°:1':19"	
Nov^r	2	Road to Athabaska River	53°:8':3"	115°:8'
	3	– d° –	53°:7':51"	115°:57¼' 114°:54':15" 115°:3':30"
	13	– d° –	53°:16':36"	
	21	– d° –	53°:24':42"	117°:30' 116°:40':15" 116°:54':15"
	26	McLeod's River, where we left it	53°:30':39"	
	28	Brook between McLeod's and the Athabaska River	53°:37':54"	
Dec^r	1–6	Athabaska River, at the Shed Depot of Goods (Longitude of 4 Observations)	53°:33':33"	117°:36':34"
1811 Feb^{ry} & March		Sortie of the Canoe River	52°:8':1"	118°:18':18"
April	23	North End of the Frozen Lake	51°:59':46"	
	24	– d° –	51°:59':41"	
May	2	South End of the Frozen Lake	51°:54':50"	117°:46':56"
	9	where I fished, at the Meadows of the Lakes, Kootanae River	51°:4':7"	
	11	Kootanae River, where we first hunted	50°:42':38"	

Date		Place	Latitude (N)	Longitude (W)
		in crossing the Mountains, 1809		
	12	Horse Hill Campment	50°:39′:35″	
	19	Great Kootanae Road, McGillivray's River	48°:22′:17″	
June	15	Spokane House, on the Skeetshoo River		117°:27′:45″ 117°:22′
	17	Road to the Columbia by Mars	48°:4′:4″	
	18	– d° –	48°:20′:42″	
	21–28	Ilthkoyape Falls (Longitude mean of 7 Observations & April 21, 1812, 2 Observations)	48°:37′:22″	117°:54′:58″
July	6	Columbia River	47°:32′:42″	120°:57′
	8	close above the Junction of the Shawpatin and Columbia Rivers	46°:12′:35″	119°:13′:15″
	9	Columbia River by Antares	45°:50′:45″	
		by Saturn	45°:51′:33″	
	10	Columbia River	45°:44′:54″	120°:49′
	11	(civil day)		121°:14′
	12	(civil day) at the foot of the Long Falls;		121°:48′:45″
		at the head of the Great Rapid	45°:39′:47″	
	14	put up		
		by Saturn	46°:10′:5″	
	16	Fort George		123°:48′:15″
	24	Wilarbet River	45°:49′:38″	
	25	Columbia River, at the Fine Lawn	45°:38′:29″	122°:35′:45″ 122°:52′:15″
	26	Campment	45°:34′:22″	122°:16′:30″ 122°:27′:45
Augst	2	Campment		119°:46′:15″ 120°:25′:30″

Date		Place	Latitude (N)	Longitude (W)
	4	Campment		118°:39':30"
				118°''
				49':45"
	7	Shawpatin river, at Noon	46°:25':23"	
		Campment		119°:11':30"
	8	Shawpatin River, at Noon	46°:36':26"	118°:22':15"
		Campment, laid up our Canoe		119°:21':15"
				118°:50':30"
	9	– d° –	46°:36'	
		Shawpatin River mean Latitude and Longitude	46°:36':13"	118°:49':51"
	13	Spokane House mean Latitude and Longitude (4 Observations)	47°:47':4"	117°:27':11"
	23	Ilthkoyape Falls	48°:38':1"	
Sept'	1	– d° –	48°:38':14"	
	3	Columbia River	48°:52':18"	
	4	– d° –	49°:2':7"	
	5	– d° –	49°:17':5"	
	6	– d° –	49°:21':16"	118°:51':15"
	7	– d° –	49°:35':30"	118°:43':45"
	8	– d° –	49°:58':24"	
	9	– d° –	50°:18':55"	118°:30':2"
	12	– d° –	51°:5':13"	
	13	– d° –	51°:17'	
	14	– d° –	51°:30':14"	
Oct'	4	Headwaters of the Athabaska River, Mr Wm Henry's Campment by Aquilae	52°:53':24"	
	5	– d° –		
		[sun's] LL	52°:54':5"	
		by Pollux (2 Observations)		118°:35'

Remarks on The Oregon Territory

PRO Letters FO5/441: Thompson to Sir James Alexander,
10 June 1845

Mr Falconer has given a clear view of the apparent claims of both
nations to the Oregon Territory, yet it appears neither nation has
placed any real confidence in their respective claims, for Mr Falconer
justly observes, "There can be no question that mere discovery is not
alone a complete title to possession."[5]

In 1790, Great Britain and the United States agreed to the joint
occupation of the country, from Latitude 42° North to Latitude
47° North: that is, the joint occupation of a Territory bounded on the
south by the parallel of 42° North, on the North by the parallel of 47°
North, on the East by the Rocky Mountains, and on the West by the
Pacific Ocean. (I have the treaty, but cannot now find it, and must depend upon my memory.)

This treaty was for ten years, subject to either party disallowing it
by giving one year's notice: in 1801 it was renewed for 10 years, and
in 1818 again renewed for an indefinite time, but as yet neither party
has given a year's notice, and President Polk has put an end to it, by
claiming the whole of the Oregon Territory.

In 1792, Lieutenant Broughton RN, under the sanction of the British
Government and by its orders, formally took possession of both banks

---

5. Thomas Falconer, editor of the *Westminster Review*, had written a pamphlet
   on the Oregon question in 1845 that was critical of current Anglo-American
   negotiations – see Merk-OQ (292–4, 307). Sir James Alexander, a Royal
   Engineer stationed in Montreal, lent the pamphlet to Thompson and asked for
   his comments on it. These "Remarks" were sent to William R. Jackson, secretary of the Royal Geographical Society, who forwarded them to the Foreign
   Office. Lord Aberdeen remained obdurate: Thompson received neither pension nor recognition from the British government.

of the Columbia River,[6] and on this formal possession Great Britain founds its claim to the Oregon, altho' no settlement was formed and the country directly abandoned, nor to this day, do I believe, that on the part of the Crown there is a Magistrate, a Court &c &c, necessary to constitute a Colony.

It is a great pity Mr Falconer did not take the treaty of 1790 and its renewals into his consideration. It is contended that Mr Gray was not in the Columbia River, but only in an arm of the sea: had Lieutenant Broughton been as well acquainted with Rivers as he was with the Ocean, he would have made no such assertion; an arm of the sea we naturally [assume] to be salt water, whereas this "arm of the sea" is fresh water, formed by the Columbia River overflowing low lands, which is common to all Rivers. And it required six days for Mr Gray to clear the Bar of the River.[7]

Astoria was a trading Factory for Furs, situated close to the Westward of Tongue Point on the expanse of the Columbia called an arm of the Sea, composed of private individuals in 1810, and in 1813 sold to the North West Company, also private individuals. Yet from this sale, authorized by the British Crown (I do not believe it) it became a British Colony, without a Magistrate or any legal authority to uphold the laws of a Colony. Three days after the sale, the *Racoon* sloop of War arrived to take Astoria, but found it in possession of the North West Comp[y]. The crew were very much disappointed, as they expected prize money, but the Captain quieted them.[8]

---

6. Vancouver's lieutenant ventured up the Columbia River as far as Point Vancouver six months after Robert Gray, a fur trader from Boston, had visited the estuary in May 1792. Cf. Broughton's account of claiming territorial possession, as copied in the VPL journal: "Previous to his Departure, ... he formally took Possession of the River & the Country in the Vicinity in his Britannic Majesty's Name, having every Reason to believe that the Subjects of no other civilized Nation or State had ever entered the River before."

7. Cf. Broughton's account, as copied in the VPL journal: "Mr Gray stated to us ... that in the course of last Summer, he had ... entered the River or rather the Sound & had named it after the Ship he then commanded (The Columbia). The extent Mr Gray became acquainted with on that occasion is not further than what I have called Gray's Bay, not more than 15M from Cape Disappointment"; and the description of the estuary in the *Columbia*'s journal for 12 May 1792: "Observ'd two sand bars making off, with a passage between them to a fine river ... The river extended to the NE as far as the eye could reach, and water fit to drink as far down as the *Bars*, at the entrance" (Howay-CR, 396–7).

8. For details of the takeover of Astoria in 1813, see Ronda (277–300).

At the peace of 1814, altho' Astoria was a Factory of private persons, yet the United States obliged the Crown to give it up, and its limits to be for future discussion, which have not yet been settled: here was lost a good opportunity for the Crown claiming the trading settlements I made in 1807 & subsequent years.

The convention in 1818 was that of joint occupancy.[9] At the end of ten years, Mr Canning and Mr Huskisson proposed that "the boundary beyond the Rocky Mountains should pass from those Mountains Westward along the 49th parallel of Latitude to the Northeasternmost branch of the Columbia River, and thence down the middle of the stream to the Pacific": this was not agreed to. I doubt much if I could point out any such branch of the Columbia River, for all the Eastern branches are Southward of the Columbia River.

President Munroe, in his Message of December the 2nd 1823 says, "The occasion has been found proper for asserting that henceforth the American Continents [a]re not to be considered as subjects for European Colonization." President Polk declared the same in bolder language, and this is *the sole principle*[10] the Crown has to contend with; every thing else is argument to no purpose.

The boundaries offered by Great Britain show a defective knowledge of the Territory. There is but one boundary which ought to be satisfactory to England, & ought to content the United States (if this is possible). This boundary is from where the parallel of the 49th degree of Latitude touches the East side of the Rocky Mountains; [from this point] the boundary shall pass along the Mountain Southward to the 47th degree of Latitude, and on this 47th parallel of Latitude, across the Rocky Mountains and continue until this parallel of Latitude intersects the Columbia River, thence down the middle of the said River to the Pacific Ocean. By this Great Britain cedes all the territory South of the 47th parallel of Latitude to the 42nd parallel, from the Pacific to the Rocky Mountains: this ought to content them.

The proposition of Mr Canning for the Boundary to pass down the Northeasternmost branch of the Columbia to this River shows that Mr Canning had no map of the Country before him, for all the Branches of the Columbia *lie Southeastward* or *Northwestward*.[11]

---

9. For a detailed account of British-American negotiations concerning the Oregon Territory, see Merk-OQ (*passim*).

10. This underlining is Thompson's own.

11. These words have been underlined in pencil, probably by someone in the Foreign Office, who added the following marginal note: "What can this twaddle mean? See [a]ny map of McGillivray's River." According to Arrowsmith's map (see the detail of the 1818 state included in this map section),

The very devious courses of the Columbia River, and of all its numerous branches to join it, show the necessity of a good map of the
Oregon Territory founded on actual survey. The proposition of Lord
John Russell to make McGillivray's River a boundary plainly shows
he must have had very erroneous maps before him, for this River has
a *most devious* course to the Columbia, and in a high Latitude of that
Territory.[12]

The speeches of Earl Aberdeen, Lord John Russell, and Sir Robert
Peel, are all very good on general principles, but will never determine
a boundary over the Oregon Territory. There appears a total want of
knowledge of that Territory; it may be beneath these great men to
study the Maps of the Columbia River; or they may have erroneous
maps.

Even the Saleesh River and its Lakes (on which I passed two
winters) is too devious a boundary.

England has long been too forward to conciliate the United States.
Let this now be given up, and let the United States now propose
a boundary over the Oregon Territory which may be modified,
accepted, or not allowed, & [let the British] no longer leave their offers
open to the United States.

The single determined principle of the United States is, that no
foreign power has any right to any part of North America, and whatever they may grant to the British Crown will be expediency, to be
resumed again as soon as possible. On the other hand the Crown
ought to assume a right to the whole Territory, by formal possession
taken by Lieutenant Broughton RN in 1792, and whatever is granted
to the United States to be [a] matter of favor, not of right.

Let the British Crown assume its natural dignified attitude, and no
longer expose itself to the refusal of the United States.[13]

"McGillivray's River" (Kootenay River) flowed southwest into the Columbia
at the south end of the Arrow Lakes: "McGillivray's River" was thus the
"Northeasternmost branch."

12. Again the underlining is in pencil; the same reader has added the following
note: "The Question is not whether it has a devious course, but that it reaches
49°N." The Arrowsmith map (1818) shows the junction of the Kootenay and
Columbia Rivers to be on the forty-ninth parallel.

13. Sir James Alexander endorsed Thompson's "Remarks" as follows: "I lent
Mr D. Thompson Falconer's Pamphlet on the Oregon and requested him to
make notes on it, as he was the first to visit it from the East of the Rocky
Mountains in 1801 [sic]. Subjoined are his ideas of the Boundary &c."

List of Sources

List of Sources

DAVID THOMPSON: MANUSCRIPTS

Journals. Toronto: Archives of Ontario F443 (cited as "AO journals").
Journal, Vancouver: Vancouver Public Library (cited as "VPL journal").
  "Extract from a *Voyage of Discovery Round the World* by Captain George Vancouver, regarding the North West Coast of America." 1800.
  "Account of an attempt to cross the Rocky Mountains by Mr James Hughes, nine Men & myself, on the part of the N.. W^t Company; in order to penetrate to the Pacific Ocean." 1801.
  "Sketch of Captn Lewis's Voyage to the Pacific Ocean by the Missesourii & Columbia Rivers from the States of America." 1807–08.
"Journey to the Rocky Mountain." 1801. Ottawa: National Archives of Canada (cited as "NA report").
"Narrative of the Establishment on the Scources of the Columbia, addressed to Mr Duncan McGillivray, Director to the N.W.. Co^y, and the Gentlemen of the upper Fort des Prairies." 1807. Cambridge: Royal Commonwealth Society Library (cited as "RCSL report").
"Remarks on the Countries westward of the Rocky Mountains, with references to the rough Chart, by D.T. Terrebonne. 19 April 1813." Cambridge: Royal Commonwealth Society Library (cited as "PRO remarks").
Letter to Duncan McDougall, Robert Stuart, and David Stuart, 15 July 1811. New Haven: Yale University Library (Coe Collection).
Letters, 1839–43. Ottawa: National Archives of Canada MG19 A8 (cited as "NA letters").

Letters, 1843–45. London: Public Record Office FO 5/415 (ff. 49–50, 55–6), 5/418 (ff. 25, 27, 29), 5/441 (ff. 99–102) (cited as "PRO letters").

DAVID THOMPSON: EDITIONS

Bridgwater, Dorothy Wildes. "John Jacob Astor Relative to his Settlement on Columbia River." *Yale University Library Gazette* 24 (1949): 47–69.

Burpee, Lawrence J., ed. "Some Letters of David Thompson." *Canadian Historical Review* 4 (1923): 105–26.

Coues, Elliott, ed. *New Light on the Early History of the Greater Northwest: The Manuscript Journals of Alexander Henry and of David Thompson.* 3 vols. 1897. Reprint. Minneapolis: Ross and Haines, 1965.

Elliott, T.C., ed. "Journal of David Thompson." *Oregon Historical Quarterly* 15 (1914): 39–63, 104–25, 216.

– "David Thompson's Journeys in the Spokane Country." *Washington Historical Quarterly* 8 (1917): 183–7; 9 (1918): 11–16, 103–6, 169–73, 284–7; 10 (1919): 17–20.

– "David Thompson's Journeys in Idaho." *Washington Historical Quarterly* 11 (1920): 97–103.

– "David Thompson and Beginnings in Idaho." *Oregon Historical Quarterly* 21 (1920): 49–61.

– "The Discovery of the Source of the Columbia River." *Oregon Historical Quarterly* 26 (1925): 23–49. (transcription of the "RCSL report")

– "David Thompson's Journeys in the Pend Oreille Country." *Washington Historical Quarterly* 23 (1932): 18–24, 88–93, 173–6.

Glover, Richard, ed. *David Thompson's Narrative.* Toronto: Champlain Society, 1962 (cited as "Glover").

Hopwood, Victor G., ed. *David Thompson: Travels in Western North America, 1784–1812.* Toronto: Macmillan, 1971.

Howay, F.W., ed. "David Thompson's Account of his First Attempt to Cross the Rockies." *Queen's Quarterly* 40 (1933): 333–56.

Schoefield, E.O.S., ed. *Report of the Provincial Archives of British Columbia (1912).* Victoria: King's Printer, 1913.

Tyrrell, J.B., ed. *David Thompson: Narrative of his Explorations in Western America, 1784–1812.* Toronto: Champlain Society, 1916 (cited as "Tyrrell").

White, M. Catherine, ed. *David Thompson's Journals Relating to Montana and Adjacent Regions, 1808–1812.* Missoula: Montana State University Press, 1950.

Wood, W. Raymond, ed. "David Thompson at the Mandan-Hidatsa Villages, 1797–1798." *Ethnohistory* 24 (1977): 329–42.
– and Thomas D. Thiessen, eds. *Early Fur Trade on the Northern Plains: The Narratives of John Macdonell, David Thompson, François-Antoine Laroque and Charles McKenzie.* Norman: University of Oklahoma Press, 1985.

OTHER SOURCES: MANUSCRIPT

Hudson's Bay Company Archives, Winnipeg: Provincial Archives of Manitoba (cited as "HBCA").
Masson Collection, Ottawa: National Archives of Canada (cited as "NA MG19").
Duncan McDougall, "Astoria Journal, 1810–13", Philadelphia: Rosenbach Museum and Library (cited as "Rosenbach AMS 1293/11").

OTHER SOURCES: PRINTED

[Atcheson, Nathaniel]. *On the Origin and Progress of the North West Company of Canada, with a History of the Fur Trade.* London: Cox and Baylis, 1811.
Belyea, Barbara. "The 'Columbian Enterprise' and A.S. Morton: A Historical Exemplum." *BC Studies* 86 (1990): 3–27.
Bowditch, Nathaniel. *The Improved Practical Navigator*, rev. Thomas Kirby. London: J. and J. Hardy/D. Steel, 1802.
Broc, Numa. *Les Montagnes vues par les géographes du XVIIIe siècle.* Paris: Bibliothèque nationale, 1969.
Butler, William. *The Great Lone Land.* 1872. Reprint. Edmonton: Hurtig, 1968.
Cautley, R.W. "Characteristics of Passes in the Canadian Rockies." *Canadian Alpine Journal* 12 (1922): 158–62.
Cheadle, Walter. *Journal*, ed. A.G. Doughty and Gustave Lanctôt. Ottawa: Graphic Press, 1931.
Cook, James. *Journals*, ed. J.C. Beaglehole. 4 vols. Cambridge: Cambridge University Press for the Hakluyt Society, 1955–74.
Coues, Elliott, ed. *New Light on the Early History of the Greater North West: The Manuscript Journals of Alexander Henry and of David Thompson.* 3 vols. 1897. Reprint. Minneapolis: Ross and Haines, 1965.
Cox, Ross. *The Columbia River*, ed. Edgar I. Stewart and Jane R. Stewart. Norman: University of Oklahoma Press, 1957.
Cutright, Paul Russell. *Lewis and Clark: Pioneering Naturalists.* Urbana: University of Illinois Press, 1969.

Dalrymple, Alexander. *A Plan for Promoting the Fur-Trade, and Securing it to this Country, by Uniting the Operations of the East-India and Hudson's Bay Companys.* London: George Bigg, 1789.

Davidson, G. Charles. *The North West Company.* Berkeley: University of California Press, 1918.

Dempsey, Hugh A. "David Thompson under Scrutiny." *Alberta Historical Review* 12, no. 1 (1969): 22–8.

Douglas, David. *Journal Kept During his Travels in North America,* ed. W. Wilks and H.R. Hutchinson. 1914. Reprint. New York: Antiquarian Press, 1959.

Ferris, Warren Angus. *Life in the Rocky Mountains,* ed. Leroy R. Hafen. Denver: Rosenstock, 1983.

Franchère, Gabriel. *Journal of a Voyage to the Northwest Coast of America,* ed. W. Kaye Lamb. Toronto: Champlain Society, 1969.

Franklin, John, *Narrative of a Journey to the Shores of the Polar Sea, 1819–20–21.* 1823. Reprint. Edmonton: Hurtig, 1969.

Fraser, Simon. *Letters and Journals,* ed W. Kaye Lamb. Toronto: Macmillan, 1960.

Gadd, Ben. *Handbook of the Canadian Rockies.* Jasper: Corax Press, 1986.

Garry, Nicholas. "A Detailed Narrative of his Travels in the North West Territories of British North America." *Transactions of the Royal Society of Canada* 2 (1900): 73–204.

Gass, Patrick. *A Journal of the Voyages and Travels of a Corps of Discovery,* ed. David McKeehan. Minneapolis: Ross and Haines, 1958.

Glover, Richard. "The Witness of David Thompson." *Canadian Historical Review* 31 (1950): 1–25.

Gough, Barry M., ed. *The Journal of Alexander Henry the Younger, 1799–1814,* vol. 1. Toronto: Champlain Society, 1988.

Graham, Andrew. *Observations on Hudson's Bay,* ed. Glyndwr Williams. London: Hudson's Bay Record Society, 1969.

Green, Jonathan S. *Journal of a Tour on the North West Coast of America.* New York: Heartman, 1915.

Harmon, Daniel. *Sixteen Years in the Indian Country,* ed. W. Kaye Lamb. Toronto: Macmillan, 1957.

Harris, R. Cole, ed. *Historical Atlas of Canada,* vol. 1. Toronto: University of Toronto Press, 1987.

Hearne, Samuel. *Narrative of a Journey from Prince of Wales's Fort on Hudson's Bay to the Northern Ocean.* 1796. Reprint. Amsterdam and New York: N. Israel and Da Capo Press, 1968.

Heckrotte, Warren. "Aaron Arrowsmith's Map of North America and the Lewis and Clark Expedition." *The Map Collector* 39 (1987): 16–20.

Hector, James. *On the Physical Features of the Central Part of British North America, and on its Capabilities for Settlement.* Edinburgh: Neill, 1861.

Hind, Henry Youle. *Northwest Territory Progress Reports.* Toronto: John Lovell, 1859.

Hopwood, Victor. "David Thompson and his Maps." *Proceedings of the Seventh Annual Conference of the Association of Canadian Map Librarians (1973).* Ottawa: Association of Canadian Map Librarians, 1974.

Howay, F.W., ed. *Voyages of the "Columbia" to the Northwest Coast, 1787–1790 and 1790–93.* Boston: Massachusetts Historical Society, 1941 (cited as "Howay-CR").

Hutton, James. *System of the Earth, Theory of the Earth, Observations on Granite.* 1785–88–94. Reprint. Darien, Conn.: Hafner, 1970.

Isham, James. *Observations on Hudson's Bay,* ed E.E. Rich. Toronto: Champlain Society, 1949.

Jackson, Donald, ed. *Letters of the Lewis and Clark Expedition.* 2 vols. Urbana: University of Illinois Press, 1978.

Johnson, Alice, ed. *Saskatchewan Journals and Correspondence.* London: Hudson's Bay Record Society, 1967.

Kane, Paul. *Wanderings of an Artist among the Indians of North America.* 1859/1925. Reprint. Edmonton: Hurtig, 1974.

Lavender, David. *Winner Take All: The Trans-Canada Canoe Trail.* New York: McGraw-Hill, 1977.

Leonard, H.L.W. *History of the Oregon Territory from Its First Discovery to the Present Time.* 1846. Reprint. Fairfield: Ye Gallion Press, 1980.

Luebke, Frederick C., Frances W. Kaye, and Gary E. Moulton, eds. *Mapping the North American Plains.* Norman and Lincoln: University of Oklahoma Press and University of Nebraska Center for Great Plains Studies, 1987.

Lyell, Charles. *Principles of Geology.* 3 vols. 1830. Reprint. Lehre: Cramer, 1970.

McGillivray, Duncan. *Journal,* ed. A.S. Morton. Toronto: Macmillan, 1929.

– and William McGillivray. "Some Account of the Trade Carried on by the North West Company." In *Report of the Public Archives of Canada (1928).* Ottawa: King's Printer, 1929.

[McGillivray, Simon/Samuel Wilcock]. *Notice Respecting the Boundary between His Majesty's Possessions in North America and the United States.* London: McMillen, 1817.

Mackenzie, Alexander. *Journals and Letters,* ed W. Kaye Lamb. Toronto: Macmillan for the Hakluyt Society, 1970.

MacLaren, I.S., ed. "Journal of Paul Kane's Western Travels." *American Art Journal* 21, no. 2 (1989): 23–62.

Masson, L.R., ed. *Les Bourgeois de la Compagnie du Nord-Ouest.* 2 vols. 1889–90. Reprint. New York: Antiquarian Press, 1960.

Merk, Frederick. *The Oregon Question: Essays in Anglo-American Diplomacy and Politics.* Cambridge: Harvard University Press 1967 (cited as "Merk-OQ").

– ed. *Fur Trade and Empire: George Simpson's Journal, 1824–5,* Cambridge: Harvard University Press, 1931 (cited as "Merk").

Milton, William Fitzwilliam, and Walter Cheadle. *The North-West Passage by Land.* London: Cassell, Petter and Galpin, 1865.

Morse, Eric W. *Fur Trade Routes of Canada: Then and Now.* Toronto: University of Toronto Press, 1973.

Morton, A.S. "The North West Company's Columbian Enterprise and David Thompson." *Canadian Historical Review* 17 (1936): 266–88.

– "Did Duncan McGillivray and David Thompson Cross the Rockies in 1801?" *Canadian Historical Review* 18 (1937): 156–62.

– *A History of the Canadian West to 1870–71,* rev. Lewis G. Thomas. 1939. Reprint. Toronto: University of Toronto Press, 1973.

Moulton, Gary, ed. *Journals of the Lewis and Clark Expedition, Atlas.* Lincoln: University of Nebraska Press, 1983.

Nelson, George. *"The Orders of the Dreamed",* ed. Jennifer S.H. Brown and Robert Brightman. Winnipeg: University of Manitoba Press, 1988.

Nicks, John. "David Thompson." In *Dictionary of Canadian Biography,* vol. 8. Toronto: University of Toronto Press, 1985.

Ogden, Peter Skene. *Snake Country Journals, 1824–25,* ed. E.E. Rich. London: Hudson's Bay Record Society, 1950.

– *Snake Country Journals 1826–27,* ed. K.G. Davies and Alice Johnson. London: Hudson's Bay Record Society, 1961.

[Ogden, Peter Skene]. *Traits of American Indian Life & Character, by a Fur Trader.* 1933. Reprint. New York: AMS Press, 1972.

Paley, William. *Natural Theology.* New York: American Tract Society, [1802].

Playfair, John. *Illustrations of the Huttonian Theory of the Earth.* 1802. Reprint. Urbana: University of Illinois Press, 1956.

Quaife, Milo M., ed. *The Journals of Captain Meriwether Lewis and Sergeant John Ordway.* 1916. Reprint. Madison: State Historical Society of Wisconsin, 1965.

Ray, Arthur J. *Indians in the Fur Trade.* Toronto: University of Toronto Press, 1974.

Rich, E.E., ed. *Simpson's 1828 Journey to the Columbia.* Toronto: Champlain Society, 1947.

Roberts, Kenneth G., and Philip Shackleton. *The Canoe*. Toronto: Macmillan, 1983.

Robertson, John. *The Elements of Navigation*. London: F. Wingrave, 1795.

Ronda, James. *Astoria and Empire*. Lincoln: University of Nebraska Press, 1990.

Ross, Alexander. *Adventures of the First Settlers on the Columbia*. 1849. Reprint. Ann Arbor: Xerox University Microfilms, 1966.

Saussure, Horace-Bénédict de. *Voyages dans les Alpes*. 4 vols. Neuchâtel: Samuel Fauché, 1779–95.

Schaeffer, Claude E. *Le Blanc and La Gassé: Predecessors of David Thompson in the Columbian Plateau*. Browning, Mont.: Museum of the Plains Indian for the United States Department of the Interior, 1966.

Sebert, L.M. "David Thompson's Determination of Longitude in Western Canada." *The Canadian Surveyor* 35, no. 4 (1981): 405–14.

Smith, Allan H. "An Ethnohistorical Analysis of David Thompson's 1809–1811 Journeys in the Lower Pend Oreille Valley, Northeastern Washington." *Ethnohistory* 8, no. 4 (1961): 309–81.

Smyth, David. "David Thompson's Surveying Instruments and Methods in the Northwest 1790–1812." *Cartographica* 18, no. 4 (1981): 1–17.

Southesk, James Carnegie, Earl of. *Saskatchewan and the Rocky Mountains*. Edinburgh: Edmonston and Douglas, 1875.

Spaulding, Kenneth. ed. *On the Oregon Trail: Robert Stuart's Journey of Discovery, 1812–1813*. Norman: University of Oklahoma Press, 1953.

Spry, Irene, ed. *The Palliser Papers*. Toronto: Champlain Society, 1968.

Stewart, W.M. "David Thompson's Surveys in the Northwest." *Canadian Historical Review* 17 (1936): 289–303.

Stuart, Robert. *The Discovery of the Oregon Trail*, ed. Robert Ashton Rollins. New York: Scribner's, 1935

Thwaites, Reuben Gold, ed. *Original Journals of the Lewis and Clark Expedition*. 7 vols. 1904–5. Reprint. New York: Antiquarian Press, 1959.

Townsend, John Kirk. *Narrative of a Journey across the Rocky Mountains to the Columbia River*. 1970. Reprint. Lincoln: University of Nebraska Press, 1978.

Tyrrell, J.B. "The Re-Discovery of David Thompson." *Transactions of the Royal Society of Canada*, 3d series, 22, no. 2 (1928): 233–47 (cited as "Tyrell–RCS").

– "David Thompson and the Columbia River." *Canadian Historical Review* 18 (1937): 12–13.

– ed. *The Journals of Samuel Hearne and Philip Turnor.* Toronto: Champlain Society, 1934 (cited as "Tyrrell–HTF").

Umfreville, Edward. *The Present State of Hudson's Bay,* ed. W.S. Wallace. Toronto: Ryerson Press, 1954.

Vancouver, George. *Voyage of Discovery to the North Pacific Ocean and Round the World.* 4 vols. 1798. Reprint. Amsterdam and New York: N. Israel and Da Capo Press, 1967.

Verner, Coolie, and Basil Stuart-Stubbs. *The Northpart of America.* Toronto: Academic Press Canada, 1979.

Wallace, W.S., ed. *Documents Relating to the North West Company.* Toronto: Champlain Society, 1934.

Whitrow, G.J. *The Natural Philosophy of Time.* London and Edinburgh: Nelson, 1981.

Williams, Glyndwr, ed. *Hudson's Bay Miscellany 1670–1870.* Winnipeg: Hudson's Bay Record Society, 1975.

Wilson, Bruce G. *Colonial Identities: Canada from 1716 to 1815.* Ottawa: National Archives of Canada, 1988.

Wood, Raymond, and Thomas D. Thiessen, eds. *Early Fur Trade on the Northern Plains: The Narratives of John Macdonell, David Thompson, François-Antoine Laroque and Charles McKenzie.* Norman: University of Oklahoma Press, 1985.

Index

This index is a list of the proper names of individuals, groups, and places found in the journals, maps, and corresponding notes.

Aberdeen, Earl of, 293–4, 320

Acton House, 192, 300–1

Adams, Mount, 272, 275, 281

Adams, Point, 156–7, 279

A hoaks pa River [Willow Creek], 284, 306

Allaire, Michel, 170–1, 287

Arrow Lakes, 287, 289, 295–7, 303. *See also* Ear bobs Lake

Arrowsmith, Aaron, 265, 295–7, 319–20

Astor, John Jacob, 155, 264, 273–4, 280, 287

Astoria, 273, 277–8, 287, 318–19

Athabaska Pass, 136, 212, 250, 258–61, 287, 290, 307. *See also* Portage

Athabaska River, 117, 123–4, 126, 133, 252–3, 299, 300–2, 307

Athapescow River. *See* Athabaska River

Atsina. *See* Fall Indians

Bad River. *See* Bow River

Baptiste's Brook [Baptiste River], 96, 239

Battoche, 129–32, 135

Beau Parler, 98, 241

Beauchamp, 3, 181

Beaulieu, 49–50, 58, 65, 79–80, 108, 111–12, 115, 170, 209, 231, 342

Beaulieu's Brook [Yaak River], 90, 237

Bellaire, 170–1, 287

Bercier, 35, 38–9, 42–5, 49–50, 53, 56, 63–4, 67, 76, 98, 119, 209, 226, 231, 242, 249

Bighorn River, 211

Bird, James, 192

Blackfoot Indians [Siksika], 69, 182, 226–8, 230, 295, 300–1, 303

Blaeberry River. *See* Portage River

Blood Indians [Kainah], 3, 14, 69, 182

Blue Mountains, 166. *See also* Shawpatin Mountains

Boat Encampment, 262–3, 290

Boggy Hall, 96, 117, 120, 239–40

Boisverd, 43, 49, 209, 242, 282

Bostonan, 107, 243

Boulard, 3, 12, 17, 39–40, 51, 53, 55, 58, 65, 85, 105, 181, 195, 204, 209, 216, 225, 235, 243, 283

Bourdeaux, Michel, 142, 148, 159, 168–9, 204, 286

Boussé, 117, 124–31, 249

Bow Hills, 13, 196, 300–1

Bow River, 13, 16–18, 198, 200, 300–1, 303–4, 308

Bow Rivulet [Ghost River], 19, 201, 304

Brazeau Range, 210

Brière, 118, 239

Bruneau, Baptiste, 117–18, 120–1, 123, 126, 129, 131–3, 249

Buché, 43, 59, 65, 68, 98, 102, 106, 108–9, 209, 222, 239, 242, 243

Buffalo Dung Lake [Chip Lake], 120

Caledonia River, 296–7, 303

Campment du Prèle, 101

Canada, 119, 121, 130, 249
Canadians [North West Company], 22
Canal Flats. See McGillivray's Portage
Canoe River, 133, 140, 176, 178, 258, 262, 290, 303
Capot Barré, 86
Cartier, 170, 287
Cascades, 276, 281
Celilo Falls, 274
Charles the Iroquois, 142, 170–1, 173, 177, 204
Charron, 12, 195
Chinook Indians, 157, 276, 278–9, 301, 303
Chip Lake. See Buffalo Dung Lake
Clatsop. See Klatsap/Klatsup Indians
Clearwater River, 3, 300–1, 304
Clément, 36, 39–40, 49–50, 56, 65–6, 76, 99, 209, 231, 241
Cline River. See Muleton Rivulet
Coeur d'Alene. See Point Heart Indians, Skeetshoo Indians
Columbia Lake, 222, 308
Columbia River, 142, 145, 152, 158, 166–7, 169, 178, 262, 268, 295, 300–9. See also Kootanae River, Oregan River
Côté, Joseph, 118–19, 130, 132, 138, 140–2, 170, 204, 249, 255, 262–3
Cotton na haws [Kutenai], 193–4, 300–1. See also Kootanae Indians
Coxe, 283, 288
Cree. See Nahathaway Indians
Crépeau, 102, 239

Dalles [lower Columbia River], 154, 160, 273–4; lower [upper Columbia River], 175, 289; upper [Dalles des morts, upper Columbia River], 177, 289. See also Portage
Daniel, Pierre, 3, 181
D'Eau, Baptiste, 119, 129–30, 132, 138–41, 249
Delcour, Baptiste, 118, 130, 177, 249
Deschutes River. See Wunwowe River
Desjarlaix, François, 130, 132, 137, 139, 141, 225, 250
Disappointment, Cape, 156, 279
Dog Campment, 214, 307
Dumond, 12, 195
Du Nord, 117–18, 127–8, 132, 135–41, 204–5, 250, 260

Dupré, 99, 239, 241

Ear bobs Lake [Arrow Lakes], 296, 301
Eet too woy Plains, 245, 305
Elk River. See Stag River
English [Hudson's Bay Company], 10, 192

Fall Indians [Atsina? Hidatsa?], 272, 300–1, 303
Fidler, Peter, 183, 189, 219, 227, 295
Fine Meadow Rivulet [Tobacco River], 79–80, 85
Finlay, Jaco, 40, 49, 104–6, 110, 166, 168, 170, 196, 209–10, 215, 235, 241, 243, 263, 285
Fisher River. See Rock River
Flat Bow Indians [Kutenai], 227–9, 235, 301, 303
Flat Bow Lake [Kootenay Lake], 301, 303. See also McGillivray's Lake
Flat Head Indians [Interior Salish], 15, 18, 81, 85–6, 88, 106–10, 199, 219, 236, 244, 286, 301, 303
Flathead Lake. See Saleesh Lake
Flat Head River [Clark Fork River], 106, 301, 303
Flat Heart Brook [Wood River], 140–1, 178, 241, 259, 262
Fort Augustus, 69, 99, 228, 230, 242, 258, 303
FDP/Fort des Prairies. See North West Company. See also Fort Augustus, Terre Blanche House
Fort George [Astoria], 156, 303; [North Saskatchewan River], 73, 229–30, 303
Fort Peles, 120
Fort William, 194, 225, 228, 290. See also Kaministiquia
Fraser River, 303

Gladu, 30, 202
Gooseberry Hill, 52, 102, 217
Grand Coulee, 265
Grand Picota, 171
Gray's Bay, 279
Grégoire, François, 142, 204
Green Wood Indians [Nez Percés], 111, 115

Hamelin, 173, 177, 287
He Dog, 3, 181

Hector, James, 213
Henry, Alexander, 118, 137, 141, 241
Henry, William, 122, 137, 141, 178, 263
Hidatsa. *See* Fall Indians
Highwood River. *See* Spitchee River
Hood, Mount, 275, 281, 300–1
Howse, Joseph, 212, 296
Howse Pass, 44, 68, 111, 194, 213, 250, 259, 304, 307. *See also* Portage
Howse River, 211
Hudson's Bay Company, 192, 295. *See also* English
Hughes, James, 21–32, 41, 50, 190, 202, 207, 201

Ignace the Iroquois, 142, 145, 204
Ilthkoyape Falls [Kettle Falls], 142, 169, 263, 265, 286, 305
Ilthkoyape Indians, 170
Inspaelis Indians, 148, 306
Interior Salish. *See* Flat Head Indians, Saleesh Indians
Iron, The, 36
Iroquois Indians, 15, 102, 198, 290

Jaco. *See* Finlay, Jaco
Jaco's Brook [Shunda Creek], 36, 97, 210, 241, 307
John Day River. *See* Torks Paez River
Joseph the Nipissing, 177

Kainah. *See* Blood Indians, Kenna Koon, Meadow Indians
Kaministiquia, 218. *See also* Fort William
Kettle Falls. *See* Ilthkoyape Falls
Kenna Koon [Kainah], 304
Kicking Horse River. *See* Rapid River
Kinville, 122, 250, 286
Kisisaskatchewan River [Saskatchewan River], 124–5
Klatsap/Klatsup Indians [Clatsop], 157
Klickitat River. *See* Nar ma neet River
Kootanae House, 76, 99, 102–3, 220, 230–1, 242, 304, 308
Kootanae Indians [Kutenai], 3–11, 15, 21, 50–71, 80, 85, 88, 105–6, 108, 160, 185, 189–90, 193, 207–8, 282, 303
Kootanae Lake [Windermere], 51, 53, 58, 75, 93, 95, 222, 231, 235, 308
Kootanae Plains [Kootenay Plains], 39–46, 98–100, 206, 307

Kootanae Pound, 45, 100
Kootanae River [Columbia River], 49, 52, 67, 75, 99, 101, 133, 135, 138–40, 215
Kootenai Falls, 235
Kootenay Lake. *See* McGillivray's Lake
Kootenay/Kootenai River. *See* McGillivray's River
Kullyspel House, 116, 242, 247, 305
Kullyspel Indians, 168, 170
Kullyspel Lake [Pend Oreille Lake], 244–5, 303, 305, 309
Kutenai. *See* Cotton na haws, Flat Bow Indians, Kootanae Indians, Lake Indians, Spokane Indians

L'Amoureux, 130, 132, 135, 141, 250
La Brèche, 170
La Course, 130, 250
Lac La Pluye [Rainy Lake], 225
La Fontaine, 119–20, 130, 250
La Gassé, 3, 6, 11, 102, 171, 181, 193, 218–19, 239
Lake Indians [Kutenai], 55, 66–70, 85, 87–8, 91, 102, 105, 113, 219, 235–7, 308–9
La Ramme, 23, 202, 204
Le Blanc, 11, 193, 218–19
Le Bon Vieux, 169–70
Le Camble, 56, 80, 88, 90, 93, 95–6, 99, 231, 239, 241
Le Chien Foux, 109
Le Muet, 63
Le Tendre, Baptiste, 141, 250
Lewis and Clark expedition, 189, 207, 216, 227, 229, 264, 272, 274, 279, 282, 285, 295
Lewis's River [Lewis and Clark River], 156; [Snake River], 301, 303. *See also* Shawpatin River
Little Hunter, 65, 68
Little Red Deer River, 182, 201
Lolo, 171
Long Plain, 35
Loyer, Charles, 171
Lussier, 58, 64, 79–80, 88, 90, 92–3, 95, 231
Lussier's Rivulet [Lussier River], 94, 237, 308

McDonald, Finan, 35–6, 39, 43, 45, 49–52, 55, 59, 62–4, 68, 95, 98,

102, 105–8, 110, 116, 171, 175, 181,
209, 239, 243, 247, 287
McDonald, John, 286
McDonald of Garth, John, 194
McDonald's River [Moyie River], 90–3,
106, 233, 236–7
McDougall, Duncan, 155, 274, 277–8,
280
McGillivray, Duncan, 12, 15–17, 19, 21,
31, 33, 34, 87, 181, 195, 202, 246,
295, 307
McGillivray, William, 34, 280, 295–6
McGillivray's Lake [Kootenay Lake],
173, 219, 235, 308. See also Flat
Bow Lake
McGillivray's Portage [Canal Flats],
72–3, 76, 94–5, 104, 227, 229, 231
McGillivray's River [Kootenay/Kootenai
River], 67, 70, 72–3, 76, 93, 95, 104,
114, 172, 175, 207, 229, 243, 288,
296–7, 303, 308–9, 319–20
Mackenzie, Alexander, 295–6
McLeod's River [McLeod River], 124
McMillan, James, 98, 100–1, 239
Maligne River, 258
Martin, 171
Meadow Indians [Blackfoot
Confederacy], 70, 111, 170, 229
Meillet, 29–30, 202, 205
Méthode, 102, 119, 129, 239, 250
Miette River, 259
Milk river. See Missisouri River
Missisouri River [Missouri River], 15,
182, 199, 264, 295, 300
Mistaya River, 211
Monde, The, 81
Morrin, 3, 181
Mousseau, 79–80, 88–9, 95, 102, 110,
118, 130, 231, 239, 243, 250
Moyie Lake, 237
Moyie River. See McDonald's River
Muleton Rivulet [Cline River], 41, 211,
307
Muleton Plains, 40
Mult no mah River [Willamette River],
301, 303. See also Wil ar bet River

Nahathaway Indians [Cree], 21, 31, 36,
202, 207, 241, 303
Nar ma neet River [Klickitat River], 161,
283, 306
Nelson, Mount, 304, 308

Nelson's Mountains [Purcell Range], 68,
93–4, 106, 237, 302
Nez Perce. See Green Wood Indians,
Shawpatin Indians
North Branch [North Saskatchewan
River], 44, 300–1, 303, 307
North West Company, 22, 34, 58, 96, 98,
100, 117, 142, 152, 196, 219, 264,
273–4, 277–8, 280, 286, 287, 290,
318; Athabaska department, 226,
238; Columbia department, 238; Fort
des Prairies department, 50, 137,
140, 228, 239, 241; Saskatchewan
River department, 241

Occhenawga Indians [Okanogan], 170
Occhenawga Lake [Okanogan Lake] 175,
289, 303
Occhenawga River [Okanogan River],
146–7, 171, 267, 303
Ojibwa. See Seauteaux Indians
Okanogan. See Occhenawga Indians
Old Bear, 3, 10, 181
Old Chief, 60, 67, 70, 85
Oregan River [Columbia River], 300
Oregon Territory, 294, 310, 317–20

Pacific Fur Company, 155, 271–2, 274,
277–8, 280, 287
Pack River, 244
Palouse River, 285
Pangman, Peter, 97, 240
Pareil, Pierre, 119, 130–2, 139–42, 170,
204, 250, 255, 262–3
Parizeau, Ignace, 96, 239
Peagan Indians [Peigan], 62–6, 69, 85,
105, 195, 219, 223–4, 230, 234–5,
286
Peigan. See Meadow Indians, Peagan
Indians, Pekenow Indians
Pekenow Indians [Peigan], 3–14, 182
Pembina River, 120, 251, 258, 300–1
Pend Oreille Lake. See Kullyspel Lake
Pend Oreille River. See Saleesh River
Pichette, 118, 250
Pishkowish River [Wenatchee River],
267, 306
Pointed Heart Indians [Coeur d'Alene],
108–10, 116, 301, 303
Portage [Athabaska Pass], 136; [Dalles,
lower Columbia River], 154, 160;
[Dalles des Morts, upper Columbia

River], 289; [Howse Pass], 44, 68, 111
Portage River [Blaeberry River], 49, 100, 215
Priest Rapids, 269
Priest River, 247
Purcell Range. See Nelson's Mountains

Rainier, Mount, 300–1, 303, 306
Rainy Lake, 225, 238, 274, 282, 290. See also Lac La Pluye
Ram River. See South Branch
Rapid River [Kicking Horse River], 51, 101–2, 117
Rattlesnake Rock, 164
Red Berry Campment, 45, 100
Red Deer's Horn's Meadow, 103
Red Deer's River [Red Deer River], 4–6, 12, 20, 184, 190
Regnie, Baptiste, 12, 195
Rivé, 170–1, 287
Rock River [Fisher River], 82–3, 233–4
Rocky Mountain House, 3, 33–4, 117, 125, 130, 181–2, 192, 195, 201, 203, 208, 240
Rocky Mountains, 4, 13, 17–18, 119, 123, 184, 196, 200–1, 214, 299, 301, 303
Rook, The, 21
Round Plain, 35, 97

Sac o tow wow, 14–15, 198
St Helen's, Mount, 275–6, 281, 300–1, 306
St Mary's River. See Torrent Rivulet
Saleesh House, 242, 247, 263, 290, 305
Saleesh Indians [Interior Salish], 55, 60, 65, 69, 199, 219, 286
Saleesh Lake [Flathead Lake], 250, 303, 305
Saleesh River [Clark Fork/Pend Oreille rivers], 172–3, 219, 243–5, 247, 288, 290, 295, 303, 305, 309, 320
Sanpoil. See Simpoil Indians
Sanpoil River, 265
Saskatchewan River, 22, 29, 33, 38, 98, 117, 182, 197, 203, 205–6, 299–304, 307. See also Kisiskatchewan River, North Branch, South Branch
Sauvie Island, 281
Seauteaux Indians [Ojibwa], 15, 49–50, 198, 239, 243

Shawpatin Indians [Nez Perces], 69, 151–2, 161, 166, 228, 247, 272, 306
Shawpatin Mountains [Blue Mountains], 151, 270
Shawpatin River [Snake River], 151–2, 166, 271, 285, 295, 301, 303. See also Lewis's River
Sheep River, 199
Shoshoni. See Snake Indians
Shunda Creek. See Jaco's Brook
Siksika. See Blackfoot Indians, Meadow Indians
Simpoil Indians [Sanpoil], 142–5, 266
Skeetshoo Indians [Coeur d'Alene], 169
Skeetshoo Lake [Coeur d'Alene Lake], 305, 309
Skeetshoo River [Spokane River], 115, 305, 309
Skirmish Brook [Wild Horse River], 94, 237, 308
Smeeth howe Indians, 148
Snake Indians [Shoshoni], 152, 166, 272–3, 301, 301
Snake River. See Lewis's River, Shawpatin River
South Branch [Ram River], 203–5, 210, 304, 307; [South Saskatchewan River], 299–300, 304, 307
Spitchee River [Highwood River], 14–15, 17, 181, 198, 300–1, 303, 308
Spokane House, 168, 263, 285, 290, 303, 305, 309
Spokane Indians [Kutenai], 115, 168, 301
Spokane River, 142, 169, 303. See also Skeetshoo River
Stag River [Elk River], 78–9, 105, 233, 308
Stillwater River, 233
Stone Indians [Assiniboin/Stoney], 123, 303
Stuart, David, 155–62, 277–8, 280, 282–3
Stuart, Robert, 155, 277–8

Terre Blanche House, 241
Thomas the Iroquois, 117, 119–20, 123, 125, 132, 135–7, 250
Thompson's Rapids, 265
Thunder, The, 106, 181, 243
Tobacco Meadows [Tobacco Plains], 79, 233

Tobacco River, 105, 233. *See also* Fine
    Meadow Rivulet
Toby Creek, 217–18, 221–2, 231
Tongue Point, 155, 157, 277
Torks Paez River [John Day River], 163,
    284, 306
Torrent Rivulet [St Mary's River], 73,
    77–8, 93–4, 104, 230, 308
Turnor, Philip, 183

Ugly Head, 67, 70–1, 86, 90–4, 227–8

Vallade, 132, 137–9, 141, 250
Vancouver expedition, 279, 295–300,
    317–18
Vancouver, Point, 155, 159, 300
Vaudette, 132, 135, 137, 250
Villiard, 129, 132–3, 263

War Tent, 36–7, 97–8, 205

Waw thloo las Indians, 155
Wenatchee River, 267
We yark eek Indians, 155
Whirlpool River, 258–60
White Mud Brook, 117
Wil ar bet River [Willamette River],
    158–9, 275, 281, 306
Wild Horse River. *See* Skirmish Brook
Willamette River. *See* Mult no mah River,
    Wil ar bet River
Windermere, Lake, 218
Wolverene, 36–9, 181
Wood River. *See* Flat Heart Brook
Wun wow we River [Deschutes River],
    162, 283, 306

Yaak River. *See* Beaulieu's Brook
Yellow Bird, 117–18, 121, 125–6, 129,
    131, 181, 239, 250